DAM BUSTERS

The True Story of the Inventors and Airmen Who Led the Devastating Raid to Smash the German Dams in 1943

James Holland

Atlantic Monthly Press
New York

First published in Great Britain
in 2012 by Bantam Press
an imprint of Transworld Publishers

Printed in the United States of America

ISBN 978-0-8021-2169-1

Atlantic Monthly Press
an imprint of Grove/Atlantic, Inc.
154 West 14th Street
New York, NY 10011

Distributed by Publishers Group West

www.groveatlantic.com

13 14 15 16   10 9 8 7 6 5 4 3 2 1

For the Chad's Boys:
Simon Barber, Peter Bell, Justin Gilbert & Stuart Mills

Contents

Maps and Figures

Author's Note

The Dams Raid is truly an incredible story. Really. An amazing weapon, and 133 men and nineteen Lancasters heading out at tree-top height, at night, over enemy territory and dropping their bouncing bombs to smash the German dams. It's a fabulous tale of daring, ingenuity and raw courage.

I must, at the outset, thank Rowland White, an old friend and author himself, for suggesting I write a book about it. But I will also admit that my immediate response to him was, 'Haven't there been hundreds of books about this already?' As he pointed out, however, the answer is no. There have been only two significant works on the Dams Raid in the past thirty years, and only ever one narrative history and that was Paul Brickhill's *The Dambusters*, written in 1951, before the files relating to the raid had been declassified. Mostly, our knowledge of the raid comes from the film, starring Richard Todd and Michael Redgrave, which is regularly repeated on television, and deservedly so; it's a great film, but as is often the way with movies, accuracy is not the prime concern, and in ninety minutes much detail has to be necessarily left out.

Last summer, in between writing the book, I was also involved in making a BBC film. People often stopped and asked what we were doing. When we told them, nine times out of ten, the response was the same: 'What are you going to call the dog?' It seems sad in a way that from this extraordinary raid there are just three names that people remember: Barnes Wallis, Guy Gibson and Nigger, the dog. What about all the others involved? All those young men who flew the raid, most of them now gone and forgotten?

The dog, of course, was the least important figure in the story, yet it is a homage to the power of Hollywood that the offices of No. 2 Hangar at Scampton, from where 617 Squadron was formed and flew the Dams Raid, now lie derelict and forlorn, while, out front, Nigger's grave is surrounded by freshly painted iron railings, the grass is kept trim, and the flowers are bright and watered. The slab marking the spot mentions the raid against the 'Möhne and Eder Dams' – the two featured in the film. There is no mention of the Sorpe, also attacked that night.

As I have been uncovering the often forgotten details behind the Dams Raid, I have been struck by what a difference they make to the story. The bare bones are much the same, but add the flesh, and an even more remarkable tale quickly emerges – a story of politics and personalities as much as science and ingenious engineering, a story of very special but ordinary men rather than the 'Top Gun' of Bomber Command. Gibson and Wallis were real people rather than caricatures – more complex, more contradictory. More interesting. The timing of the raid and its place in the wider war effort, and the Second World War as a whole, adds another layer. This was a far more complex, more nuanced episode than perhaps we might think.

To my very best ability, this is as accurate a portrayal as I have been able to make it, although there are, in the course of official records, documents and personal testimonies, a number of inconsistencies and contradictions. Occasionally, I have made assumptions, which represent my opinion and judgement as to what most likely happened. I have end-noted all direct quotations apart from those with people I interviewed myself, but I have not noted statistics or figures. There is, however, a full list of sources at the back.

The Dams Raid remains a fabulous story – the achievement even more extraordinary, even more daring and full of breathtaking courage than I had first realized. I hope this book conveys something of that.

James Holland
January 2012

Cast List

Admiralty

Lt-Commander L. Lane, RNVR
Directorate of Miscellaneous Weapons Development

Rear-Admiral E. de F. Renouf
Director of Special Weapons, the Admiralty

Air Ministry

Group Captain J. W. Baker
Director of Bomber Operations (DB Ops) at Air Ministry

Air Vice-Marshal Norman H. Bottomley
Assistant Chief of the Air Staff (Ops) (ACAS)

Group Captain Sydney O. Bufton
Deputy Director of Bomber Operations (D/DB Ops) at the Air Ministry

Air Marshal Sir Wilfrid Freeman
Vice-Chief of the Air Staff, Air Ministry

Air Vice-Marshal Frank Inglis
Assistant Chief of the Air Staff (ACAS (I))

Air Chief Marshal Sir Charles Portal
Chief of the Air Staff

Air Vice-Marshal R. S. Sorley
Assistant Chief of the Air Technical Requirements (ACAS[TR]), Air Ministry

Wing Commander Fred Winterbotham
Head of Air Intelligence Section, MI6

A. V. Roe

Roy Chadwick
Chief Designer at A. V. Roe (and designer of Lancaster)

Ministry of Aircraft Production (MAP)

Air Vice-Marshal F. J. Linnell
Controller of Research and Development (CRD) at MAP

Benjamin Lockspeiser
Deputy Director of Scientific Research (D/DSR) at MAP. Civilian

Air Commodore Bernard McEntegart
Deputy Controller of Research and Development (D/CRD)

Air Commodore G. A. H. Pideock
Director of Armament Development (D Arm D) at the MAP

Dr David Pye
Director of Scientific Research (DSR), MAP. Civilian

Norbert Rowe
Director of Technical Development (DTD), MAP. Civilian

Sir Henry Tizard
Scientific advisor to MAP. Enemy of Prof. Lindemann

Group Captain W. Wynter-Morgan
Deputy Director of Armaments (D/D Arm D), MAP

Ministry of Home Security

A. R. Collins
A scientific officer in the Concrete Section at the Road Research Laboratory
(RRL), part of the Ministry of Aircraft Production (MAP)

Dr A. H. Davis
Assistant Director at the Road Research Laboratory

Dr W. H. Glanville
Director of the Road Research Laboratory (and pro-Wallis)

Prime Minister's Office

Professor Frederick A. Lindemann (Lord Cherwell)
Scientific Advisor to the Prime Minister

RAF Bomber Command

Air Vice-Marshal the Hon. R. A. Cochrane
Air Officer Commanding (AOC) No. 5 Group, Bomber Command

Air Marshal Sir Arthur Harris
Since February 1942, Commander-in-Chief, Bomber Command

Air Vice-Marshal Robert Oxland
From February 1943, Senior Air Staff Officer (SASO)

Group Captain H. V. Satterly
SASO, 5 Group

Air Vice-Marshal R. H. M. S. 'Sandy' Saundby
Senior Air Staff Officer (SASO), Bomber Command, later Deputy Commander-in-Chief

Vickers-Armstrong

Sir Charles Craven
Chairman, Vickers-Armstrong

Captain R. C. Handasyde
Assistant Chief Test Pilot, Vickers-Armstrong

Major Hew Kilner
Managing Director, Vickers-Armstrong Aviation

Squadron Leader 'Shorty' Longbottom
Test pilot seconded from the RAF

Rex K. Pierson
Chief Designer, Vickers-Armstrong Aviation Department, Weybridge

Captain 'Mutt' Summers
Chief Test Pilot, Vickers-Armstrong

Barnes Wallis
Assistant Chief Designer, Vickers-Armstrong Aviation Department, Weybridge

617 Squadron
Avro Lancaster aircraft: Codes AJ
Order: Pilot, Flight Engineer, Navigator, Wireless Operator, Bomb-aimer, Front Gunner, Rear Gunner (mid upper turret not fitted)

'G' ED932	W/C G. P. Gibson DSO DFC
G-George	Sgt John Pulford
	F/O Harlo 'Terry' Taerum RCAF
	F/L R. E. G. 'Bob' Hutchison DFC RAAF
	P/O F. M. 'Spam' Spafford
	P/O George A. Deering RCAF
	F/L R. A. D. Trevor-Roper DFM
	(Deering had been commissioned before the operation, and Taerum promoted to F/O, without their knowledge.)

'A' Flight

'A' ED887	S/L H. Melvin 'Dinghy' Young DFC & bar
A-Apple	Sgt D. T. Horsfall
	F/S C. W. Roberts
	Sgt L. W. Nichols
	F/O V. S. MacCausland RCAF
	Sgt G. A. Yeo
	Sgt W. Ibbotson

'B' ED864	F/L W. (Bill) Astell DFC
B-Baker	Sgt J. Kinnear
	P/O F. A. Wile RCAF
	WO2 A. Garshowitz RCAF
	F/O D. Hopkinson
	F/S F. A. Garbas RCAF
	Sgt R. Bolitho

'J' ED906	F/L David J. Maltby DFC
J-Johnny	Sgt W. Hatton
	Sgt V. Nicholson
	Sgt Anthony J. Stone
	P/O Jack Fort
	F/S V. Hill
	Sgt H. T. Simmonds

'L' ED929	F/L David J. Shannon DFC RAAF
L-Leather	Sgt R. J. Henderson
	P/O Danny R. Walker DFC
	F/O Brian Goodale DFC

F/S Len J. Sumpter
Sgt B. Jagger
P/O Jack Buckley

'E' ED927   F/L Robert N. G. Barlow DFC RAAF
E-Easy   P/O S. L. Whillis
               F/O P. S. Burgess
               F/O C. R. Williams DFC RAAF
               P/O A. Gillespie DFM
               F/O H. S. Glinz RCAF
               Sgt J. R. G. Liddell

'H' ED936   P/O Geoff Rice
H-Harry   Sgt E. C. Smith
               F/O R. MacFarlane
               Sgt C. B. Gowrie RCAF
               F/S J. E. Thrasher RCAF
               Sgt T. W. Maynard
               Sgt S. Burns

'C' ED910   P/O Warner Ottley DFC RCAF
C-Charlie   Sgt R. Marsden
               F/O J. K. Barrett DFC
               Sgt J. Guterman DFM
               F/S T. B. Johnston
               Sgt H. J. Strange
               F/S Freddie Tees

'F' ED918   F/S Ken W. Brown RCAF
F-Freddie   Sgt H. Basil Feneron
               Sgt D. P. Heal
               Sgt H. J. Hewstone
               Sgt S. Oancia, RCAF
               Sgt D. Allatson
               F/S G. S. McDonald, RCAF

'K' ED934   P/O Vernon W. Byers RCAF
K-King   Sgt A. J. Taylor
               F/O J. H. Warner
               Sgt J. Wilkinson
               P/O A. N. Whitaker
               Sgt C. Mc. A. Jarvie
               Sgt J. McDowell RCAF

'B' Flight

'Z' ED937
Z-Zebra

S/L Henry E. Maudslay DFC
Sgt J. Marriott DFM
F/O R. A. Urquhart DFC RCAF
WO2 A. P. Cottam RCAF
P/O M. J. D. Fuller
F/O W. J. Tytherleigh DFC
Sgt N. R. Burrows

'M' ED925
M-Mother

F/L John V. Hopgood DFC & bar
Sgt C. Brennan
F/O K. Earnshaw (Canadian)
Sgt J. W. Minchin
P/O J. W. Fraser RCAF
P/O G. H. F. G. Gregory DFM
P/O Anthony F. Burcher DFM RAAF

'P' ED909
P-Popsie

F/L Harold B. 'Mick' Martin DFC RAAF
P/O Ivan Whittaker
F/L Jack F. Leggo DFC RAAF (Squadron Navigator)
F/O Len Chambers RNZAF
F/L R. C. 'Bob' Hay DFC RAAF (Squadron Bombing Leader)
P/O B. 'Toby' Foxlee DFM RAAF
F/S Tammy D. Simpson RAAF

'W' ED921
W-Willie

F/L J. Les Munro
Sgt F. E. Appleby
F/O F. G. Rumbles
Sgt Percy E. Pigeon RCAF
Sgt J. H. Clay
Sgt William Howarth
F/S H. A. Weeks RCAF

'T' ED825
T-Tommy

F/L Joe C. McCarthy RCAF
Sgt W. Radcliffe RCAF
P/O D. A. MacLean RCAF
Sgt L. Eaton
Sgt G. L. Johnson
Sgt R. Batson
F/O D. Rodger RCAF
(MacLean had been commissioned before the operation, without his knowledge.)

'S' ED865   P/O Lewis J. Burpee DFM RCAF
S-Sugar   Sgt G. Pegler
              Sgt T. Jaye
              P/O L. G. Weller
              W/O2 S. J. L. Arthur RCAF
              Sgt W. C. A. Long
              W/O2 J. G. Brady RCAF
              (Arthur had been promoted to W/O2 before the operation,
              without his knowledge.)

'N' ED912   F/L Les G. Knight RAAF
N-Nuts   Sgt R. E. Grayston
              F/O H Sidney Hobday
              P/O R. G. T. (Bob) Kellow RAAF
              F/O E. C. Johnson
              Sgt F. E. Sutherland RCAF
              Sgt H. E. O'Brien RCAF
              (Kellow had been commissioned before the operation,
              without his knowledge.)

'O' ED886   F/S W. C. (Bill) Townsend
O-Orange   Sgt D. J. D. Powell
              P/O C. L. Howard RAAF
              F/S G. A. Chalmers
              Sgt C. E. Franklin
              Sgt D. E. Webb
              Sgt R. Wilkinson

'Y' ED924   P/O Cyril T. Anderson
Y-York   Sgt R. C. Paterson
              Sgt J. P. Nugent
              Sgt W. D. Bickle
              Sgt G. J. Green
              Sgt E. Ewan
              Sgt A. W. Buck
              (Anderson had been commissioned before the operation,
              without his knowledge.)

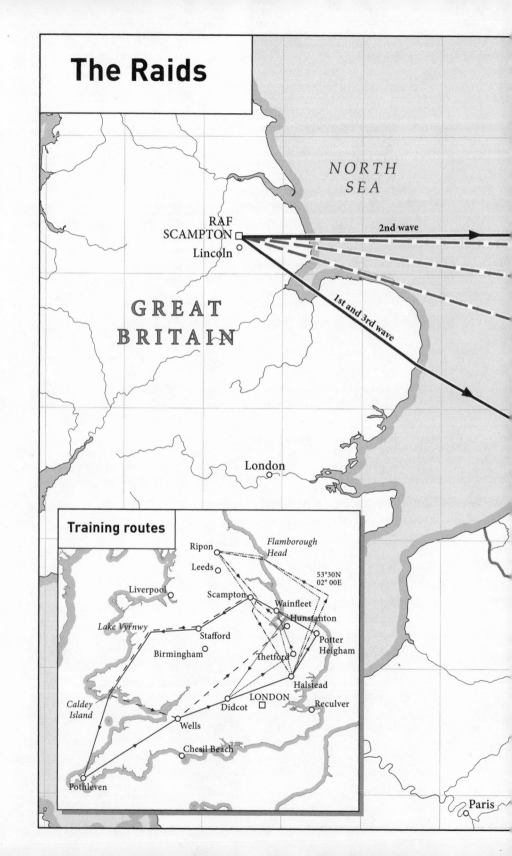

The Raids

NORTH
SEA

RAF
SCAMPTON
Lincoln

GREAT
BRITAIN

London

2nd wave

1st and 3rd wave

Training routes

Ripon
Leeds
Liverpool
Scampton
Lake Vyrnwy
Stafford
Birmingham
Flamborough Head
Wainfleet
Hunstanton
53°30N
02° 00E
Potter Heigham
Thetford
Halstead
Caldey Island
Didcot
LONDON
Reculver
Wells
Chesil Beach
Pothleven
Paris

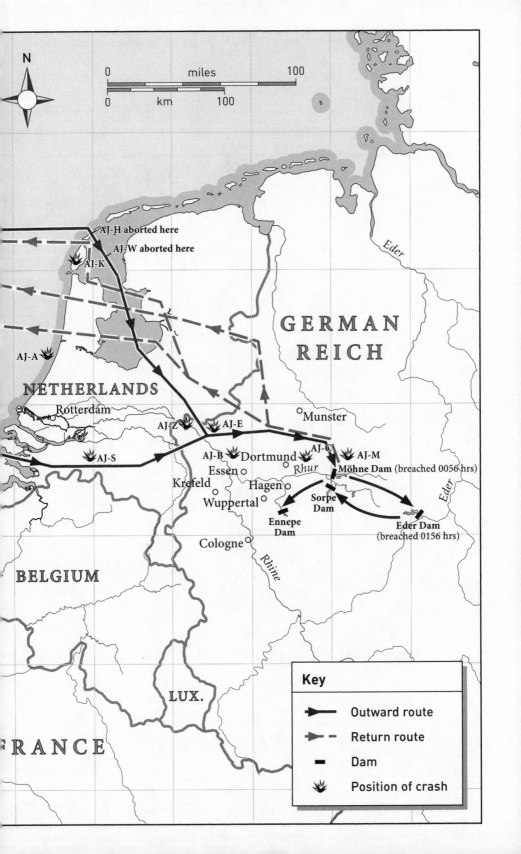

N

miles
0   100

km
0   100

AJ-H aborted here
AJ-W aborted here

AJ-K

Eder

GERMAN
REICH

AJ-A

NETHERLANDS

Rotterdam

Munster

AJ-Z   AJ-E

AJ-B   Dortmund   AJ-C   AJ-M

AJ-S   Essen   Rhur   Möhne Dam (breached 0056 hrs)

Krefeld   Hagen   Sorpe

Wuppertal   Dam   Eder

Ennepe   Eder Dam

Dam   (breached 0156 hrs)

Cologne

BELGIUM

Rhine

LUX.

FRANCE

Key

Outward route

Return route

Dam

Position of crash

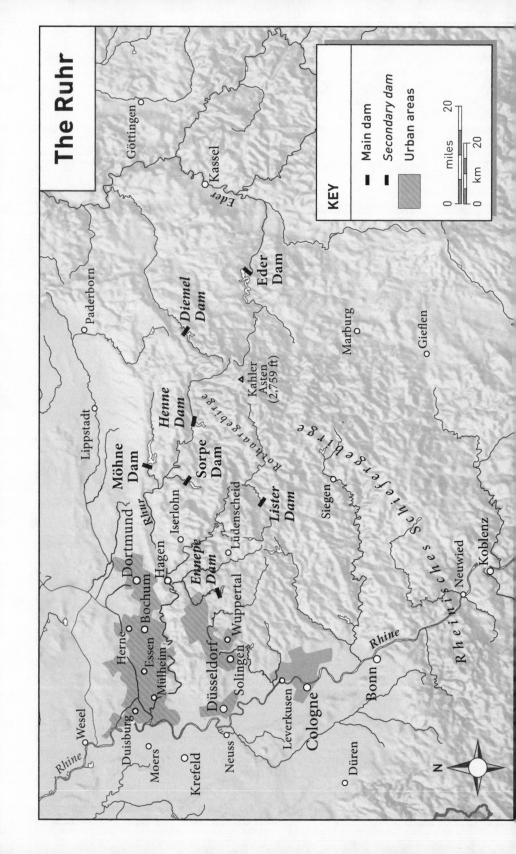

The Rull

KEY

	Main dam
	Secondary dam
	Urban areas

miles 20

km 20

N

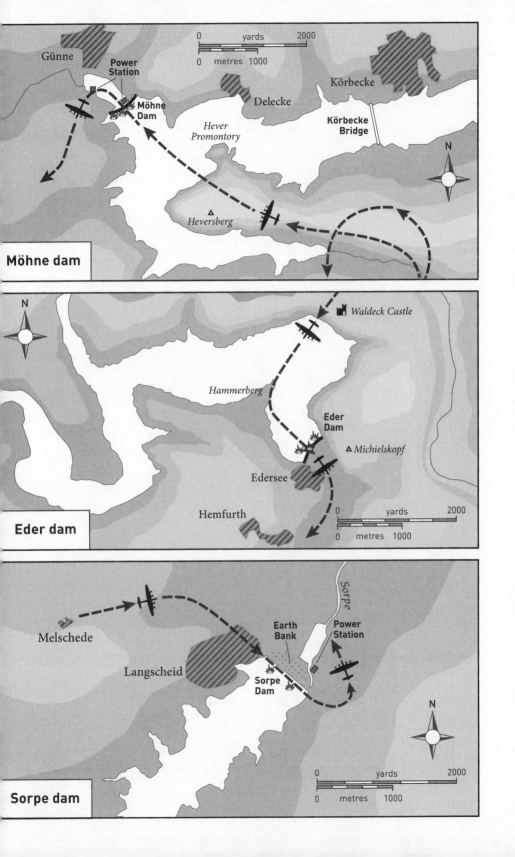

Möhne dam

Günne

**Power
Station**

**Möhne
Dam**

*Hever
Promontory*

Delecke

Körbecke

**Körbecke
Bridge**

N

△
Heversberg

Eder dam

N

🏰 *Waldeck Castle*

Hammerberg

**Eder
Dam**

△ *Michielskopf*

Edersee

Hemfurth

0   yards   2000

0   metres   1000

Sorpe dam

Sorpe

Melschede

**Earth
Bank**

**Power
Station**

Langscheid

**Sorpe
Dam**

N

0   yards   2000

0   metres   1000

0   yards   2000

0   metres   1000

ATTACKING THE DAMS

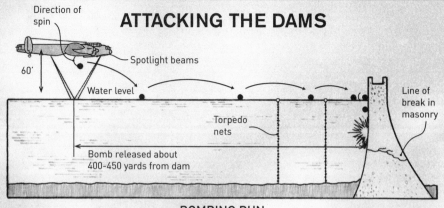

Direction of spin

60'

Spotlight beams

Water level

Torpedo nets

Bomb released about 400-450 yards from dam

Line of break in masonry

BOMBING RUN

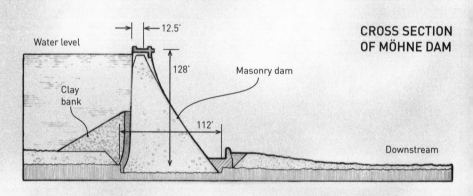

CROSS SECTION OF MÖHNE DAM

Water level

Clay bank

12.5'

128'

112'

Masonry dam

Downstream

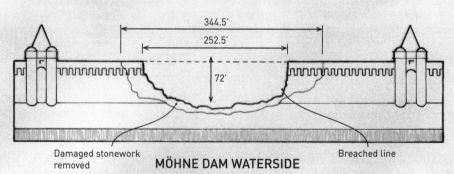

344.5'

252.5'

72'

Damaged stonework removed

Breached line

MÖHNE DAM WATERSIDE

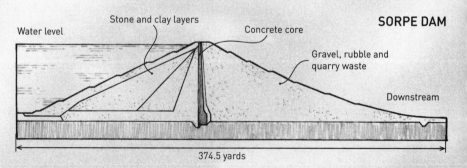

SORPE DAM

Water level

Stone and clay layers

Concrete core

Gravel, rubble and quarry waste

Downstream

374.5 yards

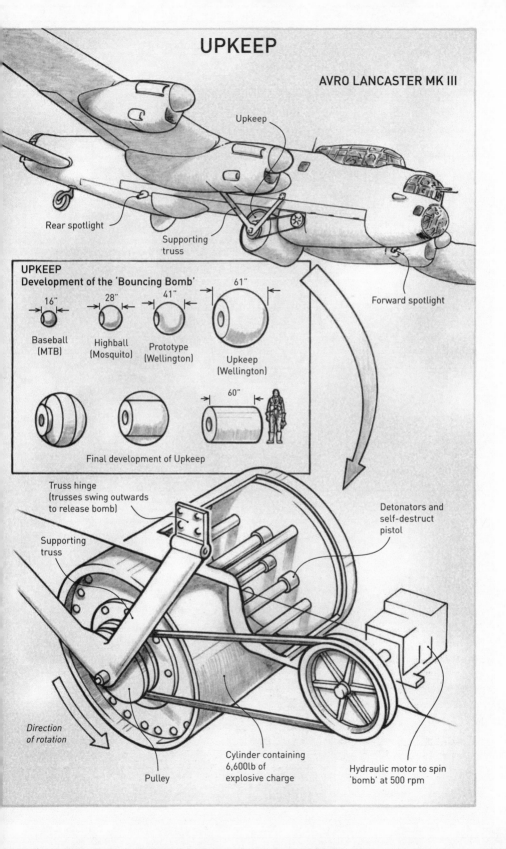

UPKEEP

AVRO LANCASTER MK III

Upkeep

Rear spotlight

Supporting
truss

Forward spotlight

UPKEEP
Development of the 'Bouncing Bomb'

16"

28"

41"

61"

Baseball
(MTB)

Highball
(Mosquito)

Prototype
(Wellington)

Upkeep
(Wellington)

60"

Final development of Upkeep

Truss hinge
(trusses swing outwards
to release bomb)

Detonators and
self-destruct
pistol

Supporting
truss

*Direction
of rotation*

Pulley

Cylinder containing
6,600lb of
explosive charge

Hydraulic motor to spin
'bomb' at 500 rpm

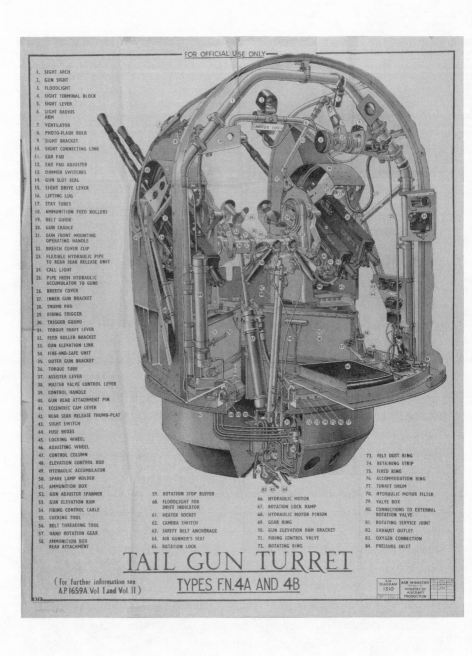

1. SIGHT ARCH
2. GUN SIGHT
3. FLOODLIGHT
4. SIGHT TERMINAL BLOCK
5. SIGHT LEVER
6. SIGHT RADIUS ARM
7. VENTILATOR
8. PHOTO-FLASH BULB
9. SIGHT BRACKET
10. SIGHT CONNECTING LINK
11. EAR PAD
12. EAR PAD ADJUSTER
13. DIMMER SWITCHES
14. GUN SLOT SEAL
15. SIGHT DRIVE LEVER
16. LIFTING LUG
17. STAY TUBES
18. AMMUNITION FEED ROLLERS
19. BELT GUIDE
20. GUN CRADLE
21. GUN FRONT MOUNTING OPERATING HANDLE
22. BREECH COVER CLIP
23. FLEXIBLE HYDRAULIC PIPE TO REAR SEAR RELEASE UNIT
24. CALL LIGHT
25. PIPE FROM HYDRAULIC ACCUMULATOR TO GUNS
26. BREECH COVER
27. INNER GUN BRACKET
28. THUMB PAD
29. FIRING TRIGGER
30. TRIGGER GUARD
31. TORQUE SHAFT LEVER
32. FEED ROLLER BRACKET
33. GUN ELEVATION LINK
34. FIRE-AND-SAFE UNIT
35. OUTER GUN BRACKET
36. TORQUE TUBE
37. ASSISTER LEVER
38. MASTER VALVE CONTROL LEVER
39. CONTROL HANDLE
40. GUN REAR ATTACHMENT PIN
41. ECCENTRIC CAM LEVER
42. REAR SEAR RELEASE THUMB-PLAT
43. SIGHT SWITCH
44. FUSE BOXES
45. LOCKING WHEEL
46. ADJUSTING WHEEL
47. CONTROL COLUMN
48. ELEVATION CONTROL ROD
49. HYDRAULIC ACCUMULATOR
50. SPARE LAMP HOLDER
51. AMMUNITION BOX
52. GUN ADJUSTER SPANNER
53. GUN ELEVATION RAM
54. FIRING CONTROL CABLE
55. COCKING TOOL
56. BELT THREADING TOOL
57. HAND ROTATION GEAR
58. AMMUNITION BOX REAR ATTACHMENT

59. ROTATION STOP BUFFER
60. FLOODLIGHT FOR DRIFT INDICATOR
61. HEATER SOCKET
62. CAMERA SWITCH
63. SAFETY BELT ANCHORAGE
64. AIR GUNNER'S SEAT
65. ROTATION LOCK

66. HYDRAULIC MOTOR
67. ROTATION LOCK RAMP
68. HYDRAULIC MOTOR PINION
69. GEAR RING
70. GUN ELEVATION RAM BRACKET
71. FIRING CONTROL VALVE
72. ROTATING RING

73. FELT DUST RING
74. RETAINING STRIP
75. FIXED RING
76. ACCOMMODATION RING
77. TURRET DRUM
78. HYDRAULIC MOTOR FILTER
79. VALVE BOX
80. CONNECTIONS TO EXTERNAL ROTATION VALVE
81. ROTATING SERVICE JOINT
82. EXHAUST OUTLET
83. OXYGEN CONNECTION
84. PRESSURE INLET

TAIL GUN TURRET

TYPES F.N.4A AND 4B

(For further information see A.P.1659A. Vol. I and Vol. II)

AIR DIAGRAM 1310 — AIR MINISTRY — MINISTRY OF AIRCRAFT PRODUCTION

Prologue

FOUR O'CLOCK, ON FRIDAY, 17 April 1942. A clear, pleasant spring afternoon of bright blue sky, high, wispy cloud, and just a slight haze. Approaching Cherbourg, on the Cotentin peninsula of Normandy, were twelve twin-engine Boston medium bombers, flying at around 12,000 feet. High above them, flying a protective top cover, were a group of three squadrons of fighters – some thirty-six in all.

At one minute past four, as the dry docks of the French port appeared, and with their bomb bays already open, the Bostons each dropped four 500-pound bombs.

German radar had, however, already picked up the raid as it had crossed the Channel, and immediately some eighteen Messerschmitt 109 single-engine fighters had been scrambled from Jagdgeschwader 2, the 'Richthofen Wing', based near Le Havre, further along the Normandy coast. No sooner were the bombs whistling down towards the port than Me 109s reached Cherbourg and were diving upon them. As the bombs exploded below, vast clouds of dust and grit and debris spiralling into the sky, the air had become a mêlée of aircraft, the bombers frantically turning for home and taking what evasive action they could while the Spitfires above dived down upon the German fighters in turn. Machine-gun and cannon tracer streaked across the sky, then suddenly one of the

Bostons, both engines aflame, was screaming downwards, a long trail of dark smoke following in its wake, but then so too was a Messerschmitt, and then another. White contrails streaked the deep blue afternoon sky, wisping smoke gradually dispersed, and another Messerschmitt seemed to be in trouble and plunging out of the fray, more smoke following in its wake. The remaining eleven Bostons, however, were now back out over the Channel, heading for home, those that had been clattered by bullets nursing their wounds, while the Spitfires chased off the remaining German fighters.

Just eleven minutes later, around 150 miles further east, another twelve Bostons were attacking two targets at Rouen, six bombing the shipyard and half a dozen more hitting the power station at Le Grand Quevilly to the south-east of the city. Again, the raid had been picked up by German radar and, this time, more than thirty Focke-Wulf 190s and Me 109s from Jagdgeschwader 2 and 26 had been scrambled from their bases at Beaumont le Roger to the south and Abbeville to the north. Fifteen of these had already been spotted by the second fighter group of escorting Spitfires and had been warned off.

Bombs crashed down on Rouen as light flak pumped upwards. More dust and smoke billowed into the air and then a fuel tank at the shipyard was hit and exploded in a burst of angry flame and thick black smoke. With the German fighters keeping out of the fray, the Bostons closed their bomb bays and headed for home, a further seventy-two Spitfires from RAF Fighter Command's 11 Group patrolling the Channel and protecting the skies as the bombers droned out over the sea. The attacks together had lasted just fifteen minutes.

As the Bostons were turning for home, seven Lancaster bombers from 44 Squadron were approaching Selsey Bill, a promontory east of Portsmouth on the south coast of England, en route to Augsburg, deep in Bavaria in southern Germany. With the Isle of Wight stretching away to their right, the seventh Lancaster, the reserve, left the formation and turned for home, no doubt with a mixed sense of relief and disappointment; amidst the fear and apprehension was a sense of pride and excitement among most of the crews that they should be part of such a special and important operation. The chosen six flew on, leaving England behind and dropping low over the Channel.

The four-engine Lancasters were new to RAF Bomber Command; 44 Squadron had been the first to receive the new much-vaunted heavy bomber, the initial three arriving on Christmas Eve the previous year.

The squadron was known as 'Rhodesia' because at least a quarter of its personnel were from the African state, and it was no coincidence that, before the First World War, Arthur Harris, now Commander-in-Chief of Bomber Command, had spent some of the happiest years of his life out there. Perhaps a little bit of favouritism had come into play, but there had to be one squadron that received the first production Lancasters, and the Rhodesia Squadron had as good a claim as any other; certainly, as one of 5 Group's principal squadrons they had already toiled hard and sacrificed many. Although neighbouring 97 Squadron, at Woodhall Spa, had been next to re-equip with Lancasters, it had been 44 Squadron who had taken them first into battle, carrying out mine-laying operations off the north German coast on 3–4 March. Now, along with six Lancasters from 97, they were taking part in the new bomber's first daylight operation and the first inland since Bomber Command had switched to night-bombing operations back in 1940.

But already this mission, codenamed Operation MARGIN, was not going entirely to plan. The Lancasters from 44 Squadron had been due to rendezvous with those from 97 Squadron over Grantham, but they had failed to do so. Although the crews had been training for two weeks, the squadrons had had just one practice link-up – again, over Grantham, three days earlier. They had not managed to find each other then, so perhaps it was no great surprise that they had failed to do so now that the training was over and the operation was happening for real. Bomber crews were used to operating at night, in no formation whatsoever, but, even on a clear sunny day, the sky remained a very big place and seven large aircraft, despite their size, could be hard to spot from more than a few miles.

So when 44 Squadron's Lancasters had reached Grantham and seen no sign of those from 97, Squadron Leader John Nettleton, flying *B-Baker*, and officially leading the entire two-squadron formation, had decided his flight should press on. He was conscious that time was of the essence, and in any case had never really thought of the operation as being really combined. Yes, they had carried out the same training as those from 97 Squadron, but apart from a few joint meetings had never actually trained *together*. Both flights knew the target and how to get there; it did not strike Nettleton as particularly necessary that they should fly there as one.

But the failure to rendezvous, however, was the least of Nettleton's worries. Unbeknown to him, it was the timings of the operation, which he had been told were so crucial to the mission's success, that were already going badly awry.

The Boston attacks on Cherbourg and Rouen had been launched primarily as a diversion. MARGIN's planning team at Bomber Command Headquarters in High Wycombe had been all too aware of the dangers of a daytime operation, but they were equally conscious that the biggest threat came from the only two enemy fighter groups still based in north-west France, JGs 2 and 26. If a diversionary raid could be launched just before the Lancasters flew over the French coast, then the German fighters in the area could be drawn away from them. Furthermore, if Nettleton's crews flew low – under 500 feet – they would pass undetected under the enemy's radar. And if they flew really low – under a hundred feet – they would be even safer from enemy fighters. 'It should be borne in mind,' noted Air Vice-Marshal Elworthy, Senior Air Staff Officer (SASO) at Bomber Command Headquarters in his Operation Order No. 143, 'that flying at ground level presents the most difficult problem to the attacking fighters'.

In any case, Elworthy was pretty confident that not only were German fighters thin on the ground – and in the air – over Normandy, but that by flying in close formation (something they did not do in night ops), the Lancasters would offer a pretty strong defensive shield. 'The fire power of a section of three heavy bombers,' he added, 'is such as to deter all but the most determined of enemy fighters.'

Combined operations of bombers and fighters operating over the continental coast were not uncommon. 'Circuses', as they were called, were frequent, with swarms of Spitfires offering protection for the bombers. And Elworthy had been most explicit about the timings: zero-hour was to be the time the Lancasters crossed the Normandy coast at Dives-sur-Mer. 'The circus operations,' he wrote, 'will be so timed that the bombing of Cherbourg and the target in the Pas de Calais area will take place simultaneously at Z minus 10.' In other words, the German fighters would then be busy tangling with 11 Group's Spitfires at the moment the Lancasters sneaked over the French coast. Further inland, the heavy bombers would, it was reckoned, probably have only light anti-aircraft fire to deal with, but by continuing to fly low and at speeds of some 250 mph, there was every chance the bombers would be past these before the gunners on the ground ever knew about them.

Fighter Command had also been generous with its support. No fewer than three wings, of some nine squadrons, making a total of around 108 Spitfires, had been detailed for the diversionary circus, which would be stacked up over the targets and out over the Channel at heights ranging from 10,000 to 24,000 feet. It was no wonder the enemy fighters of JG 26 had skulked off as soon as they saw them. On the face of it, nothing, it seemed, had been left to chance.

And yet for all this, somehow, somewhere along the line, the timings as dictated by Bomber Command and those issued for the diversionary circus by Fighter Command had drastically diverged.

On 12 April, four days after Elworthy had issued his operation order, Air Commodore Simpson, the SASO at Fighter Command HQ, had issued his own ops order to the three fighter wings, and had changed the timing of the circus attack to Z minus 50 rather than 10 minutes. This major error had not been corrected by the morning of the raid, when details of the operation were issued to the Tangmere, Kenley and Northolt fighter wings. As far as Fighter Command was concerned the targets were due to be bombed at 1600 hours, four o'clock in the afternoon, fifty, not ten, minutes before the Lancasters were due to cross the coast. Clearly anxious about this mix-up, HQ Bomber Command had hurriedly fired off a cypher message at 1245, almost three hours before any of the aircraft were to be airborne. 'Operation MARGIN Zero hours 1650,' ran the signal, and for extra clarification it then ran, '(1650 Double Summer Time). Acknowledge. Please confirm by phone.'

No acknowledgement was ever received.

At around 4.45 p.m., only five minutes earlier than Elworthy's plan, the six Lancasters from 44 Squadron were now approaching the French coast. Flying in two inverted 'V' formations – or 'vics' – with Nettleton's aircraft, *B-Baker*, leading, they climbed slightly to clear the coast, not at Dives, but a little further east along the coast at Villers-sur-Mer, then changed course south towards their next marker on the outward journey, the French town of Sens, around 200 miles away. Not far behind them, but a little further to the west, the six Lancasters from 97 Squadron, led by Squadron Leader John Sherwood, were also approaching the French coast, at Dives. It was just then that Sherwood reckoned he saw the boys from 44: just a glint in the sunlight, tiny dots away to his left. It was his one and only sighting.

Nettleton's co-pilot, the 21-year-old Pilot Officer Pat Dorehill, saw nothing of their fellow Lancasters, but was in no way concerned about that. In fact, Dorehill was rather enjoying himself. He had been excited by the entire operation. After all, it had meant two weeks off ops and plenty of practice, flying both formation – which none of them had done since flight training – and low-level. It had been terrific fun. Nor was he the sort of person to get 'windy' about ops. A bit apprehensive before take-off, perhaps, but nothing more; there were no pre-flight superstitions or mascots for him.

A Rhodesian, like Nettleton, Dorehill had been at university when war had broken out, and had been planning to go into mining, but had immediately volunteered for the Air Force instead. Like most Rhodesians, he was fiercely patriotic, and wanted to do his bit, and, since he had enjoyed watching the weekly Imperial Airways flying boats and South African Junkers passenger planes flying over, thought that becoming a pilot himself would offer plenty of excitement and adventure. He had not been disappointed.

After gaining his wings in Rhodesia and having already been singled out as having the right temperament for bombers, he had shipped over to England to finish his training. By the autumn of 1941, he was posted as a sergeant pilot to 44 Squadron, where he began flying the increasingly obsolete twin-engine Hampdens. Despite the lack of armament on the Hampdens, Dorehill had approached the prospect of operational flying with his usual phlegmatism. He was, by nature, an optimist; other people might get the chop, but not him, and having survived some fifteen ops, his old four-man crew had been split up and Dorehill posted a month earlier onto Nettleton's crew as co-pilot in preparation for his conversion to Lancasters.

'Co-pilot' was, however, something of a misnomer. The Lancasters were not dual control. Instead, Dorehill had to perch on a fold-down seat just below and at ninety degrees to the right of the pilot. Most of the time, he tended to stand instead, with the seat folded back up against the side. His role was to observe Nettleton, to help with pre-flight checks before take-off and to watch various dials and complete tasks such as the switch from one set of fuel tanks to another. In between, there was time to look out through the Perspex canopy and tear-drop viewing pane that enabled him to see straight down to the ground below.

And as they sped over France at around a hundred feet off the deck, that was quite a view. There was Caen to his right, and the Normandy countryside spread out around him. From that low height, he could see people below look up in wonder at these low-flying beasts, with their 102-foot-wide wing span and four throbbing Rolls-Royce Merlin engines, hurtling past at some 250 mph. Dorehill was enjoying himself.

The briefings for the operation had been given at 1100 hours that morning. U-boats, they were told, were causing untold destruction out at sea, especially to the Atlantic lifeline, and there were more on their way. At Bremen, at Kiel, and at Hamburg along the German Baltic coast, more and more submarines were being built. But, it was explained, those U-boats required engines – diesel engines to be precise. And these engines, invented by Rudolf Diesel in 1892, were principally built in Augsburg, Doctor Diesel's former home town, at the Maschinenfabrik Augsburg-Nürnberg, better known as the M.A.N. Works. From Lincolnshire, this was a 1,600-mile round trip, a huge distance even for the Lancaster.

At Woodhall Spa, most had guessed the operation would be a lengthy one: the long-distance training flights had suggested that, and there had been rumours that morning that the fuel tanks were being filled to maximum capacity. However, when the curtain had been pulled back and the target revealed, the chosen crews had all broken out into spontaneous laughter. Flying Officer Ernest 'Rod' Rodley, pilot of *F-Freddie*, could not believe the powers-that-be would be so foolish as to send twelve of its newest bombers all that distance and in broad daylight. 'We sat back and waited calmly for someone to say, "Now the real target is this,"' he noted. 'Unfortunately it was the real target.' As the realization set in, the briefing room became very quiet.

A few miles away at Waddington, the briefing for the 44 Squadron crews had prompted not laughter but certainly a sharp intake of breath. 'Don't be overawed by the distance to the target,' they were told. 'The RAF must strike this blow to help our seamen, and your Lancasters are the only aircraft that can strike it – with a fighting chance.' Nor would they be flying entirely in daylight. The plan was that they should hit the target in dusk and then fly the return leg under cover of darkness. Pat Dorehill had been surprised by the choice of target – he'd heard a rumour that they would be attacking the German battleship *Tirpitz*, but had not been overly concerned by the danger. The plan seemed sound enough to him, and he was convinced by the argument that six Lancasters flying together would offer a very robust defence. 'If we were attacked,' he says, 'I thought we would be able to give as good as we got, so I wasn't too bothered.'

Furthermore, he had complete faith in Nettleton, whom he was now standing beside as they turned south-east. Some light flak had opened up just as they had crossed the coast, but none of the planes appeared to have been hit. Nettleton dropped lower still, just above the rooftops, and Dorehill could now see people stopping to wave, while in the fields cattle and other livestock ran in fright as the Lancasters roared over them.

Soon after, they found themselves following the line of a railway and there was a train, heading south-east. Nettleton's gunner asked whether they could open fire, but their skipper told them to hold off. He didn't want ammunition being wasted. The railway was now on a raised embankment so that the Lancasters were flying almost alongside, rather than above, the train.

It was soon after this that they were approaching Beaumont-le-Roger. *V-Victor* was at the back of the formation, on the port side of the second vic, but her pilot, Warrant Officer John Beckett, now suddenly spotted the glint of fighters returning to base away to his left. They had been told at the briefing to observe strict radio silence except in emergency, but Beckett reckoned this was an emergency all right.

'One-oh-nines!' he exclaimed over the R/T. 'At eleven o'clock high!'

During the briefings, the crews had been assured that the route was due to miss any enemy airfields, and yet the course from the coast to Sens was always going to run pretty close to Beaumont-le-Roger, a major Luftwaffe fighter airfield since the summer of 1940 and well-known to the RAF, so it is strange that the prescribed route should have run them so close. Perhaps had 44 Squadron crossed at Dives-sur-Mer, like Sherwood's Lancasters in 97 Squadron and as specified in the original operation order, they might have missed it; but at Waddington they had been briefed to cross at Villers-sur-Mer, six miles further along. It probably made all the difference. Even so, the navigators would have planned their route carefully beforehand, with pencil lines marked onto maps. Draw a straight line from Villers-sur-Mer to Sens, and it will pass right over Beaumont-le-Roger. Yet, for some reason, Beaumont had not been flagged up.

As it was, the railway they were following also led directly to Beaumont. Out on the airfield, the Lancasters were both heard and then spotted. Otto Happel, a signaller at JG 2, the 'Richthofen' HQ, heard the shouts, and immediately put a warning out over the radio to the Focke-Wulf 190s of the II. Gruppe that were now coming back into land from the earlier scrap with the Bostons and Spitfires. Commanding JG 2 was Major Walter 'Gulle' Oesau, one of the Luftwaffe's leading aces, with more than a hundred kills to his name. He had been in the HQ building at the time, but Happel now watched him rush out and run as fast as he could to his Me 109, which was always kept at immediate readiness. Right behind him was Fritz Edelmann, his wing man. Within a couple of minutes, Oesau and Edelmann were hurtling down the runway in hot pursuit of the bombers.

Ahead of them was Kommandeur Heino Greisert, commander of II. Gruppe, and several of his pilots in their FW 190s, rather than Me 109s, who had been coming into land, undercarriage down, when they had heard Happel's warning. Greisert had immediately opened the throttle, retracted the undercarriage, and pulling back on the stick had climbed once more in hot pursuit.

'Roger, wing men keep tight!' Nettleton had called out in response to Beckett's warning. Standing beside Nettleton, Pat Dorehill had turned around, peering out of the astrodome at the enemy fighters as they initially appeared to be landing, but then he saw the undercarriage of the lead fighter fold up back into the wings and the machine surge forward.

Moments later, Crum's Lancaster, *T-Tommy*, at the rear right of the formation, was under attack, a bullet hitting the canopy, Perspex splinters spitting around the cabin. Now, however, the lone attacker had been joined by more, and suddenly a Focke-Wulf was bearing down on Beckett's plane. None of the crew of *V-Victor* could have known it, but this was Kommandeur Greisert himself, another ace, and in moments his cannon shells had struck. Flame lashed out from one of the engines, spreading in a trice as the fuel tanks caught alight and enveloping the fuselage so that the stricken Lancaster appeared to be engulfed by angry fire. Beckett's plane slowly dropped height, flame and smoke trailing behind, before plunging into a field, ploughing a vicious furrow and then smashing into some trees and exploding into a million pieces of metal and oil, rubber and incinerated flesh.

In *T-Tommy*, Crum was still desperately trying to fly, but over his intercom he could hear someone shouting that they were hit. The port wing was on fire, while large holes of torn and flapping metal had been ripped out of the fuselage. Crum jettisoned the bombs, and immediately the Lancaster seemed to momentarily lift, but it was too late. In the nose, front gunner Sergeant Bert Dowty watched with mounting horror as the ground rushed towards them. *My God!* he thought. *We're going to crash. Crummy's going to fly us straight into the deck!* Instinctively, he drew his knees up, waiting for the crash and what he knew must surely be his last moments. But then the Lancaster seem to glide, just above the stall, and with the ground ahead now clear of trees, Crum managed to slide the still burning Lancaster gently onto its belly. With a screech and groan of thirty tons of metal scraping across the ground, *T-Tommy* finally came to a halt. While the crew clambered out, Dowty found himself trapped in the nose, the escape hatch now resting on the ground. Taking the Browning machine gun from its mounting, he swung it at the Perspex, but could not get enough of a swing to hit it hard enough. Beginning to panic, Dowty then saw a bloodied Crum clamber down into the nose and hack a hole with a crash axe. Pushing their way out, Crum turned to Dowty and said, 'You know the drill. Destroy the kit and clear off. I want to see what's happened over there.'

Dowty watched his pilot run towards *V-Victor*'s crash site. Beckett had been his closest friend.

In *B-Baker*, Pat Dorehill was watching the battle from the astrodome, while both he and Nettleton were receiving a running commentary from Flight Sergeant Harrison, the rear gunner. With both *Victor* and *Tommy* down, the German fighters were concentrating on Flight-Lieutenant Nick Sandford's plane, *P-Peter*. Sandford had been one of the first pilots to convert to Lancasters and was one of the most skilled in the squadron, yet he could not shake off the 190s on his tail. Swerving and yawing the aircraft as much as he dared, he then dropped even lower, flying at zero height. At one point he even flew the Lancaster *under* a line of power cables. Three fighters followed him, but with his controls now damaged and engines on fire, even Sandford was unable to hold the great beast steady. A moment later, a wing tip clipped the ground and the Lancaster cartwheeled and exploded in a ball of fire, killing the crew instantly. It was the Richthofen's thousandth recorded kill.

'We're down to three, Skipper,' came Harrison's voice over the intercom in *B-Baker*.

Pat Dorehill had seen the blast of fire from the disintegrating Lancaster and crew. All three of the second section had now been shot down and the German fighters were still swarming around the surviving lead section. Worse, far from returning the kind of robust fire that had been predicted, the three Lancasters were discovering that they were horribly out-gunned. On Nettleton's starboard side, *H-Howe*'s six machine guns were all jammed, no doubt from over-heating, while, in *B-Baker*, Harrison's rear two machine guns had also jammed. Although the mid-upper gunner was still firing, the machine-gun bullets were nothing like as effective as the Focke-Wulfs' and Messerschmitts' combined machine guns and 20mm cannons.

For the attacking German fighters, it was all too obvious that the right-hand Lancaster – *H-Howe* – was the weakest, and it was this one that Major Oesau, now joining the fray, targeted. Closing until he was at almost point-blank range, he opened fire with both his cannons and machine guns, swinging the nose so that it raked the width of the aircraft.

In *B-Baker*, Pat Dorehill, still standing in the cockpit beside Nettleton, could now see the destruction of the fourth Lancaster in the formation in graphic detail. Flames were streaking along the wing and rapidly growing so that in moments the fuselage was awash with fire too. Dorehill watched as Dusty Rhodes, the pilot, struggled desperately to keep the stricken aircraft airborne, and then suddenly it seemed to climb, before swooping back down again directly towards *B-Baker*. Dorehill flinched but then it was gone, diving underneath their starboard wing and crashing with another deadly explosion. 'It only missed us by a fraction,' says Dorehill. 'And you could see their faces in the cockpit. It was quite gruesome.'

The two remaining Lancasters flew on.

Around them, however, the enemy fighters still swarmed. Dorehill now noticed vapour trails from the starboard wing, a sign of a fuel leak, but no sooner had he told Nettleton than another Messerschmitt roared down upon them, machine guns firing, and slid between them as they brushed the treetops. Another German fighter attacked, this time Oesau's wingman, Edelmann, his cannons spent and so drawing as close as he dared to use his machine guns. A splinter flew across the cockpit. 'What the hell?' said Dorehill, clapping a hand to his neck. But he was lucky – a graze only. Nettleton began laughing, the tension, strangely, momentarily relieved by the expression of indignation rather than pain on Dorehill's face. Behind them, machine guns from their own aircraft and from *A-Apple* on their port continued to chatter, and at last a lone bullet seemed to hit the pursuing Messerschmitt. With a puff of smoke from the engine, Edelmann broke off and suddenly their pursuers were gone, ammunition and fuel spent.

It was now 5.15 p.m. and just two of the six 44 Squadron Lancasters remained, Nettleton's *B-Baker* and Flying Officer John Garwell's *A-Apple*. Nettleton and Dorehill wondered, briefly, whether they should head south and turn back over the Bay of Biscay, but then they dismissed the idea. There was a mission to do, after all. Those deaths would really have been for nothing if they gave up now, and, it seemed, the self-sealing lining on the fuel tanks had worked, for the vapour trail had gone. So they kept going, low over France, heading towards Switzerland and Lake Constance.

No other fighter aircraft troubled them, but they did fly over an army barracks or depot and, as far as Dorehill was concerned, the men below seemed to be ready for them because a volley of small arms greeted them. Not one bullet hit *B-Baker*, but *A-Apple* was peppered with small arms, so much so that his starboard wing tip was completely shredded and flapping uselessly. The men on the ground appeared to have been expecting them, but had they guessed the target was Augsburg or had the Germans been fooled into thinking it was probably Munich? Only time would tell.

They reached Switzerland without further incident, and flew low over Lake Constance, steam rising from the dark water, the sky above deepening as dusk approached. Then briefly they climbed over the Vosges Mountains, heading north-east before dropping once more as, at long last, Augsburg came into view nestling in a valley beneath forested hills.

Not only was the navigator carefully plotting the course, but both the bomb-aimer and Dorehill, next to Nettleton, also had maps. Dorehill reckoned his was pretty good – a scale of 1:500 – and he soon saw the canal that snaked through the town, and which led, as its course ran north-west, to the M.A.N. Works beside it. Already light flak was pumping into the sky, tracer arcing towards them. The two front gunners returned fire, but thankfully both Nettleton and Flight Lieutenant McClure, the bomb-aimer, had already spotted the distinct shape of the M.A.N. factory. With a low whirr, the bomb bay doors opened.

With the big wings and four engines of the Lancaster spread out either side of the cockpit and with the nose in front, neither Dorehill nor Nettleton could now see the target. They had to trust entirely in McClure, who was staring directly at the ground below through his bombsight. Flak and small arms continued to pepper the sky around them, sirens droned from below, the town now fully awake to the arrival of the two Lancasters, but McClure had his mind closed to all but the task in hand. 'Steady,' he told his pilot, then said, 'left, left.' And then, 'Bombs gone!'

Suddenly the Lancaster lurched upwards as the weight of the bombs left its belly, and both Nettleton and Dorehill began counting, knowing that on the beat of eleven seconds, the time-delayed fuses would ignite and the bombs explode. And then a flash of light behind them and the ripple of explosions, as Nettleton continued banking to the west. At the M.A.N. plant, parts of the roof and the upper floor were hurtling into the sky as the blast tore through the factory. From the rear, Harrison reported a direct hit. It was 7.55 p.m., still dusk, and the M.A.N. plant was disappearing behind a cloud of dust and debris.

But as Nettleton now looked around for Garwell, he could no longer see him off his port wing.

'Can you see *A-Apple*, rear gunner?' he asked Harrison over the intercom.

'Starboard quarter, Skipper, a bit above us,' came the reply, 'I think he's got a fire in the fuselage.'

Dorehill could now see the burning Lancaster himself. All around Augsburg were hills, mostly wooded hills, with little or no opportunity for making a forced landing. It was clear Garwell's plane was not going to survive – not with flame billowing from the fuselage, not at such low height; not with thick, choking smoke, billowing into the cockpit. Somehow, though, Garwell managed to find an open field, and the next moment it was sliding and grinding its way across the grass until finally it came to a halt as it broke in two. All but one escaped unhurt. Theirs had been a very lucky escape.

Soon after *B-Baker* had turned for home, the six Lancasters of 97 Squadron reached Augsburg after a largely uneventful flight, but the town's gunners were alert and ready and soon flak was pouring into the air towards them. Flying Officer Rodley, in *F-Freddie*, had been sitting on an inverted tin helmet the whole way and now, as he approached the still smoking factory, was glad for it, however uncomfortable, as bullets and shards of flak clattered along the underside of the Lancaster. Black puffs of exploding heavy flak were also peppering the sky. At the briefing, they had been told the 88mm guns could not be brought to bear on low-flying aircraft, but it didn't seem that way now.

Realizing the assembly shed – their main target – was too narrow for three Lancasters flying side by side to attack together, Rodley now fell back behind the leader, Squadron Leader Sherwood, dropping his bombs a fraction later. Emerging through the smoke, he now saw white vapour trailing from Sherwood's Lancaster, *K-King*, then it immediately turned black and a moment later flames were billowing from the aircraft. He saw the flaming Lancaster slowly swing to the starboard and heard one of his gunners call out, 'Christ, Skipper, he's going in. A flaming chrysanthemum!' Even before their bombs had exploded, *K-King* had crashed into the ground, the Lancaster breaking up in bursts of angry flame. Despite this, and unbeknown to Rodley, Sherwood alone had survived. Still strapped to his seat, he had been flung out of the cockpit, his fall broken by the pines growing around.

Now the final section of three, some way behind Sherwood's section, reached Augsburg. Already, as they neared the town, Warrant Officer Mycock's Lancaster was hit, mortally, as it turned out, in the front turret, with fire spreading rapidly. Despite this, Mycock flew on, and even managed to drop his bombs on target.

The pilot was still at his controls when it suddenly swung to port and plunged into the ground, bursting into flames. All on board were killed. Another of the three, Flying Officer Deverill's aircraft, *Y-York*, had also been hit in the starboard wing and his outer port engine had also stopped, but at least it was still flying. And at least it was now nearly dark.

Before midnight, all four Lancasters from 97 Squadron had safely made it back to Woodhall Spa, including Deverill's *Y-York*, which had flown the entire leg on three engines. None of them had returned unscathed; all had battle damage of various degrees of severity. But while the surviving crews were tucking into bacon and eggs, across Lincolnshire, at Waddington, the silence of the night had been stultifying. Not one Lancaster had returned.

As midnight came and went, and with still no distant hum of engines to break the silence of the night, the duty staff had been stood down. The lights in the hangars were switched off. Not one of the crews, it seemed, would be returning.

But *B-Baker* had not been lost, but was lost – hopelessly lost. The return leg had, thankfully, been uneventful except for one thing: they had been unable to get a bearing that would fix their position.

Perhaps, then, they had been flying the wrong course, even though Pilot Officer Sands, the navigator, had already carefully worked out the bearings for the route home. Nettleton had begun to lose faith in the master gyro-compass, from which the cockpit gyro was set, and so Dorehill now clambered back, over the two wing spars, towards the rear of the fuselage to the hatch, next to which the master gyro-compass was kept, hanging freely in a wire cage to prevent it from being knocked about. Nettleton had wondered whether perhaps, at some point, the compass had been knocked so badly that it had stuck at an angle that had given it misleading readings from then on. Dorehill, however, found nothing wrong with it at all and, having clambered back, reported this to Nettleton. The skipper, even so, decided to use the P4 compass instead from then on. This was a secondary, magnetic compass that lay underneath the main panel to the pilot's left. It was reliable enough in straight and level flight, but the needle flickered in any turn and was tricky to read at night.

At any rate, when they finally crossed the coastline, they were pretty certain it didn't look like France. Eventually, at half past midnight and with fuel low, Nettleton admitted defeat and ordered Sergeant Charlie Churchill, the wireless operator, to get a fix.

'Can I use SOS, Skipper?' asked Churchill.

'Use what you like, but get us home,' Nettleton replied. Churchill tapped out the familiar dots and dashes but for what seemed like a painfully long time there was nothing. He tried again, tapping out the signal once more, and then, at last, to his enormous relief, he received a reply and moments later an answer to his request for range and bearing information to the airfield.

'Course is zero-seven-zero, sir,' Churchill relayed to Nettleton. 'They're sending us to Squire's Gate.'

Sands was studying the map. 'That's just south of Blackpool,' he told them. 'It means we're over the Irish Sea.' They had overshot England altogether.

At 0059, on the morning of 18 April 1942, *B-Baker* safely touched down on the grass airfield of Squire's Gate after some ten hours in the air, the last of just five out of twelve Lancasters to return.

The Augsburg Raid was finally over.

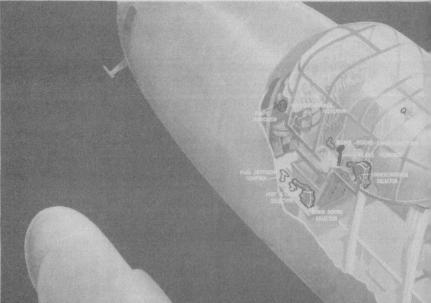

UNDERCARRIAGE

NORMAL OPERATION

NOTES

EMERGENCY OPERATION

METHOD 1 METHOD 2

WING FLAPS

EMERGENCY OPERATION

METHOD 1 METHOD 2

NORMAL OPERATION

UP
NEUTRAL
DOWN

RTP

LANCASTER I II III

(al Use Only)

Part I

TOWARDS GREENLIGHT

1

Signs of Progress

WEDNESDAY, 27 JANUARY 1943. Speeding along the quiet country Chiltern back roads at just after 8.30 in the morning was a black two-seater Bentley sports saloon, with a lighted sign on the front that said 'Priority'. Despite the speed with which the Bentley was travelling, there was no especial reason for its driver to be making such haste, but that was how Air Marshal Sir Arthur Harris liked to drive, whether it was him at the wheel – which it often was – or his chauffeur, Maddocks. He enjoyed driving and at a furious pace, and the Bentley, especially when handled skilfully, was happy to oblige.

The route from Springfields, the C-in-C's house, to Bomber Command Headquarters was just a shade over four miles, so that at 8.35 a.m., just a few minutes after leaving his wife and young daughter at home, Harris was tearing through the village of Walter's Ash, and moments later, turning into the main entrance of RAF High Wycombe and then accelerating once more, along the road towards his office at No. 1 Site, various staff officers and WAAFs hurriedly moving off the road and out of the way of the speeding black beast.

No. 1 Site consisted of a number of buildings, purpose-built in the 1930s and completed by 1940, when it became Bomber Command HQ, and it was outside one of these, a three-storey building of little charm but considerable functionality, that the Bentley finally came to a halt. Stepping out, Harris passed into the Air Staff Block, and straight to his office, which was on the ground floor, along with those of his other senior staff. Waiting for him was his personal secretary, Assistant Section Officer Peggy Wherry, a WAAF known to be almost as formidable as her boss. Handed a folder of the night's most important signals, he then pulled out a cigarette, quickly read through them, then, just before nine, stepped out of the office again and back to his Bentley for the daily conference.

This was held in the deep underground bunker that was the Headquarters Operations Room. It was only a few hundred yards away, but Harris always drove. He hated walking anywhere. As a young man in Rhodesia, he had fought with the 1st Rhodesian Regiment against the Germans in South-West Africa and during the campaign had marched some 500 miles across the Kalahari Desert in pursuit of the enemy. Poorly equipped, and poorly fed and watered, they had all struggled with extreme fatigue and even hallucinations, and it was then that the 23-year-old private vowed to never again walk a single step if he could get any form of vehicle to carry him. It was one of the reasons he had headed back to England and joined the Royal Flying Corps once the campaign was over.

At home, 'Bert' Harris would be witty and jocular, talkative, tender towards his wife and daughter, and a considerate host to the many hundreds of luminaries and VIPs that made their way to Springfields. The life and soul, in fact. At the office, however, he could not have been more different. He had a bull of a face – square, with piercing pale eyes and light, greying, gingery hair and a trim moustache, and the kind of immediate presence that pullulated with authority. At the office, he might allow himself an occasional smirk, but he was altogether more serious, more austere. A man who never played for popularity, who suffered no fools and wasted none of his valuable time on unnecessary words or civilities.

By the time he had walked down the long steps into the 'Hole', as the Ops Room was known, he expected all those who were to attend the daily conference to be there. He had no truck whatsoever with those who were late. Rarely did he raise his voice; he did not need to. A terse comment or even a stony glare was enough to show his displeasure.

The Ops Room was rectangular with an ops board on the facing wall, and a large map covering the far end wall, and all over-looked by a viewing gallery above. At this morning's 'High Mass', however, a chair and desk had been placed in the centre of the room, around which stood the C-in-C's senior staff. There was a pronounced hush as he entered the room, took off his cap, sat down, and took out and lit another of his American cigarettes. Next to him stood the ruddy-faced and moustachioed Air Vice-Marshal Robert 'Sandy' Saundby, his Senior Air Staff Officer (SASO), as well as his deputy, the Air Commodore Ops, the Deputy SASO, his naval and army liaison officers, his Intelligence Officer, Senior Engineer Staff Officer and Armament Officer, and, last, but by no means least, Dr Magnus Spence, his Chief Meteorological Officer.

'Did the Hun do anything last night?' he asked.

The Intelligence Officer briskly told him then handed him a list of priority targets, most of which had come from the Air Ministry in London, staff officers of lower rank than Harris, and whom he instinctively disliked; he did not think it was their role to try and tell him his job, however indirectly.

Harris studied the list, then, after conferring with Saundby, announced that the night's raid would be directed at Düsseldorf. He then turned to Dr Spence. This particular conversation was always a critical part of the conference. Mounting a raid required no small amount of investment in terms of fuel, bombs, aircraft, and, of course, men's lives. It was imperative that as far as possible every operation should have the greatest possible chance of success, and Harris always grilled Spence deeply; the C-in-C reckoned he had a good nose for weather. Even so, he always deferred to Spence's final word on the matter, although on this occasion it was straightforward enough: the weather looked promising, Spence told him. He forecast clear skies over the target. Harris was satisfied with that.

Next came the allocation of aircraft. It looked as though there would be under 200 available, of which only 120 or so would be Lancasters. Crews were not expected to fly two nights in a row, and 157 bombers had been sent to attack the U-boat pens at Lorient on the French Atlantic coast the previous evening. Nor was Bomber Command, in January 1943, a large force. Harris had just over 500 aircraft of all types, of which little more than 300 were 'heavies' – that is, four-engine bombers such as the Lancaster, Stirling and Halifax. In fact, he could call on fewer than a hundred more aircraft than he had had when he had taken over as Commander-in-Chief of Bomber Command just under a year before. Of the three RAF home commands – Fighter, Coastal and Bomber – it was Bomber Command that remained the smallest, even though Harris's bomber force remained the primary weapon of attack against Hitler's Germany.

Almost a year in office and yet Harris still could not launch his all-out bombing offensive against Hitler's war machine. Expansion had been painfully slow. It was all very frustrating and largely due to factors beyond his control. Not only was Bomber Command a small force, but he had been obliged to use what crews and aircraft he did have for a number of other purposes besides the strategic bombing of the Third Reich. The biggest threat to Britain had been seen to be that posed by the U-boats in the Battle of the Atlantic, but in the first half of 1942 further resources had been sucked up by the escalating and worsening war against Japan in the Far East and then, in June, by the near-annihilation of the Eighth Army in North Africa, the only place where Britain was actively engaging German troops on land. Not only were bombers needed in the Mediterranean and Middle East, but Harris was expected to repeatedly attack U-boat pens, and to use vast amounts of his meagre forces laying sea-mines.

In addition to the diversion of resources, there were also issues of training crews and rebuilding morale after the mauling the Command had received in the first years of the war, while the failure of the Manchester bomber had also hugely delayed expansion. Much of the Command's hopes in 1941 had rested on this twin-engine bomber designed by Roy Chadwick at A. V. Roe, but the engines had proved under-powered and completely un-suitable for the airframe. The Lancaster, powered by four

Rolls-Royce Merlin engines, had been developed out of the failure of the Manchester, but this all took time, as did the production of increasing numbers of the four-engine wonder-bomber that Harris believed the Lancaster was; in this new bomber, he at last had an aircraft that would be able to carry not just a handful of lightweight incendiaries, but really big bombs – bombs weighing as much as 10,000lb, possibly even bigger than that. Bombs that could cause really large amounts of destruction.

Nor had Harris had enough airfields, or even airfields that could handle four-engine heavies – stations which were needed not only for the operational squadrons but for the Heavy Conversion Units where crews were trained to operate these bigger bombers. Back in October 1941, the Air Ministry had accepted that airfields needed to be built with runways adequate for heavy bombers, but not until more than a year later was this policy actually implemented, by which time many of them had to be given over to the American bomber units which were starting to arrive in England. No one was grumbling at the arrival of the Americans, least of all Harris, but this still had consequences for the speed of expansion of Bomber Command.

Yet perhaps the biggest stumbling block of all was the lack of effective navigational aids. A device codenamed GEE had been tested over Germany in 1941 and had started being fitted into aircraft by early 1942. This was a radar pulse system that enabled a navigator on board an aircraft to fix his position by measuring the distance of pulses from three different ground stations in England. It was hoped that this would allow accurate navigation to targets, especially in the Ruhr industrial heartland in western Germany. GEE had helped, but in practice it had proved nothing like as accurate as the scientists had hoped, its range was short – the Ruhr was about the limit of its reach – and it was certainly not good enough to aid blind flying. This meant that Harris's bombers were still dependent on clear skies and preferably a decent moon, which in turn made the bombers an easier target for the German flak guns and night fighters. Furthermore, by the summer, the enemy had already worked out how to effectively jam GEE.

But, at last, two potentially exciting new radar devices had been developed – devices which, it was hoped, would finally allow Harris's crews to navigate both blind and accurately to the target. The first was codenamed 'Oboe'. This relied on a radio signal pulse repeater in the aircraft linked to two ground stations back in the UK. In other words, it was in effect a development of GEE. It still had limited range and could only cope with the signals from no more than six aircraft per hour, but tests had repeatedly proved its accuracy and it was also seemingly impervious to enemy jamming.

There were neither enough sets nor the capacity for Oboe to be used with an entire bomber force, but it could be employed with Harris's small numbers of Mosquitoes. These were very fast, light-weight twin-engine aircraft and part of Harris's Pathfinder Force, or PFF as it was known. The idea was that the Mosquitoes, using Oboe, would fly ahead of the main bomber stream, then over the target lay down ground markers, flares that would burst in a cascade just above the ground, and far more accurate than the parachute flares that had originally been used by the PFF Mosquitoes. These would then show the bombers following in their wake where to drop their bombs.

And that night's raid against Düsseldorf was to be the first time PFF Mosquitoes would be using Oboe. It was, as Harris was well aware, potentially a major step forward.

Satisfied that the bomb loads and time over target had been agreed, Harris stood up without a further word, replaced his cap and left. Details of routes and squadron allocations were for Saundby and his other senior staff officers to sort out; Harris's job was to lead, to provide direction, not trouble himself with the kind of details that could be perfectly well handled by others.

Harris drove back towards his office. Back in 1940, when he had been Deputy Chief of the Air Staff, he had been watching the Blitz one evening from the roof of the Air Ministry with Air Marshal Sir Charles Portal, then only newly appointed Chief of the Air Staff. Bombs were falling and London was burning and aglow with flames. 'Well,' Harris said, turning to Portal, 'they are sowing the wind.' A year and a half later, he was commander of Bomber Command and the man given the task of leading the strategic bombing campaign against Germany. The decision to carry out area bombing of German cities was not his – that had been made higher up the chain of command, and was one that Portal, as Chief of the Air Staff, was perhaps the biggest proponent. Yet Harris was an unwavering bomber advocate. He believed, quite zealously, that the best way to win the war was by destroying German cities. Destroy the cities, he believed, and Germany's capacity to produce war materiel would be destroyed as well. With no war materiel, Hitler would no longer be able to continue the war. Such a policy would cost the lives of many aircrew, but the losses would be nothing compared to the great slaughter of men lost in another drawn-out land war like that of a generation earlier – a war in which Harris fought. Whether such a bombing campaign would break the morale of the German people on whom these bombs would inevitably fall was, to his mind, neither here nor there. 'It was not necessary,' he noted, 'to take these possibilities into account; bombing, there was every reason to suppose, would cripple the enemy's war industries if it was carried out for long enough and with sufficient weight.'

It was the 'sufficient weight' that was the crux of the matter. For all the damage the Germans had caused during the Blitz, it had *not* been carried out with sufficient weight – Coventry and one or two other raids being the exceptions. The Luftwaffe had only had twin-engine bombers, capable of carrying no more than comparatively light payloads of bombs. A Dornier 17, for example, one of the mainstays of the Luftwaffe bombing fleet, could carry just 2,205lb of bombs; the Heinkel 111 could manage just over 4,000lb. In sharp contrast, the current Lancasters could manage 14,000lb. Nor had the Germans had anything like enough aircraft. They had invented the Blitz, Harris reckoned, without ever appreciating its strategic possibilities. And as for morale – in Britain, this had improved with the Blitz; the German bombing campaign had helped forge a unity of purpose among the British people and a determination to fight on, to never surrender. It *might* be possible to break the morale of a people, but only when cities lay totally devastated.

No, it was perfectly clear to Harris. The best way to win the war was to divert as many resources as possible into the strategic bombing campaign. To build more and more heavy bombers, with bigger and more destructive bombs, and to wipe as many cities as possible from the face of the earth.

The advent of Oboe was an important step forward, and in a few days' time a further blind navigation aid would be used on an operation too: H2S, which was effectively the first ever ground-mapping radar. The 'echo map' created by the radar pulse returns on board the aircraft was crude, and target identification required considerable skill, but it was not limited by range and had the potential to be accurate up to just a little over a mile. It was known as 'Home Sweet Home', a nickname which suggested the high hopes held for it. These two tools, at long last, would give his bombers the chance to bomb with the kind of accuracy that had simply not been possible before.

The past eleven months had been a time of rebuilding and retraining, of experimentation. But now, after nearly a year in the job, Harris believed his bomber force was almost ready to start the strategic bombing campaign in earnest. What was important was to maintain that resolve and not be diverted from the task and method of achieving that aim. Singleness of purpose; that was the key. And that meant lots of heavy bombers dropping lots of bombs on German cities. As far as Harris was concerned, it was as simple as that.

Some 150 miles north, in the largely flat Lincolnshire countryside, the crews of 97 Squadron were readying themselves for another day. The airfield was still only a year old, built as a satellite of the much larger RAF Coningsby a few miles down the road, and although it lay to the south of the little spa town, on specially cleared open ground in the middle of nowhere, for the officers RAF Woodhall Spa had one very big advantage: the mock-Tudor Edwardian mansion, Petwood House, which had been requisitioned the previous year and now served as the Officers' Mess. Not only was the house itself extremely comfortable, but it had extensive grounds complete with croquet pitches, tennis courts and a swimming pool.

It was partly for this reason that the 23-year-old Pilot Officer Les Munro found he had little cause to venture out to the surrounding towns of Boston and even Lincoln whenever he was not flying. The son of a sheep station shepherd from Gisborne, on the north-east corner of New Zealand's North Island, Munro tended to spend his time when not flying or on ops at Petwood, socializing in the Mess or playing cripette and shove ha'penny and swimming in the grounds. He reckoned it was a pretty good place to relax in between the intensity of flying combat operations over the Third Reich. In any case, he did not have a car, wasn't a great one for drinking endless pints of beer, and, in the cold of winter, it made sense to him to stay put as far as possible.

By ten o'clock, he and the other officers in the squadron had breakfasted and had taken a ride down through Woodhall and south to the airfield. Munro reported into the Flight hut with Pilot Officer Jock Rumbles, his navigator and the only other officer in his crew, where the news had already arrived that they would be flying that night, and to Düsseldorf. Take-off was due to begin at 1800 hours.

Munro had joined the squadron back in December. He was a tall, broad-shouldered man, quiet and thoughtful, but his face was always ready to crease into a big smile. His father hailed from Scotland, from the woollen mills of Glasgow, but at the turn of the century had contracted TB and emigrated to New Zealand, and in due course was employed as a shepherd on Marshlands sheep station, some sixteen miles from Gisborne. There he had met and married Munro's mother. Marsham Station was a pretty remote spot, although it had a pub, a small school and a general store, but the Munros were a further five miles away from there, so that the young Les had a ten-mile round trip to school. At home, there were no neighbours, so he and his younger brother and sister had to make their own fun. Money was scarce and the children were all expected to help about the place. It was a hard – and isolated – life.

Later, money was so short he had to give up high school, and at sixteen left to work on a dairy farm. Two years on, by the time war broke out, he was working on a mixed sheep and cropping farm not far from Gisborne, and from there he used to see the commercial aeroplanes fly over fairly regularly. By April 1940, when he turned twenty-one, his younger brother, Ian, had already joined the army, but Les decided by then that he wanted to become a pilot. Unfortunately, his truncated schooling meant that he did not have the right qualifications. He was told he could be aircrew instead. 'But I had my mind set on being a pilot,' he says. Showing the kind of determination that would stand him in good stead later, he immediately took a correspondence course, got his mathematics up to scratch, and was then finally accepted for pilot training.

Unusually, Munro volunteered to be a bomber pilot, rather than a fighter pilot as was the preference of most – it appealed more to his conservative nature, and it was to Canada that he was now sent to complete his pilot's training. When he left on 20 October 1941, it was the first time he had left the North Island's shores. The United States, Canada and Britain – the mother country – were different worlds. He saw the film star Alexis Smith in Los Angeles, flew over the snowy wilds of Saskatoon, then finally crossed the Atlantic to Liverpool on the *Cape Town Castle* in early March 1942, with his wings on his tunic and a commission to boot.

After a brief stay at the transit base in Bournemouth, Munro had been posted to No. 29 Operational Training Unit in North Luffenham, in Rutland, and it was there that he gained his first crew. Pilots and crew had all assembled in a large room at the station and been told to sort themselves out. It was an ad hoc method, but generally tended to work. It certainly did for Munro, who immediately teamed up with his navigator, Jock Rumbles, a Scot who had emigrated to South Africa before the war, but had returned and joined the Royal Air Force, and his mid-upper gunner, Bill Howarth. Finding the wireless operator and bomb-aimer took a bit more time, but soon enough there was the full crew of five, and so began the job of converting onto the Vickers Wellington twin-engine bomber.

The Wellington had come into service in September 1939, and since then had been a mainstay of Britain's bomber force. Although the Wellington had been designed by Vickers Aviation's Chief Designer, R. K. Pierson, its entire structure was a spiralling metal geodetic design, that had been invented by Vickers' Assistant Chief Designer, Barnes Wallis. The problem with the geodetic design was that it was used only by Vickers, which caused problems with outsourcing production, and it was time-consuming to build too; however, the advantages were enormous. The metal lattice gave the structure immense strength and enabled it to take incredible levels of punishment without the airframe collapsing. Moreover, it was a lightweight design for the size of aircraft, which gave it a load and range-to-power ratio that was superior to those of other similar-sized machines. Certainly, Les Munro thought it was a decent enough aircraft, good to fly, and strong too, as he was soon to discover.

Back at the end of May, Air Marshal Harris had launched the first ever 'thousand-bomber raid' against Cologne. Although Bomber Command had been only 400 aircraft strong at the time, by scouring the Operational Training Units (OTUs) and other commands, and by using a number of, frankly, completely obsolete aircraft, they had managed to reach the magic figure of a thousand bombers. It was a high-risk *coup de théâtre*, but one that was seized upon – as Harris had hoped – by the media and which was broadly a great success: heavy damage had been inflicted on an important target and it seemed the German high command had also been gratifyingly horrified. Harris had not only given his Command a tremendous boost, but had done much to convince the sceptics that Bomber Command really could, after all, pose a serious threat to Germany's war machine. Two more raids followed – neither quite reaching the magic one-thousand mark but close enough – and although the results were mixed, Harris had been determined to continue periodically launching large-scale raids, not least in an effort to keep Bomber Command's image high within the media and hence the population as a whole.

So it was that on the night of 10 September 1942, some 479 air-craft were assembled for a large raid on Düsseldorf, and among those drawn in to take part were Les Munro and his crew from 29 OTU. Without feeling too nervous, Munro and his crew had taken off, successfully reached Düsseldorf, dropped their bombs and headed home, their first operational sortie successfully completed. They had been fortunate: of the thirteen OTU crews from Upper Heyford, five had been lost. Crews at OTU were not yet with operational squadrons because they had not finished their training.

It was no wonder, then, that their casualties were higher than most.

Just two nights later, however, on 13 September, Munro and his crew had been called on again to join 445 other aircraft on a raid on Bremen on the north German coast. Another risk for the trainee crews was that their aircraft tended to be ex-operational machines that were no longer really in good enough condition to be carrying out ops. For the Bremen raid, Munro had been allocated an old Wellington that he believed was too old and too unsound to fly with a heavy bomb load. Yet despite expressing concern, he was told to take the Wellington and like it.

Doing as he had been ordered, Munro duly took off, but despite having the throttles wide open, he simply couldn't get the Wellington to climb more than about thirty feet. 'I struggled and struggled,' he says, 'but I just couldn't gain height in it.'

Cursing to himself, he cleared the runway only to hear the bomb-aimer call out, 'Trees ahead!' At one moment it looked as though they would plunge straight into them, but instead they just clipped the tops as they passed, then lost height and, with his undercarriage already retracted, Munro felt the plane come to a halt. It wasn't, he had to admit, the gentlest of landings, but fortunately Wallis's geodetic design held the aircraft together and none of the crew was injured. However, in moments the Wellington was on fire, and Munro and the rest of the crew were scrambling clear and running to safety before the first of the 500lb bombs on board exploded. Just ahead of them, Munro now saw, had been a heavy brick wall and farm buildings. They had avoided ploughing into them by a whisker.

The following day, Munro was told to take another Wellington up and to fly over the crash site, but, in truth, he was not dwelling on his harrowing brush with death the day before. 'We just got on with things,' he says.

Now, over four months later, he was preparing to fly to Düsseldorf again, not in a Wellington, but in a bigger, four-engine Lancaster and with a seven- not five-man crew. His first op with 97 Squadron had been on 2 January – a mine-laying operation off the Gironde – and now he was about to take part in his eighth. Thirty finished missions constituted a completed tour, so he and his crew still had some way to go. Experience, of course, was hugely important, but bomber pilots and their crews needed more than that. They needed to be the right kind of character. They needed to have a kind of phlegmatism and imperturbability, and iron determination. Les Munro had all those.

In the afternoon he and the crew carried out a night-flying test in the squadron's *R-Roger*. The gunners checked the guns and the hydraulics of the turrets, the wireless operator, Sergeant Pigeon, his radio sets, while Munro made sure the aircraft was performing correctly. All seemed as it should. Later in the afternoon came the briefing. All pilots, wireless operators, navigators and bomb-aimers in the briefing room. A large map, photos of the target. Details of what times they should be over the target and the news that they would be preceded by Oboe-carrying Mosquitoes. Further details: the bombing course, a briefing from the Met Officer, warnings about new flak positions, and then, at the end, a 'Good luck'. The scraping back of chairs and then up the road to the Mess and the operational meal: bacon and real eggs, a mug of tea.

It was dark now. The truck then took them down to the airfield again, where Munro and Rumbles met the rest of the crew and were taken out to their aircraft, but during the run-up of the engines prior to take-off it became clear that there was something not right – a problem with one of them – so they were hastily transferred to another Lanc, this time *X-X-Ray*. And they would be flying her without having done a night-flying test.

Four hours and fifty minutes later, Munro touched *X-X-Ray* back down again. There had been a thin sheet of cloud over the target, and had it not been for Oboe and the new target indicators, the raid would almost certainly have been a failure. His bomb-aimer had dropped his 8,000lb bomb from 22,500 feet – more than four miles high – and had been satisfied they had delivered it on target. Certainly the 124 Lancasters and thirty-three four-engine Halifaxes appeared to have done well. Ten industrial businesses were destroyed, and twenty-one lightly damaged; nine public buildings were destroyed or seriously damaged; 456 houses were destroyed, and a further 2,400 lightly damaged. The city's opera house was flattened. Sixty-six people were killed and 225 wounded, and twenty-three of the dead were soldiers, killed on a train when it was hit at the main railway station by high-explosive bombs.

Oboe, the first of Harris's new tools, was working.

The next day, Thursday, 28 January 1943. At around 12.30 p.m., in a darkened room in Vickers House, the London headquarters of Vickers-Armstrong, the armaments manufacturers, a group of about ten men – some wearing civilian suits, others the blue uniform of the RAF – sat in silence as a film projector whirred into life. After a brief moment of spotted and streaked blank film, some grainy monochrome footage of the bomb bay of a Wellington bomber appeared on the wall in front of them, and then, moments later, a large 46-inch-diameter ball was fitted onto specially adapted apparatus in the bay. In slow-motion footage, this ball was then released.

Brief commentary was being given by one of those there: a tall, big-featured man in his fifties, with thick, white hair. The film then switched to a scene over water, along the Fleet, the lagoon behind Chesil Beach in Dorset. Moments later, a Wellington, flying low, hove into view and dropped one of these spheres into the water, only for the steel casing around it to break on impact. A second run was shown; the result was the same.

Now, the white-haired man explained, the Wellington would drop a similar-looking sphere, although this time the ball was wooden and without the steel casing. The film then showed three further runs, the Wellington releasing the ball at around 290 mph at varying heights between forty and seventy feet above the water.

And on these three occasions, they saw the spheres, visibly spinning, hit the water, then bounce, still propelled forward, then hit the water and bounce again. And again. And again, so that by the time they finally came to rest, they had travelled between 1,100 and 1,200 yards.

What they had witnessed was a new weapon – a bomb that could bounce and skim across the surface of water for up to two-thirds of a mile, an astonishing distance. A bomb that could be released at distance from a target and, theoretically, then skip over any protective torpedo net in its way. And getting past torpedo nets suddenly opened up two very important targets that had hitherto been seen as too difficult to strike. These were the German capital ships lying in the Norwegian fjords, and the German dams, huge feats of engineering that were not only iconic structures within Germany, but, more importantly, provided the lifeblood of the Third Reich's industrial heartland.

2

A Method of Attacking the Axis Powers

THE TALL, WHITE-HAIRED man providing the commentary was the Assistant Chief Designer at Vickers Aviation and the inventor of the geodetic aircraft design, Barnes Wallis. His primary task at Vickers was to work alongside Rex Pierson, long since the company's principal aircraft designer. It was Pierson who had designed the Vimy heavy bomber in 1917, and although the geodetic construction was Wallis's brainchild, Pierson had been responsible for the design of first the Wellesley bomber and then the Wellington.

Their current project and number one priority was a new four-engine heavy bomber design, with the Air Ministry specification B.3/42, but which had already been given the name 'Windsor' by the team at Vickers. Pierson and Wallis had been working towards a heavy bomber for some time and had tendered for the B.12/36 contract back in 1936, which had eventually been won by Short Brothers' Stirling. They had tried again three years later, and again in 1941, before finally winning the B.3/42 contract towards the end of 1942. The Windsor was to be based on Wallis's geodetic lattice design, would be capable of high-altitude flight of some 30,000 feet and speeds in excess of 300 mph, would be armed with six 20mm cannon – as opposed to .303 Browning machine guns – and be able to carry a massive 15-ton bomb load. This would make it the most powerful heavy bomber in the RAF, something of which all those at Vickers – and indeed the Ministry of Aircraft Production – were keenly aware. In other words, there was no small amount of pressure to press on with the design and have the Windsor in production just as soon as was humanly possible.

Yet Wallis had always been a deep thinker and a particularly inventive engineer. Unlike Rex Pierson, who devoted all his undoubted talents to aircraft design, Wallis had for some time spent much thought and energy in developing non-conventional means of forcing Germany out of the war. Despite the day-to-day pressures of his work at Vickers, he was, in fact, well placed to do so. Although number two to Pierson, he was a distinguished engineer who had made his name designing airships, most notably the giant *R.100*. The age of airships had passed, but as Assistant Chief Designer, rather than Chief Designer, he was given a fair degree of latitude: he had earned the high regard of his peers, yet at Vickers the buck stopped with Pierson. So long as Wallis fulfilled his aircraft design duties, Sir Charles Craven, the Chairman of Vickers, was willing to allow Wallis time working on other, more experimental projects. His cause had been further helped when, during the Blitz, the design offices at Vickers' Weybridge headquarters were evacuated a few miles east to the Burhill Golf Club, which had been requisitioned by the Ministry of Aircraft Production. While the drawing team – and there were some fifty draughtsmen to help him and Pierson – were set up in the adjacent squash courts, Wallis was given a grand room on the first floor of the Club House, a former Georgian country mansion. There, surrounded by lush fairways and wooded parkland, he was a world away from the beady eyes of the Air Ministry and Ministry of Aircraft Production, and, for that matter, even Sir Charles Craven and the Vickers Board.

Thus, between his official commitments for Vickers, he had been able to spend the best part of the war researching and developing his ideas for new potentially war-ending weapons, whether during long office hours at Burhill or in his attic office at his family home in Effingham, a few miles away, or by working alongside scientists and other engineers at the Ministry of Aircraft

Production research laboratories. It still meant a punishing workload.

Now, at the end of January 1943, it seemed as though all that time and effort, the endless setbacks and all the frustrations that had gone with them, were finally about to bear fruit. The short film he had shown of his proposed weapon and the four trials that had been conducted on the Dorset coast proved the bouncing bomb was no longer merely theory, a blueprint only on a draughtsman's board. It was real. And it could work.

Yet although he had proved its feasibility as a weapon, he was fully aware that the hardest hurdle of all had yet to be jumped: convincing the decision makers to put it into action. His plan was to use two different versions of the weapon. The first, which since the beginning of the year had been codenamed 'Highball', would be a smaller bomb, twenty-eight inches wide, that could be dropped by Mosquitoes and be used by RAF Coastal Command working alongside the Admiralty as an anti-shipping weapon. The great German battleships the *Bismarck* and *Scharnhorst* might have already been sunk, and the *Gneisenau* put out of action, but the biggest of all, the *Tirpitz*, still skulked untouched in the Norwegian fjords. Equally, Highball could be used in the Far East, against the Japanese Imperial Navy, or against hydro-electric power stations situated, like the German capital ships, in the Norwegian fjords. The opportunities were considerable.

The second version was considerably larger than the one used during the trials, at some sixty-one inches wide, and had been codenamed 'Upkeep'. This bomb, Wallis hoped, would be used for an attack on the German and Italian dams. Low-flying aircraft would swoop in over the Möhne and Tirso dams, for example, and at the right height and speed would drop a rotating bomb, which would then bounce across the water, over the torpedo net, hit the dam wall, sink beneath the surface and then explode, and in the process cause a seismic breach in the dam wall, through which the millions of cubic tons of water behind would flow, wreaking havoc and destruction and denying the enemy the use of the reservoir, which held vast amounts of 'white coal' (water), an essential ingredient in the industrial processes that supported the German and Italian war machines.

However convinced Wallis may have been about the potential of Upkeep and the feasibility of such an attack, there were two massive obstacles to overcome. The first was that RAF Bomber Command operated at night, and usually at bombing heights of more than 18,000 feet, yet Upkeep could only work if dropped at the kind of low level last seen during the Augsburg Raid the previous April – a raid that had proved that, even with special training and the most assiduous planning, the aircraft involved would be lucky to reach their destination. Also, the kind of accuracy that would be needed so that Upkeep skipped over the torpedo nets and hit the dam wall in precisely the right spot was, frankly, the stuff of dreams. Current bomb crews were doing well if they got within a mile of the target, but Wallis was expecting his Upkeep to be dropped on a sixpence.

The second major obstacle was time. For the best chance of a breach, the dams needed to be full, and that was in May and early June. If the attack was not made this year, it would have to wait until 1944 until it could be attempted again. Since Wallis's intention was to hasten the end of the war, a twelve-month delay rather defeated the whole point of the exercise. But it was now almost February. Even Wallis, ever the optimist, knew that to carry out such an attack would not only require specially trained crews, but specially adapted Lancaster bombers, and he still hadn't even drawn up the plans for this bigger version of the spherical bomb – a bomb that had to be larger than the trial version in order to hold the amount of explosives calculated to cause a breach in the dam.

It was a tall order, to say the very least, and now, as Air Marshal Sir Arthur Harris was finally about to launch his all-out bombing offensive against the Third Reich, Wallis was expecting him to agree to a diversion of resources on an operation that was, at best, fraught with risk. Not only was the raid itself a very tall order, but so would be convincing the top brass that it was worth their backing.

At least, though, he now had his film – and on that few minutes of celluloid a visual demonstration of the weapon's essential feasibility. Furthermore, he had his own unshakeable faith in the weapon's potential, and had become a fine salesman of his own ideas, which, allied to a healthy dose of optimism, and the tenacity of a terrier, had helped him win over a number of important supporters and get the project as far as it had come already.

In January 1943, Wallis was fifty-two, and in many ways had a rather donnish appearance. His thick and rapidly whitening hair was never slickly brilliantined as was the case with so many men, and seemed to rise off his head with an obvious lack of vanity. He never wore a hat, so the thickness of the hair was more evident somehow. He often wore spectacles, and from his big frame his suits, more country than city, seemed to hang rather than suggest any hint of urbane tailoring. His features were gentle, and his manner affable.

Yet although first impressions may have suggested he was the archetypal absent-minded professor, nothing could have been further from the truth. Wallis had a brain that was both highly organized and pragmatic. He was a brilliant mathematician and draughtsman, and something of a perfectionist – a man who could remember figures and details with extraordinary precision. He also possessed steely resolve and determination; after all, this was a man who never went to university, who learned many of his skills through experience and huge amounts of dedicated hard work, and who later completed a degree, in his spare time, in three months. Learned and widely read, through his combination of talent, brains, hard graft and determination he had become one of Britain's best-regarded aircraft designers.

The genesis of this new weapon was to be found at the beginning of the war, as Wallis had applied his mind to a way in which Germany might be brought down swiftly without the appalling slaughter that had been such a feature of the last world conflict. Wallis, a devout Christian, was also a strong patriot. He was as well a man who liked to solve problems, and no matter what he turned his mind to – whether it be helping build a new sports field for his village in Surrey, or new aircraft designs – he never gave less than his all.

Moreover, Wallis was also extremely resourceful, and spent much time firing off letters of enquiry to various experts, specialist firms or friends in the know. In September 1940, for example, he had written to Glenfield & Kennedy Ltd of Kilmarnock, asking for technical details about control gates on hydro-electric dams. A couple of months later, he was contacting Brewer & Son, patents agents in Chancery Lane, asking for information about the Möhne Dam. He also wrote to a firm called High Duty Alloys, of Slough. If he did not know the answer to something, he searched until he did.

His highly practical mind recognized the importance of contacts, too, and he worked hard to maintain them. Among the many he had made before and since the beginning of the war, few had been of greater help than Group Captain Fred Winterbotham, Head of Air Intelligence at MI6, which was why he was among the first to see Wallis's film. Winterbotham, perhaps more than any other, had followed the extraordinary story of this new weapon from the very beginning and, despite being in the Secret Intelligence Service, had consistently proved to be one of Wallis's greatest champions.

Charming, clever and well-travelled, Winterbotham had by the age of forty-five, as he now was, already led an extraordinary life. A soldier turned pilot in the First World War, he had returned home from France and taken a law degree at Oxford, but realizing he did not have the patience for office work turned to farming, trying his hand in Rhodesia and Kenya. At the end of the twenties, he came back from Africa and was soon recruited into air intelligence in the RAF, and spent much of his time before the war as a spy in Germany, meeting most of the senior Luftwaffe commanders from Erhard Milch to Albert Kesselring and even Göring and Hitler. The intelligence he managed to gather proved invaluable, as did his pioneering development of high-level aerial espionage.

Tall, urbane and excellent company, Winterbotham made it his business to keep up to speed with all the latest scientific and intelligence developments, whether it be code-breaking, new radar systems or potential new weapons. Like Wallis, he understood the importance of networking and was fabulously well connected. He also used his knowledge, connections and great charm to make sure he knew or had the ear of almost everyone in the corridors of British power, be it the Air Ministry or the Prime Minister's office.

The two men had met in early 1940, thanks to a mutual friend,

Leo D'Erlanger. A highly successful city banker, D'Erlanger was fascinated by aeronautics and had for some time been a friend of Wallis's, and had made a striking impression on the latter's four children by once bringing them a pink gramophone. On 23 February in that first year of the war, he had come for lunch at the Wallis house in Effingham and this time brought with him a friend, Fred Winterbotham. D'Erlanger hoped the two might have much in common and that the one might be a useful contact for the other.

So it proved. Welcomed into the Wallis family home, Winterbotham was immediately charmed by both Wallis and his wife, Molly, and by the rush of their children about the place and endless clamour and sound of the piano and other musical instruments. More than that, he was intrigued by Wallis's idea and, soon after, invited him to lunch at the RAF Club in Piccadilly. There, Wallis talked about the efficiency of the anti-submarine depth charge that detonated under water. It was not the blast that did the damage, Wallis explained, so much as the shock wave that was transmitted by the water itself. No one appeared to have thought of it, but since the beginning of the war Wallis had been spending much of his spare time learning about bombs and the physics of high explosives, and now reckoned the same principle might be applied to a weapon detonating underground.

He had also been learning about the winding shafts of German collieries and the construction of different types of dams. All this research led him to one basic premise: that the key to ending the war was to take out Germany's power source. If its coal mines, oil depots, hydro-electric stations and water supplies – or 'white coal' – could be destroyed, then there would be no war industry. With no war industry, Germany would no longer be able to wage war.

Like Air Marshal Harris, Wallis passionately believed that air power could bring about the end of the war. But whereas Portal and Harris and other advocates of bombing believed the only way to destroy the enemy's industry was to attack the factories and cities, Wallis thought that approach was fatally flawed, because even in the Ruhr factories and industrial plants were spread out. Wallis's premise was sound enough, but the nub was how to achieve something simply beyond the limitations of current technology and weaponry.

Wallis, however, reckoned it *was* achievable. What he had been working on back in 1940 was the development of a deep-penetration bomb with a big enough explosive charge to create a miniature earthquake. Such a bomb would be huge and would need an equally huge bomber to carry it, but both he and Pierson had been working on a six-engine aircraft since before the outbreak of war. If such an aircraft and such a bomb could be built, then it would be possible, Wallis believed, to drop this weapon on German coal seams, dams, oil depots and other power sources. And destroy them.

After this first lunch in the RAF Club, Wallis and Winterbotham began to meet regularly and became increasingly good friends, so much so that Wallis soon permitted Winterbotham to call him by his Christian name, a singular honour bestowed only on those closest to him. Wallis, on the other hand, never called Winterbotham 'Fred'; the Victorian in him preferred surnames as a means of address.

Because of Winterbotham's position in MI6, he was already aware that scientists in both Germany and the United States were beginning to develop ideas for big bombs and believed that some time in the future these would become reality. Yet he was also won over by Wallis's rational thought processes and powers of persuasion, and therefore promised to provide him with intelligence data gathered from Germany, which he duly did. At the same time, Wallis recruited various scholars, friends and relations to scour through German textbooks, called on fellow members of the Institute of Civil Engineers, and procured information about explosives from the Ordnance Board. There were enquiries, too, to the English Steel Corporation and other specialist firms. As Wallis's research progressed, so Winterbotham became convinced that such a deep-penetration bomb was sounding increasingly plausible and that if there was a chance of it working, then it was worth developing without delay. The problem was that Wallis's reputation as an aeronautical engineer would only count for so much; somehow he needed to get his theories heard by people of influence and for them to rise above the many half-baked schemes that were endlessly being proposed – and ignored.

This was where Winterbotham could help. He had a friend working at the Prime Minister's Office who promised to put Wallis's proposals to Professor Lindemann, the Prime Minister's Chief Scientific Advisor.

The response, in early July 1940, was lukewarm, and it was suggested that Wallis should approach Boeing or some other American firm for support. Wallis was infuriated. 'In those very early days,' noted Winterbotham, 'Barnes could not envisage the possibility of anybody not falling in with his ideas at once.' Yet Winterbotham urged him to continue his work, encouraging him to put his thoughts together in a full and reasoned paper that could then be circulated.

Working tirelessly over the course of the following year, Wallis eventually produced, in March 1941, *A Note on a Method of Attacking the Axis Powers*, which he then distributed widely to his contacts in the world of aviation and at the Air Ministry and Ministry of Air Production.

'If strength rests in dispersal,' Wallis argued, 'concentration is weakness.' Man could choose where to place his factories and power stations, but natural resources, such as coal seams, could not be dispersed. 'If their destruction or paralysis can be accomplished,' he asserted, 'THEY OFFER A MEANS OF RENDERING THE ENEMY UTTERLY INCAPABLE OF CONTINUING TO PROSECUTE THE WAR.' He provided a natty illustration to make the point: a diamond shape, with power stations, oil refineries, gas works and hydro-electric power at the narrow end, then widening into 'dispersed industrial processes', tapering again to 'war effort', and finally, at the other narrow point, 'ability to wage war'.

It was, of course, the dispersed industrial processes that Portal and Harris were attacking and now intended to obliterate with the American Air Force's assistance and once Bomber Command had expanded sufficiently. Thanks to the help of Winterbotham and others, however, and armed with all kinds of detail and statistics, Wallis now knew considerably more about Germany's natural resources, and where and how they might be attacked. And with this information he had also greatly developed his ideas for his deep-penetration earthquake bomb.

His calculations led him to assert that a ten-ton bomb, designed with a sharp pointed nose and shaped rather like one of his airships, and dropped from 40,000 feet, could plunge some 135 feet into the ground. The subsequent explosion would cause a miniature and concentrated earthquake, which could provide precisely the levels of destruction that would be needed to destroy any underground oil storage depot, coal mine or, even, a massive dam such as the Möhne that fed water into the Ruhr Valley. A ten-ton bomb of this design, he claimed, would create a lethal area of destruction of twenty-nine acres. He accepted that gaining that kind of accuracy was difficult, but he argued that some 4,000 acres could be completely destroyed by sweeps of five aircraft each carrying a ten-ton bomb. In other words, vast fleets of bombers would no longer be needed. Just a handful, delivering these lethal weapons, could cause the kind of widespread devastation to Germany's power sources that could never be achieved by a mass of bombers carrying conventional bombs.

He also provided a solution for how to deliver this massive bomb from such heights: the six-engine Victory bomber. Rex Pierson had, before the war, put forward a design for such a bomber with a massive 235-foot wing span – the Lancaster's was 102 feet – and capable of carrying twenty tons of bombs, which had been based on Wallis's ideas. This had initially been rejected – after all, the RAF hadn't even got any four-engine bombers in service at that time – but Wallis, typically, refused to give up the idea and, as it happened, while working on the *Note* had received a certain amount of encouragement for his Victory bomber from none other than Lord Beaverbrook himself, the Canadian press baron, who was not only a great friend of the Prime Minister's but had, back in May 1940, been made Minister of Aircraft Production.

This had been thanks, once again, to Winterbotham, who had urged Beaverbrook to see Wallis back in July 1940. However, at the subsequent meeting, Beaverbrook surprised Wallis by asking him to go to America to study the work they were doing on pressurized cabins. Wallis pointed out that he already knew about such matters and that his time could be better spent staying in England.

'What would you do in England for us?' Beaverbrook asked him.

'Build you a monster bomber to smash the Germans,' Wallis replied.

Wallis explained his ideas. The latest version of the Victory bomber would have a wingspan of 160 feet, have a pressurized cabin, and be capable of flying at 40,000 feet.

Beaverbrook had been intrigued and asked him to provide fuller details, which Wallis gave him the following day. This, however, was July 1940, with the Luftwaffe already attacking Britain and, it seemed, a German invasion possible any day. One of the first orders Beaverbrook had issued when he took over as Minister of Aircraft Production back in May was that, from that moment on, only five types of aircraft should be manufactured – three types of bomber and two fighters. This dictum, however necessary in the immediate crisis, was already affecting future plans for four-engine bombers, so Wallis's plans for a six-engine beast that could only carry one very specialized bomb were never going to get immediate and full backing. Nonetheless, Beaverbrook did promise co-operation from the Ministry of Aircraft Production as Wallis worked on his plans, which included the help of their scientists at the Road Research Laboratory. This was a sprawling complex of offices, wind tunnels, water tanks and open-air experimentation sites in Harmondsworth in west London, that had been first opened in 1930 by the Ministry of Transport for doing exactly what its name suggested: researching better road-building techniques. Now, however, it was almost entirely turned over to use by the Ministry of Aircraft Production.

Britain's air power was overseen by not just one ministry, but two, and involved a vast number of different offices. Head of it all was the Minister for Air, Sir Archibald Sinclair, who although he had served in the last war was now a civilian and a member of the War Cabinet. Alongside him was Air Chief Marshal Sir Charles Portal, Chief of the Air Staff and the RAF's most senior officer. Under the overall direction of the Air Ministry, there were the three home Commands – Bomber, Coastal and Fighter – and then the various overseas Commands, not least Middle East, whose headquarters were in Cairo.

Separate, but obviously working alongside the Air Ministry, was the Ministry of Aircraft Production, known as the MAP. This ministry did what its name described, but also invested much time and resources into research and into helping companies such as Vickers, Avro (or A. V. Roe, as the company was more formally known), Supermarine *et al.* to develop new aircraft and weapons. Overseeing all research and development at the MAP was Air Vice-Marshal Francis Linnell, the Controller of Research and Development, known as CRD. Under him were two directorates – Scientific Research and Technical Development. The Director of Scientific Research (DSR) was Dr David Pye, a civilian and a man of no small amount of influence, and his deputy, Benjamin Lockspeiser, was another key figure in the chain.

Operating under the eye of Pye and Lockspeiser was the Road Research Laboratory, led by another civilian, Dr W. H. Glanville, and his deputy, Dr A. H. Davis, and in October 1940, as Wallis was working on his ideas for a deep-penetration bomb and high-altitude bomber, they instructed A. R. Collins, Scientific Officer in the 'Concrete Section', to carry out tests to examine the possibility of destroying the Möhne Dam, one of the largest in Germany and whose reservoir fed water into the Ruhr and had, since before the war, been seen as a key target. These men in the MAP, whether scientists, servicemen or former businessmen, not only helped develop new aircraft, weapons and technology, but also acted as a kind of filter who could apply their understanding of current strategies with expertise. Barnes Wallis was not the only man in England independently trying to develop new weapons and technologies, and a great deal of the proposals that were sent into the MAP and Air Ministry were little more than fantasy. Even someone like Wallis, well-connected and a senior designer at Vickers, could not be expected to know the kind of issues and constraints that affected so much decision making when it came to the development of new weapons or aircraft.

However, Beaverbrook and others did clearly think that Wallis's ideas were worth pursuing, albeit tentatively. In August 1940, he had gained the help of the Aeronautical Research Committee, and had been allowed to use the wind tunnel at the National Physical Laboratory at Teddington for tests on his proposed deep-penetration bomb. A few months later, Wallis also met with Glanville, Davis and Collins at the Road Research Lab to explain the progress of his own research. While there, he told them that among the power source targets he had been considering were the two largest dams in Germany, the Möhne and Eder, and the Tirso in northern Italy. He gave Collins a copy of a German book that contained all the dimensions of the Möhne.

Not only did Collins and his team of four begin explosives tests against models of dams, but other scientists at the Road Research Lab also carried out experiments on Wallis's behalf on the effect of shock waves on underwater structures. With regular visits and correspondence, Wallis was able to draw on these tests and research for his *Note*, and yet he could not help feeling frustrated. Time was marching on. 'As a result of the continued opposition that we have met,' he wrote to Air Marshal Tedder, an early supporter at the MAP but now about to be posted to the Middle East, 'it has been necessary to resort to these laborious and long winded experiments in order to prove that what I suggested last July can in reality be done.' That had been at the end of November 1940, but despite Wallis's impatience, people were taking notice, not just at the MAP but at the Ministry of Home Security too, which had secured a 'real live dam' in the Elan Valley in Wales for conducting further experiments. At the beginning of January, R. E. Stirling of the Research and Experiments Department wrote to Sir Henry Tizard, Chief Scientific Advisor to the MAP and one of the most respected scientists in the country. 'Will you back me in this,' wrote Stirling about the purchase of the dam, 'by sending a letter express-ing the interest of MAP and stressing the importance from your side?'

Then in February, Dr David Pye, the DSR at the MAP, formed an ad hoc group of four civilian scientists and one air commodore called the Aerial Attack on Dams Advisory Committee, or AAD for short. This had been prompted by discussions with Wallis and by the experiments being carried out by Collins *et al.* at the Road Research Lab.

Furthermore, by March, Wallis had finally produced the detailed and reasoned paper that Fred Winterbotham had urged him to write. And Winterbotham thought it quite brilliant. Wallis ran off some hundred copies, which were sent to Professor Lindemann, various people at the Air Ministry and at the MAP, even to certain journalists; four copies were also sent to America. Winterbotham once again did all he could to place copies in the hands of the right people. Wallis had also begun talking to Wing Commander Sidney Bufton, then Deputy Director of Bomber Operations at the Air Ministry, and had sparked enough interest for him to visit Wallis at Burhill, where he was promptly given a copy of the *Note*.

Much as Winterbotham had expected, however, the response from the Air Ministry was once again cautious. The problem was the difficulty of fulfilling current commitments – not least the development of new navigational aids and the four-engine bomber – without undertaking any project, especially one of such magnitude and one that, despite very convincing reasoning, relied on the kind of bombing accuracy that was massively beyond what most in the RAF considered possible. Professor Lindemann, on the other hand, believed that no such aircraft or bomb that size could be built in time to be used in the war.

Meanwhile, on 11 April, Dr Pye convened a meeting with the AAD Advisory Committee members and also Sir Henry Tizard, who had been given a copy of the *Note* by Winterbotham. The reason for the meeting was specifically to discuss the feasibility of Wallis's suggestions. They concluded – tentatively – that his calculations seemed sound enough, but their immediate stumbling block was how to detonate a bomb of some fifteen feet in length in such a way that the whole length of the bomb exploded at the same moment – a feature that was necessary in order to achieve a shock wave of the intensity required.

On 21 May, Wallis heard, via a letter from Sir Henry Tizard, that both the deep penetration bomb and the Victory bomber had been officially rejected by the Air Staff. Wallis was distraught. No matter what others said about timings, costs or the problems of diverting from existing projects, he was so convinced about the rightness of his ideas, he could not see why they should not be fully endorsed immediately and take priority over all other projects. This was not arrogance. It was because he passionately wanted the war to end as quickly as possible and believed he had the ideas to achieve that.

This, then, was Wallis's nadir, and yet despite his despair, the *Note* had gained him widespread attention within the corridors of power. The Big Bomb and the Victory bomber may have been rejected for now, but from these plans new lines of thinking were being developed. Wallis was not a lone voice; there were others still trying to develop some of his principles – and particularly his suggestion of attacking the enemy dams. The *Note* had sown some seeds, and from these plans another weapon would be developed.

Less than two years later, he would be able to show people more than a few drawings and some calculations. He would be able to show film footage of the bomb itself.

3

Bouncing Bomb

BOMBER COMMAND HAD drawn young men from all around the world: New Zealanders like Munro, South Africans, Australians and lots of Canadians. But not too many Americans. There were one or two, however, men such as Don Curtin of 106 Squadron and Joe McCarthy of 97.

McCarthy was twenty-two, 6 feet 3 inches tall and 16 stone, which made clambering into the Lancaster and along its fuselage and over the spars no easy matter, but once in the pilot's seat in the cockpit he was comfortable enough. With big, broad shoulders and blond hair, McCarthy was something of a giant.

Brought up in the Bronx in New York City, a second-generation Irishman, McCarthy had joined with Don Curtin, his great friend from back home. Both were competitive swimmers and had been lifeguards on Long Island. Both men had also begun learning to fly and had been well on their way to getting their flying licences. But with money tight and with a growing suspicion that the US would soon enough get itself into the war anyway, it had seemed like a good idea to cross over into Canada and join the RCAF. That way, they could learn to fly and get paid to do so. In any case, both men loved flying, loved the thought of adventure and liked the idea of getting to see something of the world. The danger – the sense that they might not get through it – never really entered their minds too much.

A little over a year later, both McCarthy and Curtin were among those whisked out of their OTUs to take part in the raid on Düsseldorf. For Curtin, this was certainly a baptism of fire. On the route out, his Hampden was attacked by a German night fighter. Somehow, he managed to evade his attacker, and despite the damage to his aircraft flew on to the target, dropped his bombs and headed for home, only to be attacked by a further enemy night fighter. Again, Curtin managed to get them away, but not before three of his crew were wounded.

For McCarthy, the trip was altogether less anxious, and soon after they were finally separated and sent to their respective squadrons, Curtin, with a DFC to his name already, to 106 Squadron under Wing Commander Guy Gibson, and McCarthy to 97, where he had quickly made an impression. It wasn't only the British who tended to conduct themselves with an understated reserve – it was part of the culture throughout Bomber Command, no matter what your nationality, but that wasn't McCarthy's way. He liked being the life and soul and using the kind of colourful language that any young man growing up in the Bronx would use. One attribute he did share with Munro, however, was his imperturbability. He might be loud and outspoken in the Mess, but at the controls of his Lancaster he was as quietly determined and unflappable as any.

He was certainly well liked by his bomb-aimer, an altogether more diminutive Englishman, George Johnson, known to all, inevitably, as 'Johnny'. His background could not have been more different. Born in a small village in Lincolnshire, he had been raised on a farm, largely by his father and five much older siblings; his mother had died when he was young. The relationship with his father had always been difficult. 'He and I seldom talked,' says Johnny, 'and I had more good hidings than good dinners.' He managed to largely escape home when, aged eleven, he was offered a scholarship to the Lord Wandsworth Agricultural College in Hampshire, an establishment set up for agricultural children who had lost one parent or more. He thrived at the school, captaining the cricket and football teams and showing a particular aptitude for sciences. After gaining his matriculation, he sat a Royal

Horticultural Society exam, passed, and was pursuing a career as a park keeper when war was declared. By the following summer, he realized he wanted to be part of it – rather than sitting on the sidelines – so joined the Air Force.

He was sent overseas for training, first to Florida, then Alabama in the United States, and initially to be a pilot. America – or at least, the US Army Air Corps – did not make a great impression on him, however. He had detested initial training and his American instructors. 'Stupid discipline,' he says, 'and stupid marching. I didn't take to it at all.' And despite making a solo landing, he did not make the pilots' course either. Johnson didn't blame the instructors for that. 'I didn't have the aptitude or the inclination,' he says; it had never been a burning passion, not even as a boy. But he was beginning to feel he was wasting time, and so opted to retrain as an air gunner instead, knowing it was the shortest aircrew training course. That meant returning to England. After a very cold Christmas in New Brunswick, he was shipped back across the Atlantic, completed his training and in March 1942 was posted straight to 97 Squadron, bypassing his OTU, and instead becoming a supernumerary air gunner. He missed the Augsburg Raid, but flew a number of ops before the opportunity arose to retrain again on a local bomb-aimer's course.

He joined a crew that was nearing the end of its tour together and on their last flight found themselves flying in terrible weather. On the return trip, the weather turned for the worse and, having dropped down to 10,000 feet and taken their oxygen masks off, they were suddenly struck by a bolt of lightning. Johnson was completely blinded by the flash, and his first thought was that he must already be dead. But then his wits began to return and, with them, his sight, and the Lancaster was screaming in a plunging dive, everything was shaking, and the Perspex in the bomb-aimer's nose compartment was burned brown.

Eventually, the pilot managed to level out at 2,000 feet and they safely made their way home. 'They were all very edgy,' says Johnson, 'because it was their last flight.'

But not Johnson's. However, an American had joined the squadron, and he needed a bomb-aimer, so Johnson was transferred to McCarthy's crew. 'I thought, oh Christ, a bloody American!' he says. 'Yet from the first time we met, we just gelled. He was big in size and big in personality and he was big in pilot ability.' Johnson quickly learned to trust him and vice versa. 'It was subconscious faith in Joe,' says Johnny, 'that convinced me we were always going to come back.'

Inevitably, though, they had had their fair share of close calls. On the night of 17 January, they had flown the long trip to Berlin – it was the second trip there in a row by Bomber Command – and over the city, where the flak was always intense, they were hit and lost their inner port engine. The Lancaster still flew, but it made flying physically very demanding for the pilot. McCarthy turned for home, but on the way back they were hit again and lost the second port engine, so were now flying on just the two starboard engines. By trimming the aircraft and reducing the throttle, it was still possible to keep the machine airborne, but it was even harder to fly, and because it was travelling more slowly the trip was even longer. The physical strain on McCarthy was immense.

As they crossed the coast, it was clear they were not going to make Woodhall, so McCarthy called 'Mayday' and they were picked up by Tangmere, in Kent, a sector airfield in Fighter Command. Worrying that they might crash on the runway and so block it for any other possible aircraft coming in, he told the crew to get into the crash positions and then landed on the grass away from the runway.

'We landed OK,' says Johnson, who as bomb-aimer at the front of the aircraft had a bird's-eye view as they had come in to land. The stricken Lancaster stayed at Tangmere until they'd repaired it. 'A crew eventually came down to pick us up,' adds Johnny. 'They said, "What are you doing here?"' The whole crew had been posted missing.

They were flying ops again a week later; it would have been sooner had it not been for two trips cancelled because of bad weather. If a crew was fit and able, they flew, no matter what. It was relentless. Absolutely relentless.

On Tuesday, 2 February 1943, four days after the first showing of his film reel, Wallis held another screening, this time for Professor

Lindemann, now Lord Cherwell. Two days earlier, on 30 January, he had sent Churchill's scientific advisor a copy of his latest paper, *Air Attack on Dams*, and Cherwell had responded quickly, welcoming the chance to see Wallis's film footage of the Chesil Beach trials. The man who had shown such dismissive scepticism at the publication of Wallis's *Note on a Method of Attacking the Axis Powers* was, at long last, showing some interest.

The decision by the Air Ministry to drop both the deep-penetration bomb and the Victory bomber had been nearly two years before, but back then, in May 1941, Wallis had not given up his ideas. Tizard had encouraged him to continue his work on the ten-ton bomb, and then in June 1941 he had attended the second meeting of the AAD committee. Beforehand, Wallis had managed to speak privately with Dr Pye and persuaded him to continue supporting further experiments on how the German and Italian dams might be destroyed.

Tests had continued throughout the autumn of 1941, with underwater charges detonated in various strengths and sizes and at varying distances from the face of the dam. No one thought it possible to accurately get a charge against the dam wall, so the experiments were to determine what size charge was needed to destroy the dam away from the wall, and at what distance such a charge might work. The problem was that the experiments proved that, to cause a breach, the charge needed to be bigger than could practically be carried.

One faint sign of encouragement had been with a new type of plastic explosive, which, when detonated a foot away from the model dam wall, caused significantly more damage than gelignite. But damage was not the same as outright destruction; as Collins had reported, the damage was certainly still not significant enough to justify an attack on the real dam. Nor was Collins entirely convinced that proportional damage would be achieved when the amount of explosive was scaled up for a real dam.

However, there was still the 35-foot-high 'real live' gravity dam in the Elan Valley in Wales, smaller than but similar in construction to the Möhne and Eder dams and which had, with Sir Henry Tizard's encouragement, duly been bought from the Water

Department of Birmingham City Corporation. It had been built at the turn of the century on the Nant y Gro stream to provide water for the construction of a larger, main dam and was now redundant. It was the ideal place to conduct further experiments.

So when the AAD committee had next met, in December 1941, with both Collins and Wallis attending, they had agreed that the tests at Nant y Gro should go ahead. Nonetheless, Wallis had sensed enthusiasm was wavering, and feared that MAP funding at the Road Research Lab might well soon be withdrawn. At the time, it seemed likely that the upcoming tests would probably be the last chance to prove there was any merit at all in the plans to destroy the enemy dams. At the end of 1941, it had appeared that the project was about to fizzle out.

On the night after Wallis showed Lord Cherwell his film, Tuesday, 2 February 1943, Bomber Command sent 161 bombers to Cologne, the scene of the first thousand-bomber raid the previous summer. Among the 116 Lancasters that took off, nine were from 97 Squadron's B Flight.

This was Les Munro's tenth operational mission, and at 1813 that evening he opened the throttles of *W-Willie* and sped off down the runway at Woodhall, the Lancaster loaded with one 4,000lb bomb and twelve SBCs – 'small bomb containers'.

Taking off alongside him were Joe McCarthy, Johnny Johnson and the crew of *C-Charlie*. It was a cloudy January night, bad enough to have normally grounded the bomber force; however, this raid on Cologne was another landmark for Air Marshal Harris and his men in Bomber Command. This time, the bomber stream was guided not only by Oboe-carrying Mosquitoes but by H2S-carrying Lancasters too. Both *C-Charlie* and *W-Willie* reached the target without trouble. Munro could see cloud over the target, but green marker flares were just visible, so Sergeant Cummins released their bombs over that. They could not see their own bursts, but the city was glowing with fires.

In *C-Charlie*, McCarthy had also arrived to discover the city covered by patchy cloud, but Johnson had spotted the red markers and had dropped their bombs on those, and seen the strange orange light of fires beneath the cloud. McCarthy then headed for home. Both crews were back around the same time, just under five hours after they had taken off. A quick debrief, something to eat, and then bed. Another mission successfully completed.

And as far as 97 Squadron was concerned, it had been a successful night – all nine had safely returned; only five had failed to make it home out of the entire force. Yet the following day, at Bomber Command HQ, it seemed the night's raid had not been as accurate as they had hoped. Despite Oboe and H2S, no clear concentration of markers had been achieved. Damage had been caused across Cologne, but none of it especially serious. In fact, study of reconnaissance photographs showed that not a single industrial site had been hit at all.

It was, to put it mildly, disappointing.

Bomber Command's early experiments with its new navigational aids might not have been going to plan, but Barnes Wallis was feeling altogether more gung-ho about his new wonder weapon. In this first week of February 1943, an attack on the dams had never looked more likely. It wasn't only Lord Cherwell and Freddie Winterbotham who had now seen the film. A number of people had watched it, not least Air Marshal Sir Wilfrid Freeman, Assistant Chief of the Air Staff and number two to Portal. And the film was impressive: to see a Wellington delivering a spherical bomb that bounced high and long across the still waters of the Fleet could hardly fail to impress.

Events were now moving swiftly. After showing Lord Cherwell the film on 2 February, Wallis had seen Benjamin Lockspeiser, who had now taken over from Dr David Pye as Director of Scientific Research at the MAP. Wallis urged Lockspeiser to give him permission to start design work on the bigger bomb, codenamed Upkeep, which would be carried by a Lancaster. The following day, Wednesday, 3 February, Lockspeiser rang and told Wallis that Air Vice-Marshal Linnell, Controller of Research and Development, had given a partial go-ahead: preliminary work could begin on design work for the Upkeep.

The idea for the bouncing bomb had evolved following that

third meeting of the AAD committee, back in December 1941. Wallis had, by the beginning of 1942, realized that a completely different approach was needed. But what? The seemingly un-solvable problem was how to get a big enough charge of explosive close enough to the dam to cause a fatal breach. He had originally accepted that an explosion against the face of the dam would be most effective. This was basic physics, and was why any explosive charge was always, where possible, placed against the structure it is trying to destroy rather than away from it. He had, however, rejected this option from his *Note* because he could not see how it could ever be achieved. Even so, in all the various experiments, meetings and correspondence that had gone on throughout the previous year, the possibility of exploding a charge against the dam wall had repeatedly arisen. Wallis had even consulted an RAF weapons expert, Wing Commander Baker-Carr, who confirmed that it would be quite possible to sink a charge with a time-fuse – that was, after all, what an anti-submarine depth charge relied upon. Baker-Carr had even been brought along to the June meet-ing of the AAD committee. One of the conclusions of the next meeting, in December 1941, had been that 'A charge of 220 lbs would be adequate to cause serious damage to stressed dams if exploded in contact with the face.' But how to achieve it? Wallis's big-bomb, high-altitude bomber had been rejected, and although a torpedo dropped from the air had been suggested, the enemy dams were protected by anti-torpedo nets.

The ongoing tests by Collins's team at the Road Research Lab were based on the assumption that delivering a charge right on the dam wall would be next to impossible. In fact, the assumption was that it would be unlikely to get any charge beyond the anti-torpedo net – which, of course, was precisely why the Germans had put them in front of their dams. Perhaps, though, the current stock of bombers in the RAF might be able – possibly – to deliver enough aerial mines, for example, which, when exploded together before the anti-torpedo nets, might create a fissure in the dam wall that, with the pressure of millions of cubic tons of water, would then subsequently force a breach. That was the hope. So far, though, the scale models suggested otherwise.

It was now early April 1942, and the Wallis house in Effingham was full of children, home for the Easter holidays. Wallis and his wife, Molly, had four, but they also looked after Molly's nephews, whose parents had been killed in the Blitz. Outside on the patio, his youngest daughter, Elizabeth, had set up a game of marbles with a tub of water. As she flicked the little glass spheres, the good marbles went into the water, the naughty marbles went onto the paving.

Later, Wallis could never recall what it was that had prompted him to think of skipping a bomb across water, but his daughter's game is as probable as anything. Every great thought needs a spark or a falling apple.

Wallis now set up a home-made catapult, a tub of water and a table on the patio at the back of their home in Effingham, commandeered some of Elizabeth's marbles, and with the children's help began firing them from the catapult, watching them bounce across the tub of water, over a taut piece of string running across the tub, and onto the table.

Ricocheting missiles across water was nothing new. The Navy had fired cannon balls this way to gain extra distance since the seventeenth century and certainly in Nelson's day. Wallis had also heard of an RAF Coastal Command crew skip-bouncing a bomb in the Channel. But no one had thought to use a specially designed bouncing bomb that could skip over water – and, most importantly, over an anti-torpedo net – to strike a specific target.

A few days after these experiments, he once again turned to Group Captain Fred Winterbotham, whose support had continued without waver, and explained his latest idea. Winterbotham grasped the significance of the bouncing-bomb concept but urged his friend to develop it further before talking about it to too many people. 'I begged him to come up with a properly baked pie,' he noted, 'no under-cooked blackbirds, please!'

Wallis heeded his advice. More home-spun experiments were carried out. He also discussed his ideas with colleagues, and it seems possible that one, George Edwards, the Vickers Experimental Manager and a keen cricketer, was responsible for suggesting Wallis apply backspin to the sphere. As a spin bowler, Edwards knew that the more revolutions applied to a cricket ball through the air, the higher it would bounce off the ground. At any rate, it seemed likely the same principles would apply to a spinning ball on water.

Wallis was not convinced, but at the end of April he quietly took his catapult to the nearby Silvermere Lake, just east of Cobham, with his secretary, Amy Gentry, a former ladies' rowing champion, to help. Applying Edwards's backspin theory, he discovered that an unspun missile bounced four or five times, but one that was rotating managed as many as fifteen. It was a significant breakthrough. He also wrote up his thoughts and research in *Spherical Bomb, Surface Torpedo*, a new paper that was complete by the middle of May 1942.

Ironically, in his paper, Wallis referenced a study on the bouncing theory by a German scientist, but in his own paper he showed that if a missile hit the water at an angle of incidence of less than seven degrees, it would ricochet. The missile would bounce at an increasingly lower angle of incidence until eventually it would come to a halt. Wallis also included details about the density of the missile and suggested using a double skin. The inner canister would contain the charge, the outer both the charge and a layer of air, kept in place by wooden struts. He also predicted a range of three-quarters of a mile, which would allow an attacking aircraft to drop it and turn away, and pointed out that a spherical bomb would mean less of its surface hitting the water, which in turn would allow it to travel further. It was a comprehensive and convincing paper. As Winterbotham had hoped, there was nothing half-baked about it whatsoever.

Meanwhile, at the Road Research Lab, Collins and his team had been working on two 1:10 scale models of the Nant y Gro dam in the Elan Valley. On 18 April, an explosion was detonated nine inches from the dam wall and eighteen inches deep, which caused a certain amount of damage. At the beginning of May, they went to Wales, accompanied by Wallis and his wife. At no point does Wallis appear to have mentioned his bouncing-bomb idea, because although this new potential weapon solved the problem of how to get the charge to the dam wall, Wallis believed it would still not be possible to get enough explosive in the right spot with one aircraft.

It would simply be too heavy for a single Lancaster to carry.

At Nant y Gro, the first full-scale experiment was carried out with a charge away from the dam wall, just as had been done on the scale model at the Road Research Lab, but with ten times the amount of explosive. The results were much the same: damage, but no breach.

'A solution to the problem was, however,' noted Collins, 'found almost by chance shortly afterwards.' His team had to destroy one of the damaged scale models and did so using a contact charge, because, of course, a contact charge was always more effective. However, with the water in the model reservoir still behind the dam, they were stunned by the effect of the explosion. Bits of the concrete model were flung far and wide and the water gushed through a wide breach.

Immediately, Collins realized something of great significance had happened. Because any gravity dam has the same proportions, it was possible to simply scale up the amount of explosive. If Collins was right, then it should be possible to destroy the Nant y Gro Dam with far less explosive than he had hitherto realized.

Hastily, they began further tests at the Road Research Lab with different-sized contact charges and at different heights. They realized that the accidental smashing of that first model had been no fluke, and were soon able to conclude that on the 1:10 scale model of the Nant y Gro dam a four-ounce charge detonated at twelve inches below the surface of the water was enough to cause a breach. This meant that if they increased the sizes tenfold, a similar test on the actual dam should, in theory, achieve a similar breach.

The second test on the actual dam was planned for Friday, 24 July. Wallis was, naturally enough, invited to witness the test, although not until the 16th. He replied that he would attend if at all possible. 'At present,' he wrote, 'I am working under such heavy pressure that it seems unlikely that I shall be able to get away,' then somewhat huffily added, 'May I point out that the notice you give is very short.'

As it happened, Wallis was able to witness the test, which was duly carried out as planned by army engineers and filmed with high-speed cameras from the Royal Aircraft Establishment (RAE) at Farnborough.

It proved every bit as successful as Collins and his team had hoped. A huge spume of water spray erupted into the air and then, a moment later, a huge hole was punched out of the dam wall. This was a massive breakthrough, literally and metaphorically. In any concrete or masonry gravity dam – such as Nant y Gro or the Möhne and Eder dams – the section above an arbitrary horizontal plane is always a scale model of the entire dam. In other words, the cross-section of the Nant y Gro Dam was, in effect, approximately a scale model of the Möhne and Eder. Consequently, it was possible for Collins to apply the results of this stunning experiment to a gravity dam of any height and size. Still armed with Wallis's details of the Möhne Dam, in August Collins wrote a report in which he concluded that a contact charge of some 7,500lb, thirty feet deep, would be enough to blow a gaping breach through a depth of some forty-four feet of a dam wall, an amount of explosive that was considerably less than had previously been imagined would be needed. This was a massive game-changer.

And a 7,500lb bomb did not need the Victory bomber to carry it. A Lancaster could manage it easily.

4

Sink the *Tirpitz*

I T WAS, ON THE FACE of it, odd that Collins should have discovered the dramatic effect of a contact charge against the face of the dam without Wallis having put him up to it first. After all, by the time of the first full-scale test at Nant y Gro, Wallis had already carried out his marble test and was some way into developing his bouncing-bomb ideas.

But, at this stage, Wallis had not approached the MAP or Air Ministry with his *Spherical Bomb* paper, because he had been thinking of it not as a weapon to use against dams, but rather ships – enemy capital ships, like the German battleship *Tirpitz*. So, on 22 April, he had taken Winterbotham along with him to discuss his findings with another old friend and contact, Professor Patrick Blackett, an experimental physicist and currently Scientific Advisor to the Admiralty.

Blackett was impressed but felt the bomb should not be limited to naval use only. Perhaps it might not work against dams, but against locks or other targets it might prove highly effective, and so immediately told his old friend Sir Henry Tizard all about it. This was just as Winterbotham had planned; he wanted the Air Ministry to become interested but felt it would be better to come from an independent authoritative source, rather than direct from himself or Wallis.

Sure enough, the very next day, Tizard visited Wallis at Burhill. Like Blackett, he was impressed and promised his support, a major stepping-stone to securing formal backing. Along with Professor Lindemann, Tizard remained the most influential scientist in the country.

With Tizard's help, Benjamin Lockspeiser, Deputy Director of Scientific Research at the MAP, had agreed to let Wallis use the two experimental ship tanks at the National Physical Laboratory at Teddington. These tests began in June and continued intermittently over twenty-two days right through until September. Further backspin tests showed not only that it increased the distance with which the missile was propelled forward before hitting the water, but also diminished the amount it plunged downward on its first impact with the surface, and increased the distance the sphere would travel while skimming across the water.

Tizard was not the only one to visit Teddington to watch these trials; so did a run of other movers and shakers within the MAP, Air Ministry and Admiralty, including Rear-Admiral Renouf.

Admiral Edward de Faye Renouf was Director of Special Weapons at the Admiralty. Now fifty-five, he had been a highly successful torpedo officer and had continued to rise up through the ranks during the interwar years, with a reputation for easy charm, intelligence, hard work and devotion to duty, so that by 1940 he had been promoted to rear-admiral and was in command of a cruiser squadron in the Mediterranean under Admiral Cunningham.

It was not to prove a happy command. In June 1940, shortly after the Italians declared war, his squadron had come under submarine attack while at anchor in Suda Bay, in Crete. Renouf had been criticized for not keeping his ships at a sufficient state of readiness. Worse was to follow, however. In January 1941, he had been commanding the cruisers HMS *Gloucester* and *Southampton* as part of Operation EXCESS, a two-part convoy to the strategically important outpost of Malta. The Luftwaffe had recently deployed to Sicily and this had been the first time German bombers had attacked British shipping in the Mediterranean. Renouf's cruiser force had been given the task of escorting a battle-crippled ship to Malta, which it successfully fulfilled, but as they sailed east to rejoin the rest of Cunningham's fleet, they came under very heavy air attack, and both the *Gloucester*, Renouf's flag, and *Southampton* were hit. Struck twice and soon ablaze, the *Southampton* had to be abandoned and sunk by torpedo.

The bomb that had struck the *Gloucester*, meanwhile, had gone straight through the roof of the director tower, right behind the bridge, where Renouf had been standing with his senior officers, yet had miraculously not exploded. Incredibly, this was the second time that Renouf had been on the bridge when struck by a dud bomb. Having cheated death twice, his nerves started to fail him, and a couple of weeks later, having safely returned to Alexandria, he was relieved of his command and flown home. Cunningham reckoned Renouf had a temperament 'always inclined to nervousness', but while recognizing that he had an undoubted ability 'and capacity for hard work', he could not recommend him for further command at sea.

Back in England, however, after a ten-month stint in a naval hospital, his intellectual capacity, wide-ranging understanding, and knowledge of both naval and other matters were considered just what was needed for a good Flag Officer. Renouf, recovering from his breakdown, had been reprieved – and justly so, because he soon proved an incisive and imaginative Director of Special Weapons.

It was another member of his staff, Lieutenant-Commander Lane, from the Directorate of Miscellaneous Weapon Development, who had alerted Renouf to the new bouncing bomb that Wallis was developing. In June 1942, he had been to see him about another of Wallis's ideas – a smoke-laying glider – but before long was being told about the bouncing bomb. Lane reported his discussions to Renouf, who then contacted Wallis and arranged to see the tests being carried out at Teddington.

Renouf was immediately struck by the possibilities of this weapon, and showed up again the very next day, this time with Lieutenant-Commander Lane and others in tow. Wallis set up a wax model of a battleship for their benefit and from several hundred feet further along the tank, began firing two-inch balls, which struck the side of the ship and then, with the backspin, rolled down against its underside.

Renouf and his colleagues were tremendously impressed, and immediately took steps to see how it might be developed further. A meeting was arranged with Sir Charles Craven, Wallis's boss, where Renouf urged Vickers to give some kind of unofficial priority to this work on Wallis's weapon. Already he wanted Wallis to develop a model that could be carried by a twin-engine Mosquito. The Navy's Fleet Air Arm did not operate these aircraft, but this does not appear to have worried Renouf unduly at this stage.

At any rate, this sudden and urgent interest from Renouf and the Admiralty could not have come at a better time. For all Tizard's support, both Dr David Pye and his number two at the MAP, Benjamin Lockspeiser, were less than enthusiastic, even though, by now, Wallis had fully realized that his bouncing bomb *could*, in theory, be used against enemy dams. A Lancaster could drop the bomb some distance from the dam, and it might then ricochet over the anti-torpedo net to the dam wall. After hitting the crest of the dam, it would sink in close contact with the water-side face of the dam and explode.

There was a massive gulf, however, between what might be possible in theory and the practicalities of getting air crew all the way to the dam and then dropping the bomb with the kind of precision required if there was to be any chance of success. Both Pye and Lockspeiser grasped the feasibility of such a weapon but, quite apart from the practical problems of delivering the weapon, were nervous about any diversion of resources to such a radical bomb that could only be used on water. It had also been agreed that any newly developed bomb had to conform to existing 'stowage conditions'. 'The general argument,' Lockspeiser wrote to Tizard on 16 June, 'was that it is quite impractical and uneconomic to modify our bombers in large numbers for the special purpose of carrying any particular bomb.' Dr Pye was also now convinced that an aerial attack on the dams was little more than pie in the sky – not because it could not, in theory, be achieved, but because there seemed far too many hurdles to overcome and too many imponderables for it to be worth the kind of hard-pressed resources it required.

The Admiralty shared none of these concerns, however, and, with the energized Admiral Renouf leading the way, not only funded Vickers' development of the 'rota-bomb' but also helped put pressure on Air Vice-Marshal Linnell at the MAP to allow Vickers to convert one of their Wellingtons for a series of tests. Renouf's team also asked the MAP for twelve experimental bombs, and on 22 July the Oxley Engineering Company was given the brief to construct them. With such backing from the Admiralty, the MAP had little option but to oblige. It may have been the Ministry of Aircraft Production, but that did not make it solely the hand-maiden of the Air Ministry; the MAP served the Admiralty too.

A month later, on 25 August, Wallis was attending a meeting at the MAP with, among others, Captain Davies of Renouf's staff, Lockspeiser, Group Captain Wynter-Morgan, the Deputy Director of Armaments at the MAP, as well as 'Mutt' Summers, a former Supermarine Spitfire prototype test pilot and now with Vickers. Top of the agenda were a series of full-scale trials. A location – the calm lagoon behind Chesil Beach, in Dorset, known as the Fleet – was chosen, while other details, such as which film camera should be used, the necessary security passes and special sensitive altimeters for the Wellington, were also discussed. It was agreed that the trials should take place a month hence, at the end of September.

This was to prove overly optimistic. By mid-September, the Oxley Engineering Company had made only one bomb, which was being prepared for spinning tests on the ground, while modifi-cations on the Wellington had also not been completed. In October, further delays were caused by Wallis becoming ill and, unusually for him, being forced to spend a few days at home recovering. However, by the end of the month, the modified Wellington was at last ready for flying trials, although there were further glitches with the substitute fillings for the trial bombs instead of the explosive that would eventually be used, should all go to plan. By 20 November, after an endlessly anxious period of intense trial and error, Wallis told Lockspeiser that, assuming no further difficulties arose, he expected the live trials to begin within a fortnight.

On Wednesday, 2 December, Mutt Summers, with Wallis on board, took the modified Wellington for a test flight over the

Queen Mary Reservoir, with a trial bomb on board in order to test the spinning gear. All seemed to go well, and two days later, at 1.40 p.m. on Friday, 4 December, the Wellington took off again from Weybridge with Mutt Summers as pilot, Richard Handasyde as co-pilot, and with Wallis as bomb-aimer. With the bomb-bay doors removed and the special bomb spinning gear fixed, they flew straight to the agreed test range at Chesil Beach.

The first live trial was finally under way, but as Wallis was keenly aware, without Admiralty support his 'rota-bomb' would not have got even this far. But while the Navy believed this was a new and exciting anti-shipping weapon, Wallis still had his mind on an attack on the dams. He still believed, as strongly as he ever did, that cutting off Germany's power source was the best way to defeat the Third Reich. Destroy the Möhne and even the Eder dams, and perhaps others would come round to his way of thinking too.

5

Sitting on the Fence

THURSDAY, 4 FEBRUARY 1943. At Bomber Command Headquarters, a letter had arrived for Air Marshal Sir Arthur Harris from Air Vice-Marshal Bottomley, Assistant Chief of the Air Staff (Ops) at the Air Ministry – and this time, not the usual daily interference from the desk wallahs in London, but a new Combined Chiefs of Staff approved directive.

'Your prime objective,' the Directive instructed, 'will be the progressive destruction and dislocation of the German military, industrial and economic system, and the undermining of the morale of the German people to a point where their capacity for armed resistance is fatally weakened.'

This new Directive had been drawn up during the Casablanca Conference in January, when the Combined Chiefs of Staff – the most senior military leaders of Britain and the United States – had met in North Africa to plan future strategy. American military strength was growing, but so too was Britain's war machine. A British army had, in early November, comprehensively defeated a combined German–Italian army at El Alamein – the fighting in Egypt had seen the first major defeat of German ground forces by the British since the beginning of the war. A few days after the Panzerarmee Afrika was forced to flee westwards into Libya, a combined Anglo-US force had landed in north-west Africa. Morocco and Algeria, controlled by pro-Axis Vichy France, had been defeated and the French forces joined the Allies. Now the Allies were fighting in Tunisia, the Anglo-US First Army pressing forward from the west, the British Eighth Army pushing Field Marshal Rommel's Panzerarmee from the east. On 21 January, the same day that the new Directive had been approved, Tripoli, a key city and major port in western Libya, had fallen to the Allies. Axis forces in North Africa were being squeezed by a giant Allied pincer. Soon – in a few weeks, maybe a month or two – the Axis would be forced out of North Africa altogether.

The war news was looking brighter in the east, too. Eighteen months earlier, it had looked as though Stalin's Russia was finished, that Hitler would be victorious in the USSR, but now a corner had been turned. The German advance in the east had stalled, and at Stalingrad they had been caught in a massive encirclement.

For the first time since the start of the war, the ultimate defeat of Nazi Germany was beginning to look not just possible, but probable. After victory in North Africa, the Allies would invade Sicily in an attempt to hasten Italy's exit from the war and then they would turn to mainland Europe. A key part of this policy was to continue to tighten the ring around Germany, to never let up the pressure. More and more US bombers would be arriving in England. Together with Bomber Command they would continue to pound Germany.

Harris's new Directive also outlined a number of priority targets: German U-boat construction yards, the German aircraft industry, transportation networks, oil plants and other targets in the enemy war industry. There was, however, no specific mention of dams, or coal mines or any other power sources. Nor was there any direction given as to how this air offensive should be carried out.

As far as Harris was concerned, it was a ringing endorsement of all that he had been pressing so hard for since taking over the Command the previous February. It was a Directive designed for the tools that he had: increasing numbers of heavy bombers and larger bombs and improving navigational aids. And that meant the area bombing of Germany's major industrial cities.

Harris had spent the best part of a year building up his Command to carry out precisely what the Directive was demanding, and although it still was not the force he hoped it would become, and although early use of Oboe and H2S had been disappointing, he was sure that performance could and would improve. The key, now, was for both the Chiefs of Staff and the Air Ministry – indeed all of Britain's war leaders – to give him the kind of focused support he needed. His force was almost ready. So long as there was no more meddling, and no more diversion of resources, he felt certain he could deliver what they asked.

Harris was completely unaware that a new weapon that could bounce across water was being developed. He knew nothing of the endless meetings that were taking place, the trials off Chesil Beach, the inter-service jockeying that was going on between the Air Ministry, Admiralty and Ministry of Aircraft Production.

As it happened, it now appeared that he might never know either. After the giddy excitement for Wallis of the previous few days, he now rang Lockspeiser to find out whether there was any news on the development of the larger bomb, codenamed Upkeep. Preliminary design approval was one thing, but what Wallis wanted was a decision on *developing* the weapon. Lockspeiser promised to speak to Air Vice-Marshal Linnell at the MAP and get back to him. This he did that afternoon, 12 February 1943, and the news was not good. Linnell was apparently concerned that Upkeep would interfere with work on the Vickers Windsor four-engine bomber, so was going to prepare a memo which he then would circulate as a means of canvassing opinion within the Air Ministry.

The following day, Wallis headed back down to Weymouth to watch the fifth live trial along the Fleet. The first, back on 4 December, had been aborted, but although there had been problems with his bomb disintegrating on impact and other issues of height and speed, the trials had proved that the weapon would work. The fourth trial had taken place on 23 January and had recorded a 'skip' of thirteen bounces, and then one of twenty. Further modifications had been made on the casing since then, and on this final test trial the dummy bombs were smooth wooden balls, dropped from between 80 and 145 feet at around 300 mph and with the spheres revolving at between 425 and 450 revolutions per minute. The skimming distance achieved was remarkable: some 1,315 yards.

For Wallis, the lack of wholehearted support was unfathomable. The trials and the test the previous summer at Nant y Gro proved that the weapon could work. He had his film reel and accompanying latest paper, *Air Attack on Dams*, which involved highly detailed and authoritative research. In it, he pinpointed five dams in the catchment area of the River Ruhr, which in turn fed into Germany's industrial heartland. These were the Möhne, the largest, and singled out by Wallis in his *Note*, but also the Sorpe and much smaller Lister, Ennepe and Henne. Together, they held back some 254 million cubic metres of water, a staggeringly large amount. Their destruction, he argued, would wreak mayhem. It would severely disrupt heavy industry, vast amounts of damage would be caused by the floods, and the domestic and industrial water supply for some 5 million Germans and the heart of the Ruhr Valley industrial area would be greatly affected.

Wallis, admittedly, knew little about the other calls on resources, but as far as he was concerned, an attack on the dams with his larger bomb was now a no-brainer, but a decision needed to be made quickly. Time, he had stressed in his paper, was very much of the essence. The tests at Nant y Gro had showed that for the dams to be properly breached, the water level needed to be at its highest, and that was in May or June. If the go-ahead was given, he promised, it would be possible to develop a Lancaster to drop the Upkeep bombs 'within a period of two months'. *Possible*, maybe – but that would be cutting it fine. Very fine indeed. But if they did not launch an attack within the next three months, then they would have to wait another whole year. The point was to cause as much havoc to Germany as possible in an effort to hasten the end of the war. To wait a further year would be to defeat the whole point of the operation. If such an attack were to be launched, it needed to be now, this year, 1943.

On 12 February, Wallis learned that Linnell had finally set down his thoughts and sent them to Air Vice-Marshal Sorley, the Assistant Chief of the Air Staff (Technical Requirements). Linnell pointed out that the bouncing-bomb project was technically feasible, but certainly not yet guaranteed. He outlined the time constraint, and made the valid point that it was essential that if the attack went ahead it would need to be in sufficient strength to ensure success because the element of surprise would be essential. He also expressed his concerns about delays it would cause to the Windsor bomber project. His memo was neither for nor against going ahead. Linnell was sitting firmly on the fence.

Realizing his project was slipping away, Wallis wasted no time in despatching, via special messenger, a letter and two copies of his *Attack on Dams* to Fred Winterbotham, the man who had already done so much to push Wallis's ideas into the hands of men of influence that he had jokingly described himself as 'Wallis's impresario'. Winterbotham had been recently in north-west Africa – landing in Algiers two days after the invasion in November – briefing senior commanders on Ultra (the decodes of German Engima traffic) and other intelligence matters. However, he had returned by the time Wallis had been ready to show his film reel and was still in London.

'We have just worked out some of our results from the last experiment at Chesil Beach,' Wallis wrote in his letter, 'and are getting ranges nearly twice those which would be forecast from the water tank, that is, with a Wellington flying at about 300 miles an hour and dropping from an altitude of 200 feet, we have a registered range of exactly three-quarters of a mile.' He had then underlined the last point and added two exclamation marks. The problem of making a bomb for a Lancaster and fitting it was one that was easily solved, he said. 'It follows,' he added, 'that sufficient bombs for the Lancaster experiment (if, say, thirty machines were to be used, to destroy simultaneously five dams, that is, six machines per dam to make certain of doing it) can be completed within two or three weeks, and it is modifications to the aircraft itself which will take the time.' He signed off, 'Yours in great haste', then added in handwritten ink pen, 'Help, oh help.'

What Wallis was asking was for Winterbotham, once again, to use his influence and connections within the corridors of power to urge the Air Ministry into action. His friend chose to write to Air

Vice-Marshal Inglis on 16 February. The Air Ministry had four Assistant Chiefs of the Air Staff: General, Policy (P), Technical Requirements (TR), Operations (Ops) and Intelligence (I). Inglis was Intelligence, and as such a direct colleague of Winterbotham's. 'You may remember I spoke to you some months ago about an invention, for which I was partly responsible,' wrote Winterbotham, throwing his own reputation behind it. It was a weapon, he said, originally devised for attack against Axis warships, but which would be ideal against 'any target where there was from a quarter to one mile of approach water surface'. He added, 'The Admiralty became enthusiastic, and through the C.C.O. and the Prime Minister, the Naval side for use against Axis ships has been rapidly developed.' In one sentence he had suggested Churchill's direct involvement (which was not true) and implied that the Navy had already got one over the RAF. 'Little enthusiasm, however,' he continued, 'appears to have been shown by the RAF in the MAP, and my fear is that a new and formidable strategic weapon will be spoiled by premature use against a few ships, instead of being developed and used in a properly coordinated plan.' This was an important point. 'I am wondering,' he wrote, 'whether the CAS or ACAS (P) have really been fully informed of the successful development of this invention.' In other words, Inglis had a duty to get Wallis's *Air Attack on Dams* paper to Portal without delay. It was a masterful letter, full of cunning and suggestion. Not for nothing was Winterbotham a highly respected Air Intelligence Officer within MI6.

Winterbotham was probably right in supposing that Portal had not yet been fully briefed, but his subordinates would have been wary, at such a critical time in the bomber offensive, of burdening the Chief of the Air Staff with something that many supposed still had little chance of ever seeing the light of day. Men like Lockspeiser, newly appointed Director of Scientific Research, and Air Vice-Marshal Linnell, the Controller of Research and Development, were hedging their bets, carefully trying not to be seen to support a dud project, while at the same time giving sufficient support should enough momentum gather behind it.

The day after Linnell's memo – 13 February – the project was

considerably opened up at a meeting held at AVM Sorley's office –
the ACAS (TR) – at the Air Ministry in King Charles Street,
Whitehall, to discuss the proposed Upkeep and Highball projects.
This was no small gathering. Seven staff officers from the Air
Ministry were joined by three representatives from the MAP –
Lockspeiser included – as well as Group Captain Sam Elworthy
from Harris's staff at Bomber Command HQ, and two from the
Admiralty. Their discussions proved hardly a ringing endorsement.
Group Captain Bufton, Deputy Director of Bomber Operations at
the Air Ministry, made it clear that he believed it was impracticable
to fly at the low height required to drop the Upkeep at night and
over the dams, which were, of course, in the heart of the Third
Reich. As someone who had flown bomber operations during this
current conflict, his opinion was not to be taken lightly.
Lockspeiser suggested that developing the smaller Highball first
would be the best way of developing the larger bomb, and when
AVM Sorley then suggested that production of the bigger Upkeep
was some six months off, no one demurred.

The meeting concluded with several of those attending being
asked to go away and investigate further. Lockspeiser was asked to
find out what kind of speed, height and range from the target the
Lancasters would be expected to operate at were an attack on
the dams to go ahead, while Group Captain Bufton was given the
task of investigating the entire operational project of an attack
against the dams. He was to discuss this with Wallis and other
representatives of Bomber Command. Finally, Group Captain
Elworthy was to now put Bomber Command HQ fully in the
picture.

The following day, Sunday, 14 February, Air Marshal Harris was
finally briefed about the proposed attack on the dams. As it
happened, Harris had already been investigating the possibility of
destroying a large dam by dropping a number of mines near to the
dam wall, although had been told this would be impossible.

Harris's reaction to Upkeep was predictable and emphatic.
'This,' he scribbled at the foot of a memo from his SASO, AVM
Saundby, 'is tripe of the wildest description. There are so many ifs
and buts that there is not the smallest chance of it working.'

The Commander-in-Chief of the RAF's bomber force could not have been clearer. No matter what was being discussed in the corridors of the Air Ministry and the MAP, there would be no such operation taking place if he had anything to do with it. His machines – and his bomber boys – were too valuable to be wasted on mad schemes cooked up by half-baked scientists.

6

Bomber Boys

WHEN AIR MARSHAL HARRIS took over in February 1942, he had been keenly aware that his new Command was not receiving the best press, either nationally, in the newspapers and on radio and film news coverage, or internally. The Butt Report of the previous June, instigated by Lord Cherwell, had shown, from the study of some 600 photographs, that no more than a third of all bombs dropped by Bomber Command hit within five miles of the target. This was a devastating revelation, and flew in the face of reports by the bomber crews themselves. And although the report never claimed to be infallible, the consequences were far-reaching and seriously undermined confidence in Bomber Command on the part of Britain's war leaders, not least Churchill. The Prime Minister had, even during the dark days of May and June 1940, seen Britain's bomber force's potential as a key means of taking the fight to the enemy. To have this faith in the bomber arm so starkly shaken was a damaging blow, and he immediately urged Portal to give the report his 'most urgent attention'.

In truth, bombing was still, in 1941, in its infancy, and in many ways the Butt Report gave the kind of spur that was needed to improve training and develop science. Nonetheless, the griping and criticism continued. This, Harris knew, had to stop. 'I must bring to your urgent and earnest attention,' he wrote to Portal just two weeks into the job, 'the deplorable effect on morale of the spate of largely ignorant and uninstructed chatter against our bombing policy and against the general efficiency and co-operativeness of the Air Force.'

Bomber Command needed to be in the media for the right reasons, as Harris fully recognized. This was one of the main reasons for launching the thousand-bomber raids, and, just as he had hoped, they had received immediate and emphatic support from the British media. Moreover, they allowed both Churchill and Harris to publicly talk up Bomber Command's growing strength. 'This proof of the growing power of the British bomber force,' announced Churchill, 'is also the herald of what Germany will receive, city by city, from now on.' Harris himself became very much the public face of Bomber Command after the raids, and although he preferred action rather than words, he accepted that from time to time he needed to be a visual and more vocal C-in-C – a champion of his men and their efforts. He even put his name to a leaflet dropped over Germany, which was then translated and printed in newspapers in Britain and the United States and cited on the BBC. 'We are bombing Germany, city by city, and even more terribly, in order to make it impossible for you to go on with the war,' he wrote. 'That is our object. We shall pursue it remorselessly . . . Soon we shall be coming every night and every day, rain, blow or snow – we and the Americans.'

There were a number of people willing to criticize Harris for adopting this kind of bombastic rhetoric, normally the preserve of the Nazis, but it was scarcely less forthright than most of Britain's newspapers and war magazines. *The War Illustrated* hailed the attack on Cologne as the 'Greatest Raid in History', recounting with barely contained glee the account of an RAF bomb-aimer who described endless fires and shattered buildings as he had flown over. 'Gone forever is the Cologne that we knew,' the magazine quoted one German newspaper as having reported.

Harris shrugged off the criticism. Some might find it distaste-ful, but it showed intent and aggression, and while there may even have been criticism in Parliament, the stock of Bomber Command – in the public consciousness at any rate – was rising.

Nor was Harris the only member of his Command to speak out. Far more frequent were brief accounts of particular raids made by the crews who flew them. John Nettleton, for example, awarded a Victoria Cross for his part in the Augsburg Raid, broadcast an account of his experience for the BBC. So too did many others. Harris was also well served by the BBC journalist Richard Dimbleby. 'Mr Dimbleby can talk to anyone he likes,' Harris told his staff, 'go where he likes, and see anything he likes, and be directly responsible to me.'

Dimbleby repaid this show of good faith when, in January 1943, he travelled as a passenger during a raid on Berlin. An attack on the German capital had been something of a surprise when it had been announced at the briefing at Syerston, where 106 Squadron was based, on the afternoon of 16 January. Bomber Command had not been there for over a year, but it was a long trip and the flak was known to be intense.

It was Dimbleby's first trip in a bomber and his aircraft came under flak attack as they crossed the Dutch coast, bursting 'in little winking flashes'. He found he couldn't really hear it above the roar of the four Merlin engines. Pushing on unscathed, they eventually neared Berlin, Dimbleby mesmerized by the searchlights crisscrossing the sky looking like a 'tracery of sparkling silver'. The amount of flak shocked him – it was far worse than anything they had experienced up to that point, and as one burst close by, he felt the Lancaster lurch upwards, 'as if a giant hand had pushed up the belly of the machine'. He watched one Lancaster drop a load of incendiaries. 'And where a moment before,' said Dimbleby, 'there had been a dark patch of the city, a dazzling silver pattern spread itself. A rectangle of brilliant lights, hundreds, thousands of them, winking and gleaming and lighting the outlines of the city around them. As though this unloading had been the signal, score after score of fire bombs went down and all over the dark face of the German capital these great incandescent flowerbeds spread themselves. It was a fascinating sight.'

The Lancaster he was in was carrying just one 8,000lb bomb, but it was to be an agonizing experience waiting to drop it: on the first run, the bomb-aimer could not see the aiming point so the pilot decided to go around again. This meant taking a wide circuit and starting the entire bomb run a second time, a decision never made lightly. But on the second run, the aiming point was still obscured so they went around a third time. Many pilots were not so assiduous, but on this third attempt, and with the Lancaster still, thankfully, undamaged, the bomb was finally released.

Immediately, the pilot began corkscrewing away into the night. For Dimbleby, this was too much. Buffeted and rocked, his stomach lurched and a moment later he was vomiting down the ladder into the bomb-aimer's compartment in the nose.

In his subsequent broadcast, Dimbleby paid tribute to the 'six, brave, cool and exceedingly skilful men' he had flown with, but finished by praising all the crews of Bomber Command. 'Perhaps I am shooting a line for them,' he said, 'but I think that somebody ought to. They and their magnificent Lancasters, and all the others like them, are taking the war right into Germany. They have been attacking, giving their lives in attack since the first day of the war.'

This was certainly true of the young 24-year-old pilot Wing Commander Guy Gibson, who had flown his first operational sortie on 3 September 1939, the day when Britain's war started. Since then, he had completed 154 operational sorties, including ninety as a Beaufighter night fighter and sixty-four bomber raids. The normal tour for most aircrew was thirty ops, and then, after a period as an instructor or with a desk job, a second tour of twenty. So Gibson had already comfortably surpassed what should have been required of him.

Despite his youth, Gibson had been CO of 106 Squadron since the previous April. That he had been given notice of his new command just a month after Harris had taken over as C-in-C was no coincidence. As Air Officer Commanding 5 Group in the first year of war, Harris had quickly spotted in Gibson the kind of 'press on' attitude and cool imperturbability that he believed made the best bomber pilots. When, in the summer of 1940, Gibson had been posted from bombers, Harris had promised that once he had done his stint with night fighters, he would give him the best command he possibly could.

Unfortunately for Gibson, in November 1941, when he learned

he would soon be posted as an instructor, Harris had been Deputy Chief of the Air Staff and unable to influence operational postings. Instead, Gibson had taken himself off to St Vincents, in Grantham, the HQ of 5 Group, and had pleaded to be allowed back on bombers. It had, as he commented, been a waste of time, and he had duly been sent to 51 OTU at Cranfield. But on taking over Bomber Command, Harris had wasted no time. For Gibson, being an instructor had been a form of purgatory. He missed the camaraderie of the bomber squadron and, in any case, was driven by a compelling urge to always prove himself. Good friends of his were getting killed; why should they be giving their lives while he was stuck as an instructor?

Fortunately for him, Harris had urged AVM Slessor, then AOC 5 Group, to take him on. 'You will find him absolutely first class,' Harris told Slessor, 'and as this is a two-year-old promise now in fulfilment, I am sure you will agree to its consummation.' Gibson, still only twenty-three at the time, was given his first command, and with it some eighteen ever-changing crews and 500 men. And a year on, Gibson had repaid Harris's faith. Under his energetic and youthful command, he had moulded 106 Squadron into one of the very best in all Bomber Command. More to the point, after a further twenty-five operational missions since taking over the squadron, he was still alive.

'A good trip and fairly successful,' Gibson jotted in his log book after the long raid to Berlin and back with Richard Dimbleby. Yet the very next day, he had visited the RAF Hospital at Rauceby in a state of intense agitation. Although Syerston, where 106 was based, was some twenty miles west of Rauceby, Gibson had increasingly taken to driving over whenever he could to see Corporal Maggie North, a nurse with whom he had recently begun an intense friendship. They had met at the beginning of December, on a bleak night for Syerston. Gibson and the Station Commander, Group Captain Gus Walker, had been watching aircraft taking off when Walker spotted through his binoculars that a parked Lancaster from 61 Squadron had its bomb bay open and that incendiaries were dropping out, and some were igniting. Worried there was a 4,000lb 'cookie' on board, Walker dashed off, clambering into his car and driving as fast as he could to warn the crew. Gibson had watched him get out of his car and wave his hands, and he was twenty yards from the aircraft when the big bomb exploded. 'There was one of those great slow explosions,' noted Gibson, 'which shot straight into the air for about 2,000 feet and the great Lancaster just disappeared.' Gibson assumed his friend had been blown to pieces, but in fact, the blast had taken off an arm and blown him 200 feet backwards. But he was still alive.

A surgeon and two nurses, one of whom was Maggie North, hurried from Rauceby, where Gibson helped them tend the badly injured Group Captain. The next day, he had visited Walker in hospital and there spoke with Maggie North. After talking with her for some time and learning about the many burns victims they dealt with at the hospital, Gibson asked her for a drink.

'Yes, but . . .' faltered Nurse North.

'Yes, but what?' asked Gibson. She explained that she was only a corporal. There were strict codes about mixing with officers, even between sexes.

'Bugger that,' said Gibson. 'We'll go anyway.'

Gibson was already married – he had been since November 1940, to a dancer, Eve Moore, eight years his senior. He had been just twenty-one when they'd met and she had thought he looked as young as a schoolboy, but Gibson had become infatuated, his ardour heightened by the enormous casualties being suffered by Bomber Command at the time and his own conviction that he, too, was shortly to meet his death. Yet he had not died and his wartime commitments had ensured they had spent little of their married life together. Gibson's infatuation remained, but there had never been any meeting of minds. His life on the squadron, and as a bomber pilot, was too remote from his life with her. Like so many aircrew, Gibson was unable to talk to his wife about his experiences.

Maggie North, however, was different. She came face to face with the violence and trauma felt by the bomber crews every day at the hospital. The wards were filled with young men and boys burned beyond recognition, or badly mutilated by wounds. She understood. With Maggie, Gibson could escape from the crushing responsibility of commanding a squadron while repeatedly facing death himself. He no longer had to be the indefatigable and cheery leader. With Maggie, he could be himself. For her part, Maggie North was flattered by his attention but also drawn to this complicated young man, full of good heart one day, wistful and fragile the next.

On this occasion, the afternoon of 17 January, Gibson had appeared at Rauceby unannounced – as was often his way – looking washed out. A sister found Nurse North for him, and told her that her visitor looked troubled. 'I've seen that kind of thing before,' she told her. 'You better go to him.'

She found him sitting in his car, staring through the windscreen and chewing on the stem of his unlit pipe. He was also shaking, quite uncontrollably.

'Please hold me,' he asked her. She did so, folding her arms around him until eventually the shaking stopped.

'Ops last night?' she asked.

Gibson nodded, but said nothing more. It might have been the Berlin op that had prompted the brief breakdown, but more likely it was the loss of two of his best crews four days earlier over Essen. Gray Healey, especially, had been a close friend and an outstanding pilot. He was a quiet, gentle soul, but a pillar of strength within the squadron – and to Gibson. Maurice Phair, an American, had been nearing the end of his first tour, while Healey was halfway through his second. Michael Lumley, Healey's wireless operator, was a more lively personality and had been one of the great characters of 106. Gibson had waited up all night hoping that Healey might return. He was still officially missing, and there was always the slight hope that they had been taken prisoner, and Gibson had written a long letter to Healey's mother suggesting just that. Writing condolence letters was another of the added strains of command. For one so young, the burden of command was immense.

On Sunday, 14 February – St Valentine's Day – Gibson flew an operation for the first time since the Berlin raid. His workload had increased since Gus Walker had been blown up; Gibson not only greatly liked and respected him, but relied on him too, for the Station Commander had eased Gibson's administrative burden enormously. He had also been the one person to whom Gibson was willing to defer; no other person was allowed to make the slightest inroad on his authority.

Yet with or without Walker by his side, Gibson had always been keen to be a very visual CO, and a man who led by example, and that meant flying as often as he could. He liked his pilots to share that same 'press on' attitude, to be outwardly, at any rate, phlegmatic and imperturbable, and to be utterly committed to the task in hand. To be 'squadron types', as he termed them. He also liked to be seen around the place. Unlike Harris, who after his morning 'High Mass' disappeared to his office, barely to be seen again, Gibson made a point of drinking with the chaps in the Mess, of joining in on sports and games, and of imposing strict, obsessive discipline. He would also stand up for his men, would back them to the hilt against any outside pressure, or if they found themselves in trouble, but came down on them like a hammer if they erred on his watch – and more often than not, that meant those who did not fall into line with his way of thinking. In this respect, he was decidedly autocratic. He believed that any aircrew should devote their time and energy to the frontline unit. Outside influences were not welcome. His own wife was not with him at Syerston and he did not approve of his pilots living with their wives; they were a distraction.

And yet since Walker had gone, he had struck up an intense, but still platonic, relationship with Maggie North, in which they would talk about a fantasy future, living a life together in 'Honeysuckle Cottage'. Entire conversations were devoted to the décor of their cottage and what they would do: gardening, fishing trips and being surrounded by dogs. By Valentine's Day, however, that fantasy appeared to be over. Gibson had learned that Maggie had been receiving the attentions of another man, a sergeant.

'Don't do it,' Gibson told her.

'Why not?' she replied. 'No one else seems to want to.'

'You don't love him,' Gibson said.

'How do you know?'

Gibson said again, 'Don't do this.'

Maggie North was confused. Gibson had made no physical move on her at all, and yet he seemed to need her, and to have created a future for them both. She wanted more, however, and Sergeant Figgins was offering it to her.

Gibson flew to Milan on 14 February. Visibility was good and Italian anti-aircraft guns were seldom as vicious as those of the Germans. In the moonlight, the great city could easily be seen and the bombing was more concentrated than usual. Gibson was carrying a film cameraman, so after dropping his bomb circled the city, watching the rapidly growing fires below, while film footage was shot. When they eventually turned for home, fires could still be seen a hundred miles away. Furthermore, Gibson and the others from the squadron brought back six photographs that showed they had dropped their bombs on the aiming point, no small achievement.

Gibson had been born in India. His father was a colonial officer in the Imperial Indian Forest Service, and eighteen years older than Gibson's mother, who had been just nineteen when they married and only twenty-three when her second son and youngest of three had been born. Aloof and remote, Alexander Gibson was emotionally distant, not only to his wife, but to his children too. At six, Guy had, like so many colonial children before him, been sent to boarding school in England, accompanied by his mother, whose marriage was already struggling. Thereafter, Gibson had little more to do with his father.

Nor was returning to England a happy experience for his mother, who had become used to the privileged life of a colonial wife, was sexually frustrated, and soon turned to alcohol for solace. Becoming increasingly depressed and volatile, his mother was unable to provide the stability her three children, and especially Guy, as youngest, needed. With his father in India and his mother suffering from a personality disorder, Gibson and his brother and sister were starved of both parental support and affection. When Gibson was fourteen, his mother was even jailed briefly for a series of drunken driving offences. After that, he had little more to do with her. Instead, during school holidays, the children were often passed from one relative to another, although mostly to their maternal grandparents in Cornwall. There, at least, Guy was provided with some emotional stability.

Gibson rarely talked of his childhood, either to his friends, or to Eve or even to Maggie North. He was close to his older brother, Alick, and his sister-in-law, Ruth, and relied upon the stability of their married home. His tragic mother, Nora, had died at Christmas 1939, horrifically burned when her dress had caught in an electric stove – just as his infatuation with the older Eve was beginning. Yet Gibson did pick brief moments from his childhood – fishing boats leaving a pier at Porthleven, the scent of honeysuckle on a summer's evening – to furnish his fantasy future. And in this future life, he would find all that had been missing up to now.

Another officer at Syerston was Flying Officer Charlie Williams, and in sharp contrast with Gibson he had had a far more emotionally fulfilling life. An Australian, and now thirty-three years old, he had grown up in a loving and close family on a sheep station on the Flinders River in northern Queensland. It was true that they had struggled when depression hit in the 1930s, but they had recovered. Through enterprise and hard work, Charlie and his older brother, Doug, had gradually taken over the mantle from their father; by the time war was declared, the family prospects seemed good.

As farmers with elderly parents, both brothers could have avoided military service, but while it was agreed that Doug would join the Army Reserve and would stay in Australia to take responsibility for the family, Charlie volunteered for the Air Force. He had already learned to fly, but in 1939 he had been thirty, single and anxious to see something of the world. Life in the outback was a remote existence – he had never been further than Brisbane in his life, but equally, like many young Australians, felt compelled to follow a higher calling. Britain was still very much the mother country, and he believed it was his duty to play his part.

Despite volunteering, it was not until February 1941 that he was called up, and then, even with his flying experience, he was considered too old to be trained as a combat pilot. Instead, he was selected to become a wireless operator/air gunner, or WAG as they were known. After training, he finally left Australia in October 1941 with an understandable mixture of excitement, apprehension and sadness, not least because his father was suffering from heart trouble. It was a long journey, via Hawaii, the United States and Canada, and then the final leg across the Atlantic, arriving in England at the end of November 1941. After signals school at Cranwell – where he had passed out with an 'above average' assessment – he had been posted to his OTU, at Cottesmore, and there had taken part in Harris's thousand-bomber raid on Cologne. Despite his training, he had gone as a tail gunner in an old two-engine Hampden, but they had found the target all right. Cologne had been a maze of fires, but as they had turned for home, their aircraft was ensnared in searchlights and heavy flak began to burst all around them. Somehow, they managed to get through, then about an hour later were caught up in even heavier flak, the Hampden clattering and lurching as shards of metal battered the airframe. Again, they managed to get through, but having cleared the enemy coast they got lost and when they eventually approached England, found themselves targets from British anti-aircraft gunners. 'We finally landed,' he wrote in a letter home, 'after being up for seven hours, feeling very tired and weary. We all had a solid rum and after briefing had breakfast and then to bed.'

By now it was 8 a.m. on 31 May, but the following day they were expected to fly again, this time to Essen. It was perhaps just as well for Williams and his crew mates, still far from ready for combat operations, that they suffered engine failure in their old crate and had to turn back. Even so, they then were ordered to take part in the third thousand-bomber raid, on Bremen on 25 June. This time, Williams spotted two enemy night fighters. They appeared to be heading straight for them, their Hampden in their sights, but before Williams opened fire, they passed by, intent on some other target. 'We were,' he wrote, 'glad to see them go.'

He had been alone among those of his OTU in being posted to 61 Squadron at Syerston, and it was as a member of the squadron that he converted to Lancasters. He had been impressed by his first flight in a Lancaster, struck by its speed and easy grace. Crewed up at last, and with a pilot who already had some operational experience, he flew his first operation with the squadron on 19 September – and it was a long one, too, to Munich. His next few missions followed in quick succession. Williams was fortunate in that he had flown in the thousand-bomber raids and emerged unscathed, but the initial handful of operations were invariably a bewildering and often terrifying experience. Luck, of course, played a huge part in whether crews survived. A chance burst of flak could strike a fuel tank on a first trip or the thirtieth. The night fighters Williams had seen over Bremen in June left them alone, but might have blasted them with high-explosive cannon shells. Statistically, the percentage chance of returning safely diminished with every flight, but, in truth, experience did make a difference. The best crews developed a sixth sense that only experience could teach them. And the more time a crew spent in an aircraft, the more natural it felt. They learned what could be done and what could not, how hard their machine could be pushed, its strengths and weaknesses. Moreover, crews became hardened. They learned what it felt like to corkscrew, with the wings bending, and the airframe shuddering; they learned to distinguish between a near miss and flak that jolted them but was harmless. Nor was the sight of a Lancaster exploding mid-air or spiralling in flames ever as shocking as it was the first time.

Williams's second trip was to Wismar on the Baltic Coast. The target had been the Dornier aircraft factory, but the weather was far from ideal and the eighty-three Lancasters sent over attacked from just 2,000 feet rather than 18,000 or more. This was later reported as a highly successful raid, but it had not seemed that way to Williams. On the way back, they flew through a series of very alarming electrical storms. This was the first time he had ever seen the phenomenon of St Elmo's Fire, caused by static electricity building up around the metal airframe. From his desk seat as wireless operator, Williams saw sparks jumping off the wings and a halo of blue jumping and flashing around the propellers. 'It is really a most frightening sight,' he wrote, 'although not dangerous.' The very next night, he was out again, this time a mine-laying operation which took a staggering ten hours fifteen minutes. The weather was once again bad, they encountered plenty of flak and when they did eventually touch down it was at Leaconfield in Yorkshire, about a hundred miles from Syerston. Williams and his crew mates did not get back until 6 p.m. the following evening. The physical and mental strain was immense. 'We were all just about done in,' he scrawled, 'after nearly 18 hours of operational flying in a week.'

By 13 February, Williams was still alive and had completed seventeen ops, so was nearly two-thirds of the way through his first tour. Many of the lads he had joined up with in Australia were now dead – half a dozen had joined the Air Force with him back home, and now all but he and his friend John were gone. So too was his friend Charlie Walker, the former Australian Test cricketer. Williams loved cricket and had played a number of games with Walker the previous summer. A mid-upper gunner, Walker had volunteered to fill a vacancy outside his normal crew, but he, the Lancaster and the rest of the crew had never returned. Williams also kept a group photograph of his air gunner's course at 14 OTU, taken the previous April. The name of each was written in white, but Williams one day wrote 'KA' – killed in action – above those he knew had already been lost. There were six marked this way already.

Williams had a stoical attitude; after all, every other aircrew at Syerston was in much the same boat. He missed home and he missed his family – he had felt an understandable bout of home-sickness at Christmas – but he had taken each day as it came, and tried not to think too far ahead. Now, however, he was, like Gibson, starting to think about a future beyond the war. Approaching his thirty-fourth birthday, Williams had never married; he had been engaged, in Australia, to a girl he met while training, but it had been a hurried wartime affair and since reaching England the letters had stopped. He had not actually broken with Millie, but it was over. That much was obvious.

But now he had met someone, a girl called Gwen Parfitt, known as 'Bobbie'. She was a secretary in Nottingham, but Williams was smitten and it seemed as though the feeling was mutual. Nottingham was only fifteen miles or so from Syerston, and Williams had a car, so it was easy enough to head over to see her whenever there was no flying and they were stood down. A shared love of books had been one of the things that had drawn them together, and Bobbie had sent him a copy of Omar Khayyam's poems. 'This, together with Kipling's "IF",' she wrote to him, 'are two of my most cherished possessions.'

In the weeks to come, their love affair would flourish. The same could not be said for Guy Gibson and Maggie North, however. On Saturday, 20 February, Gibson rang Maggie and once again implored her not to marry.

'I don't want you to do this,' he repeated.

'Guy, you are spoken for,' she told him.

A long silence. And then Gibson said, 'But I need you.'

'Eve wouldn't let you go, would she?'

Gibson sighed. 'Would you come if I asked?'

'Yes,' Maggie replied.

'Do you really mean that?'

'Yes. You know I would.'

A half-conversation, with neither really saying what they felt, both wretched and confused. Maggie North married later that same day.

By that time, however, far away to the south, events were moving fast, although Wallis's plan for an attack on the dams using his large bouncing bomb was proving divisive. Who would prevail still hung in the balance.

7

Panacea Mongers

MONDAY, 15 FEBRUARY 1943. 'DB Ops was requested to investigate the whole operational project ("UPKEEP"-versus-dam),' it had been minuted at the Air Ministry meeting of two days before, 'with the assistance of such expert advice as he might require, including, if necessary, Mr Wallis and represent-atives of Bomber Command.' Wasting no time, Group Captain Bufton had thus set up another meeting, this time with both Wallis and the Vickers test pilot, Captain Mutt Summers, present, as well as Group Captain Elworthy from Bomber Command, Lockspeiser and various others, including William Halcrow, a civilian engineer and friend of Wallis's whom he had frequently consulted since first working on the *Note*.

It was Bufton who had, two days earlier, queried the feasibility of flying such a distance to the German dams. It was a perfectly reasonable point. 'Buf', as he was known, had already been some months into the job of Deputy Director of Bomber Operations when the Augsburg Raid had taken place, and although it had been a Bomber Command initiative, the disastrous loss of aircraft and crews had not been forgotten. A daylight raid on Le Creusot, in France, had taken place the previous autumn – both Guy Gibson and Charlie Williams had taken part – but nothing at that kind of 100-foot level had been attempted since Augsburg. Nothing even remotely that low. And there was also the issue of accuracy. Bufton had been the driving force behind bringing the Pathfinder Force into being, designed specifically to improve accuracy, but Wallis's plans seemed to hinge on being able to drop the Upkeep on a sixpence.

Even so, Bufton was more open-minded than many, and an innovator within the RAF. Back in the spring of 1941, he had had lunch with Wallis at the RAF Club and had later visited him at Burhill. Wallis had also given him a copy of the *Note*, and more recently one of his *Air Attack on Dams*. Bufton may have been a 35-year-old staff officer, but he had also been an RAF high-flyer, literally and metaphorically, having been a bomber pilot and having already commanded both 10 and 76 Squadrons before taking over as Station Commander at RAF Pocklington. He was thus unusual among highly placed staff officers in that he had operational combat experience from the current conflict. If there was a realistic way of improving Britain's bombing capability, then he was always willing to back it.

Bufton thus had come to that meeting on the Monday morning with an attitude that was sceptical but open-minded. What he really wanted to discover was this: (1) Were the tactical limitations of the weapon, i.e. the height, speed and accuracy at which the Upkeep needed to be dropped, too great to make a night operation impracticable? (2) If so, could the weapon be modified to overcome these limitations? And (3), what were the timing restrictions involved with regard to water levels in the dams?

Wallis answered in detail, although in essence, he said, he estimated the bomb could be released from 250 feet at about 250 mph at any point between three-eighths of a mile and three-quarters of a mile.

Group Captain Elworthy did not mention that Harris believed the whole scheme was a load of tripe, but instead expressed the C-in-C's concern about taking away Lancasters to be modified. Wallis answered that only one Lancaster would be needed for full-scale trials. 'After the operation has taken place,' he said, 'the aircraft could be made fit for normal operations in a matter of twenty-four hours.' He also pointed out that the three smaller bombs which had been made for the Mosquito trials had been designed and produced in just one week. The large bombs for the Lancasters could be produced in two months, he reckoned, so long as they were given the right priority and that Avro was willing to cooperate. Elworthy, clearly beginning to come round, reckoned two to three weeks would be enough to train the crews needed for the operation. Targets were then examined. Wallis suggested that as well as the Möhne Dam, the Eder Dam, some forty-five miles east-south-east but with double the capacity, would also be an important target.

Wallis appeared to have won his audience over. 'It was agreed,' Bufton later reported, 'that the operation offered a very good chance of success, and that the weapons and necessary parts for modification should be prepared for thirty aircraft.' It was also agreed that so long as the operation took place before the end of June, the water levels would be right for an attack.

Bufton and Lockspeiser were among those who then followed Wallis to Teddington to see scale trials in the water tank at the National Physical Laboratory. Wallis also showed them his film reel. Bufton was impressed, and at a convivial lunch afterwards Wallis stressed upon him that a raid on the dams should have very little effect on the B.3/42 Windsor bomber project.

'In my opinion,' concluded Bufton in a long memo to his direct surperior, Air Vice-Marshal Bottomley, 'the prospects offered by this new weapon fully justify our pressing on with development as quickly as possible.'

Wallis had now won over a key part of the Air Ministry.

Unbeknown to Wallis, however, Bufton's support was something of a double-edged sword. Air Marshal Harris took a dim view of young upstarts at the Air Ministry telling him what to do, especially when they were quite a few rungs down the ranking ladder, but that was what he regularly had to put up with from the 'Three B's' – Bufton, Bottomley and Baker. They sounded more like a firm of provincial solicitors than members of the air staff, but, of the three, only Bottomley, as Assistant Chief of the Air Staff (Ops) was an Air Vice-Marshal. Both Baker, a Director of Bombing Operations, and Bufton, as Baker's deputy, were Group Captains.

Group Captains! And yet they felt they had the right to send missives to Bomber Command HQ, directing Harris how to use his aircraft. He found them exasperating.

Of the three men, however, it was Bufton who particularly got on his nerves, and if there was one way above all that was guaranteed to turn Harris off any madcap plan to attack the dams, it was a recommendation from this troublesome young know-it-all, Sydney Bufton.

The truth was, Bufton had humiliated the C-in-C, and badly so, something Bert Harris was not going to forget in a hurry. This had happened the previous summer, over the matter of whether or not to create a Pathfinder Force (PFF). The idea of having a specialist squadron or group who would operate ahead of the main bomber stream and then lay target markers as a guide to the others following behind had been discussed as early as the summer of 1941, well before Harris took over Bomber Command. It had been discovered that, during the Blitz, the Luftwaffe had done just this with two specialist bomber groups, KG 100 and KG 26, and so it had been mooted – and had gained the support of Lord Cherwell – that several 'fire raising' squadrons might be developed along similar lines to those of the Germans.

This was a tactic that Bufton believed, very strongly, was absolutely essential. He had flown too many bomber operations himself where the target had been almost impossible to find, and although navigational aids were improving, he knew from practical experience that these were unlikely to be enough. So, on joining the Air Ministry as Deputy Director of Bomber Operations in November 1941, he immediately set about writing a paper in which he urged the formation of a 'target-finding force', whose aircraft would be the first to be equipped with GEE and the still being developed Oboe. 'They should start training, thinking and developing tactics,' he wrote, 'with a view to acting in a target-finding role.'

While stirring interest – not least in Lord Cherwell once again – there was little sign that anyone was prepared to push Bufton's ideas. So, at the end of February, and with Harris newly ensconced as C-in-C Bomber Command, Bufton pressed the point again in a memo to Group Captain John Baker, his immediate boss at the Air Ministry. Bufton pointed out that the current criticism of Bomber Command's efforts stemmed from a failure to carry out tactical directions and control of their bomber force. 'I urge therefore most strongly,' he wrote, 'and with the utmost urgency that we should immediately form a Target-Finding Force, cut out the dead wood from Bomber Command, and so tighten the sinews of control that the bomber force may be wielded and directed as a sharp, flexible, hard-hitting unit.' He also suggested that a target-finding force would enable attacks to be made on precision targets and even listed a few, such as several synthetic-fuel plants and the ball-bearing factories at Schweinfurt.

Bufton's report received rather more enthusiasm within Air Ministry circles this time around and eventually wound up on Harris's desk. Of course, this was precisely the kind of paper Harris loathed: unasked for and unwanted and written by a junior officer, who, despite his combat experience, did not know the whole picture. In any case, he fundamentally disagreed with the idea of creating a specialist target-finding force by creaming off the best crews of all the bomber groups into what would be a *corps d'élite*. This, he believed, would not only be bad for morale but would never really work because, human nature being what it was, the Groups would want to retain their best crews, and the best personnel themselves would also object to leaving squadrons in which they had half-completed tours and were looked up to, in order to be sent to new squadrons and have to start all over again.

These objections were more valid than Bufton was prepared to acknowledge. Bomber Command was still small, and there was no doubt that taking away the best crews would be keenly felt. Harris also reckoned that bombing techniques would improve by appointing certain crews as 'raid leaders' or giving the honour to the squadron that achieved the best bombing results each month.

Bufton, however, believed this was something of a false argument. Crews would not have to start their tours again if they were moved into a new target-finding force, while crew rotation within squadrons happened all the time, through tours being completed, through promotions and, of course, through casualties.

He disagreed that pulling out a good crew would dent morale.

On the other hand, what most definitely *would* improve morale would be better results. It would stop the criticism and make the huge sacrifice more obviously worthwhile. And creating a target-finding force would be the best way to get those results, because by putting the best crews together, they would then have an opportunity to discuss, develop and co-ordinate their technique. Furthermore, they could operate with the best and latest navigational aids, such as GEE, and eventually Oboe and H2S could be quickly introduced to these few aircraft without waiting until there were sufficient supplies for the entire Command – which was another reason why adopting Harris's plan of using the best squadron in the group to lead the way would not work; not every aircraft was yet equipped with GEE.

Bufton's determination ensured that this was a debate that would not go away. Harris, therefore, decided to try and deal with it once and for all, by organizing a conference at Bomber Command and inviting all his five bomber group and two training group commanders and their SASOs – all of whom he knew he could rely on to back him – and Baker and Bufton from the Air Ministry.

The conference opened with Harris reeling off his arguments about morale and then argued that if crews were collected into a target-finding force they would inevitably lose their chance for promotion. At this Bufton, who had had two brothers shot down, lost his cool and, banging the table with his hand, said, 'Sir, you will never win the war like that! These people don't know if they will be alive tomorrow and they couldn't care less about promotion.' This was extraordinary behaviour in front of the C-in-C, and it says much for Harris's *sang-froid* that he merely looked at his watch and suggested it was time for lunch.

When they reconvened, the C-in-C suggested a vote. 'I need hardly tell you,' he told them, 'that I am fundamentally opposed to the idea, but I wouldn't mind hearing your views.' Needless to say, Harris's men all voted against the idea. 'It was highly significant to my mind,' noted Bufton later, 'that I, an observer, was the only person present at the conference with experience of night bombing in the war. This major, and purely tactical, problem was discussed, and a decision made, in the absence of any person with the relevant operational experience.'

Bufton was convinced that had the conference been full of experienced aircrew rather than desk wallahs, a quite different decision would have been reached, so he decided to go behind Harris's back and canvass opinion himself. Having sent out copies of his proposals for a target-finding force together with a short questionnaire to a dozen squadron and station commanders, the response was as he expected. 'TFF an urgent requirement,' wrote one. 'Have discussed idea of TFF with many senior captains who all entirely agree,' wrote another. 'A unit comparable with KG100 is vital,' said another. 'A *corps d'élite* even if it were unpopular is absolutely essential.' 'The Army has never suffered from having Guards Regiments.' And so on. All were unanimously behind Bufton, so he sent their copies straight to Harris and then, getting no response, followed it up with another, even more comprehensive letter, in which he summed up the whole argument.

His survey, however, was every bit as loaded as the conference Harris had convened earlier. The dozen people questioned were all known to Bufton and like-minded. There were plenty of squadron commanders he did not question. And squadron leaders did not fully appreciate the paucity of aircraft and crews that Harris was having to juggle in the first months of his command. He was not disagreeing with a target-finding force *per se* but, rather, its form and structure.

By June, there had still been no response, but then Bufton had been visited by Air Marshal Sir Wilfrid Freeman, at the time standing in for Portal, who was away on leave. Bufton told him that he was frustrated by the lack of progress with the Pathfinder Force and lent Freeman his folder on the matter.

'This last letter, have you had a reply?' Freeman asked.

'No, sir,' Bufton replied.

'Do you know why?'

'No, sir.'

'Because there isn't a reply,' said Freeman. 'You've beaten Bert at his own game. CAS will be in on Monday. We've got to have a Pathfinder Force and I'll talk it over with him.'

Events moved swiftly after that. The very next day, Freeman met with Bufton and Sir Henry Tizard, who gave his support, and then Freeman drafted a letter for Portal to send to Harris. 'In the opinion of the Air Staff,' ran the note, 'the formation of the special force would open up a new field for improvement, raising the standard of accuracy of bombing, and thus morale, throughout Bomber Command.'

Harris could ignore junior staff officers, but not the Chief of the Air Staff. Meeting with Portal the very next day, Harris was forced reluctantly to concede, while Bufton was asked to draw up a list of crews for this new force. The Pathfinder Force came into being on 15 August 1942. Harris viewed this humiliation as a commander in the field being overruled 'at the dictation of junior officers in the Air Ministry'. Certainly it was Bufton who had been the driving force behind creating the PFF, but it was cool logic and good sense overcoming entrenched obstinacy that had ensured the decision went in favour of creating the new force.

And that decision had been the Chief of the Air Staff's, Air Chief Marshal Sir Charles Portal, for he was the most senior air officer in the RAF and his word was final.

Harris, however, not only disliked being told what to do by young know-it-alls but also deeply disliked what he termed as 'panacea mongers'. These were those – scientists, upstarts like Bufton and others – who believed there was some panacea out there that could solve all the difficulties imposed by the current technological limitations and enable Bomber Command to become a precision bomber force. Thus 'panacea targets' were those that Wallis had originally suggested in the *Note*, or those synthetic-fuel plants that Bufton had mentioned. It was true in February 1942, when Bufton had been drafting Harris's Directive on behalf of Portal, that the aim was the destruction of Germany's morale and industrial cities through area bombing. However, Bufton had always meant to turn to precision bombing as soon as the tactical capabilities of the bomber force permitted. This was a distinction that Harris did not agree with. By February 1943, despite the advent of new navigational aids, and, yes, even the PFF, Harris believed his bombers were still only capable of area, not precision, bombing – much more efficient area bombing, which was why he was planning a new, concentrated effort against the Ruhr for the beginning of March. The first year of his command had been a time of trial and experimentation, but now it was time to focus on the main task: bludgeoning Germany into submission, and without Bufton and his ilk offering 'panacea targets' or madcap bouncing-bomb ideas. These people, as far as Harris was concerned, were not in the day-to-day business of running a Command such as his and therefore should not be butting in and telling him how to do his job. Nor should they be revving up scientists into believing that they, too, held the key of some fantasy bombing panacea.

So when Harris learned that at a meeting chaired by his old *bête noire*, Sid Bufton, it had been recommended that *thirty* Lancasters be modified for a low-level precision attack on the German dams using a new bouncing-bomb wonder weapon, and just before the launch of the Command's all-out offensive against the Ruhr, the reaction was explosive. To put it mildly.

8

Portal Power

THURSDAY, 18 FEBRUARY 1943. After 'High Mass' that morning, Harris had as usual driven in his Bentley back to his office and there had received a call from Air Vice-Marshal Francis Linnell, the Controller of Research and Development at the MAP. Linnell had not been at Bufton's meeting three days earlier, but Lockspeiser had been and had presumably told him of what had been discussed. In any case, Lockspeiser had been on the distribution list for the minutes. Linnell must have seen these. Linnell had been promoted to Assistant Chief of the Air Staff (Ops), Bottomley's current post, in February 1941, when Harris was still Deputy Chief of the Air Staff. The two men knew each other well – and, in fact, before joining the Air Ministry, Linnell had been Air Officer Administration at Bomber Command, one of the senior posts at High Wycombe. At the MAP, it was Linnell's job to oversee future development, but he was still a bomber man first and foremost and, top of his list, was the Windsor bomber. Furthermore, no matter how impressive the weapon or the film show reel of the Chesil Beach trials, he doubted whether such an operation against the German dams was practicable. Finally, he was also an ally of Harris's. Whether Elworthy had already reported back to his boss the details of the meeting is not clear, but Linnell certainly did.

Whether Harris actually choked on his morning coffee when he heard the news is not known, but having come off the phone to Linnell, he clearly decided it was time to stop this nonsense once and for all. At his headquarters in High Wycombe, there was, of course, only one person to go to, and that was the Chief of the Air Staff, Air Chief Marshal Sir Charles Portal. Despite overruling Harris over the PFF the previous summer, Portal had been one of the main architects of the strategic air offensive and the two men had always had a close working relationship. Portal was fully aware of Bomber Command's plans for a March assault on the Ruhr and Harris was certain he would support him in getting this madcap scheme stopped in its tracks.

'Dear CAS,' Harris wrote. 'Linnell rang me up this morning about the Highball proposition.' He told Portal of his call from Linnell. 'He is as worried as I am about it.' That the C-in-C appeared to be unaware of the difference between Upkeep and Highball was neither here nor there. Size of bomb wasn't the issue; it was the principle of the entire loony scheme. 'He says,' he continued, 'that all sorts of enthusiasts and panacea-mongers are now coming round MAP suggesting the taking of about thirty Lancasters off the line to rig them up for this weapon, when the weapon itself exists so far only within the imagination of those who conceived it.' This much was true. The trial bomb was smaller than Wallis's proposed Upkeep, but bigger than Highball, and, of course, not a bomb at all, as it was inert.

'I cannot too strongly deprecate any diversion of Lancasters at this critical moment in our affairs, on the assumption that some entirely new weapon, totally untried, is going to be a success.' And now, getting into his stride, Harris let rip. 'With some slight practical knowledge and many previous bitter experiences on similar lines,' he continued, 'I am prepared to bet that the Highball is just about the maddest proposition as a weapon that we have yet come across – and this is saying something.' He was saying this with some understanding of what was involved with delivering Wallis's weapon. 'The job of rotating some 1,200 lbs of material at 500 rpm on an aircraft,' he pointed out, 'is in itself fraught with difficulty. The slightest lack of balance will just tear the aircraft to pieces, and in the packing of the explosive, let alone in retaining it packed in balance during rotation, are obvious technical difficulties.' This was true enough.

'I am prepared to bet my shirt,' he continued, '(a) that the weapon itself cannot be passed as a prototype for trial inside 6 months, (b) that its ballistics will in no way resemble those claimed for it; (c) that it will be impossible to keep such a weapon in adequate balance either when rotating it prior to release or at all in storage; and (d) that it will not work when we have got it.

'Finally, we have made attempt after attempt to pull successful low attacks with heavy bombers. They have been, almost without exception, costly failures.'

Harris's arguments were not at all unreasonable, and the final point was possibly the most valid of all. The Augsburg Raid was the obvious example. There was no question now of flying low level during daylight hours, but was Portal really going to sanction a mission that involved precious Lancasters flying at under a hundred feet, over enemy territory, beyond the Ruhr – the most heavily defended part of Germany other than Berlin – and at night and with a bonkers new weapon that had still not even been made?

'In these circumstances,' Harris stated with dismissive condescension, 'while nobody would object to the Highball enthusiasts being given one aeroplane and told to go away and play while we get on with the war, I hope you will do your utmost to keep these mistaken enthusiasts within the bounds of reason and certainly to prevent them from setting aside any number of our precious Lancasters for immediate modification. Lancasters make the great contribution to our bomber offensive, which we have to carry on so continuously against such great odds. The heaviest odds arise from the continual attempts to ruin Lancasters for some specialist purpose or to take them away for others to use.'

Having got that off his chest, Harris would have no doubt assumed that would be the last he heard of the matter. In that, however, he was to be sorely mistaken.

These were busy days for Barnes Wallis. On 18 February, he was at the National Physical Laboratory at Teddington, where he was making a further show reel, this time of underwater shots of the sphere hitting the 'dam' wall, and then, with the backspin, rolling down against the dam face. The next day, he had a meeting with Renouf and others at the Admiralty, two more meetings at 1 p.m. and 2.30 p.m., and then another screening of his original film as well as this new footage to a large gathering at Vickers House. This time, the audience included not only Sir Charles Craven but two of the most powerful men in the country: the heads of two of the armed services, Admiral Sir Dudley Pound and Air Chief Marshal Sir Charles Portal.

This was certainly enough to convince the First Sea Lord to give the Highball project, at any rate, his full backing. Renouf, as far as he was concerned, had been quite right to champion the development of this weapon so wholeheartedly, and a week later, on 27 February, he made his views clear on paper. 'It is considered that the potential value of the High Ball is so great,' he wrote, 'and the need for having it ready by May is so urgent, that not only should the trials be given the highest priority, but that their complete success should be <u>assumed now</u>.' As if this endorsement was not enough, Pound then added, 'the High Ball is the most promising secret weapon yet produced by any belligerent and may even have a decisive effect on the war.' He recommended that the Chiefs of Staff prepare a plan for use of the Highball against the 'main units of the German Fleet and the Ruhr Dams simultaneously about the end of May'.

It was hard to imagine how Admiral Pound could have been more supportive. In fact, it was striking how unanimously excited those in the Admiralty were about the prospects of Highball. Admiral Renouf had seen its potential and having given it his full backing had skilfully steered ever-growing support for it among the Navy's senior Flag Officers, culminating with Admiral Pound. Whatever inter-departmental and Command rivalries and issues there may have been, Wallis's invention was not causing any rifts.

The same could not be said for the Royal Air Force. Highball was, on the face of it, a more obviously viable weapon than Upkeep. It was smaller, could be delivered over seas whose airspace was, for the most part, dominated by the Allies, and was a weapon apparently tailor-made for attacking German capital ships anchored deep within Norwegian fjords – ships that had for some time been high on the Royal Navy's target list, but which had remained there for want of means of getting at them. Thus Highball really did seem to be the panacea they had been vainly hoping for. Furthermore, since the Highball was smaller, it was easier to carry. And more importantly, Mosquitoes were not precious Lancasters. Such was Admiralty enthusiasm, there were even discussions about another variant, called 'Baseball' – smaller than the Highball and which, Wallis suggested, could be carried by motor torpedo boats.

Even so, the differences of opinion that were now emerging with the Air Force over Upkeep were unquestionably exacerbated by conflicting views over how best to execute the bomber war, as well as character clashes and inter-departmental rivalry and factions. It was not that one view was right or wrong; the weapon of strategic bombing was still comparatively new, even in February 1943. Technology was evolving rapidly, but Portal, Harris and the senior Air Staff were still flying into the unknown. It was just that Harris believed that continuity was best: the blunt instrument he had could only improve as more and more Lancasters were built, as navigational aids became more sophisticated, as bombsights became more technologically superior, and as the US Eighth Air Force grew alongside them. Ever increasingly heavy area bombing would get the job done, would win the war. Eventually. It had to; this was something Harris believed absolutely. Endlessly searching for a more refined, more precise weapon or method of attack was a distraction, and could only detract from what was already in place. Better to stick with what one knew than risk being derailed by something that would prove a time-consuming and costly failure. In a handwritten note at the end of a memorandum from Bottomley about Upkeep, Harris had spelled out his view even more plainly. 'This is tripe of the wildest description,' he had scribbled. 'There are so many ifs and buts that there is not the smallest chance of it working.'

On both 17 and 18 February, Wallis had been spending some of his time working on the B.3/42 Windsor – it was, after all, still Vickers' priority project – but in between had managed to continue work on the bouncing bomb; he had been at the National Physical Laboratory until 7.45 p.m. on the 18th. Friday the 19th had begun with a meeting with Captain Jeans, the Director of Miscellaneous Weapons Development at the Admiralty, to discuss Baseball and Highball, then at 2.30 p.m. he had a meeting with Barrett and Munton from the MAP 're de-icing problems'. By 4 p.m., he was at Vickers, preparing his film showing, then at 5.30 p.m. he showed it to Admiral Pound and Portal. Following this, he drove to Dorking with Admiral Renouf. On Saturday, 20 February, Wallis was at Burhill, then in the afternoon there were more meetings. Finally, on Sunday, he allowed himself a day off, not least because he was suffering from a migraine. The house was quiet, which was no bad thing. Molly had gone to Salisbury with Elizabeth and Christopher, their youngest, to see Mary, who was at school there. It was normally such a noisy, clamorous place, especially during the holidays when there were suddenly six children about, and often even more when friends came over. Like any people, they were never free of troubles. Barnes was fretting about Upkeep and Highball, but Molly had been concerned the previous week about Christopher, the youngest, who was suffering from earache and a temperature; and she was worrying about her nephew, John, who was at Epsom College and mixing with the wrong sort. Barnes and Molly had taken on the extra burden of their two nephews without question or complaint. They had been orphaned, like so many others all over the world, by the war. In many ways, John and Robert's plight only underlined how lucky Barnes and Molly were. Theirs was a close and happy family. Moreover, Barnes still regarded his wife with an uxoriousness that remained undimmed after nearly eighteen years of marriage.

Theirs had been an unusual courtship. They were, in fact, cousins by marriage, although they had not met until April 1922, when Molly Bloxam had been seventeen and in her last year at school, and when Wallis, by then already thirty-five, had been out of a job. Wallis had come from a middle-class background – his father had been a doctor in the East End of London, but suffered from polio, which meant it had been hard to keep up his practice and thus money had always been tight. His second son, Barnes had only attended the public school Christ's Hospital, in Sussex, after winning a Foundation Scholarship. Despite this, he had left school at sixteen; he had always been interested in mechanics and machinery, was good with his hands, and, determined to become an engineer, believed practical experience was the best way to achieve his goal. He became an apprentice to a shipbuilding firm on the Isle of Wight, but by hard graft and flair slowly worked his way up. In 1913, he became one of the designers in the airship development programme of Vickers, by then already an established engineering company.

Tragedy struck the family when Barnes's mother died, still young, in 1911. He was devastated; he had hoped to help his parents financially, and felt haunted by his inability to do so before it was too late. A few years later, however, in 1916, and with the country still at war, his father had remarried, to Fanny Bloxam, one of his late wife's childhood friends. After the war, Fanny's brother, Arthur, brought his family to London, which included his two eldest daughters, Baba and Molly.

By 1922, however, Vickers had finished with airship production, so that the job that had prevented Wallis from seeing frontline action – he had tried to enlist on three separate occasions but on each had been recalled – was over and he was made redundant. He had decided not to waste his time so was studying for a London External B.Sc., but then, in September, took a teaching job at a young gentlemen's academy in Chillon in Switzerland. While away, and with affection growing between him and the young seventeen-year-old Molly, they began a long correspondence, in which he taught her the fundamentals of mathematics and physics as she struggled with the beginning of her degree at London University. Thus, over long letters filled with news, observations, tender thoughts and carefully explained mathematical formulas, the romance blossomed. In April 1925, three years to the day after they had first met, they were married. He was then thirty-seven, she still only twenty, but the age gap never seemed to matter.

And by that time, he was back at Vickers as Assistant Chief

Designer, working on the renewed airship programme at Howden in North Yorkshire, and doing quite well for himself. His triumph of those years had been the design of the great *R.100* airship, which, at the time, was the largest ever built. The age of airships was almost over, however, and Wallis had been brought south from Yorkshire to Vickers Aviation in Weybridge in 1930. It was then that he bought White Hill House in Effingham. The impecuniousness of his childhood and the years of his apprenticeship had left Wallis seared with the desire never to be caught short. Although generous enough, he was nonetheless extremely cautious with money and never, ever, lived extravagantly. He and Molly shared a simple bungalow in Yorkshire during the airship years at Howden. With White Hill House he made a major commitment: still half-built, but big enough for a large family, it would, he hoped, be home for many, many years.

Since then, the house had long been completed and numerous features had been added by Wallis himself, including a sliding door between kitchen and living room that depended on runners made from pram wheels, removable storage space, and the patio on which he had carried out his first bouncing marble experiments. A classic Surrey house of period design, complete with mock-Tudor beams, it was comfortable, and spacious enough for their own four children and their two nephews. More importantly, set back from the beech-lined road, and looking out onto a golf course, it was a quiet haven for Wallis, a place of solidity and security, away from the politics and machinations that were such a feature of his war work.

'Rested,' he wrote in his pocket diary for Sunday, 21 February, as he tried to rid himself of his migraine. Normally on Sunday there would have been church. Wallis not only regularly rang the village bells; he also served on the Parochial Church Council and attended services whenever he could. His faith, which was profound, meant a great deal to him. There was little chance for relaxation at the moment, but when not working Wallis enjoyed a number of different pursuits. He was a keen and very able wood carver, and also enjoyed a round of golf, or listening to music on D'Erlanger's pink gramophone – Vaughan Williams was a particular favourite. Music was important in the Wallis household. Everyone had an instrument, except Barnes, but he liked to sing, especially when Molly played the piano.

There would be reading, too – he enjoyed detective novels, Agatha Christie in particular, and *The Times*; he would often read even at mealtimes. In the afternoon, there would be a shared bottle of beer with their gardener – although only ever a half-glass. They drank little – a sherry before supper if they had any, but nothing more. He would also read to Molly. While she mended and darned clothes, he read aloud from Dickens, Austen or Hardy. Not this Sunday, though, as Molly had gone to see Mary, at the Godolphin School in Salisbury.

As parents, they were kind, warm and loving, although strict too. The children were given plenty of freedom so long as they remembered their manners, were never late at mealtimes, and never, ever rude. 'His standards were always high,' says his eldest daughter, Mary. 'You were not rude, top and bottom of it.' The children, however, did notice that their father had become perhaps more 'severe' in recent times. 'He was more distracted, more tired,' says Mary, 'and more in the study.' But this was hardly surprising. There was much on his mind, not least on this quiet Sunday, 21 February, for the following morning he was to drive up to High Wycombe to see Air Marshal Harris himself.

It seems likely that Air Vice-Marshal the Honourable Sir Ralph Cochrane, newly appointed AOC 5 Group, Bomber Command, had played some part in gaining Wallis an audience with Harris. Cochrane was an old friend and another of Wallis's many useful contacts. They had met in 1915, when Wallis had been a Sub-Lieutenant in the Royal Navy Air Service working on airships at Walney Island, and Cochrane an RNAS airship pilot. Later, as Chief of the Royal New Zealand Air Staff, he had backed the Wellington bomber, and had been one of those invited by Wallis to visit the water tank trials at Teddington.

Cochrane was also an old and trusted friend of Harris's. The two had served together in the 1920s, when Harris had been CO of 70 Squadron in Iraq, and although the C-in-C remained extremely hostile to the proposed operation against the dams, he nevertheless agreed to hear what Wallis had to say for himself.

Wallis arrived with Mutt Summers, and armed with his film reels. Barely had they stepped inside Harris's office than the C-in-C let rip.

'What is it you want?' he growled. 'I've no use for you damned inventors. My boys' lives are too precious to be wasted on your crazy notions.' Wallis was not so easily put off his stride, however, and swiftly embarked on his usual lucid and well-argued explanations of why the attack should be launched and why it was feasible. Softening somewhat, Harris then agreed to Wallis's suggestion that he watch the film reels he had brought.

In the interests of security, only four men were present at the screening: Wallis and Summers, and Harris and his right-hand man, AVM Sandy Saundby, who was given the job of projectionist. Despite initially getting himself tangled in lots of celluloid, he eventually mastered the reel and projector and the film. When the film was finished, Harris admitted that the weapon had not been fully explained to him up to that point, but he remained as against the operation as ever. 'H. very much misinformed re: job,' Wallis scribbled in his diary. Harris was, however, noticeably less hostile than he had been to begin with, and revealed to Wallis that Portal had authorized the modification of three Lancasters. Consequently, Wallis returned to Weybridge feeling not entirely despondent. His mood was further improved when he learned later that day that the MAP had given formal approval for the modification of two Mosquitoes to carry Highball.

The following day, however, came Wallis's nadir. Summoned to Vickers' Weybridge plant to see Hew Kilner, the manager, Kilner told him that they were both to head straight up to town to see Sir Charles Craven at Vickers House. Wallis's hopes had soared, but the moment he walked through Craven's door, he realized he had misjudged the situation. There was no warm greeting, no cheery smiles. Not even an invitation to sit down. Instead, Wallis was left standing in front of Craven's desk, Kilner beside him.

Craven did not mince his words. He had been speaking to AVM Linnell, who had complained about Wallis's incessant interfering. He was making a nuisance of himself and damaging the interests of

Vickers, not least the chances of the Windsor bomber. Linnell, the Controller of Research and Development, had specifically asked Craven to tell Wallis to stop this nonsense about the destruction of the dams. Wallis was not allowed a word in edgeways: Craven was telling him the orders of both the Government and the Chairman of Vickers. Eventually, Wallis managed to offer his resignation, but this just produced another tirade from the usually equanimous Craven, who repeatedly punched his fist down on his desk and cried, 'Mutiny!'

Afterwards, Wallis was so shaken that he had to stand in the corridor for a few minutes and compose himself, although when Kilner followed soon after, he again repeated his intention to resign. This was natural enough. He had received as big a dressing-down as at any time since being a boy at Christ's Hospital. The humiliation for a proud man like Wallis was terrible. All he had been trying to do was his duty to his country, and to help win the war. To make matters worse, this tirade had come from Sir Charles Craven, a man he had known and respected for years and who was normally even-tempered courtesy personified.

Clearly, what had happened was that Linnell had been speaking to Harris. From the outset, Harris had made it clear to Linnell what he thought about the plan and then, no doubt, relayed to his old colleague that Wallis had even been to High Wycombe trying to flog his idea. Harris would have told Linnell that he was as against it as ever, that he had written to Portal saying this and that he fully expected the CAS to support him.

Linnell, now confident of which way the wind was blowing, and never much keen on the project in the first place, had decided to speak to Craven, presumably throwing in a few comments about how Wallis's actions were not only damaging the Windsor bomber but also Vickers' reputation. He probably exaggerated the extent to which Wallis had been making a nuisance of himself. At any rate, something he said seems to have made Craven see the red mist.

However, what Linnell did not know, and nor did Craven, was that Portal had taken a quite different view from Harris. Winterbotham's letter of 16 February had obviously played a part, because certainly by the time he received Harris's letter of

18 February he was fully in the picture and the following day had seen Wallis's trials film and been extremely impressed. He had then written a reply to Harris's impassioned plea of the day before.

'As you know,' he began, 'I have the greatest respect for your opinion on all technical and operational matters, and I agree with you that it is quite possible that Highball and Upkeep projects may come to nothing.' Portal, unlike Harris, had grasped the fundamental difference between the two weapons. After this opening sop, however, came the 'but'. 'Nevertheless,' he continued, 'I do not feel inclined to refuse Air Staff interest in these weapons.' Upkeep, he believed, was quite a simple concept and could quickly be proved or disproved. He had therefore given the go-ahead for three Lancasters to be converted for trials. 'But there will be no further interruption of supply of Lancasters,' he promised, 'until it is known that the difficulties to which you refer have actually been overcome.' Then he added, 'Incidentally, I gather that Linnell is in favour of a limited gamble.' In this, he might have been misinformed; Linnell would hardly have spoken to Craven in such a way if so. No, it was the Air Ministry, not the MAP, where Linnell was, that was pushing forward Upkeep.

Ultimately, though, the only chance of Upkeep – as opposed to Highball – ever being taken further was on the say-so of Portal. Just as the CAS had forced Harris to acquiesce on the Pathfinder Force, so he was now overruling his bomber commander over Upkeep.

This was the power of Portal.

9

Greenlight

THURSDAY, 25 FEBRUARY 1943. The night's target had been decided at High Mass that morning, and phoned through soon after to the various groups in Bomber Command. A maximum effort: 337 bombers available. At St Vincent's, AVM Cochrane's HQ at 5 Group, the news was received then passed down to the various stations within his group, and then the various squadrons. In his office at Syerston, Wing Commander Guy Gibson received the news by telephone, then called for his two flight commanders and broke the news: it was Nuremberg.

The airfield sprang to life, just as it was doing at Woodhall Spa, where 97 Squadron was putting up nine Lancasters for the raid. Vehicles busied about the place, taking crews to their machines for their air test, while groundcrew continued preparing the aircraft for imminent take-off. Soon after, airfields all over Lincolnshire erupted with the roar of Rolls-Royce Merlin engines, starting up one by one, and then these great beasts, brown and olive drab on top, black underneath, began thundering down the runway and taking to the sky.

Half an hour after take-off, and with everything from guns to bomb doors tested, the aircraft began landing again. Taxi around the perimeter, engines off, and then crews clambering out and onto a truck to take them back to the Sergeants' and Officers' Messes for lunch. Later there was the briefing, then supper, then the mission itself.

Charlie Williams's crew were working well; they had been given a new pilot at the beginning of the month, a New Zealander, Flight Sergeant 'Woody' Woodward, and a new bomb-aimer, a nineteen-year-old, Pilot Officer Burgess. Williams and Burgess were the only two officers, but Charlie had immediately taken to Woody Woodward. He was a good pilot and Williams trusted him, which for obvious reasons was essential for the harmony and success of any crew. This night, they were airborne at 1905 along with the rest of the 61 Squadron Lancs, then it was 106 Squadron's turn. Gibson took off at 1920. A little to the north-east, at Woodhall, the 97 Squadron Lancasters began taking off just after half past seven, Joe McCarthy taking off at 1942, Les Munro finally thundering down the runway at 2005. One of the most dangerous moments of any operation was taking off, lumbering the thirty-ton Lancaster into the air, weighed down as it was by a full bomb bay. Then there was the threat of collision: hundreds of aircraft, all taking off more or less at the same time, in the dark, could easily – and sometimes did – collide.

It was a long trip to Nuremberg, scene of so many pre-war Nazi rallies: some three and a half hours at least. The forecast had been good and en route had lived up to expectations, but around half past ten, when the Pathfinders were due to arrive, there had been some haze and they were late with their marking. By the time the first bombers started to arrive, they had not completed their marking, which was, to begin with, fifteen miles short of the aiming point, from which the bomber stream would begin their bomb run to the target, and then over the target itself. Both Joe McCarthy and Guy Gibson reached Nuremberg before the PFF had finished their marking so were forced to circle, with searchlights and flak now fully alive to the roar of aircraft high overhead. 'Some aircraft failed to wait for PFF,' noted Les Munro, arriving a little after Gibson and McCarthy. Gibson, who was flying for the first time since Maggie North had got married, found the experience really quite frightening – the danger was not only from the flak but also from lots of bombers circling closely together. At last, however, the markers were lit and they began their run.

At least by this time, the haze had dispersed. 'Conditions very good for bombing,' he jotted later in his logbook. 'No cloud, excellent visibility. Target located visually and bombed from 12,000 feet. A very concentrated attack which caused huge fires and explosions.' Joe McCarthy's crew also saw the target and bombed the green target indicators. They reported two large fires, 'presumably factory'. So too did Les Munro and his crew. 'Long factory type of building seen to burst into flames,' he noted.

In the early hours of the morning they began arriving back – and none had been lost from 97, 61 or 106 Squadrons. Les Munro was back at 3.30 a.m., an hour after Gibson, McCarthy ten minutes later. Among the last to land back down was Charlie Williams's crew. They had come under heavy attack as they had returned over the French coast, and although badly shaken but not hit had then become disorientated over the Channel. 'The trip took us much longer than it should have,' noted Williams, 'and we were short of petrol and when we landed we only had four minutes' petrol left.' Luck, however, held. They made it safely, after eight hours forty-five minutes in the air. A long night.

'A good but frightening trip,' noted Gibson, by which he presumably meant successful but terrifying.

While the crews were sleeping off the raid, Barnes Wallis was heading up to London for a meeting at the MAP with none other than AVM Linnell and others. Ever since his dressing-down from Sir Charles Craven, Wallis had been wondering whether his resignation had been accepted. He had had meetings with Admiral Renouf – among others – the following day and continued working on the Highball project, but no one from Vickers had said anything more to him.

Then the previous day, Thursday, 25 February, he had received a letter from Ben Lockspeiser of the MAP asking him to attend a conference which would be chaired by AVM Linnell the following morning. This meeting had already been planned, to discuss the 'Golf Mine' – a variation that had, as its name implied, a golfball-like casing. It had been hoped that this might improve aerodynamics. In his letter, Lockspeiser had told him that

Chadwick, the Chief Designer at Avro, would also be coming along. This could only really mean one thing: that Upkeep was not dead and buried after all.

The morning meeting was postponed, so it was not until 3 p.m. that it finally got under way, in Linnell's office at the Ministry of Aircraft Production on Millbank, overlooking Victoria Tower Gardens and the River Thames. There were twelve in all, including Wallis and Roy Chadwick, Sir Charles Craven, AVM Sorley and Air Commodore Baker from the Air Ministry and Group Captain Wynter-Morgan.

Whatever private thoughts AVM Linnell may have had, or even Sir Charles Craven for that matter, much had now changed. Portal had taken considerable personal interest in Upkeep and had briefed Linnell thoroughly via AVM Bottomley, the Assistant Chief of the Air Staff (Ops). 'I consider that the potentialities of the "Upkeep"', Bottomley had written in a draft memo for the CAS on 19 February, 'will fully justify our pressing on with the development of the weapon as quickly as possible.' Portal had approved this draft. 'I think this is a good gamble,' he noted, 'and I agree with the recommendation.'

So, after years of discussing a possible attack on the dams, and after a frenzied few weeks of meetings, reports, arguments and yet more discussion, the CAS had made his ruling and all the chattering and debate had stopped. Wallis was hardly the person to gloat, but, in any case, Linnell was no less likely to mention his earlier reservations. It was now his task to act upon Portal's orders. Nor was there any more mention of Wallis being a nuisance at the MAP or of his resignation. In true British style, everyone tacitly agreed never to mention it again.

And so to business. Three Lancasters were to be modified to carry Upkeep, while the bombs themselves were also to be built. The CAS had instructed that every effort was to be made to complete both aircraft and bombs so as to allow them to be used this coming spring. He did not want this development period dragging on. If the raid was going to happen at all, it was to be this year, in 1943.

'For this purpose,' said Linnell, presumably through gritted teeth, 'the CAS has allotted priority to Upkeep over work on the B.3/42 aircraft at Vickers, and over other projects on the Lancaster at Avros.' This was the intake-of-breath moment. Everyone around the table knew Harris's Ruhr offensive was about to start; they also knew the importance of Vickers' Windsor bomber project. That Upkeep was to take priority at this time showed just how seriously Portal was taking this. 'The requirement,' Linnell told them, 'is for three Lancasters to be prepared as quickly as possible with full Upkeep apparatus for trial purposes.' Then came the second bomb-shell. 'These are to be followed by conversion sets to complete thirty aircraft. The requirement for bombs has been stated as one hundred and fifty to cover trials and operations.'

With this stunning development, Air Commodore Baker con-firmed that the final assessment of dates showed that 26 May was the latest date on which the operation could be carried out that year. It was then agreed that the programme for full delivery of all thirty modified Lancasters and 150 Upkeeps should be 1 May, so as to allow a 'reasonable' time for training and experiments.

It was now the very end of February. That meant less than three months until the very latest date for any potential raid, and just two months – eight weeks – to get the bombs and the Lancasters all ready. That was not long. That was not long at all.

The CAS had made one decision – to greenlight the project; a flurry of others were needed and right now. First, the demarcation over who was doing what part of the modifications. Eventually, it was agreed that Avro would be responsible for the strongpoint attachments to the airframe, for the bombcell fairings, for the electrical bomb release wiring, and for the hydraulic power point for the rotating motor. Vickers, meanwhile, would make the attach-ment arms that would carry the Upkeep, including the driving mechanism, and the bomb itself. It was also agreed that the work should be carried out at Vickers and that Chadwick would send a team of draughtsmen without delay. The first Lancaster to be modified would be housed at either Brooklands or Farnborough – on Vickers' watch, at any rate.

Wallis then suggested that all drawings could be ready in three weeks' time. Chadwick also offered to accompany Wallis and the other representatives from Vickers back to Weybridge for further discussion. They both promised to give an estimate as to when the first, second and third Lancasters and thirty additional conversion sets might be ready within forty-eight hours.

Having admitted there had been no prior plan or drawings for the modified Lancaster, Wallis then had to confess he had no detailed drawings for the Upkeep either. These, he reckoned, would take ten days. Sir Charles Craven spoke up, voicing his concern about the difficulty in getting the necessary materials and of machining a bomb the size of the Upkeep. Wynter-Morgan then reported that the Torpex – the explosive – needed was available and it would take three weeks to fill one hundred bombs.

These discussions had revealed just how tight the programme was, as Linnell now reminded everyone. 'Of the eight weeks available,' he said, 'at least four were already bespoken for the completion of drawings and filling of the bombs, leaving less than four for manufacture.' A more precise estimate was needed, which Mr Palmer, one of Wallis's colleagues at Vickers, promised to give by 5 March. Sir Charles Craven then stressed that there was no hope at all of completing the bombs unless absolute priority in materials was given.

After some further discussion about Highball and estimates for delivering the modified Mosquitoes, the meeting broke up. As Wallis left the building with his Vickers colleagues and with Roy Chadwick, his mind must have been racing. Three days earlier, he had been in deep disgrace and with Upkeep apparently finished. Now, the project had been given the greenlight. They meant to actually launch an attack on the dams. That was the aim – an operation within ten to twelve weeks.

As he stepped out onto Millbank, with the Houses of Parliament looming opposite and Westminster Abbey just a stone's throw away, did he ever really believe it would be possible to do all that was needed in such a desperately short period? He had airily been telling any who would listen that the project could be done in eight weeks, but how much of that had been pure bluster will never be known.

Whatever the truth, there must have been a suspicion among

several there at that meeting that Wallis had been somewhat hoist by his own petard. The stark truth of the matter was this: Upkeep had been given the greenlight before it had *even been built*. It was one thing testing a prototype, but that was considerably smaller. Whether a large version would actually work was, to a large extent, unknown. At best, the entire project was a colossal gamble.

Much also depended on the close working relationship between two normally rival firms, Vickers and A. V. Roe, and, more specifically, Wallis and Chadwick, the great aircraft designer.

There was also, in truth, much resting on Portal. The higher up the chain of command someone rose, so the decisions that needed to be made became harder. This had been a big decision, and if the Upkeep project failed, he would lose a lot of face, not only with Churchill and the Chiefs of Staff, but also with Harris.

Massive responsibility now rested on Wallis's shoulders. He had talked the talk. Now, in the coming days and weeks, he had to deliver. The race to smash those German dams was now on. The clock was ticking inexorably.

GENERAL INFORMATION

Number of Cylinders..........12.
Arrangement } Two Banks with an
of Cylinders }...inclined angle of 60°
Bore .... 5·4 ins.
Stroke .... 6·0 ins.
Swept Volume .....1648 cu.ins.
Compression Ratio.....6·0 to 1.

Supercharger
Type..... Two-Speed, Single Stage.
Gear Ratios...8·15 to 1 & 9·49 to 1
Impeller Diameter....10·25 ins.

Direction of Rotation
Propeller Shaft....Right Hand.
Crank Shaft........Left Hand.
Reduction Gear Ratio...0·420 to 1.
(Merlin 27)...........0·477 to 1)

Oil Pressure (main)
Normal.....60 to 80 lb. per sq. in.
Minimum (in flight) 45 lb. per sq. in.

Firing Order
1A. 6B. 4A. 3B. 2A. 5B. 6A. 1B. 3A. 4B. 5A. 2B.
Magnetos ..{Two B.T.H. C5SE-12S
          {or Rotax NSE 12-4
Timing (fully advanced).........
      {Starboard 45° before T.D.C.
      {Port 50° before T.D.C.
Contact Breaker Gap........
......0·012 in (fully advanced)

Sparking Plugs
24 K.L.G. R.C.5/1. Lodge R.S.5-2-3-4. or
A.C. R.23.(Merlin 24 & 25, Lodge R.S.5-5 only)
Sparking Plug Gap......0·012 in.
Carburetter...S.U type Merlin AVT40

Valve Timing
Inlet Opens....31° before T.D.C.
Inlet Closes....52° before B.D.C.
Exhaust Opens..72° before B.D.C.
Exhaust Closes..12° before T.D.C.

Tappet Clearances (cold)
Inlet ....0·010 in.
Exhaust ....0·020 in.

MERLIN AERO

Two-piece block, sin

For further informa

only)

Part II

THE RACE TO
SMASH THE DAMS

NGINE

ge, two-speed supercharger type

A.P. 1590 G & N. Vol. I.

10

The Main Offensive

FRIDAY, 5 MARCH 1943. A historic day for Air Marshal Harris and his Command, because that night's raid would mark the start of his main offensive. 'I was at last,' Harris noted, 'able to undertake with real hope of success the task which had been given me when I first took over the Command a little more than a year before, the task of destroying the main cities of the Ruhr.'

What was it about this day's raid that was so different from those in the weeks that had preceded it? To start with, he now had more aircraft. At the beginning of the year, he could call on just over 500 of all types; that figure was now pushing 700. More significantly, the number of four-engine heavy bombers had passed 400 for the first time. And heavies meant more bombs. Compared with a year earlier, these aircraft could now drop more than double the amount of monthly tonnage.

Furthermore, Oboe was now trialled and ready. The Pathfinders, too, were a more proficient force than they had been the previous year – now more skilled, more experienced at target marking. Nor had navigational techniques really been up to the task Bufton and others had given the then new target-finding force. GEE had not been the panacea some had predicted, and even Oboe had proved initially limited because the ground stations could only deal with one pair of Mosquitoes every ten minutes. This, too, had improved, because now there were two pairs of ground stations, which meant twelve target-laying Mosquitoes could operate over a target every hour.

What Harris now envisaged was a concentrated effort on the cities of the Ruhr. This part of north-west Germany was within comfortable range of Oboe, and furthermore any target could be reached during the short nights of spring and summer that would soon be upon them. Harris could not, of course, solely bomb the Ruhr because it was essential that German anti-aircraft defences and night fighters were spread across the Reich and not concentrated entirely around the industrial heartland. Even so, it meant that over the next few weeks and months, some two-thirds of all Bomber Command sorties would be directed against those cities. This was what he was already calling the 'Battle of the Ruhr'.

And it would start this night, 5 March 1943.

The target was Essen, the largest and most important manufacturing centre among a wide spread of industrial cities, and home to the all-important Krupp Works, one of Germany's largest armaments manufacturers. This was no easy target, for not only was Essen one of the most heavily defended cities in Germany, but it was often protected by a near-permanent shroud of industrial haze. With Oboe, however, this would hopefully not be a problem.

The main bomber force consisted of 442 aircraft, of which 261 were heavies. The PFF was made up from twenty-two Lancasters and eight Oboe-carrying Mosquitoes.

The plan was for the bomber stream to fly to Egmond on the Dutch coast and to a point fifteen miles north of Essen, which PFF Lancasters had marked with yellow flares. From there, the bombers would begin the run-up to the main target, which they were to reach at a rate of eleven per minute, so that the entire attack would last thirty-eight minutes. Over the target itself, Mosquitoes at intervals of three and seven minutes would drop red target indicators by using their Oboe. In between, the more numerous PFF Lancasters, with larger loads of flares, would visually – rather than by Oboe – drop green target indicators next to the red ones dropped by the Mosquitoes. Using these target indicators, the bombers then droned over the city, one after another, dropping a mixture of 4,000lb high explosives and incendiaries, the former to smash buildings, the latter to start raging fires. It was still not perfect, but bombing proficiency had improved massively during Harris's first year of trial and experiment. It was no wonder he was beginning to feel his force could make a difference.

In the event, three of the Oboe Mosquitoes turned back due to technical defects, along with a further fifty-three other aircraft, including that of Charlie Williams. 'Oxygen U/S', he wrote in his logbook. Yet despite the uncommonly large number of returns, the raid was a success. The remaining Oboe Mosquitoes laid their markers over the centre of Essen perfectly, as did the PFF Lancasters. And this despite the heavy haze over the target. Essen was bombed blind.

And what damage: 160 acres of destruction, with fifty-three separate buildings within the Krupps Works hit, and a staggering 3,018 houses destroyed and 2,166 seriously damaged. As many as 482 people were killed – more than in any other single raid to date.

Perhaps fittingly, the raid had been the Command's 100,000th of the war – a vast number. Harris was in no mind, however, that a corner had been turned. He reckoned the Essen raid was the most important attack so far carried out by Bomber Command, and promptly fired off a signal to all his men in the Command, which was written with his usual bombast. 'You have set a fire in the belly of Germany which will burn the black heart out of Nazidom and wither its grasping limbs at the very roots,' he wrote. 'Such attacks, which will continue in crescendo, will progressively make it more impossible for the enemy to further his aggressions or to hold where he now stands. The great skill and high courage with which you press home your objectives has already impressed the inevitability of disaster on the whole of Germany and, within the next few months, the hopelessness of their situation will be borne in upon them in a manner which will destroy their capacity for resistance and break their hearts.'

Meanwhile, as the Battle of the Ruhr was getting under way, there had been feverish activity on the development of Upkeep and the modified Lancaster designed to carry it. After the decision on 26 February, Wallis had wasted no time and had immediately set to work on the design of the bomb. And now that Upkeep had priority over the Windsor, he was able to draw on the help of the Vickers drawing office staff in the squash courts at Burhill. First thing the following morning, he held a meeting of all Vickers staff concerned for a briefing and to formulate plans for the Upkeep. From a design point of view, it was a large version of the trial prototype, but it still had to contain 7,000lb of explosive – three and a half tons – and be encased in such a way as to not disintegrate on impact. The finished design would be more than seven feet in diameter. It was a beast.

Two days later, when Wallis met with Group Captain Wynter-Morgan, the Deputy Director of Armaments at the MAP, and various others, he reported the drawings were almost finished: he and his drawing office staff had begun them at lunchtime on 27 February and were nearly there by teatime the following day. It was an astonishing achievement; he had suggested he would need ten days at the meeting on the 26th. What he needed to finish them was details of the hydro-static fuses, which would enable the bomb to detonate at a fixed depth, as well as self-destruction fuses should any be captured intact during the operation. The former would be standard Admiralty types, as used in anti-submarine depth charges, but loaded with twice the normal amount of composition explosive pellets.

There was immediately a problem when the Ministry of Supply estimated a two-year wait for the necessary steel to make the dies for casting the Upkeeps; Sir Charles Craven's fears about the supply of materials seemed to have been justified. However, Wallis got around this by making a smaller cylindrical core for the explosives and packing the rest of the sphere with wood. The shortage of steel was overcome by dealing directly with Oxley Engineering Company Ltd, who confirmed they had the 'capacity and rolls' to produce one hundred Upkeeps. 'Mr Hollis, the Managing Director,' Wallis wrote in a hurried note to Palmer, his colleague at Vickers at the Crayford Works, 'made the twelve 4 foot spheres for the Wellington outfit for us, and my experience then was that they gave us a very quick and good job.' Oxley would thus provide the steel, sending it direct to the Vickers plant at Elswick, where the Upkeeps would be made.

The same day, 1 March, he was also writing to Mr C. H. Smith of the Hoffman Manufacturing Company Ltd about the bearings they were making for the driving mechanism for the rotating of the Upkeep. There were normal ordering procedures in such matters, which had been followed, but Wallis wanted to add his own personal plea to Mr Smith. Thirty complete sets, he pointed out, were needed by 1 May at the latest. 'You will see, therefore, that the time for use is exceedingly short, and as someone remarked at a meeting recently, it will be a miracle if we succeed in meeting MAP requirements. However, we are determined to make every endeavour to do so.' Wallis then promised to help put him in touch with relevant authorities at the MAP for future work if he managed to deliver these crucially important ball-bearings in time. Wallis understood the benefits of showing a bit of stick and carrot, and that very same day he received a telegram from Hoffman Manufacturing asking for drawings to be sent 'URGENTLY'.

The next day was Tuesday, 2 March, and in the morning Wallis delivered by hand to Wynter-Morgan six copies of his Upkeep drawings, finished six days earlier than he had initially forecast. At 11 a.m., there was another large meeting at the MAP with Wallis, Roy Chadwick and various others from Vickers. There was still much to discuss; Wallis did not have all the answers for his Upkeep by any means: it was his concept, his design, but the transition from blueprint to reality had to be a team effort, with a number of different people and organizations co-operating and co-ordinating extremely tightly. As Wallis had implied in his letter to Mr Smith at Hoffman's, if just one link in the chain failed to deliver, the entire project could be scuppered.

As the various designers, draughtsmen and engineers began working furiously to meet their stringent deadlines, so a flurry of telegrams and letters criss-crossed their way over the country, from Vickers in Surrey to A. V. Roe in Manchester, to Vickers' plants in Elswick, Barrow and Crayford.

Wallis and Roy Chadwick, and the respective teams from

Vickers and A. V. Roe, were also working well, with the Avro Chief Designer overseeing the work on what was now called the 'Type 464 Provisioning Lancaster'. Chadwick and Wallis were, in many ways, cut from the same cloth. Both were largely self-taught, having opted for apprenticeships rather than following a university education. Chadwick was a Lancastrian, and, like Wallis, a devout Christian, with a wife he adored and two girls to whom he was devoted. Like Wallis, his achievements were numerous, and were gained through a combination of extremely hard work, a touch of genius and a streak of ruthlessness too. Both men were kindly and generous towards others, but had a hardness about them too; neither suffered fools. But nor were they possessors of uncontrolled egos, and now, at this critical moment, both worked with the kind of co-operation that was essential if the project was to reach fruition.

So it was that on 6 March, just a week after the greenlight, Wallis was able to update Sir Charles Craven with a fair degree of optimism. The roasting Wallis had received two weeks earlier had been put to bed, their normal relationship, hitherto very good, resumed. Drawings of Upkeep had been sent to Elswick, their Newcastle works, while at Barrow the first five Upkeeps had almost been finished, albeit with rough drawings sent up early the previous week; these would need reworking. He reckoned all drawing work – which included the special Lancaster – would be finished on schedule at the end of the following week. 'Everything is being done to push on with the work here,' he wrote, 'and preliminary information on materials and tools is being given to the shops who are keeping close touch with us. My impression,' he added, 'is that we shall come through all right as things are going far better than I thought would be possible.'

The organizational planning of the project was also progressing. The first issue to overcome was the parallel Highball project and any potential conflicts of interest. That Upkeep had come to fruition at all was in no small measure due to the championing of Wallis's bouncing bomb by the Admiralty, and Admiral Renouf in particular. While senior figures in the MAP, Air Ministry and Prime Minister's Office had been pooh-poohing such a weapon, Renouf had been trooping down to Weymouth to watch the trials along Chesil Beach and giving Wallis every bit of support he possibly could.

On 27 February, Renouf had hurried over to the Air Ministry and had seen Sid Bufton, pointing out that the Admiralty had already invested much in the project, not least in the early stages, and were now well advanced with plans for Highball, including trials against an old French battleship in Scotland using modified Mosquitoes. The RAF now had the German dams in their sights, but the Admiralty was planning to use Highball to sink the German battleship, *Tirpitz*. He suggested a co-ordinating committee be formed, to make sure they did not step on each other's toes.

This was quickly agreed and the Admiralty suggested Renouf be chair. However, Portal himself swiftly blocked this, insisting that since the MAP was so intimately involved, it was more appropriate that an Air Ministry man be chair. He suggested AVM Bottomley, Assistant Chief of the Air Staff (Ops). Admiral Pound demurred. The Admiralty also gave way over prioritization. Renouf was anxious to launch an attack using Highball as soon as possible, but Portal insisted Highball could not be used before Upkeep. A daylight operation, such as the Admiralty was proposing, could compromise their night-time attack on the dams.

Another decision was reached: only twenty, not thirty, Lancasters would be converted to carry Upkeeps. This was also on Portal's direct say-so. Realizing that all thirty would be segregated and kept apart from the rest of Bomber Command until after the operation, he felt this was too much to expect and, in any case, more than would be needed. This also meant a reduction of the crews needed, which in turn ensured that forming a new squadron specifically for the task of attacking the dams would be slightly more straightforward. As Portal was keenly aware, the fewer crews and aircraft that had to be taken away from Harris's direct control, the better.

The task of deciding what exactly should be targeted and what kind of force was needed to achieve it had been left to the Air Ministry. As ACAS (Ops), this naturally came under Bottomley's purview, and so he immediately gave the task of making a preliminary report to Bufton, who hurriedly began researching a list of targets, from dams – in Germany and Italy – through to enemy naval units, ship lifts and locks on the many large river ways and canals that were so crucial to Germany's war industry.

While this rush of activity was going on, the men of Bomber Command continued to fly over the Reich, oblivious, of course, to what was being planned in secret by the desk wallahs of the Air Ministry. For Charlie Williams, thoughts were now focusing largely on his new girl, Bobbie, with whom he was rapidly falling in love, and the prospect of finishing his first tour.

The trip over Essen had prolonged the wait. Because they had returned home early, the Essen trip was not a completed one so did not count towards the thirty for Williams's first tour. He had now chalked up twenty-five missions, however, and was beginning to feel the strain. He was tired and his anxiety about making it through was increasing as he neared the end of this initial tour.

Also struggling was Guy Gibson, although he never let on, barely even to himself. He missed the influence of Gus Walker, he missed the confidences of Maggie North, and his wife was far away. Bombing was also a more complex business than it had been when he had taken over 106 Squadron. As the attack on Essen had shown, routes and timings over the target were now planned in minute detail. Tactics were rapidly evolving too with the advent of Oboe and H2S and the increasingly sophisticated skill of the PFF. As squadron commander, he did not fly as many ops as the rest of his men, but quite enough all the same. And in between making sure he drank a few beers with the chaps, and bombing missions, there were more and more meetings to attend, both at Syerston and at 5 Group HQ at Grantham. At Grantham there was a new AOC as well. Gibson was sorry to see Coryton, whom he liked, move on. His successor was AVM Ralph Cochrane, a man unquestionably more than qualified for the post, but an unknown quantity. For Gibson, it meant forging a working relationship all over again, and on first impression Cochrane, a neat, narrow-featured figure, seemed to lack obvious warmth. Then there was the paperwork: reports to write, letters of commiseration. The most all other crews had to do was fly.

But this particular phase of Gibson's flying career was about to come to an end. Following Essen, and in keeping with the policy of continuing to bomb beyond the Ruhr, Bomber Command's next two operations had been against Nuremberg and Munich, but now, on 11 March, Stuttgart was chosen. And this was to be Gibson's seventy-second and final mission with 106.

Gibson and his crew took off from Syerston at 10.20 p.m. Crossing the French coast, they ran into some flak, mostly concentrated in flashes around a straggler who had strayed off course. Otherwise, Gibson thought it a perfect night for flying. There was little cloud and a three-quarter moon, which shone so brightly his cockpit was lit up almost as though it were day. Below, he saw France spread out beneath them, milky grey and partly shielded by a thin gauze of cloud.

As they droned on towards Stuttgart, Gibson began to feel hot. Heat in the Lancaster came from a vent near the wireless operator, so he yelled to Flight Lieutenant Bob Hutchison, 'Hey, Hutch. Turn off the heat.'

'Thank God for that,' Hutchison replied.

All around him – either side, above and below – he could see the Lancasters of the bomber stream forging ahead. He thought the big bombers looked as though their chins were somehow thrust forward with more purpose than he'd ever noticed before. All seemed calm. All seemed set.

Then suddenly his flight engineer, a freshman pilot, Flying Officer Walter Thompson, called out, 'Port outboard's going, sir!'

As Gibson hastily looked to his left out across the wing, he saw Thompson was right – it was packing up – and then he could feel it on the throttle. No power at all now from the port outer. In his heavily laden Lancaster, he would have to lose height.

This was ill luck. To turn around would mean the mission would not count. He would feel obliged to do another one, and then this would not be his last op with 106 after all.

Behind him, Norman Scrivener, his navigator, was at his station, watching the air speed needle dropping.

'What shall I do, Scriv?' Gibson asked.

'It's up to you, sir,' Scrivener replied.

'OK, Scriv, we are going on at low level. We will try to climb up to bomb when we get there.'

The Lancaster gently fell away, out of formation. They were now over the Reich, and flak was pumping up towards them from Mannheim, Frankfurt and Mainz. Gibson could see it bursting all around the bomber stream above him, but, fortunately, they had not spotted this lone lame duck. 'Now and again,' noted Gibson later, 'I caught sight of a Lancaster far above, four miles above, as it got into the beam of a searchlight and as a light flashed on its wings.'

As they arrived over Stuttgart, fires were already raging. Suddenly, an 8,000lb bomb hurtled past his wing tip, and a few moments later a heavy flash erupted below and then the Lancaster bounced and jolted, 'as though it were a leaf'.

Gibson was now in an extremely precarious position, directly below the bomber stream and sandwiched between the enemy ground defences and a rain of falling heavy explosives and incendiaries, any one of which could have blown his aircraft to pieces. However, flying on, they eventually reached the target and duly dropped their load, the stricken Lancaster lurching upwards at the sudden and dramatic loss of weight. Banking around, Gibson then thrust the stick forward and dived for the deck. It was now twenty past eleven.

They were still a long way from home, however; there were night fighters around, and for Gibson there was the small matter of nursing a crippled Lancaster. The next few hours were going to be both mentally testing and physically exhausting as Gibson tried to counteract the asymmetrical torque caused by the loss of the port outer engine.

Flying at 4,000 feet the entire way, they managed to avoid being picked up by either German night fighters or flak, successfully crossed the North Sea, and, nearly three and a half torturous hours after leaving Stuttgart, touched back down at Syerston. They had made it.

Later that day, Group Captain Bussell, who had replaced Gus Walker as Station Commander, recommended Gibson for a Bar to his Distinguished Service Order. This was received by Cochrane, who recommended that since Gibson's DSO had been awarded only the previous December, perhaps a second DFC, a lesser gong, would be more appropriate. When this then found its way to Harris's desk, the C-in-C scribbled in his own hand, 'Any Captain who completes 172 sorties in outstanding manner is worth two DSOs if not a VC. Bar to DSO approved.'

Gibson knew nothing of this. He woke up late that morning, his ears still ringing from the raid, and his eyes red and sore. He wanted to stay lying there, in his bed, where it was warm, and quiet, and peaceful. 'I wanted to think,' he wrote, 'and I wanted to be alone. After a year of this sort of thing I was getting a bit weary. It seems that no matter how hard you try, the human body can take just so much and no more.'

But he had to get up. AVM Cochrane wanted to see him, so having finally roused himself, he drove over to St Vincent's in Grantham in his Humber. Gibson wondered what his next posting would be. He had hoped it might be a station, where he could take some time off ops, but where he could make the most of his considerable experience. Instead, he was in for a shock. When he finally got to see Cochrane, he learned that he was being asked to write a book – a guide for the benefit of the would-be bomber pilot. He would be based at St Vincent's, and would write it there, under the guidance of 5 Group.

Gibson was flummoxed. He had never written anything of any length in his life; at school at St Edward's, Oxford, he had shown no great intellectual capacity and his academic achievements had been decidedly mediocre.

He returned to Syerston that night for his leaving party, where he got drunk with the chaps and made, by his own admission, a rather poor speech, before spending another day and a bit clearing things up and handing over to John Searby, one of his former flight commanders. On 14 March, having expected – and been due – some leave with Eve in Cornwall, he was summoned back to Grantham and once more drove to St Vincent's. The building was Victorian, a large, comfortable private residence, complete with different-sized gables and tower and spire, that had been requisitioned by the Air Ministry. It had an air of quiet, cool efficiency, with a very different atmosphere from what he was used to, lacking the boisterous hubbub of a frontline bomber station.

He was soon shown into Cochrane's office, and was congratulated on the Bar to his DSO, the news of which had just come through. And then, before Gibson had barely a chance to reply, the AOC 5 Group leaned towards him.

'How would you like the idea,' Cochrane asked him, 'of doing one more trip?'

11

Special Squadron

SATURDAY, 13 MARCH. The weekend, but few involved with Upkeep were resting at home. There was work to be done, urgent work. The men at Vickers Aviation had even assured their colleagues at A. V. Roe that they were working Sundays too. In this race against time, there were no such things as weekends.

Nor was there any slacking at the Air Ministry, where, on this Saturday more than two weeks after Upkeep's greenlight, Group Captain Bufton submitted his preliminary target survey to his boss, AVM Bottomley. Dams in southern Italy and Sardinia had been considered, but they would involve a diversion of Lancasters and Upkeeps to the Mediterranean, which was logistically out of the question, so the idea had been discounted. Dams in northern Italy, such as the Tirso, had been examined too, but the range was considered too far for such an operation. Bufton had also looked into developing their own Highball operations using RAF Mosquitoes. In the end, though, he and his team had decided that two targets, in particular, seemed most suitable: the Möhne and the Eder. 'The former is much more important,' he concluded, 'and tactically the more suitable. We should, therefore, ensure that an adequate effort is devoted to this objective before considering the possibility of an attack upon the Eder Dam.' In his covering note to Bottomley, he added, 'The attached survey is necessarily a rapid one, but it embraces the important objectives and indicates the limited scope for the employment of the new weapon. I feel a lot of time would be wasted if we go to the lengths of making a minute examination of all possible targets.'

Having been given provisional approval for his targets, Bufton had then discussed the proposed operation with Air Vice-Marshal Robert Oxland, who had recently taken over as Senior Air Staff Officer (SASO) at Bomber Command on Saundby's elevation to Deputy Commander.

After discussing matters with Harris and Saundby, Oxland reported back to Bufton that the C-in-C was vehemently opposed to the forming of a special Highball-carrying Mosquito squadron, pointing out quite reasonably that Highball was more appropriate to an anti-shipping role. He had, he pointed out, accepted the Lancaster project but felt that it was now up to Coastal Command or the Navy to undertake any operations with Highball. On the other hand, Harris and his staff had already begun setting things in motion to form a 'special squadron'.

In fact, despite Harris's earlier protestations, the C-in-C had responded well to Portal's decision. It was a feature of Harris's approach to command that he would fight tooth and nail against any suggestion he disagreed with, but once a decision had been made, he accepted it and got on with the task of carrying it out to the best of his ability. He had shown this over the decision to form the PFF the previous summer, and he was doing the same with the Upkeep project too. Two days later, Bottomley, in his role as Assistant Chief of the Air Staff (Operations), sent a loose directive to Harris, outlining the proposed employment of both Highball and Upkeep. The proposed target was 'probably' the Möhne Dam, and 'possibly' the Eder. 'If the Möhne attack is to take place by 26th May,' wrote Bottomley, 'it is essential that no delay should occur at any stage in the development, training and planning and it is therefore desired that your command should now be closely associated with these three aspects of the preparations.'

In fact, Harris was already several steps ahead of Bottomley, and it says much about the C-in-C that he and his staff had already taken the initiative despite their reservations about the project. In truth, smashing the German dams fitted in well with his plan to pulverize the Ruhr, and if it were to succeed would be a massive feather in the cap of his Command. Perhaps Harris had begun to think it might not be such a crackpot idea after all.

Bufton had reported to Bottomley on 17 March that Harris and Saundby had not yet decided in which group the special squadron would be, as this depended on the availability of an airfield and accommodation. In fact, this was not the case; 5 Group had been chosen – it was Harris's old command during 1940 and was his premier Bomber Group, just as 11 Group had always been the top dog within Fighter Command. Now that those at Bomber Command were committed, they were going to fulfil their part of the bargain to the absolute best of their ability.

And they had also found a base, which conveniently enough was within 5 Group. RAF Scampton, just to the north of Lincoln, was a grass airfield but due to have concrete runways laid. In antici-pation of this, 49 Squadron had already moved out, leaving 57 Squadron in sole possession of a station that could comfortably house two squadrons. No doubt somewhere would have been found within 5 Group, but this certainly simplified matters.

In fact, Cochrane had been told by Harris on 15 March that he would not only have to find a new squadron, but would also oversee its development and training. Harris had already nominated Gibson to lead the squadron, which was why, when the now ex-106 Squadron commander went to see him after leaving Syerston, Cochrane wasted no time in coming straight to the point. For Harris, the decision must have been a straightforward one. He had rated Gibson in 1940, and he had, as far as he was concerned, led 106 Squadron magnificently, fully justifying the belief he had held in him, despite his youth. Gibson had that 'push on' quality that Harris liked in his pilots, and an iron determination. It was just one operation and one trip. What was needed was efficiency, drive and guts, and Gibson had all those things. Moreover, he had just finished a tour. Making him CO of this new special squadron would not upset the applecart. And in any case, who else was there? Nettleton VC? He was in the middle of his second tour so not avail-able. Nor was Leonard Cheshire, another young star of the

Command, who despite not being in 5 Group was an obvious candidate for the post. No, there was no other person who combined, so perfectly, availability with absolutely the right attributes for the job. It *had* to be Gibson.

Even so, Cochrane would have preferred not to force him, hence the slightly nonchalant manner in which he put it to him, as though he were doing Gibson a favour as a reward for all that he'd done at 106. *Surely this is better than flying a desk?*

Had he known how exhausted Gibson was? How in need of a decent spell of leave? Cochrane was new to the position; he did not know Gibson as well as his predecessor, Coryton, had done, and yet few knew him well at all. Most only saw the man Gibson liked to portray: the indefatigable bomber commander, a man imbued with a rigid sense of duty and honour and steely determination. A man who would love the chance for just one more trip.

At the question, Gibson had gulped, thinking: *More flak, more fighters.*

'What kind of trip, sir?'

'A pretty important one,' Cochrane told him, 'perhaps one of the most devastating of all time. I can't tell you any more now. Do you want to do it?'

Gibson told him he thought he did, although initially he had the impression Cochrane meant that night. He couldn't quite remember where he had left his flying kit.

But, to his surprise, nothing happened. There was no more mention of it and, for two days, Gibson kicked his heels around St Vincent's, wondering what the hell was going on. Then eventually, on the third day, Cochrane sent for him again.

It was now Friday, 19 March. In the AOC's office there was another man, an air commodore. Cochrane greeted Gibson affably and introduced Charles Whitworth, a young-looking man with a round, fleshy but amiable face and dark hair. Greetings over, Cochrane offered Gibson a Chesterfield and told him to sit on one of the chairs in front of his desk.

'I asked you the other day if you would care to do another raid,' Cochrane said. 'You said you would, but I have to warn you that this is no ordinary sortie. In fact, it can't be done for at least two months.'

Gibson groaned inwardly. It had to be the *Tirpitz*, he thought to himself, and wondered why he'd ever agreed.

'Moreover,' Cochrane continued, 'the training for the raid is of such importance that the Commander-in-Chief has decided that a special squadron is to be formed for the job.' He wanted Gibson to help form this squadron. It was, he said, going to be based at Scampton, where Gibson had served with 83 Squadron at the beginning of the war, and Whitworth was going to be the Station Commander. There was a great deal of urgency, Cochrane told him. It was essential to get the squadron right away then get cracking with the training.

'But what sort of training, sir?' asked Gibson, quite reasonably. 'And the target? I can't do a thing—'

Cochrane cut him short. 'I'm afraid I can't tell you any more just for the moment.' He was to get his squadron together, get them flying and then he would be briefed some more.

'How about aircraft and equipment?'

This, Cochrane told him, was being dealt with by Squadron Leader May, the 5 Group Equipment Officer. He was then dismissed with a warning that secrecy was 'vital'.

Outside, Whitworth said cheerily, 'See you at Scampton,' then added, 'If you come over in a couple of days, I'll get everything fixed up for you.'

Gibson was left standing outside Cochrane's office feeling quite dumbfounded, but once Whitworth had departed for Scampton he went upstairs at St Vincent's to discuss with one of the 5 Group officers his wish-list of pilots that he would like to bring with him to this new squadron.

The new squadron had been given the temporary name 'Squadron X', the standard holding title until a number could be officially designated. Also agreed between Bomber Command HQ and 5 Group were the guidelines for selecting personnel. The majority were to have completed one if not two operational tours, and the rest to be specially selected. This was a job for experienced crews, and men who had already demonstrated both skill and considerable aptitude. Groundcrews were to be drawn from Group resources as far as was humanly possible, and all were to have had experience on Lancasters. Since there were not yet any modified Type 464s, aircraft for training would also have to be drawn from the Group. This special squadron was furthermore to have priority over everything else – which, since it would not be flying a mission for two months while every other squadron in the Group continued with the nightly operations over the Reich, was a significant concession from the C-in-C.

Gibson himself arrived at Scampton around teatime on Sunday, 21 March. He had still not had any leave or seen Eve. Parking his Humber outside the Mess, he strutted inside, his dog at his heels. A black labrador called Nigger, the dog was rarely far from his master, except when Gibson was flying. It was something of a tradition for squadron commanders to have a dog, many becoming unofficial squadron mascots. What's more, because they were the boss's dog, they had security passes few others were granted; wives might not have been allowed on base, but the CO's dog was. At 106, Nigger had been spoiled by the chaps; his party trick was to drink beer in the Mess from his own bowl. Fortunately, wartime ale was not as strong as it might have been, and Nigger never seemed too worse for wear.

The Mess at Scampton was a large brick building, with bar, games room, large rectangular reception room and even larger dining room along the front, and with two wings of officers' rooms extending behind. Functional and solid, the Scampton Mess was similar in design and layout to many others built around the country in the previous ten years.

Having been given his rooms, Gibson bustled about, re-familiarizing himself with the station. A small man, with dark hair, full lips and a full but good-looking face, he tended to compensate for his height by walking briskly and purposefully, with shoulders back and chest puffed out. It gave the impression of impatience, of a man who was in a hurry.

Scampton was a sizeable station. The Mess was to the south, and then, across a wide open expanse of grass where cricket and soccer were played, there were a number of other brick buildings, rectangular flat-roofed blocks, painted with large curving camouflage patterns. These were the accommodation blocks for the non-commissioned crews and other personnel. There were also the other station offices, including the briefing room and Sergeants' Mess. Metalled roadways linked these buildings but there were also plenty of open grassy areas. Scampton was in no way cramped.

Beyond this self-contained RAF brick village, to the north-west, were four giant hangars, numbered one to four, and to the front was the grass airfield itself. Lancasters of 57 Squadron were parked around the perimeter track; the only aircraft inside the hangars were those requiring significant attention. Day-to-day servicing was done where the Lancasters were parked, the mechanics – or erks, as they were known – beetling around the aircraft in tool- and parts-laden trucks, the clang of wrenches on metal and occasional shouts ringing out around the airfield.

The new squadron's offices were to the front of No. 2 Hangar, tacked onto the main hangar construction – a long row of rooms on the ground floor and another set, flat-roofed, above. Gibson's was the end room along the corridor on the first floor – a simple square room, metal windows on the outward facing walls, and with a desk at an angle between the two. All he found was the desk, a chair and a single telephone.

Over the following days, Scampton became a whirlwind of activity as a transformation took place. From the moment he accepted Cochrane's offer, Gibson had been busy trying to get his squadron together, first at St Vincent's and then at Scampton. He was by no means expected to do this on his own: it was a joint effort, principally between Gibson, a personnel staff officer at 5 Group called Cartwright, AVM Cochrane, his SASO, Group Captain Harry Satterly, and Group Captain Whitworth, the Station Commander.

There was a great deal to do: forming the squadron was as much of a logistical headache as trying to find someone who could make steel casing of a precise thickness for Wallis's Upkeeps. The crews were just one cog. The best part of 500 men and women in all made up a frontline squadron. Groundcrew and administration staff were way more numerous than the crews themselves; each Lancaster required a team of nearly fifty to get it airborne, of which just seven were the crew.

As well as securing ten aircraft for immediate use, tools, beds, blankets, typewriters, furniture, vehicles and stationery were just some of the other things that needed to be found; they could not take them off 57 Squadron, the other resident unit at Scampton. It was a massive undertaking.

Nonetheless, progress was being made. Two key early appointments were those of Flight Sergeant George Powell, known as 'Chiefy', and Sergeant Jim Heveron. Both were from 57 Squadron and so already at Scampton, and both were known to Gibson from his time there earlier in the war. Chiefy Powell was Welsh, softly spoken and prone to malapropisms, but was canny and efficient, and knew both Scampton and the bureaucratic workings of the RAF inside out. Powell had been head of 57 Squadron's administration and was the senior NCO, with Heveron, who was cut from much the same cloth, as Orderly Room sergeant and Powell's sidekick. They were hastily brought into the squadron in the same role, and set about overseeing the arrival of groundcrew, filtering out those not up to scratch and purloining whatever was needed. A number of chairs, for example, were pilfered from 57 Squadron. Beds and accommodation for the hundreds of groundcrew were harder to come by. Initially, they were put up in old First World War-era huts – previously empty but also condemned. The accommodation shortage was partially solved when one of the erks told him that a number of three-tiered bunks were being thrown out of another station.

An adjutant, who would, with Chiefy Powell, oversee the administration of the squadron, was appointed by 5 Group but got off on the wrong foot. For some reason, Gibson did not like the cut of his jib, and instead asked for, and got, his former deputy adjutant at Syerston, Flying Officer Harry Humphries, although he did not take over – with a promotion to Flight Lieutenant – until 1 April. This was a canny move: Gibson knew he would have more than enough on his plate without worrying about logistics. Handing that headache to a man he knew and trusted was one of the best decisions he made over the formation of the squadron. Also brought across in quick order were the chief engineer, electrical engineer, armament officer and medical officer.

Undoubtedly, however, Powell and Heveron's intimate

knowledge of Scampton helped oil the wheels of squadron formation. Scampton was also 5 Group's ground handling equipment
pool. Stores were swiftly raided and bomb trolleys, winching tools
and other essential kit soon found its way to No. 2 Hangar.

Whenever Powell or Heveron came up against a bureaucratic
brick wall, Gibson waded in, reminding startled clerks and administration officers that his new squadron had been given top priority
and threatening to take the matter higher if they did not offer
immediate co-operation. In this first week, the enormous difficulty
of forming an entire squadron from scratch was quite naturally
both an intense and a hugely stressful time, and Gibson's temper,
never the most even at the best of times, frequently exploded. He
had already something of a reputation as a martinet, and certainly
he relished the power and authority of being Head Boy. Yet if he
lost his rag on occasion, it was hardly surprising. He had been
physically and mentally exhausted by the time he had left 106
Squadron, yet a week later he was now overseeing a mammoth
operation of gargantuan responsibility. Everyone wanted a piece of
him all the time: meetings in Grantham, meetings at Scampton,
people endlessly asking him questions, wanting papers signed. Jim
Heveron brought him a pile of papers to sign one day, which
prompted a weary response.

'At the moment,' Gibson sighed, 'you could put a piece of toilet
paper in front of me and I'd sign it.'

He was still only twenty-four years old.

Another recruit was a 21-year-old WAAF, Section Officer Fay
Gillon, an officer in Intelligence Operations who was already at
Scampton working for 57 Squadron. Hearing about her, Gibson
asked her to come and see him.

'Sit down,' he told her as she came into his still-bare office.
When she had done so, Gibson then said, 'The first thing is, can you
keep a secret? I don't often ask women this.'

Gillon assured him she could, and was then grilled further. She
was married, Gibson understood, and her husband was serving
overseas. Gillon assumed that had she been unmarried he would
have thought her more likely to have boyfriends to whom she
might talk – but with a husband who was overseas, she maybe

presented less of a security risk. Whatever he was thinking, Gibson eventually said, 'Right, this is what I need.' Her duties, he said, would be to liaise with the flight commanders and navigation officer who would be organizing the training programme and the 5 Group staff at St Vincent's and make sure that all low-flying routes were cleared, not least to ensure they were not inundated with civilian protests about Lancasters flying at treetop height. The job was hers – and what was more, she was to be given an office next to that of the Navigation Officer.

Then there were the twenty-one crews needed. Getting the right pilots and crews for this special squadron was no easy matter, and nor did it follow that crews would necessarily follow their pilots – not those who were volunteering, at any rate.

Gibson quite naturally turned to his old squadron. There were a couple of names that immediately sprang to mind: men whom he knew well and trusted and who had already passed the required number of ops, and he wasted no time in ringing them and asking them to join him. David Shannon, a twenty-year-old Australian, had been a close friend and was imbued with the same kind of 'press on' spirit that Gibson liked in his pilots. The son of a South Australian Member of Parliament, Shannon had joined the Royal Australian Air Force just as soon as he turned eighteen and after training out in Australia, had travelled halfway around the world to Britain, arriving late in 1941, around the same time as his fellow Aussie, Charlie Williams. While some could find themselves caught up in transit and further training for months, Shannon was quickly posted to an OTU in Scotland flying Whitleys and then on to 106 Squadron.

Baby-faced and fair-haired, Shannon looked even younger than he was, despite the thin, wispy moustache he insisted on keeping. During his time with 106, he had viewed Gibson as an ideal role model: someone who would brook no nonsense, but who led from the front and yet was still one of the boys. Aping this spirit of in-defatigability, Shannon had already flown way more than the standard thirty ops for a first tour, but had finally just been taken off the squadron for a well-earned rest. A stint as an instructor beckoned. 'That was not to my liking,' said Shannon, 'and so I asked for a transfer to the Pathfinders.' Rather surprisingly, this was granted, and he was sent to 83 Squadron at Wyton. He had only been there a couple of days when Gibson rang and asked him to join a new squadron he was forming for a special raid. He couldn't tell him more, but would pull strings to get Shannon on board if he wanted him to. Shannon agreed immediately, as did his Canadian navigator, Danny Walker. The rest of the crew, however, did not want another change, so stayed where they were.

Another pilot from 106 was the 22-year-old John Hopgood, who, like Shannon, had been one of Gibson's 'press on' types and one of his most trusted and closest friends. From the village of Shere in Surrey, Hopgood had been educated at Marlborough, was a talented musician, and easily fulfilled the recruitment brief, having amassed forty-seven ops and thus nearly completed two tours. He would not reach Scampton for a few days yet, but he had agreed to join. A third pilot from 106 Squadron was a Canadian, Lewis Burpee, twenty-five years old and with twenty-three ops to his name, so nearing the end of his first tour. When Gibson asked him if he wanted to join his new squadron as well, Burpee and his crew agreed.

So that made four pilots, but where were the others going to come from? Twenty-one were needed, and if the operation order for the formation of the squadron was to be taken to the letter, then seven complete crews were to have reached Scampton by 24 March, seven more the following day, and the final seven between the 26th and the end of the month. It was all very well insisting on highly experienced crews, but there was simply not the time to scour every squadron in 5 Group or all of Bomber Command, for that matter. Forming the squadron had to be achieved in double-quick time, and that necessarily meant compromises.

The three pilots from 106 Squadron were the only ones personally known to Gibson, but three further pilots and crews *did* arrive on 24 March: Vernon Byers, a 32-year-old Canadian, and newly commissioned, came with his crew from 467 Squadron; Flight Sergeant George Lancaster, another Canadian, from 57 Squadron, and so already at Scampton; and Flight Lieutenant Harold Wilson from 44 Squadron. None of these three had completed a tour. Byers had just four ops to his name. Four! And yet he was accepted. The necessity of finding enough crews had ensured the exacting requirements of experience were already being put to one side. As Gibson and Whitworth were discovering, crews that were both available and had at least one tour to their credit were hard to find at the drop of a hat.

Nonetheless, by the end of the day, Wednesday, 24 March, the squadron had signed up – and with Gibson included – the seven pilots and crews demanded. At the very least, it was a start.

As crews arrived on 24 March, there was no Commanding Officer to greet them. That morning, Gibson had been ordered to St Vincent's by Group Captain Harry Satterly, where he was told he was to head south to meet a 'scientist' closely connected with the project. Satterly again stressed the utmost importance of secrecy.

Rather bemused, Gibson was driven down the Great North Road, meeting little traffic on the way, and deposited at a train station to the west of London. He then took a train to Weybridge, where he was met by Mutt Summers, the Vickers test pilot. Years before, when Gibson had first considered flying and had thought of a career as a civil test pilot, he had written to Summers, then known as the test pilot of the Supermarine Spitfire, for advice. Summers had advised him to join the RAF. Now, years later, and with Gibson a Wing Commander of a new special squadron formed for a top-secret mission, they finally met. Yet as they rumbled towards Burhill Golf Club, the two barely spoke. 'I think,' wrote Gibson, 'we were both wondering what we were doing there, anyway.'

Eventually they pulled into the long driveway that led up to Burhill, through the trees and past the old fairways and up to the main Georgian building. Passes were checked and rechecked and Gibson had to hand over his special buff-coloured security pass that Satterly had given him earlier that morning. A couple of policemen eyed them suspiciously and then they were in and climbing up the staircase that led from the hall and up to a large office on the first floor. It was by now about twenty past four in the afternoon.

Gibson thought Barnes Wallis looked 'neither young nor old, but just a quiet, earnest man'.

'I'm glad you've come,' said Wallis. 'I don't suppose you know what for.'

'No idea, I'm afraid,' Gibson replied. 'SASO said you would tell me nearly everything, whatever that means.'

Wallis looked taken aback. 'Do you mean to say you don't know the target?'

'Not the faintest idea.'

This put Wallis in an immediate quandary. He had assumed, quite reasonably, that Gibson would not have been sent all the way down from Lincolnshire to see him without being briefed, and yet it was not in his authority to divulge state secrets to those without the proper clearance.

'This is damned silly,' said Mutt Summers.

'I know,' agreed Wallis, 'but it can't be helped. But I'll tell you as much as I dare. I hope the AOC will tell you the rest when you get back.'

Gibson accepted this, and waited, agog, for what Wallis was about to tell him.

Briefly, Wallis outlined the bare bones: that there were certain objectives in enemy territory that could be destroyed if enough explosive was brought to bear at the right point. The snag, of course, was dropping the explosive accurately enough, which in turn necessarily meant it would have to be a low-level attack. The next snag was dropping the charge without blowing up the aircraft in the process.

'The other two snags are, of course,' continued Wallis, 'the danger of flak at that level and balloons, and the difficulty of flying over water at low level.'

'Over water?' Gibson said, surprised.

'Yes, over water at night or early morning when the water will be as flat as a mill pond and backed up with a lot of haze or fog all round.'

Gibson immediately began thinking of possible targets – the *Tirpitz*, or U-boat pens, sprang to mind. He didn't like the sound of either.

Wallis then switched off the lights in the room and showed him his film footage of the Chesil Beach trials and the rotating mine. Wallis pointed out that the prototype was considerably smaller than the bomb Gibson and his crews would be using. 'When we get to the big fellows,' he said, meaning the Upkeeps, 'I think we're going to get into a lot of difficulties.' The first run of these bombs were being made and would be ready in a week or so, Wallis explained. Avro's were doing a rush job to modify some Lancasters specially to carry it.

'I believe they're working twenty-four hours a day,' Wallis told him, then said, 'Now what I want to know from you is this. Can you fly to the limits I want? These are roughly a speed of 240 miles per hour at 150 feet above smooth water, having pulled out of a dive from 2,000 feet, and then be able to drop a bomb accurately within a few yards?'

Gibson told him he couldn't say for certain, but would try and would let him know as soon as possible. Soon after that, he left, with Summers giving him a lift back to Weybridge. Four hours later, he was at Scampton, with even more to think about.

Among the crews now assembling there was a core of experience – but experience of flying mostly Bomber Command missions. Missions that were flown in a very different way. Operations at 18,000 feet and more. They were used to taking off, flying on their own, at high levels of altitude, then dropping their bombs as close as possible on coloured markers many, many thousands of feet below. 'Bombing accuracy' in Bomber Command was a pretty loose term.

And yet now Wallis was asking him and his still only partially formed squadron to fly just above the trees, over enemy-occupied territory, at night, and drop a single enormous bomb that supposedly bounced on water with the kind of accuracy that no British bomber had yet achieved at any point in the entire war. Although he had flown on the Le Creusot Raid the previous October at some 500 feet, he himself had never flown an operation at the extreme low-level heights Wallis was now suggesting. Every man in Bomber Command, however, knew about the Augsburg Raid, the last time it had been tried. It had been little more than a suicide mission.

This new operation was going to be a tall order. A very tall order indeed.

12

617 Squadron

THE AD HOC COMMITTEE to chart progress on both Upkeep and Highball projects first met on 18 March. Despite being an Admiralty initiative, AVM Bottomley, rather than Admiral Renouf, as had been originally suggested, took the chair. Armed with Bufton's initial target survey, it was agreed that the Sorpe, an earthen rather than a gravity dam, and therefore harder to destroy with an Upkeep, should be ruled out, even though it fed, like the Möhne, into the River Ruhr. As with Bufton's suggestions, they agreed the targets should be the Möhne and possibly also the Eder dams. At the same time, it was agreed that an attack should be made against the *Tirpitz* or another German capital ship in the Norwegian fjords using Highball.

Caution was creeping back into the minds of the committee, however. What if Upkeep could not be launched in time before the water levels in the German dams dropped? The project would have to be delayed for a whole year and that would mean keeping specially modified Lancasters idle and doing nothing, while at the same time increasing the security risks. And then there was a further note of concern: what if both Upkeep and Highball did not work? The two weapons had not even been trialled yet. So much was riding on the assumption that they could achieve what had been predicted by Wallis and his advocates.

Bottomley followed up the meeting by contacting the Road Research Lab for as accurate an appraisal as possible of the lowest possible water level at which effective damage could be achieved in the 'certain dams'. The answer ensured that the Upkeep operation would have to take place by the end of May, and, more practically, by 26 May, which was the end of the month's moon period. That was little more than two months away – just nine weeks. Nine weeks and there were still neither finished Upkeeps nor Highballs, modified Lancasters nor Mosquitoes, nor functioning squadrons. It was hardly surprising that Bottomley and others were feeling twitchy, which came across loud and clear when he made his report to the War Cabinet and Chiefs of Staff Committee on 18 March, outlining the progress of Upkeep and Highball. 'The speed with which they have been developed,' he wrote, 'has been so high and the time available to complete them before the required date is so short, that there is a considerable element of gamble in the success of the immediate projects.' He was both expressing his opinion and covering his back, but it was a perfectly reasonable comment to make. It was a gamble – a massive gamble.

A second meeting of the Ad Hoc Committee was held at the Air Ministry's King Charles Street offices on Thursday, 25 March. 'Ad Hoc' was perhaps no longer really the right term, because at no point in the bouncing bomb's genesis had there ever been such a high-ranking number of committee members sat around one table. Not only were Bottomley and Sorley, two of the Assistant Chiefs of the Air Staff, present, but so too were Bufton and several other Air Staff officers. Admiral Renouf was there from the Admiralty, as were a gaggle from the MAP, including Lockspeiser, and also Saundby, Oxland and Cochrane from Bomber Command, Wallis and Summers from Vickers, and the C-in-C of Coastal Command, Air Marshal John Slessor.

Despite the ticking clock, the timetable was, it appeared, on track, at least in terms of the delivery of weapons and modified aircraft. Vickers and A. V. Roe had been continuing to gel well, and it was now confirmed that two Type 464 Lancasters would be ready by 21 April, six more by the 26th and the remaining twelve by 8 May. Sixteen Mosquitoes would also be ready by the same date.

Forty Upkeeps had been built and were now being filled with explosive and fuses, while a further forty and fifty Highballs were currently being filled with inert substances for trials. Two inert Upkeeps would be sent to Vickers at Weybridge in the next few days for spinning trials, while four more were due to reach Manston between 4 and 6 April, from where trials would take place.

And as for the trials, those with the Mosquitoes and Highballs would take place on 11 April, while those of the Lancasters and Upkeeps would be carried out on 17/18 April, less than a week later. It meant that not until around a month before the Upkeep operation was due to take place would they know whether the weapon actually worked, but that could not be helped.

Rough details of training were also mapped out, while the importance of security was also stressed. Both at Scampton, where the Upkeep squadron was now forming, and at Skitten, in Scotland, where Coastal Command's 'special squadron' would soon be formed for Highball, security was to be paramount. No one was to breathe a word of what they were doing. All mail would be rigorously censored and phone lines tapped.

And the two parallel projects, still supposedly running side by side, were given codenames. The Highball project was to be called Operation SERVANT. Bomber Command's Upkeep operation was codenamed CHASTISE. At last they had proper names.

Bomber Command's new special squadron had been given a name, too, as more and more flesh was added to the bones of the project. By the time Gibson returned to Scampton after his visit to Wallis at Burhill, his new squadron had been given its official number. There were several limiting factors in this. By March 1943, those up to 299 had already been spoken for. The 300s were reserved for overseas squadrons – Czech, Polish, Belgian, French and so on – while the 400s were taken by the Canadians that made up the RCAF. The 500s were regular and advanced training RAF squadrons, but had also been used up, although 599 was still up for grabs. 600–616 Squadrons were all pre-war Auxiliary squadrons, many of which had earned numerous battle honours since the start of the war. But 617 Squadron was free, and so this was what the new squadron was called. Two letters were also needed as a code for the squadron number, and which would be painted on the fuselage of each aircraft. These were 'AJ'.

By the end of Thursday, 25 March – the unit's first full day as 617 Squadron – there were, as prescribed, fourteen pilots and more-or-less complete crews. Squadron Leader Henry Maudslay, an old Etonian with over forty ops to his name, was one of those to arrive that day. Still only twenty-one, he fitted the bill perfectly and was promptly appointed one of Gibson's two flight commanders. Les Knight, a 22-year-old Australian and teetotaller, with exactly thirty ops, also came with Maudslay from 50 Squadron.

Navigator on Les Knight's crew was 31-year-old Sid 'Hobby' Hobday, from Wallington in Surrey. A commissioned Flying Officer, Hobday was considerably older than the rest of the crew, which included the usual mixture of nationalities: Knight was Australian, as was Bob Kellow, the wireless operator, while Fred Sutherland, the front gunner, was Canadian. The other three were English but they all got along well enough and certainly there had been no disagreement between them over whether they should join this new squadron together. It had caused a small amount of soul searching for Hobday, however, because he had been due to go on a new navigational course, which would have meant promotion, and so had spent a sleepless night worrying whether he should go on the course, as he'd already asked to do, or sign up for the new special squadron. It worried him that it was bad form to renege on the course having already agreed to go. 'I spent quite a long time worrying about what to do for the best,' he said, 'but I decided that the crew should come first.' And so the whole crew had stayed together and gone to Scampton.

Hobday had chosen to be a navigator. After leaving school, aged seventeen, he had got a job with Lloyds of London insurance and had also joined the Territorials, as a gunner on an anti-aircraft battery. Army life didn't suit him much, however, and nor did he particularly enjoy standing around a gun all night, often in the cold and mud, so he left and then, when war was declared, decided to join the RAF instead. His family tried to dissuade him, worrying it would be too dangerous, but his mind was made up and having always been interested in maps thought that being a navigator would be the best way for him to do his bit towards the war.

Initially, he found the training difficult. It had been some years since he had been at school and he had not done any maths since then, but he worked hard, got through his initial training and was then shipped out to South Africa to carry out his navigational course. Britain's Empire really was a huge advantage to her war effort. From many corners came food, materials and natural resources. In addition to her own manpower, there were some 250 million more people she could call upon since all the Empire's governments had shown solidarity and declared war too. And there was the space these lands afforded. Whether it be the plains of Canada or the veldt of South Africa, these were ideal training grounds for the RAF. Unlike little Britain, over-populated and with indifferent weather, Canada and South Africa held vast open country and air space and the kind of weather that, between them, ensured aircrew could be trained all year around. Germany had nothing to compare with it, nothing to compare with it at all.

Hobday loved it out in South Africa and thoroughly enjoyed the course too, and when he returned, he was a commissioned and qualified navigator. Having crewed up and been through OTU and a Heavy Conversion Unit, he and the crew were posted to 50 Squadron. That had been the previous autumn, and now, with their first tour complete, they were experienced veterans. 'We had done quite well,' says Hobday. 'I think that was the reason they chose our crew to go to 617.'

Knight and his crew might have had the kind of experience required, but such crews were hard to come by; not too many people in 5 Group had both a first tour under their belts and were available for immediate transfer. As Hobday points out, the numbers of those who finished tours was not high. 'The loss rate was so colossal.'

A change of tack was needed. They had aimed for a minimum requirement of one completed tour, but if that was not possible, then they would have to complete the squadron with what they could get. Furthermore, between them, Gibson, Whitworth and those helping to form the squadron at 5 Group HQ simply did not personally know all the crews in 5 Group; nor did they keep precise tabs on the missions chalked up by crews – that was left to the various squadron and station commanders. Thus once they *had* exhausted all those they knew about, they were then dependent on those other station commanders to find the shortfall.

Some station commanders hand-picked certain crews, but at Woodhall Spa a letter from 5 Group was put up on the squadron notice board asking for volunteers for a 'special mission'. 'When I read this letter,' says Les Munro, 'I had an immediate inclination to say yes, let's volunteer, so I called my crew together and we discussed the question of whether we should.' All but the rear gunner and bomb-aimer agreed. Flight Lieutenant David Maltby and crew also volunteered from 97 Squadron but, while they had completed thirty ops, Munro had chalked up just twenty-two. This did not stop them being accepted, however.

Another pilot to come from 97 Squadron was the American, Joe McCarthy, and his crew. Gibson had possibly been told about McCarthy by Don Curtin, who had been in 106 Squadron. McCarthy's old pal would have been an obvious choice for the new squadron but had been killed on 25 February during the raid on Nuremberg. At any rate, McCarthy had just finished his first tour and had the kind of personality and attitude that fitted Gibson's idea of what a bomber pilot should be like. Gibson actually rang McCarthy and asked him personally if he would join. McCarthy agreed so long as his crew were prepared to come too, which they were, on the understanding that it was a special squadron that was being formed for just one trip.

All three 97 Squadron pilots and crews were taken by bus from Woodhall to Scampton on 25 March.

Three more pilots arrived that day: Flying Officer Norm Barlow, another Australian, from 61 Squadron, and Sergeants Cyril Anderson and Bill Townsend from 49 Squadron. Townsend and Barlow were nearing the magic thirty-ops mark, but Anderson and his crew had just seven ops to their name – way below the experience required. And Anderson was older than most – at twenty-eight – and married too. Once again, it did not stop them from being accepted, and now Whitworth and Gibson had fourteen.

On 26 March, 57 Squadron's entire 'C' Flight was ordered across. This included Squadron Leader Melvin Young, who had only just joined 57, and who, despite considerable experience of flying in the Mediterranean, was new to Lancasters. The others were the 23-year-old Flight Lieutenant Bill Astell, who had also mostly flown in the Mediterranean, Flight Sergeant Ray Lovell and Pilot Officer Geoff Rice. Neither Lovell nor Rice had flown many ops at all. Rice had flown even fewer than Cyril Anderson, and both he and his crew protested vehemently against their transfer. Far from the special squadron being made up from volunteers and 'special', highly experienced crews, Gibson and Whitworth, in their desperation to stick to the strict timetable set them, were now accepting crews with way, way less than the minimum requirement of operations. Whether this would come back to haunt them later, only time would tell.

However, there were no such question marks over Melvin Young, even though he was only newly converted to Lancasters. In Young, Gibson found his second Flight Commander. Tall, broad, and newly married to a Californian, Young had two tours under his belt, flying Whitleys with Bomber Command and then later, in 1942, Wellingtons from Malta and Egypt. Crucially, he also had staff experience from when, after his second tour, he worked at HQ 205 Group in Egypt and earned laurels for his administrative capabilities. With an American mother, Young had been partly raised in America and had met his future wife, Priscilla, at Kent College in Connecticut. Fiercely clever, he was a rowing blue at Oxford and had been in the 1938 Boat Race crew that had beaten Cambridge. Among his other talents was an ability to down a pint quicker than any man who challenged him. In the squadron environment, this was an appealing trait.

Not only did Young have more than fifty ops to his name, he also had a Distinguished Flying Cross and Bar, and a cool head in a crisis. His nickname was 'Dinghy', as he had twice ditched his plane into the sea, the first occasion during a stint with Coastal Command when he suffered engine failure. 'The engine got very hot,' said Young, 'and so did I, and it was only a matter of a very few minutes before we found ourselves cooling rather rapidly in the

Altantic.' They had ditched within sight of land, but wind and currents soon swept them tantalizingly further away. He and his crew were forced to bob about in their inflatable dinghy in the Atlantic swell for over twenty-two hours before being finally picked up by a British destroyer. Barely a month later, during a raid on Turin, he got lost on the return leg and, unable to get a fix, ran out of fuel and was forced to ditch again. For a second time, he was in luck and not only managed to get out of the plane before it sank, but was rescued too, some five and a half hours later. The nickname was inevitable. 'My reputation for always wanting to row is bad in the Air Force,' he commented later. 'Several times I have had to park my plane in the sea and take to the rubber boats. My friends cautioned me that it was a rather expensive way of brushing up on my rowing.'

There had been a shock waiting for Joe McCarthy and his crew on reaching Scampton. McCarthy had understood that having finished their first tour, they were due some leave, but had been told that Gibson had cancelled all leave. This was a double blow for Johnny Johnson, who had been dating a girl from Torquay for some time and was due to be getting married on 3 April – a wedding in Devon that had been arranged around the promised week of leave.

'I thought, oh Christ,' says Johnny. 'There goes my wedding. There's going to be hell to pay.' McCarthy, however, wasn't having any of it and immediately led the entire crew up the stairs of the squadron offices and rapped on Gibson's door.

'Come in,' Gibson replied. The office had improved considerably. There were now shelves and drawers, a baize notice board on the wall behind him and even some flowers on the desk.

'We've just finished our first tour,' said the tall American, his crew standing alongside him, 'and we're entitled to a week's leave. My bomb-aimer here is supposed to be getting married on 3rd April and he's gonna get married on 3rd April!'

Gibson, no doubt taken aback by this forthright giant of a man, conceded – in part. They were given four days – enough, just, for Johnson to get himself down to Torquay, get married, and then hurry back to Lincolnshire.

*

Saturday, 27 March. Up until this day, 617 Squadron had been muddling through, as reams of ground- and aircrew arrived to join a new unit that, as of yet, had no aircraft and no indication of what they had been formed to do. It was a 'special squadron' formed for a specific mission, but no one seemed to know what that was. Crews kicked their heels in the Messes, the rumours getting wilder, while groundcrews were interviewed and screened by Chiefy Powell and given makeshift accommodation. The amount of men, women and equipment arriving was extraordinary. No squadron had ever been established from nothing in such a short time, but during those first few days it was all happening without anyone knowing why. Bemused aircrew supposed they would be told eventually, but when was anyone's guess.

There were all sorts of issues to be resolved. First, and most importantly, they needed Lancasters, if not the Type 464s just yet, then enough ordinary types with which to start training. Two arrived on 26 March, one from 106 Squadron, the other from 61. That was a start. Then there was the kind of training they needed to carry out, although Gibson was massively hampered by how little he knew himself and by the secrecy of what little he did know.

Now, however, on this last Saturday in March – and an entire month and a day after the project had been given the greenlight – things began to become a little clearer. Six more Lancasters arrived, borrowed and purloined from a number of different 5 Group squadrons, which made eight in all – enough for crews to start training with. That same day, Gibson also received a detailed training note from Group Captain Harry Satterly, Cochrane's SASO at 5 Group HQ. Although Gibson, after his meeting with Barnes Wallis, had a pretty good idea of what was required, Satterly's note was helpfully specific. He outlined three key requirements, each of which crews were to have mastered by 10 May:

Accurate navigation under moonlight or simulated moonlight conditions at a height which will best afford security against fighter attack. Air Position Indicators may be available for all aircraft, but training should not await their arrival.

The final approach at 100 feet and at a precise speed, which will be about 240 miles per hour. The actual speed will be notified later. It will be convenient to practise this over water.

The release of the mine visually at an estimated range judged either by a land mark on a nearby shore or by timing 'E' seconds after passing an easily identified land mark. Accuracy of release required is for all crews to be able to release this mine within 40 yards either side of the correct release point.

Satterly advised the squadron to fly low-level training flights routed over the area south and west of the Wash, extending into the north Midlands or the northern Welsh mountains. Final approach training – simulating the dropping of the bomb – could be done over the numerous reservoir lakes in these areas. He helpfully attached a list. Finally, he warned Gibson not to fly anywhere near light flak range from other airfields or other likely defended spots. Night simulation was also to be carried out, using dark goggles with the 'correct lenses'.

Gibson now felt able to confer with his new flight commanders, Henry Maudslay and Dinghy Young. In his now carpeted office in front of No. 2 Hangar, he outlined Satterly's training brief, although did not mention the bouncing bomb he had seen in Wallis's film.

Specific routes now needed to be agreed, and the authority given to be hurling big four-engine Lancasters just over the rooftops of unsuspecting civilians below, while reconnaissance trips over some of the lakes suggested by Satterly also needed to be carried out.

Gibson would rely heavily on these two men in the days and weeks to come, but Young especially. At twenty-seven, he was the second-oldest pilot in the squadron, but his age, experience and administrative skills – he even had his own typewriter – ensured that when Gibson was repeatedly called into meetings or whisked away to Grantham, Young covered for him and managed the training programmes.

It was a measure of Young's influence that Bill Astell, in both his flight at 617 and his former flight with 57, should have been sent that afternoon on the squadron's first sortie – a photographic reconnaissance flight over the suggested lakes and reservoirs.

The following morning, Astell carried out another photographic reconnaissance, and then, a few days later, Gibson flew himself, taking Young and his old friend from 106 Squadron, John Hopgood, with him. It was typical of Gibson that he insisted on flying the first low-level training sortie over water, determined to judge for himself whether flying at such low heights was practicable; no pilot of his should be expected to try something he had not already done first.

He was also flying with his new crew – his navigator had arrived that day. All were new to Gibson, except Bob 'Hutch' Hutchison, his wireless operator, with whom he had regularly flown at 106 Squadron.

They flew to the Pennines, to the Derwent Reservoir, which they had picked out from Astell's photo recce. Lying to the south of Sheffield, surrounded by high ground, and with a thin industrial haze above it from the collieries and steelworks of Sheffield, it looked to be ideal. Furthermore, the water was apparently usually calm because the lake was narrow and the valley walls sheltered it from the prevailing winds.

As they approached, Gibson dropped low and then thundered over the reservoir at 240 mph, as prescribed, and at as close to 150 feet as they could judge, 'Hoppy' Hopgood sitting beside him in the flight engineer's seat checking the altitude. They carried out a number more dummy runs, by which time dusk was falling and fog was beginning to form in the Derwent Valley. Visibility was down to about a mile, which was what Satterly had suggested in his training notes they could expect during the real operation.

Trying another run, they quickly realized it was now not so straightforward. The blue water of the reservoir had turned black, and the limited visibility was disorientating, and the altimeter ineffective. Gibson found it extremely difficult to judge his height. So low were they now flying, as they screamed over, they very nearly hit the water.

'Christ, this is bloody dangerous!' called out Pilot Officer 'Spam' Spafford from the bomb-aimer's dome at the front of the

Lancaster. He was right – they had been a sliver away from plunging into the water. In a trice they could have all been killed.

'Unless we can find some way of judging our height above water,' Gibson now said to Young, 'this type of attack will be completely impossible.'

'But why must we fly at this dead height?' asked Hopgood.

Because, Gibson explained, the weapon wouldn't work unless it was dropped at the right height and the right speed. 'That's our problem.'

And it was a problem that needed to be solved very quickly – otherwise Gibson and his crews were likely to kill themselves not over enemy-occupied territory but in the inky dark waters of Derwent Reservoir.

13

Certain Dams

B Y THE AFTERNOON OF 27 March, with most, if not all of the crews having now reached Scampton, Gibson and Whitworth realized some kind of briefing was in order. Assembling them together at No. 2 Hangar, Gibson gave a speech that was short and to the point. 'You're here to do a special job,' he told them, 'you're here as a crack squadron, you're here to carry out a raid on Germany which, I am told, will have startling results. Some say it may even cut short the duration of the war. What the target is, I can't tell you. Nor can I tell you where it is. All I can tell you is that you will have to practise low flying all day and all night until you know how to do it with your eyes shut. If I tell you to fly to a tree in the middle of England, then I will want you to bomb that tree. If I tell you to fly through a hangar, then you will have to go through that hangar even though your wing tips might hit either side. Discipline is absolutely essential.'

He reminded them of the importance of secrecy. 'We've got to say nothing,' he told them. 'When you go into pubs at night you've got to keep your mouths shut. When the other boys ask you what you're doing, just tell them to mind their own business, because of all things in this game, security is the greatest factor.' Nor would there be any leave. It was a speech that well reflected Gibson's command style: outwardly extremely confident and bullish, but one that demanded absolute loyalty and obedience. Discipline was all-important, and Gibson never batted an eye about giving anyone who strayed a severe dressing-down. He was the boss, the top dog, and no one was allowed to forget it.

He might strut about the place with his chest puffed out, acting as though he were the king of his little world, but it was a command style aped from those days at school, where captains of rugby and the Head Boy had been demigods within their narrow environment. As a schoolboy in Oxford he had had such an unremarkable time, and yet since joining the RAF he had flown as many combat missions as anyone, and deservedly won two DSOs and two DFCs and had the three rings on his sleeves of a wing commander. His approach to command had worked at 106 Squadron, but it was noticeable that the ones who tended to question his decision making – such as John Searby, who had taken over command from him – were usually older. Those who looked up to him the most were, understandably, younger – men like Hopgood and Shannon.

His first briefing over, Gibson disappeared off to his office, leaving Young to sort out the two flights, which required a degree of tact and empathy as it meant choosing who would work best with who and then allocating flying lockers and crew rooms. Gibson, who had little patience – or empathy – for such matters, was happy to leave it to his Senior Flight Commander, someone who was older, in many ways wiser, and considerably more worldly.

Three days later, on Tuesday, 30 March, Gibson and Whitworth then briefed the groundcrew, gathered together by Chiefy Powell in No. 2 Hangar. Standing on his Humber to make sure everyone could both see and hear him, Gibson repeated what he'd told his aircrews a few days earlier, and stressing the importance of security. Whitworth then addressed them.

'Many of you will have seen Noel Coward's film, *In Which We Serve*,' he said to them. 'In one scene Coward, as commander of a destroyer, asks one of the seamen what is the secret of an efficient ship. The seaman answers, "A happy ship, sir." And that is what I want you to be here. You in the Air Force use a well-known verb in practically every sentence; that verb is "to bind." I can promise you,' he said, 'that if you don't bind me, I won't bind you!'

It was hardly Churchillian, but it was the first time the ground-crew had all been together and had been given a proper chance to see their new commander. The squadron now almost had its full complement of personnel. That it had been done in little more than a week was no small achievement. Furthermore, that afternoon, Gibson's new Adjutant, Flight Lieutenant Humphries, finally joined the Squadron. The jigsaw was almost complete.

Meanwhile, in London, memos and papers were going back and forth over precisely what targets should be the focus of Operation CHASTISE. On 23 March, the Chiefs of Staff had asked Portal for a memorandum on the results that could be expected 'from an attack on certain targets'. This he provided on 27 March in a paper rather long-windedly called, *The Economic and Moral Effects of the Destruction of the Möhne Dam and the Added Effects Which Will Result from Destruction at the Same Time of the Sorpe and Eder Dams*. As its title indicated, it was a fairly comprehensive study which suggested the destruction of five dams in the Ruhr would be 'appreciable', with widespread flooding and a substantial loss of electrical capacity, that the thermo-electrical generating stations in the Ruhr would be 'seriously impaired', while the restriction of water supplies to the heavy industries of the Ruhr would have 'a most serious effect on activities in the foundries, coal mines, coke ovens, blast furnaces and chemical plants which require enormous quantities of water for their operation'. Traffic on the lower reaches of the Ruhr would be affected, while the Ruhr railway network, which crossed and recrossed the river, and ran parallel to it for much of its length, would inevitably be badly damaged by the flood water. There would also be less water available for fire-fighting during and after other aerial attacks. Destroying the Eder Dam would have less obvious economic effects, although the loss of 202 million cubic metres of water would be 'spectacular'.

Destruction of the Sorpe Dam, only ten miles south-west of the Möhne, was more problematical because of its earthen construction, but by no means impossible. Destroying the two would account for 75 per cent of the water supplies to the Ruhr and would have a 'paralysing effect upon the industrial activity in the Ruhr'. In conclusion, the paper recommended attacking both the Möhne and Sorpe and also the Eder in one combined attack.

Portal had obtained this assessment from the Scientific Advisors to the Minister of Production, and many of its findings were contained in Wallis's *Air Attack on Dams*, which implied that the authors had got much of their material from his paper. In turn, Wallis had sourced much of his information from Winterbotham in Air Intelligence, which made it about as legitimate as it could be. However, Portal felt obliged to point out in a covering note to General Brooke, the Chief of the Imperial General Staff, that while he had no reason to doubt a word of it, he could not regard it as authoritative until it had been vetted by another Ministry, that of Economic Warfare, known as the MEW.

The MEW was an important cog in the shaping of the air war, because it had for some time advised the Air Staff on bombing policy, drawing from its impressive intelligence network, which included the work being done at Bletchley and by radio listening services, agents on the ground and other sources. In fact, following the Augsburg Raid the previous April, Lord Selbourne, the Minister for Economic Warfare, had complained bitterly to the Prime Minister that the M.A.N. Diesel Works had not been on their list of practicable or viable targets, and that they had not been consulted by Harris and Bomber Command before the raid was mounted. It had caused a considerable stir at the time, although Harris had dead-batted Selbourne's gripe with considerable aplomb and the furore had passed soon enough.

However, CHASTISE was on an altogether different magnitude from the Augsburg Raid and there was no way the Air Ministry was going to send anyone to attack any German dam until they had been given the authority and approval of the MEW.

As it happened, however, the MEW had been coming around to the opinion that it was better for bombing to be concentrated on fewer targets, more thoroughly, than for the effort to be spread over a greater number of targets, and had produced a paper of its own, as recently as 15 March, called *Economic Significance of the Möhnetalsperre and Edertalsperre* (the Möhne and Eder dams), a copy of which Wallis had seen via Admiral Renouf.

At any rate, Bottomley now sent Portal's target assessment by the Scientific Advisors to the Minister of Production to his contact at the MEW to ask for their own appreciation. Such was the importance of the target and so significant was the investment being placed in Operation CHASTISE, and the risk of it all going wrong so high, no one was prepared to leave a stone unturned. This operation had to be done by the book, with final approval for both CHASTISE and SERVANT to be given by the Chiefs of Staff. That could not happen until the Ministry of Economic Warfare had passed judgement. If that meant a delay in making a decision about targets, then so be it.

Despite the question marks that still hung over the targets, on 29 March Gibson was summoned once again to Grantham, leaving the squadron in the hands of Dinghy Young. At St Vincent's, Cochrane showed him two scale models of the Möhne and Sorpe dams. He would not tell him where they were, but admitted that Wallis had spoken to him and insisted that Gibson be told what the targets were, even if not their names or precise locations. Apparently, Wallis had told Cochrane that it would be impossible for Gibson to train his squadron properly without knowing.

'However,' Cochrane told him, 'don't forget that you have got to be the only man in the squadron who can possibly know the target until the day before the attack is made.'

Gibson was surprised the targets were dams, although his immediate thought was: *Thank God it's not the Tirpitz.*

Cochrane told him he was now to head back down to see Wallis once more, although this time he was to take an aeroplane, rather than suffer a long-winded journey via train and car.

As before, Mutt Summers was there to greet him and drove him to Burhill, where Wallis seemed pleased to see him. He asked Gibson how he had got on flying so low over water. Gibson told him: straightforward enough by day but near impossible by night.

Wallis told him that Cochrane had given him the authority to reveal the targets. As Summers passed Gibson a cigarette, Wallis told him the models were of the dams in the Ruhr Valley. He mentioned the bouncing bomb that Gibson had seen in his film and explained that with really accurate bombing, it would be possible to use the Upkeeps to destroy the dams.

He also explained the difference between the Möhne and the Sorpe dams. The first was a gravity dam, which was made of concrete and masonry, and at its base was 140 feet thick and kept back the water by its weight. The Sorpe, on the other hand, was an earthen dam, sloping on both sides and filled with a concrete core. He then mentioned a third dam, the Eder, another gravity dam. As he then explained how and why the bouncing bomb would work, he showed Gibson pictures of the scale trials at the Road Research Lab.

Gibson thought this must have been rather fun. He immediately remembered being a boy in Cornwall and making sand dams across the little streams that ran across the beach. 'I could remember how we dammed up the water until it made a big pool behind the sand,' he noted, 'and I could remember how, when it was time to go home to supper, I used to smash the whole thing with one sweep of my spade, letting the water rush out down the beach. I could also remember how angry my brother used to get when I did this.'

Next, Wallis told him about the live trials at Nant y Gro and showed him photographs of the second trial carried out the previous July, and explained how the bouncing bomb would be the means of achieving this kind of breach. Then came a confession. 'My smaller scale weapons have worked,' he told Gibson, 'but we haven't had a chance to try the big ones yet – they aren't ready.' Trials were set, but, he admitted, time was short, and told him about the limitations of water levels and the May moon period.

'You couldn't get to the Ruhr by day, could you?'

'God, no,' Gibson replied.

Wallis talked him through the type of attack needed: the height, the speed, the size and weight of the mines; that they would be spinning at 500 rpm.

'That's going to be mighty difficult,' admitted Gibson. Over black water, at a constant height, when it was hard to see much at all.

'And remember this,' said Wallis, 'you'll have to drop your mines slightly before you reach the wall, so an ordinary bombsight

Above: Squadron Leader John Nettleton, who led the ill-fated low-level Augsburg Raid in April 1942. His was the only Lancaster of six from 44 Squadron to make it back.

Below: Fred Winterbotham, a former spy and an Air Intelligence Officer in MI6, was also fabulously well-connected and a crucial supporter of Wallis.

Above: Barnes Wallis. A brilliant and largely self-taught designer and engineer, he was thinking of new ways in which to destroy Germany's war machine from the outset of war.

Below: A diagram from Wallis's *Note*. Destroy Germany's natural resources, he argued, and their ability to wage war would be wiped out too.

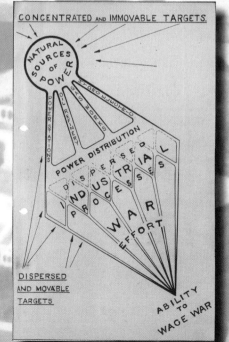

Below: Nant y Gro dam in Wales. Tests here in July 1942 proved that the German dams could be destroyed with far less explosive than had originally been thought.

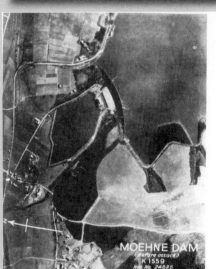

Left: The Kaiser inspects the building of the Eder Dam in 1912.

Middle left and right: The Möhne and the Eder dams from the air. These dams were two of the best-known structures in all of Germany, symbols not only of industrial and engineering might, but of the German ability to tame nature, too.

Bottom: The Möhne, pre-war.

The first dropping trials took place in December 1942, and for the larger bomb, the Upkeep, did not end until 13 May 1943, three days before the raid. A Vickers Wellington (**left**), drops the prototype spherical bouncing bomb at Chesil Beach in Dorset, while (**below**) adapted Type 464 Lancasters drop the final cylindrical bomb at Reculver in Kent.

The Type 464 Provisioning Lancaster. When Operation CHASTISE was given the greenlight at the end of February 1943, Wallis had no idea how long it would take to adapt a Lancaster specially to carry his rotating four-ton bomb. Fortunately, Roy Chadwick, the Lancaster's designer, cooperated well with Barnes Wallis, as did their respective teams at A. V. Roe and Vickers, so that the first Type 464 was delivered for testing on 8 April, just six weeks after work began.

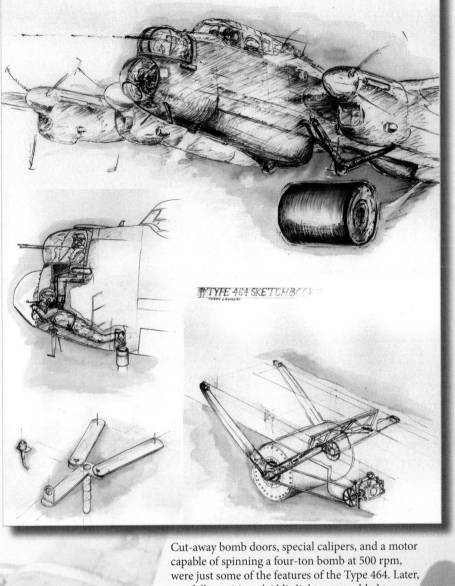

TYPE 464 SKETCHBOOK
TERRY LAWLER

Cut-away bomb doors, special calipers, and a motor capable of spinning a four-ton bomb at 500 rpm, were just some of the features of the Type 464. Later, carefully positioned Aldis lights were added to help the crews judge height off the water, while bomb-aimers were given a simple home-made wooden sight to help them judge the correct distance to drop the bomb.

Guy Gibson in his office at Scampton with David Maltby (**above**), and (**left**), his youth plain to see. He looks fresh-faced here, but by the time he took command of 617 Squadron, Gibson was mentally and physically exhausted and in dire need of a break.

Two of the crews: (**Above**): Joe McCarthy (*middle left*) with 'Johnny' Johnson (*far left*), and Les Knight and his crew (**below**), with Sid Hobday (*on the left*).

Above: Grant McDonald (*right*), one of the many Canadians flying on the Dams Raid.

Top and above left: The tough, phlegmatic New Zealander Les Munro.

Above right: David Shannon from Australia, and one of the few pilots known to Gibson.

Charlie Williams (**left**), a sheep farmer from the Australian outback, and (**right**) John Fraser, from Vancouver Island.

Below: 'Mick' Martin (*far right*) with some of his crew, including Navigation Officer Jack Leggo (*far left*), and Bomb-aimer Bob Hay (*centre*).

Some of the key players in the story of the Dams Raid …

Left: Air Chief Marshal Sir Charles Portal, Chief of the Air Staff. For all the politicking that went on with regard to Wallis's bouncing bomb, once Portal gave it his backing, CHASTISE was very quickly given the go-ahead.

Right: Air Vice-Marshal Norman Bottomley, one of the Assistant Chiefs of the Air Staff and the man overseeing the planning for CHASTISE.

Above left: Air Vice-Marshal Francis Linnell, the Controller of Research and Development at the Ministry of Aircraft Production. Linnell was a sceptic, concerned that the bouncing bombs would be a drain on resources and a diversion from other projects already in development.

Above right: Air Vice-Marshal Ralph Cochrane, the AOC of 5 Group, Bomber Command. Cochrane did all within his power to ensure that 617 Squadron had the best possible chance of success.

Air Marshal Sir Arthur Harris (**main picture and left at his desk**) – the man with the immense responsibility of leading Britain's bomber offensive. He was vehemently opposed to CHASTISE, and with good reason, but once Portal had made his decision, Harris gave it his complete support.

won't do. If you undershoot, nothing will happen, if you overshoot, the mine will go over the top. But it's best to be accurate because, if you make a mistake, the mine might hit the parapet and explode underneath your tail.' If the Upkeep was dropped accurately, on the other hand, it would explode about a hundred yards behind. 'You'll be OK,' Wallis told him. 'There's not much blast from an underwater explosion. Besides, the parapet will protect you.'

'I see,' Gibson said slowly, although he didn't. Not really. He felt completely and utterly bewildered. The limitations seemed so great. 'But all we could do,' he noted, 'was try.'

In the meantime, he still needed to muster his complete squadron. There were three more crews needed. On 30 March, Flight Sergeant Ken Brown, a 22-year-old Canadian, arrived with his crew from 44 Squadron. His rear gunner was another Canadian and just as young. Grant McDonald was from Grand Forks, in the Rocky Mountains in British Columbia, a place almost as remote as the sheep station in Queensland where Charlie Williams had been brought up. It had been a good place to be raised, with plenty of fishing, hiking and running wild, but when he'd got out of school, he wondered what he would do and so enlisted in the Army – not because of the war, but because as the second-youngest child of seven, Grand Forks held only limited opportunities for him and, at the time, it had seemed like a good idea.

He hadn't really taken to the Army, but in any case, it had always been the Air Force that he'd really wanted to join – he'd always been interested in aircraft and flying – but at the time the RCAF was not recruiting so heavily and he had been unable to get in. All that had changed with the onset of war and the Allied defeat in the West in 1940, and McDonald had managed to get a transfer. 'I really wanted to enlist as a wireless operator/air gunner,' says McDonald, 'but when I went through the initial training, they said I had to go on a pilot's course.' So he went to an initial training wing, put in some flying hours, but, like Johnny Johnson, failed to make the cut. 'My landings, in particular, were not good.' And, like Johnson, he was retrained as an air gunner.

A trip across the Atlantic in a Polish troop ship saw him arrive at Greenock in Scotland in the summer of 1942. After the holding camp in Bournemouth on the southern coast of England, he was then sent back up to Scotland, to Stranraer, for a further gunnery course, and then to his OTU at Kinloss. It was here that he crewed up with Ken Brown and their navigator, Dudley Heal. By November 1942, they were attached to Coastal Command and back down in the far south-west of England flying twin-engine Whitleys from St Eval in Cornwall. 'The anti-submarine patrols were long trips,' admits McDonald. 'They had auxiliary tanks in the fuselage, which gave them a range of up to ten hours.' Ten-hour flights, far, far out to sea. And in mid-winter too. These were tough operations.

Not until January were they finally sent back to Bomber Command and to a Heavy Conversion Unit, where they flew firstly Manchesters and then eventually the Lancaster. From there, on 6 February 1943, they were finally posted to 44 Squadron at Waddington, where John Nettleton, VC, was still commanding officer.

On the night of 27 March, they were due to fly their fourth operation with 44 as part of a big raid on Berlin, but after the briefing Nettleton took Ken Brown aside and told him that he and his crew were about to be transferred. Brown protested and said he would far rather complete his tour with 44 Squadron. This, Nettleton told him, would not be possible. It was out of his hands. Orders were orders.

That night, they still flew to Berlin, along with 395 other aircraft. Fortunately, they made the long trip back in one piece, although the raid was hardly a success. The Pathfinders laid their marking areas short of the city and not one bomb fell within five miles of the intended target, although by fluke a Luftwaffe stores depot eleven miles south-west of the city was heavily hit and destroyed. Nor were the raid's chances of success helped by the large number of dud bombs that were dropped – another perennial problem that faced Harris.

In any case, on 30 March, Brown and the rest of his crew left Waddington for Scampton, just a few miles to the north, still none the wiser as to why they, with just seven confirmed ops in all to their names, should have been posted to a completely different and new squadron. 'I don't know why we were transferred,' says McDonald. 'I still don't know how they arranged for crews like ourselves to be sent there.'

The next day, the last day of March, the twentieth pilot and crew arrived. Flight Lieutenant Mick Martin had, unlike Ken Brown, chalked up his first tour and been posted to an OTU, but had been tracked down and asked by Gibson personally to form a crew and get over to Scampton. The two had met during an investiture at Buckingham Palace, in which Martin had told him his views about the virtues of low flying. Still only twenty-three, but with a classic airman's moustache, Martin, another Australian, was precisely the sort of pilot Gibson had been after: extrovert, charismatic, imperturbable, experienced and already decorated.

It was a shame the same could not be said for all the crews now assembled at Scampton. At any rate, the intensive training that would be carried out over the next few weeks would soon weed out any pilot or crew not coming up to scratch.

14

The Conquest of Nature

AIR VICE-MARSHAL BOTTOMLEY had duly sent Portal's circulated memo on targets to the MEW, and a few days later, on 2 April, they replied with their assessment, which, broadly speaking, suggested the economic effects of destroying the three dams might not be quite so great as had been supposed. It pointed out that the immediate water source of the Ruhr area was provided by underground water-bearing strata, supplemented by colliery water and water pumped back from the Rhine and Emscher River and canal systems. What the report did point out, however, was that the longer-term effect would be dependent on how quickly the dam might be repaired and how much subsequent rainfall there would be in the following months. The nearby Sorpe was essentially complementary to the Möhne. 'For this reason,' the report stated, 'the destruction of both dams would be worth much more than twice the destruction of one.' It strongly urged an attack on both. As regards the Eder Dam, it claimed that the four power stations that would be destroyed as a result would be a 'useful measure of interference', while there would be inevitable widespread flooding and some effect on the maintaining of water levels in the Weser and Mittelland Canal.

On the basis of this rather more sober assessment, Bottomley suggested to Portal that they change the emphasis of the targets.

'You will note that contrary to our original idea,' he wrote to the CAS in a hand-delivered note on 5 April, 'the destruction of the Sorpe is regarded as the second in order of importance and especially so if combined with that of the Möhne. We should therefore plan for simultaneous attacks on these two to be followed by attacks on the Eder if circumstances allow.'

No one was denying, however, that the dams were not worthwhile targets, especially when put alongside the pounding the Ruhr was getting from Harris's continuing campaign. The 'moral effects' were also considered to be considerable. Whether destroying the Möhne and Sorpe, in particular, would constitute industrial meltdown in the area was clearly open to debate, but what their destruction would achieve was widespread flooding and destruction of houses, roads, bridges, railway lines and numerous power stations, as well as considerable damage to a number of war-industry-related buildings. To repair all this would be astronomically expensive and would, at the very least, be a major inconvenience and a diversion of resources.

There was another very good reason why the dams were a good target, however, one that was touched upon by Barnes Wallis during his second meeting with Gibson on 29 March. 'The Germans,' he said of the Möhne, 'are very proud of this dam.' In fact, they were proud of all their dams, although of the Möhne *and* Eder in particular; they were among the best-known structures in the Reich. Dams, of course, were as old as the hills. It was a German, Georg Steinfurth, who discovered the world's oldest in 1885 – the Kafara Dam south of Cairo. In Spain, the Roman dam at Cornalvo had been standing for the best part of two millennia. However, although these were ancient structures, they had not been built on the kind of scale that the Germans began building them in the latter part of the nineteenth century.

Although Germany was a new nation, just seventy years old, there was nonetheless a tradition among the German people over the previous 200 years of transforming their landscape, or conquering nature. Germany by the beginning of the war was a quite different place from how it had been just a couple of hundred years earlier, especially its lowlands. At the beginning of the eighteenth century, it was a wild place, full of low-lying marsh and fenland. Travellers likened it to Amazonia and the New World. Wild animals like boar and wolves roamed, while the Rhine, Germany's greatest river, snaked its way north through hundreds of separate channels, which were divided by endless little islands, sandbars and gravel banks. Along long stretches of its banks were damp forests, not lush farmland and industry. And because this river was so wild, because its flow of water so unpredictable and its depth so varied, it was for large parts completely impassable.

Yet as Prussia's strength grew, so did its prosperity, and with it the increased need for mobility. What a difference it would make if this wild part of north-west Germany could be tamed. One German engineer, Johann Tulla, believed he could, and so began one of the most extraordinary engineering feats the world had ever known. Quite simply, Tulla straightened the Upper Rhine. Not only was it an extraordinary achievement, it was also one of the world's biggest engineering feats. By carving out new channels and damming up the twists and turns, the flow of water improved. The Rhine took on a completely different appearance, and was now shorter by some fifty miles. Moreover, the water now flowed deep enough and fast enough to allow large-scale navigation. The Rhine, by the early part of the nineteenth century, had become one of Germany's most important arteries.

Now that the Rhine was properly navigable, the population along it rose rapidly. Further to the east, in the Ruhr area, coal seams were developed and through the nineteenth century the area grew with industrial plants springing up all around it. More and more water was needed: for the rising population to drink, and for the rapidly increasing industrial processes. Canals were built, and so too were railways, providing a network that enabled all this industry to be spread around the country.

Suddenly, there was no longer enough water consistently feeding into these rapidly growing areas. The natural cycle of water flow running into the Möhne, Wupper, Ruhr and Eder followed an irregular pattern – heavier in winter, less so in summer, but one that had become more extreme through deforestation and cultivation in their upper reaches.

Dams were the solution, although, as the Germans were discovering, by upsetting one of nature's rhythms, they were being forced to alter another. Constructing large dams had begun in Alsace as a means of building up a mass of water from the inconsistent flow of rivers running down from the Vosges Mountains. These dams, comparatively small, were so effective they paved the way for the golden decade of dam building in Germany. In the 1890s, dams were the solution to the booming industrial region of Rhineland-Westphalia.

The first large dam was the Eschbach, which provided drinking water for the growing population of Remsheid. This had been designed by the greatest of German dam builders, Otto Intze, and his stamp would be all over many of those that followed: by his death in 1904, he had built no fewer than twelve.

A regular flow of water may have been needed in the rapidly growing area of Rhineland-Westphalia, but it was even more essential a little further north in the Ruhr Valley. The annual flow of water into the Ruhr was heavy, but deforestation in the Sauerland, the mountainous region east of the Ruhr, had intensified the extremes of seasonal variation. These were also exacerbated enormously by the huge amounts of water being pumped from the lower reaches. Water was needed for drinking, not just by the populations of towns on the Ruhr, but by those on the now polluted Wupper, Emscher and Lipper. Water was also needed by the mining, metallurgical and chemical industries, for cooling, cleaning and processing. The Krupps Works in Essen, alone, were responsible for using vast amounts of water both for their manufacturing processes and for their hordes of thirsty workers.

By the turn of the century, the Ruhr Valley was in crisis. In high summer, water levels were so low, it was possible to walk across the river without getting barely wet at all. Dams were clearly the only solution. Intze built two across a couple of small tributaries, but it was not enough. After long arguments about whose responsibility it was to resolve the crisis – after all, building dams was not cheap – the Ruhr Valley Reservoirs Associaton, or *Ruhrtalsperrenverein* – was formed in 1899. This collection of interested parties collectively funded the programme of dam building that now hurriedly got under way. Seven were built by 1906 – all by Intze – but then came a move to build substantially larger dams. The first was the Lister, which, by 1912, when it opened, had a capacity of 22 million cubic metres.

Its supremacy lasted just a year, for in 1913 a new, even bigger dam, designed by Intze's star pupil, Ernst Link, was opened. It held a staggering 130 million cubic metres of water – more than the combined capacity of all of the dams built previously in the Ruhr and Wupper region. This vast edifice was the Möhne Dam.

But the Möhne was also about to be eclipsed. Forty-five miles to the south-east, an even taller, though not wider, dam was being built across the River Eder, one that would have the capacity to hold a mind-boggling 200 million cubic metres of water, ten times the amount of the Lister, which when it had been inaugurated had been the largest of its kind. The Eder Dam, when it was completed in that fateful month of August 1914, was the largest dam in Europe. Its waters stretched for seventeen miles, covering a lush, fertile valley where villages and many farmsteads had once stood. Its construction was considered such a profoundly incredible achievement, the Kaiser and his wife had been due to attend its inauguration. That had been planned for 15 August 1914. War had scuppered that plan, but during its construction, the Kaiser had visited the rapidly growing dam wall, as had his daughter, Princess Victoria.

It was no wonder these structures attracted so much attention. They personified the German conquest of nature and were symbols of German identity. Every educated person in the land knew of the Eder and the Möhne dams, as familiar as the Empire State Building became to Americans. They symbolized the emergence of a great and unified power. The *Book of Famous Engineers* was a popular book aimed as much at a youth market of aspiring young Germans as anyone, and contained a whole chapter on dam builders. Men like Otto Intze were household names in Germany, held as champions of a bright new dawn and an age of technological wonder. On no fewer than three occasions he gave private lectures to the Kaiser, who was, like most of his subjects, fascinated by technological innovations and developments.

Another popular, post-First World War tome was *In the*

Wonderland of Technology: Masterpieces and New Achievements That Our Youth Should Know. And most of them did: radios, Zeppelins, Mercedes-Benz motor cars and the Eder and Möhne dams were all written about, feats from Germany's proud era of technology.

The large lakes behind the dams became huge tourist attractions. Tens of thousands of visitors travelled to the Möhne, Eder and other dams every year. Hikers walked around the shores, anglers fished, sailors sailed, or rowed on pleasure dinghies, or took steamer trips. Others just stood at the foot of the vast walls of granite and masonry and marvelled at the wonder of such enormous constructions – constructions that looked so solid, so thick. So impregnable.

On 18 February, the day that Harris was furiously writing to Portal to try and prevent any more talk of Upkeep, the Reich Propaganda Minister and Gauleiter of Berlin, Josef Goebbels, delivered a speech at the Sportpalast in the German capital. It was packed with some 15,000 Berliners, including party officials, Red Cross workers, soldiers home on leave and ordinary civilians. It was a ticketed event, although Goebbels had made sure there was plenty of canned applause linked up to the speakers around the arena. Copies of his speech had already been given to newspapers, and it was to be broadcast live as well, blaring from the many hundreds of thousands of radios that still filled the Reich, both in homes and in public places.

The speech included ten rhetorical questions. 'The English claim that the German people have lost their trust in the Führer,' he said. 'Are you determined to follow the Führer through thick and thin and shoulder even the heaviest burden?' The answer was a massed cry of 'Yes! Führer command, we obey!' As the crammed audience in the Sportpalast was further whipped up into near-hysteria, he asked the last of his questions. 'Do you want total war? Do you want war more total, if need be, and more radical than we can even begin to conceive of today?' For anyone listening on the radio – and millions were – the answer to this final question was so loud it nearly burst the speakers.

He had chosen to make this speech at a moment of crisis. The surrender at Stalingrad had stunned both the Nazi leadership and Germany as a whole. Many who had already sensed that the tide had turned against them had become convinced this was now the case. The speech was supposed to rally Berliners and the German people, and to shore up ailing support for Hitler, and certainly agents of the Sicherheitsdient (or SD – the secret police) primed to eavesdrop at railway stations, cafés and other public places reported back that the speech had been very well received. However, what Goebbels had really got from his hysterical audience was tacit support for the continuation of war – total war, war that promised only ever greater levels of destruction.

With the fall of Stalingrad and the surrender of a quarter of a million men, the Wehrmacht had been pushed back yet further. Kursk and Kharkov, two more key cities, had fallen; then, in March, Kharkov was retaken and for the time being the Eastern Front seemed to have stabilized. That was something, but the same could not be said for North Africa. Hitler had poured more and more troops, tanks, guns and aircraft into Tunisia, but the noose was closing around them as two Allied armies caught the Axis forces from south and west. Complete defeat in North Africa was now a matter of when, not if, and with it would come the inevitable loss of another huge amount of German and Italian troops and vital war materiel. Although the Eastern Front had stabilized, Hitler had insisted on his generals launching a major counter-attack. This was due for May.

Hitler blamed Göring and the Luftwaffe above all for the failures, whether it be their inability to destroy the RAF in 1940, their inability to save Stalingrad, or their inability to defend the Reich from the aerial pirates that came over almost daily. But the Luftwaffe was as stretched as other parts of the Wehrmacht, needed in too many places at once, aircraft production unable to keep up with demand and not enough new pilots and crews being trained. Out at sea, the U-boats had been unable to stem the flow of Allied shipping across the Atlantic. A new-generation U-boat force had been authorized, but the tide was inexorably turning there too.

The intensified air assault by the RAF was also taking its toll.

The Nazi leadership – Hitler included – took assaults on the capital as a personal insult. The attack on Nuremberg on the night of 8 March – the second within a fortnight – had flung Hitler into renewed depression. Six hundred buildings had been destroyed and a further 1,400 damaged, including the M.A.N. and Siemens factories. But more than that, Nuremberg had been the place where the Nazis had held their spectacular rallies back in the 1930s. It was an ancient city and an iconic place for the Führer. The following night, Munich, the birthplace of the Nazis and their former head-quarters, was hit again. Another 291 buildings had been completely destroyed, 660 severely damaged, 2,134 partially damaged. The BMW aero engine plant was so badly hit, it was out of action for six weeks.

In the Ruhr, the piles of rubble and the death toll were also mounting. In Essen, 500 houses were completely destroyed on the night of 12 March when the city was targeted once more. The Krupps factory was hit again. It was said that soldiers home on leave in these cities could not wait to get back to the front. There were now an incredible 10,000 anti-aircraft guns in the Reich trained towards the skies. 'The same guns could have well been employed in Russia against tanks and other ground targets,' noted Albert Speer, the Reich's Armaments Minister. 'Had it not been for this new front, the air front over Germany, our defensive strength against tanks would have been about doubled, as far as equipment was concerned. Moreover, the anti-aircraft force tied down hundreds of thousands of young soldiers.' When Germany had gone to war, both Hitler and his war leaders had been as one in insisting they should not find themselves fighting on more than one front – it was what had contributed to defeat in the First World War, and yet when they had been unable to defeat Britain in 1940, Hitler, the Führer, the Commander-in-Chief of all German forces, had decided to turn on Russia sooner than he had originally intended. The defeat of France in May and June 1940 had shown him that a great power could be subdued quickly by a lightning strike of immense force. It could work against the Soviet Union too. Then he would turn back and finish off Britain.

That was the plan, except that it had not worked. The invasion of Russia in June 1941 had failed – by a whisker, admittedly – but now he faced war on three fronts: against Russia in the East, against Britain *and* America in North Africa, and against the RAF and now the USAAF over the skies of the Reich. As Speer pointed out, a third of the optical industry was now busy producing gunsights for the flak batteries, while half the electronics industry in the entire Reich was occupied producing radar and other communications net-works for defence against bombing. Because of this front over the sky, the Wehrmacht was, for the first time since the start of the war, falling behind the Western Allies in terms of modern equipment for frontline troops. When Harris had called his intensified air offensive a 'battle' he had been quite entitled to do so as far as Speer and other leading Nazis were concerned.

At the Great Dams, however, the war had seemed more distant. The young men of the surrounding towns and villages had, of course, been sent away to war, but there had been no rain of steel. At the Möhne, the gunners guarding the dam had heard the distant thunder of bombs and guns as Essen, fifty miles away, and Dortmund, just thirty, had been hit, but they had barely seen any aircraft overheard at all, and of those they had, most had been Luftwaffe.

In early April 1943, the heavy flak guns and barrage balloons that defended the dam were removed – the need was greater else-where. Leutnant Jörg Widmann, the commander of the dam's battery, was appalled, but with the assault on the Ruhr currently being carried out by the RAF, heavy defence at the Möhne Dam had seemed a waste of resources. The single-barrelled Flak 38s, 20mm light anti-aircraft guns, on both towers, and the three further flak emplacements on the field below the dam to the north-west remained, as did the twin torpedo nets, vast blankets of netted iron that stretched across its width and were submerged in the water to its front. That, it was quite reasonably believed, would protect it well enough, while the main structure of the dam was so thick, so solid, there was no Allied bomb that could destroy it. The dam wall was camouflaged too. Rows of fake fir trees had been placed in the hope of making it look like a spit of land extending from the Arnsberg forest to the south of the Möhne.

Leutnant Widmann, however, was under no illusion about the

importance of his battery of light flak. 'Listen boys,' he told his men, 'you really have no idea at all of your responsibility and exactly what depends on the Möhne Dam. It supplies all the factories in the Ruhrgebiet.'

Unteroffizier Karl Schütte was not quite so alarmed about this downgrading of defences. A 23-year-old Luftwaffe NCO, he was a local boy and the son of a farmer. Back in 1940 and 1941, he had been among those Luftwaffe anti-aircraft units posted close to the Channel coast awaiting the invasion of Britain. When the invasion had been called off for good, he had been pulled back and had eventually been given command of the Flak 38 on the North Tower. In some ways, he regretted being so out of the action, but was sensible enough to realize that in all other respects he had fallen on his feet. The posting to the Möhne was a cushy number, known by the boys as the 'Flak Sanatorium'. The surroundings were very pleasant, there was almost nothing to do except clean the guns and play cards, and compared with some units discipline was reason-ably relaxed. The men had pretty good digs, too – they even had a sauna – and because they were surrounded by farmland, they usually managed to get their hands on more fresh food than most Germans. Certainly, it beat the normal Wehrmacht rations, which were universally considered to be both revolting and insufficient. Although it was pretty boring most of the time, Schütte had the good sense to realize it was one of the best postings any man in the Wehrmacht could hope to be given.

The Möhne lay in the north-west corner of the Sauerland, just as the hills began to soften. Further south and east lay the heart of this part of Westphalia, a beautiful area of green, rolling hills, and before the war a haven for outdoor pursuits, not least for those from the great cities of the Ruhr, eager to escape the industrial smog and effluence to fresher, cleaner country air. Among the hills and lush, gentle valleys, people would come to hike and camp and, in winter, even ski on some of the larger hills around the little towns of Sondern and Willingen.

Forty-five miles from the Möhne as the crow flies, in the south-east of the Sauerland, lay the snaking Edersee, some sixteen miles in length, and once a peaceful rural valley, but now a vast reservoir.

Near the great dam, the lake bulged before curling south towards the dam itself. Above, to the north, high on a spur overlooking the lake, stood the small country town of Waldeck, and next to it, on a promontory, the Schloss Waldeck, with its high, thick stone walls and grey slate roofs and towers. The old castle seemed to stand sentinel over the dam below. Down on the water, the dam was further protected by a curling spit that stretched out into the lake, so that anyone standing on the dam wall could barely see more than a mile of the long winding reservoir behind. Ahead of the dam, directly beyond, lay another curving ridge of high ground. Trees – forest, in fact – surrounded the reservoir, climbing from the water's edge to the top of the hills around. No wonder the Germans had left the dam free of anti-aircraft defences; the terrain provided all the protection it could possibly need.

The locals were proud of their dam, and understandably so. Everyone knew that the Kaiser had been to visit. In the little village of Hemfurth, just to the south of the dam, there was even a little track that led to an outcrop in the trees where Kaiser Wilhelm had once stood and watched the construction of the dam. For a quiet corner of Westphalia, that was something. People still spoke of it thirty years later.

'The Kaiser was expected to come to the inauguration,' says Karl Schäfer, then a sixteen-year-old schoolboy living in the village of Giflitz, a few miles downstream from the dam. 'But then war broke out.' Now the Eder Dam was in the middle of its second major war, not that the war had reached it either back then or now. A set of torpedo nets had been put in, but that was all. In the villages around about, the young men had inevitably been sent off to war, but this was a part of Germany that had remained far less touched by the conflict than most. Occasionally, the air raid sirens went off, and, even more occasionally, they might hear the faint drone of aircraft in the distance, but Karl Schäfer barely ever saw one. 'They were flying to Kassel,' he says. 'They didn't want anything here.'

But Schäfer was mistaken. The Allied bombers may have been uninterested, but not all British aircraft were. Flying over the dams had been the high-altitude Spitfires of 542 Squadron, based at RAF

Benson in Oxfordshire. These were mostly Mk IXs, left bare of any machine guns or cannons, and armed only with either 20- or 36-inch focal length cameras capable of 500 prints. Without the guns, the wings could be filled with an extra 215 gallons of fuel, allowing them to fly deep into the Reich, photographing potential targets, the results of bombing, troop movements, new structures – anything, in fact, that might add to the intelligence picture of what was going on inside the Reich. 'Our standard procedure for all high-level flights,' says Frank 'Gerry' Fray, a flight lieutenant in 542 Squadron, 'consisted of the take-off and climb to operational height, just below the contrail level.' This meant above 30,000 feet. The aperture was set by the groundcrew before take-off, depending on weather forecasts and the time expected over the target. It was essential to allow an overlap, so the interval between shots was set by the pilot when nearing the target and based on estimated ground speed over the target area. The idea was to obtain a 60 per cent overlap.

Fray's first photo recce for 542 Squadron had been back in July the previous year, but since February he and his colleagues had been flying over the German dams, taking pictures, and were back again on 4 and 5 April. Once back at Benson, the photographs were then sent to the Central Interpretation Unit at RAF Medmenham in Buckinghamshire, for detailed and careful analysis. Water levels, the removal of guns from the Möhne, the strange conical pretend fir trees, and the singular lack of defences at either the Eder or Sorpe had all been minutely analysed. Locals like Karl Schäfer or gunners like Karl Schütte may have felt as though the war was ignoring them. But it was not – at least, not as far as the RAF was concerned.

15

Low Level

THURSDAY, 1 APRIL 1943. This day, another new squadron came into being: attached to Coastal Command and equipped with Mosquitoes, 618 Squadron was formed at RAF Skitten, a satellite airfield of RAF Wick, in the far north-east of Scotland – as close, in fact, as a Coastal Command base could feasibly get to Norway, where most of Germany's remaining capital ships lay anchored, and where they made nuisances of themselves, threatening Arctic convoys and typing up Royal Navy ships keeping watch on them.

The previous summer, when the Admiralty had first shown interest in Highball, Admiral Renouf had immediately begun thinking about the great German battleship *Tirpitz*, which at the time had been based near Narvik, and at the end of February had been at Trondheim, even further south on Norway's western coast. At Trondheim, the great ship was within Mosquito range. Tantalizingly, just a couple of weeks earlier, *Tirpitz* had been joined by the only other German battleship, the *Scharnhorst*, as well as the heavy cruiser *Lützow* and a number of German destroyers; suddenly, the bulk of the Kriegsmarine's surviving surface ships were all together, and ripe for the plucking. But to the Admiralty's immense frustration, no sooner had the *Scharnhorst* and *Lützow* joined the *Tirpitz* than they sailed further north and were now skulking in the Altafjord, high in Norway's Arctic Circle. From there, they had attacked the British weather station and refuelling base at Spitzbergen, and although Arctic convoys had, for the time being at any rate, ceased, the German ships remained an irritating threat that tied down a number of British vessels which could have been used elsewhere.

Narvik had been within range, just, for the Mosquitoes, but Altafjord was not – or rather, it was, but only as a one-way ticket. This was the deep frustration for Renouf and the Admiralty planners who remained overseers of the entire operation. On the face of it, an operation against enemy shipping using Highball had seemed a considerably more straightforward exercise than one using Upkeep deep into the Reich, yet as the new Mosquito squadron was formed, the conundrum of how to actually get to the *Tirpitz* and others and then safely fly away again had not been solved. There was talk of using Russian airfields as staging posts, but nothing had been decided. There were other difficulties too. Because of the dark background of the surrounding mountains, it would be impossible to see the targets clearly enough at night, even with a full moon. Therefore, the attack would have to be in daylight, at low level, when the attacking Mosquitoes could expect the full weight of the ships' anti-aircraft firepower. To make matters worse, at low level and that far north, the Mosquitoes would find themselves beyond radar reach. Navigation would be difficult. In fact, even at the end of February, it was beginning to look like a suicide mission.

After Upkeep had been given the greenlight on 26 February, the Air Staff had moved swiftly to ensure Upkeep took precedence, but however hard this may have been on Renouf and his colleagues who had championed the bouncing bomb way before the Air Ministry, it was the right decision. Even when the *Tirpitz* had been at Trondheim, it was clear that far from being the easier operation to mount, SERVANT now looked like being considerably more difficult than a raid on the German dams – and even that still looked like a very long shot indeed. The problem was that if the *Tirpitz* attack went first and failed, then the Germans would almost certainly take rapid steps to improve the defences around the dams.

Since then, Renouf had fought the Admiralty's corner, with the First Sea Lord's blessing and support, and it had been agreed that 'every effort' should be made to launch the two operations simultaneously, although CHASTISE would be launched if SERVANT was ready in May, but not the other way around.

The new squadron was to begin training with as much urgency as 617 Squadron, and Renouf was determined the upcoming trials would be a success, but the clock was ticking for those planning SERVANT every bit as much as it was for those planning an attack on the German dams. If only the *Tirpitz* hadn't sailed so far north . . .

And as March gave way to April, 617 Squadron was now training in earnest, although only just. Wednesday, 31 March, marked the first full day of training for the operation, as Astell's photographic mission had been a reconnaissance flight rather than an official training sortie. This meant the crews now had between six and eight weeks before the live operation. This was not long, particularly since there were currently just ten Lancasters, which needed to be shared by twenty-two crews.

A loosely structured training programme had been devised by Gibson and his two flight commanders. The first week would focus on low-level flying and navigation, the second on flying at 150 feet over still water at night and bombing practice. From the third week, crews would practise the entire operation. By 4 April, twenty-six low-level daylight cross-country flights had been completed and 204 practice bombs had been dropped on a target from a hundred feet at a speed of 240 mph, mostly at floats on the Derwent Reservoir or on posts in the mud at the Wainfleet bombing range on the northern edge of the Wash. Four days later, they had amassed sixty-two cross-country sorties, which had included bombing practice. Most had carried out at least two training flights, some even five. In terms of bombing accuracy, Mick Martin's crew were doing the best with an average error of thirty-four yards, with the novice crew of Geoff Rice coming a surprising second. The two worst, by some margin, were Flight Lieutenant Wilson's crew with an average error from the target of ninety-seven yards, and Sergeant Bill Townsend's crew with ninety-five yards.

They were, however, practising without either an effective altimeter or bombsight. Once these problems were resolved, it would be time for the Squadron as a whole to pay more attention to results.

The idea had been to carry out a number of sorties in formation, but the shortage of aircraft largely prevented this. As had been the case with the Augsburg Raid, it was still felt the squadron would be safest flying in vics of three, but because none of the crews was used to flying in formation, it did need some practice.

That would have to come later. For the time being, crews would set off on their own, on long and very specific sorties. The idea was, as far as possible, to simulate the kind of flying they would be doing on the actual raid, in terms of both height and duration. Navigation was a key element because, flying at a hundred feet, GEE would be unlikely to work. Instead, they would have to depend on map-reading and the more traditional form of navigation, dead reckoning, or DR, as it was known. 'It is very difficult to navigate,' says Sid Hobday, navigator on Les Knight's crew, 'at about sixty to a hundred feet.' Dead reckoning was originally a sailor's art, and had been adapted for aerial navigation. In a nutshell, DR was the method the navigator used to determine his position at any given moment, by calculating the ground speed and the track made good since his last position.

The calculations would all be done beforehand, as well as en route. This was where the Meteorological Officer was so important. The Met Office provided highly detailed weather maps of Britain and Europe, at ground level and a range of altitudes, and on a three- or four-hour basis, which was then in turn fed out to the various RAF Stations and to the Met Officer. Forecast wind speeds could then be fed into the navigator's calculations. At all altitudes there was usually some wind to take into account, so the navigator would have to work out his course in relation to the speed and direction of the wind. Even a heavy Lancaster, flying at 240 mph, would be blown sideways by the wind. This was known as drift. In many ways, the aircraft was rather like a boat crossing a flowing river; the rower would aim at a point along the bank above where he actually wanted to land.

A navigator would make a similar calculation and aim off

accordingly. The direction the aircraft was intending to go was known as the 'heading', while the direction it was actually heading was the 'track'. Only when a wind was dead behind or dead ahead would the track and course be the same, although the air speed would vary depending on whether an aircraft was flying with a head- or tailwind.

Since there was no instrument inside the aircraft which indicated wind speed and direction, the only way wind speed could be calculated once airborne was by dropping flares over the sea and watching for drift, or by taking a fix and recalculating the heading, although that was dependent on successfully finding a new visual fix. Usually, a course would be plotted beforehand in pencil onto a map. A trip around Britain would not be a round loop – rather, it would be plotted as a series of straight lines, the direction changing on a fixed point, such as a town, or lake or other landmark. When the landmark was recognized, then the navigator had achieved a visual 'fix'; a 'fix' referred to the position of the aircraft.

Navigators would always use maps, which in many ways looked rather like ordinary road maps, and more often than not to a scale of 1:500,000. Few villages were marked on these, but all main roads, rivers and railways – obvious landmarks that could be spotted from the air – were. Operating at heights of 18,000 feet or more, as was usually the case, navigators were increasingly expected to do so blind, which was why radar-based navigational aids were so important. If a navigator could not use a visual fix, he would use a radio fix instead, as could be provided by GEE.

This new squadron, however, would, at the heights they were to operate, have to navigate visually, which was why it was essential the raid should be mounted during the moon period in May. The light of the moon would be a considerable help that was not to be underestimated. Even so, navigating accurately at such low heights was extremely difficult even in broad daylight. As those flying on the Augsburg Raid had discovered to their peril, an aircraft only needed to be a few miles off, and the carefully planned route that avoided enemy airfields, flak positions or other defences would be for nothing. It was very difficult to get one's bearings at such a low height, too, because the distance one could see was so reduced –

which was why they needed to train so hard and thoroughly. As Sid Hobday points out, any kind of navigation was hard at that height – even using maps. The countryside passes by quickly and yet one was too low to look very far ahead at all. As well as maps, they did, of course, have compasses, but navigators were also dependent on other members of the crew, especially the bomb-aimer, with his direct view of the ground below and ahead, helping. Johnny Johnson, bomb-aimer with Joe McCarthy's crew, always took a map on those cross-country flights and tried to help the navigator, Don MacLean. 'Don would say, "We should be seeing so and so",' says Johnson, 'and I'd look for it.' If he could see it, he would let MacLean know, otherwise he would try and work out how far away they were and then they would make the necessary adjustment. 'We got around on that sort of basis,' he says. Flying bombers was always a team effort, but already the crews were working more closely together than they had been used to.

David Shannon flew his first cross-country mission on 6 April, a long trip that saw him fly to Sudbury in Suffolk, then back up to Langham in the Midlands, and on to Ripon in North Yorkshire, then back south to Didcot, near Oxford, and then north-east towards Wainfleet, where they practised dropping bombs on the ranges there, carrying out four low passes, and then finally back to Scampton. Two days later, on 8 April, he flew another long trip, criss-crossing over the country, their fixes being Stafford, Lake Vyrnwy in Wales, Caldy Island off the Pembrokeshire Coast, Porthleven, Wells in Somerset, Halstead in Suffolk, Potter Heigham on the Norfolk Broads, and then another bombing practice at Wainfleet. It took five hours, about the length it was reckoned the actual raid would take, but was thoroughly enjoyed by the crew. It was a lovely day, they were in their shirt sleeves rather than dolled up like Michelin men in thick sheepskins, and they were hurtling over Britain at breathtakingly low heights. 'It was really a great sport to fly over the channels in Lincolnshire,' said Shannon, 'to scare the people on the boats and on the banks.'

Most others were finding low-level flying pretty good sport too. 'It was something, all right,' says Grant McDonald, who as tail gunner on Ken Brown's crew had a fine view. 'The ground goes by very, very quickly.'

In this first couple of weeks of training, life began to take on a fairly standard routine. Les Munro tended to get up around eight or even nine in the morning. He had been given his own room, one of the many off the long corridors on both the ground and first floors that lined a wing running off the main part of the Mess. He had a single bed, a desk, a cupboard with hanging space and drawers, and shared a bathroom. Breakfast was in the dining room in the main block, where he would meet up with Jock Rumbles, the only other officer in his crew and his navigator, and perhaps some of the other officers, then head down to Flights. This was a five-minute walk. Munro was in 'B' Flight under Henry Maudslay, who despite his young age had actually been his instructor at the Heavy Conversion Unit at Wigsley. 'Flights' were the Squadron Offices to the front of No. 2 Hangar, although there was a specific flight office. In there, Maudslay had a desk and a phone, and there were a few chairs and lists of crews and training schedules.

At Flights, Munro would learn what he was doing that day – which in those first couple of weeks would be a cross-country flight with some bombing practice at Wainfleet incorporated into the exercise. Both he and his navigator would be given a briefing, then, depending on the allocation of aircraft, he would let the rest of the crew know what they were doing. After that they were left pretty much to get on with it on their own. Munro had little to do with Maudslay or the other pilots, for example, except those he might see in the Mess in the evening or at meals. There were no tactical discussions where pilots or crews semi-formally sat down and shared experiences, thoughts or ideas. 'We discussed the flying socially,' says Munro, 'when you were off duty.' Otherwise the only instructions they were given was the height they were to fly, the route, and that they were to practise some bombing runs too.

There were now a number of standard routes, not dissimilar to those flown by Shannon, but which also involved flying up through the Lake District and to Scotland. For Len Sumpter, Shannon's bomb-aimer, this new type of flying was fascinating. He had completed just thirteen ops before joining the squadron, and these had been carried out at around 20,000 feet. His role had been to drop the bombs and nothing much else. 'But on 617,' he says, 'where you are low level all the time, you have to keep your brain on the job. You couldn't afford to relax; you couldn't afford to think of anything else.' He was very quickly keenly aware that if the pilot did not concentrate at all times, they might easily hit a tree or a pylon.

Trying to warn military and civilian authorities about this sudden rush of low-level flying was Section Officer Fay Gillon. It was, of course, an impossible task. Rather than warning the relevant people about the flying that was due to take place, Gillon found herself repeatedly apologizing after the event.

As a pilot, however, Les Munro was thoroughly enjoying the low flying. 'I took to low flying like a duck,' he says. 'It's an exhilarating experience.' Gibson had told them to fly at treetop height. 'But,' says Munro, 'it wasn't long before most guys were flying below that.' Although both Scampton and the city of Lincoln, four miles to the south, were on a plateau of higher ground, much of Lincolnshire was flat and low. Many of the canals and dykes were built up with embankments that were higher than the surrounding countryside. 'And, you know,' says Munro, 'you could tuck a Lanc down inside these and fly down a canal.' He also enjoyed beating up nearby Metheringham, airman's slang for buzzing over at extreme low level. The airfield, to the east of Lincoln, was under construction, so Munro didn't bother climbing but instead flew over fast and low right over the main runway. Unfortunately, AVM Cochrane, AOC at 5 Group, had been inspecting the work at the time and had been far from amused. Back at Scampton, Munro got a telling-off but nothing more. 'I was told to behave myself,' he says, 'and not do it again.'

Johnny Johnson was also enjoying the thrill of low flying and as bomb-aimer had probably the best seat in the aircraft. Joe McCarthy, like Les Munro, was taking low-level flying to new extremes. Height was hard to judge because the altimeters were simply not accurate enough at those kinds of levels. To ensure they were definitely not flying at more than a hundred feet, he tended to stick below that, somewhere between sixty and eighty feet. Sixty feet was less than twenty metres – the length of a cricket pitch. It was nothing. No height at all.

They would often fly down past Sutton Bridge in the Fens on

their way to the bombing range off Wainfleet, not far to the north. Before they reached the actual bridge itself, a set of power cables crossed over the canal. Just for fun, McCarthy would take the Lancaster even lower and fly under the cables, then pull up over the bridge. 'It was great,' says Johnson, 'it really was.'

On one occasion, they were leaving Wainfleet and flying at not much under a hundred feet, when Johnson, sitting in the nose of the Lancaster, had the shock of his life. Suddenly, a Lancaster thundered past – *underneath*. 'There wasn't an awful lot of room for movement,' says Johnson. 'Joe wasn't very pleased about that.' They suspected the culprit had been Les Munro, although he denied it at the time. So, had it been him flying a thirty-ton Lancaster at less than thirty feet off the deck?

'I can't quite remember,' says Munro, 'but that is not to say it didn't happen.'

Flying under power cables and other Lancasters obviously had its fair share of dangers, as did sticking to Gibson's treetop height guideline. Maudslay came back from one cross-country flight with bits of foliage stuck in the tail-wheel. He wasn't the only one.

But another danger was birds. A number of plovers lived in the large open expanse of grass that was the runway and were often being hit, which could cause damage to the Lancasters as well as curtailing the plovers' lives. On one occasion, a pheasant smashed the Perspex in David Shannon's cockpit. A bird also went through Norm Barlow's windscreen. 'Caused the pilot to lose control for a few seconds,' noted Charlie Williams, Barlow's wireless operator, 'and we hit the top of a tree.' Fortunately, the aircraft was undamaged.

On 6 April, the final crew had arrived – that of Pilot Officer Warner Ottley, just twenty years old, but who had completed a full tour with 207 Squadron. With the kind of 'press on' attitude that Gibson wanted, he was, on paper at any rate, an ideal pilot for the new squadron. He was arriving late, however, but already Gibson and his flight commanders were wondering whether one or two of the pilots were up to scratch. Taking Ottley was thus probably a risk worth taking.

And there were still some individual crew members only just

joining 617 Squadron. These included Charlie Williams, who reached Scampton the following day, Wednesday, 7 April, joining as wireless operator on the Australian Norm Barlow's crew.

Williams had had a frustrating few weeks. Back in January, he had been ill and been stood down from ops until he was recovered. That meant the rest of the crew were several ahead of him and had thus finished their first tour before him. There was no question of Williams leaving the squadron with them; he had to do thirty ops, and that was all there was to it.

First, though, there had been leave – nine days of it, which he had spent partly with his cousins in Reading before he managed to take Bobbie away for a weekend to Blackpool. It was soon over, however, and then he was back at Syerston, as a supernumerary – a spare. This was difficult; flying ops depended on trust and mutual respect, but it was hard to establish these key ingredients without knowing the crew. His first op in this role was to have been to Duisburg, but when the weather turned, they alone were stood down – it was felt the pilot, a freshman, was too inexperienced.

Finally, however, he completed his tour, and with a big one: a raid on Berlin. Again, the pilot had been a new boy, on his first ever raid as skipper. 'But he was quite OK,' wrote Williams, 'and we did not have any trouble at all.' Even so, trips to Berlin were never casual affairs. Intense flak, the constant danger of night fighters, and carnage down below. A great number of fires were raging over the city, thick swirls of black smoke were rising thousands of feet. 'It was a long and very tiring trip,' noted Williams, 'and we did not get to bed until 6am.'

That had been the first tour finished, but Williams had made a decision about his future. His father was seriously ill and he was pining badly for home; he wanted his war service over and done with as soon as possible, so instead of taking a six-month breather as an instructor, decided to begin his second tour right away. With the summer coming, he reckoned he would have it done in three or four months. He was also madly in love with Bobbie and was already thinking she was the girl he would like to marry. With luck, he could take her back to Australia with him.

Williams had not been the only one thinking this way. So too was Norm Barlow, who had been his Flight Commander at 61 Squadron and had also just finished his first tour. He had seen the call asking for volunteers for the new special squadron being formed, and decided to put himself forward. Not all his crew had agreed to come with him, however, and there had been a place for a wireless operator. As fellow officers at Syerston, the two men knew each other well, so when Barlow offered him the opportunity to join his new crew, Williams leapt at the chance; after all, it was far better to see out his second tour with a highly experienced pilot than be lumbered with a freshman.

Yet Williams had not completed his tour at the same time as Barlow so was made to wait before making the transfer to Scampton, finally arriving on 7 April, more than two weeks after some, and a week into the training programme.

Williams might have been granted his wish to start his second tour right away, but that did not mean he was in any way happy to arrive at Scampton. He was now more than forty miles from Bobbie in Nottingham, rather than a dozen, and although he had his own car, fuel was rare, even to an officer in the RAF. Furthermore, the squadron had embarked on an intense training programme that made free time scarce and any leave out of the question. Nor could he explain to her what he was doing – security, as he had been immediately made aware, was extremely tight.

That evening, he wrote to her. He was missing her desperately, her absence made worse by the unfamiliarity of a new crew and new squadron colleagues, and the sparseness of the room he had been allocated along one of the long corridors of the Officers' Mess. 'Things are in a bit of a mess here,' he wrote. 'The Mess is full to overflowing and all I can get is a room for the night with a bed and nothing else in it.'

Meanwhile Gibson was as busy as ever. There were regular trips to St Vincent's, meetings at Scampton, weekly reports to write, letters to write, yet more letters to sign. There were those visits to see Wallis. There were also a number of technical issues that needed resolving, and resolving quickly.

The first related to bomb-aiming. He had been making enquiries, because he now knew after his second visit to see Wallis that the Upkeep would have to be released at a fairly precise distance from the dam, but there was no bombsight in existence within the RAF that would work for an operation of this kind. On 2 April, however, he had been in his office when he suddenly received an unexpected visitor. This was Wing Commander Dann of the MAP, who immediately began telling him about the sighting difficulties on the Möhne and Eder dams, and warned him that a new anti-submarine bombsight would not do either.

Gibson, who had repeatedly stressed to everyone the importance of security, was absolutely horrified to hear Dann talking about the dams so openly.

'How the hell do you know all this?' he snapped.

Dann explained himself. He was, he told Gibson, the Supervisor of Aeronautics at the Aircraft and Armament Experimental Establishment, and had been told about the project specifically so that he could help. He had spoken to no one about it. Gibson began to calm down and to listen to what he had to say. Taking out a piece of paper, Dann began drawing various lines and at first Gibson wasn't sure what he was driving at. But eventually he realized Dann was describing a very simple range-finder. Aerial photographs of the Möhne and Eder had shown there were two towers on each, which proved to be around 600 feet apart. It should be possible, Dann explained, to build a simple triangular device, like a two-pronged fork. The bomb-aimer would look through an eyepiece at one end and on each of the prongs would be a nail. By working out the scales mathematically, it would be possible to make the device to precisely the right scale so that as they approached the dam, when the two nails lined up exactly with the two towers, that would be the exact distance to drop the Upkeep. It was simple, but ingenious. Gibson called in one of his ground personnel and asked him to make one right away. 'Within half an hour,' noted Gibson, 'the instrument section had knocked up the prototype of the bombsight.'

That afternoon he took Dann up to Derwent Reservoir, where there were also two sluice towers. The trial showed the simple wood device worked well, and, having landed back down at Scampton, Dann headed back to London, one problem seemingly solved.

Gibson was delighted and told Bob Hay, the Squadron Bomb Leader, to brief all the bomb-aimers about the device. These wooden, hand-held bombsights were quickly made and handed out, while at Wainfleet poles were rigged up to simulate the towers – not that the crews knew what they represented. They also used the two sluice towers on the Derwent Reservoir for aiming.

Johnny Johnson found the device worked well for him, but not all the crews were happy with it. Len Sumpter, bomb-aimer in David Shannon's crew, found that, when trying it out, he could not keep his arm steady. There was the vibration and movement of the Lancaster, and he had one hand over the bomb-release button, and at the same time was trying to hold the device. He talked it over with Les Knight's bomb-aimer, Edward Johnson, and they worked out an alternative. The Perspex on the vision panel was held in by screws. They realized they could loosen these, tie a bit of string around each screw, then tighten them again. On the Perspex itself, they used a grease pencil to make two marks. They then brought the string back to their eye to make a triangle like the wooden bomb sight. This could be adjusted to exactly the right depth from the target, then when the marks on the Perspex lined up with the flags at Wainfleet, they knew when to release the bombs. 'This worked just as well,' says Len Sumpter. 'And you could lean your arm on the arm rest, and just lie there with this against your eye, without wobbling.'

The second problem relating to bomb-aiming was the thorny issue of how to make sure the Upkeep was dropped at precisely the correct height. Gibson had been worrying about this since his near-death experience on Derwent Reservoir, and knew that unless it could be adequately resolved it would make the operation impossible to carry out successfully. Trailing a wire with a heavy weight on the end had been considered, but proved unworkable. In daylight it was easier to judge height, but at night, with the eyes straining and the lack of light distorting vision, it was impossible. Dinghy Young tried again, but returned every bit as shaken as Gibson had been. 'It's no use,' Young told Gibson. 'I can't see how we're going to do it.'

Young wondered about installing electric altimeters. This was difficult for Gibson; he was aware that such an altimeter would only work over sea, but not in a valley where there were too many hills around to interfere with the mechanism. Gibson, unable to reveal they would not be attacking from the sea, told Young he would try, and left it at that. Instead, he spoke to Satterly again, urging him to somehow, some way, find a solution.

As with the bomb-aiming device, the answer, when it came, was a simple one. It was Benjamin Lockspeiser, the Director of Scientific Research at the MAP, who suggested using two spotlights, which would be set in such a way that when the lights were at 150 feet, they would converge into a figure of eight.

In fact, the idea was nothing new. Harris had used the method when commanding the flying boats of 210 Squadron, and when told by Cochrane that the spotlights were being tested dismissed the idea. It hadn't worked, he told Cochrane, because the spots went through the surface of the water. Since the start of the war, Coastal Command had tried the method again to help them depth-charge U-boats, but once again it had not worked, this time because the water had been too choppy. Lockspeiser, however, thought it might just work on the calm waters of a lake. Tests were immediately carried out at the Royal Aircraft Establishment at Farnborough in Surrey.

Eventually, after a bit of trial and error with the positioning of the two Aldis lamps – the standard lights used on runways – a workable configuration was found: one lamp in the bomb-aimer's camera position and the other in the bomb bay. These would be angled slightly to starboard so that the convergence of the lights could be seen easily through the starboard cockpit blister, a teardrop bubble of Perspex through which the navigator or flight engineer could look down at the ground – or water – below.

Gibson sent Henry Maudslay down to Farnborough with one of the Lancasters, and within twenty-four hours was back again, the two Aldis lamps fitted. At dusk, Gibson watched him take the aircraft up. The Lancaster climbed, banked and turned, and then came hurtling back across the airfield, the two spotlights shining brightly. 'He looked so low in his great aircraft,' noted Gibson, 'that if he turned on to his side one wing would rip along the ground.'

He thought it looked rather frightening, but when Maudslay had landed again, he told Gibson it had been quite easy and suggested the navigator should worry about the height calculations and leave the pilot to concentrate on flying. That was good enough for Gibson, and within days all their aircraft were fitted. Proper night training could now begin in earnest.

With all the other pulls on his time, the one person who was struggling to get enough flying was Gibson himself. This in turn put even more pressure on him and his crew. He had always intended to lead the squadron on the operation itself, but he had an almost entirely new crew and, if they were not careful, would be the least trained. Gibson might have seventy-two bomber missions to his name, but he was no more experienced in low-level night flying than anyone else. He also needed time for his crew to gel.

The only option was to head out later in the day, and practise in the late part of the evening and at night, even though, to begin with, most others were practising navigation and low-level flying by day. It was an added pressure for Gibson and his crew. They would fly up towards the Lake District and on to Scotland, Gibson marvelling at how much open expanse of country there was. And there was, it seemed, an upside to all this evening and night-time flying. 'It's a good thing flying with the Wingco,' Gibson heard Trevor-Roper, his gunner, say. 'It keeps us off the booze.'

On 12 April, Gibson was called away from Scampton once again, this time to see the trials of the Upkeep that were being tested for the first time. These were to take place at Reculver, off the north Kent coast. Barnes Wallis and the team at Vickers had been working flat out, but now had arrived at the moment of truth. Nearly seven weeks after the project had been given the greenlight, and after nearly two whole weeks of special training, those running the project would finally discover whether they had a weapon that could actually work.

16

Trials and Tribulations

MEANWHILE, HARRIS'S BATTLE of the Ruhr continued. In the Messes at Scampton there was some needling from 57 Squadron crews, who were continuing to fly regular ops while those in 617 Squadron seemed to be doing nothing but larking around scaring the wits out of the unsuspecting good folk of Lincolnshire.

Harris was broadly pleased with the way his intensified air offensive was going. Oboe and H2S, while not perfect, were certainly making a huge difference. So too were the Mosquitoes that carried Oboe. Mostly operating between 28,000 and 30,000 feet, they were too high for the enemy flak and too fast to be troubled by German night fighters. As a result, they suffered almost no casualties whatsoever, and were able to do what they were meant to do – fly straight and level over the target and drop their target markers – without much interference.

In between other raids, the Ruhr was certainly receiving a pounding. Many of these cities – such as Essen and Duisburg – had grown up around older medieval centres. Essen was unusual in that the Krupps Works were right in the centre and a specific target, but, that exception aside, Harris was using his force to strike the centres of these towns, where the buildings were more densely built-up and thus more susceptible to attacks with massive amounts of incendiaries – bombs which would ignite on hitting the ground. The idea was that enough of them would then start fires that could develop into a heavy conflagration. The aim was to use a combination of these with much heavier, high-explosive bombs. 'The objective of the campaign,' noted Harris, 'was to reduce production in the industries of the Ruhr at least as much by the indirect effect of damage to services, housing and amenities, as by any direct damage to the factories and railways themselves. At this stage of the war,' he added pointedly, 'there was no alternative method or means of attacking German industry.'

It was also true that, overall, the numbers of Bomber Command casualties was down – from 5.4 per cent in 1942 to 4.2 per cent. Neither of these figures may sound too severe, but accumulatively they were much more so, as the crews were discovering. Those flying Pathfinder Mosquitoes might have been as safe as any flying in the RAF, but those in the bomber streams were certainly not.

In part this was because they were operating at heights well within range of those 10,000 high-velocity anti-aircraft guns now packed along the coast and around the cities below them, and in part because they were not fast enough to escape their hunters in the sky, the Luftwaffe's radar-armed night fighters – aircraft that were equipped with cannons as well as machine guns.

In contrast, British bombers were primarily designed to drop as many bombs as possible. Crew comforts were minimal, and so was crew protection. The fuselage was made of lightweight and thin steel, and the only armour plating was behind the pilot's seat. Worst of all, British bombers were armed only with light machine guns – Browning .303 calibres, which used the same ammunition as a British rifle. The actual bullet – as opposed to the casing and charge that propelled it – was tiny and weighed little more than a gram. Although these had a theoretical range of some 1,500 yards, unless they were fired within about 400 yards, and preferably even less, there was little chance of them causing any serious damage. As early as 1925, it had been claimed that 'a .303 bullet has but little effect on any aeroplane', and this at a time when aircraft were slow and largely made of wood and fabric. This view of the inadequacy of the .303 was absolutely correct and had in no way changed by the outbreak of war. The Lancaster had eight of these machine guns: four in the tail, two in the dorsal turret, halfway along the fuselage, and two in the nose.

The German ploy was to let the pilot be vectored towards a target, fly underneath and then climb up and rake it with a combination of cannons and machine guns. The Messerschmitt 110 night fighter variant, for example, had two 20mm cannons and two 30mm cannons, as well as two machine guns. This was awesome firepower. A 20mm cannon alone could destroy a Lancaster with one carefully aimed shot, but a 30mm was a bigger beast altogether. Cannon shells came in different forms. Some were armour piercing – a pointed multi-layered metal head – while others were high explosive. This meant they would penetrate the target and then explode. They would shatter a Merlin engine or blast huge holes. If they hit the bomb bay before the bombs had been dropped, the effect was even more devastating.

Cannons and .50 calibre machine guns could have been put in the RAF's bombers, but the arguments against them were the extra weight and drag and the difficulty of developing the right turrets in which to mount them. The truth was that those capable of effecting such a change were far too wedded to the need to carry ever-larger payloads. This was a false economy. Had the bombers been able to fly higher – as was planned with the Windsor – and had they been better armed, the casualties would have been lower. Fewer planes lost, and fewer men too. The feeble armament of the Lancasters – and other heavy bombers for that matter – was nothing short of a disgrace.

The bald facts were that less than half of the crews survived their first tour of thirty ops, and only one in five made it through a second of twenty. It was a chilling statistic, and although most men did not know it as such, they were keenly aware that the odds were against them. Some were too young – too optimistic – to believe that it could possibly happen to them. Death was something so incomprehensible. Occasionally, crews would see other aircraft explode mid-air, or plummet downwards in flames, but it was rare to see dead comrades. Instead, back at the airfield, those who had been in the Mess the previous evening suddenly were not there any more. Guy Gibson thought he would not survive, and certainly the odds were massively stacked against him. He was also more directly exposed to death because, as a squadron commander, he had to write so many letters of condolence and had been flying for so long. He'd seen first hand how many crews had failed to return. He'd lost many good friends.

Les Munro was phlegmatic, but not afraid of death. 'I was a fatalist,' he says. 'I accepted that there was a danger I might lose my life, but I knew there was nothing I could do about it. It didn't worry me, the fact that we were flying into danger, risking my life. What will be will be was my attitude.' Nor did he struggle with fear, as many did. In fact, there was only one time when he really felt afraid, and that was during his first operation, a mining raid on the Gironde River in France and, on the face of it, one of the more straightforward bombing missions he had done. As they approached, he could see the hills around and the water below and it looked very dark and ominous. For a moment, he was gripped by fear, but then it passed. After that, he reckoned he was always too busy to worry about being afraid. Johnny Johnson was also a fatalist, but an optimist too. 'I didn't feel afraid,' he says, 'and I never felt I wasn't coming back. I was sure I was going to come back every time.' Grant McDonald, the rear gunner in Ken Brown's crew, was of much the same view. 'I took it in my stride,' he says. A few nerves occasionally, but he was hardly rigid with fear when flying ops. 'If you were getting worried all the time, you shouldn't really have been there.'

Few would deny, however, how physically and mentally draining it was flying bombing missions over the Reich. One minute you were on familiar turf, surrounded by comparative comfort, albeit of a rather basic variety. On the base, there were film shows to watch, games to play, and nearby pubs to visit, dances to go to, and girls to chat up. The next moment, you were airborne, high over enemy territory and subject to a largely random and violent death at any moment.

A first tour typically took four or five months, and by the end of it most crews felt they needed a break. Just a couple of miles from Scampton lay RAF Skellingthorpe, home of 50 Squadron, where Flight Lieutenant Schofield's crew had just finished their first tour of thirty completed operations with what their bomb-aimer, John Fraser, called a 'quiet stooge to Stuttgart'. Schofield, known as 'Pop' – he was over thirty – was, Fraser noted, tired by the end of it. 'He doesn't seem very keen to go back on ops – thinks too much of his wife at home. Too old for a fast life.'

In contrast, Fraser, a twenty-year-old Canadian, had decided, like Charlie Williams, to get going and start his second tour right away without a six-month break instructing, and then get back home. 'After being on "ops",' he wrote, 'instructing would be one of the most binding jobs in the world.' And something being 'binding' in RAF slang was about as damning an insult as could be.

On 15 April, Fraser wrote to his mother and sister back home in understandably contemplative mood. A country boy from the wilds of Vancouver Island off the west coast of Canada, he had initially found Britain a strange and deeply unfamiliar place despite the imperial ties that bound the two countries. 'And so this war still goes on,' he wrote. 'Just a year ago yesterday that I landed on this foreign soil and first heard murmurs of pounds, shillings and pence over shop counters, saw cars driving the wrong side of the road – today these differences plus a hundred other oddities have become quite familiar. One can become accustomed to strange things.'

Fraser had volunteered when war was declared, dreaming of becoming a pilot. However, he had, as a boy, proved a highly able mathematician and even won a scholarship at school. This mathematics prowess had proved his undoing, because as soon as he joined the Air Force, he was promptly whisked off for training as a navigator. He took it well – there were seven men in a heavy-bomber crew, after all, and each played his role. 'The pilot can fly us,' he wrote in one of his letters to his family, 'but I'll get us home.' Ironically, by the time he had joined 50 Squadron in England, he'd been switched to bomb-aimer.

He had still been very young when he reached Britain a year earlier. Although it was a sense of adventure and curiosity as much as anything that had led him to volunteer in the first place, Britain in 1942, in its third year of war, had seemed like a million miles away from the land of freedom and plenty back home. He had grown up hunting and fishing, with plenty of meat on the table and surrounded by woods and sea. In England there were rationing, rules and war weariness. It was a different world, but now there was unmistakable regret to be leaving the squadron and so much that had become familiar to him. 'To leave the squadron now,' he wrote, 'is just like leaving school after grade 12 – we know all the boys – the mess is just like home.'

There was another reason why Fraser was now feeling more at home in England. He too had fallen in love with an English girl. He had met Doris Wilkinson while completing his training at RAF Finningley. She was a secretary living and working in nearby Doncaster and over the course of the winter their romance blossomed, even once he was posted further south to 50 Squadron. Now, his tour finished and about to leave the squadron, he was looking forward to a week of leave. A week spent with Doris. A week in which they were due to be married. They were both still very young, but in wartime, there was no time like the present . . .

John Fraser, of course, was completely unaware of the frenetic and urgent developments going on at two of Britain's leading air-craft manufacturers. So too were the crews, Gibson excepted, who were now into their second week of training for a mission about which they had no idea, but about which rumour and speculation were rife. Most seemed to think it was an attack on the *Tirpitz*, a battleship which every serviceman and schoolboy in Britain knew about. Other rumours were that the target was U-boat pens. One target not mentioned had been the German dams.

By the second week of April, there were between five and seven weeks left before the operation *had* to take place, and for Barnes Wallis that meant that every hour, every day, counted. Nor was he working purely on Operation CHASTISE. As had been agreed, as far as possible SERVANT was to be given equal billing, and just as he had been busily overseeing the development and production of Upkeep, so he had been doing the same for Highball. Time at the drawing board and working with the Vickers draughtsmen had to be fitted around an endless flurry of telephone conversations, hastily written letters and meetings, more often than not in

London, and which took him away from Weybridge and Burhill. Letters and telephone conversations were flying back and forth between him and Roy Chadwick at A. V. Roe almost every other day; fortunately, their easy co-operation had continued. There were also an increasing number of sub-contractors to·deal with, since the normal Admiralty- or Air Ministry-backed procurement procedures had been discarded in favour of a much faster, direct approach. This in turn caused problems, because it turned the normal accounting procedures on their head. Hew Kilner, the Managing Director at Vickers, must have been tearing his hair out as the careful day-to-day operating procedures of a large armaments business were thrown out in the interest of speed. Then there was Wallis's work on the B.3/42 Windsor, which was still very much going ahead and required his input and expertise. Frankly, it was an aircraft Bomber Command could not get soon enough; the moment Harris had a bomber that could fly above the range of German flak, the appalling attritional losses would be drastically cut. This in turn would make his force considerably more effective.

For now, however, the Windsor had to play second fiddle, and fortunately, for the most part, the enormous focus and energy being given to Upkeep and Highball by Vickers were paying off. A month on from greenlight, however, both projects seemed to be more or less going according to plan as everyone involved worked ceaselessly against the constantly ticking clock. Mosquito modification was going well, although by the beginning of April the Type 464 Lancaster was a week behind schedule. This was because, on 27 March, Wallis had sent Roy Chadwick details of the weight estimates of fittings to the Type 464 being carried out by Vickers, which were heavier than had been anticipated. This had affected Chadwick's calculations about fuel and oil capacity, which therefore had to be reconfigured; every change, every slight tweak, took time to resolve.

Fortunately, this delay did not affect the dates already set for the scale trials of the Upkeep, and by the beginning of April inert Upkeeps and Highballs had reached Vickers' works buildings at Foxwarren for spinning and balancing trials. Wallis was far more confident about the Highball, which was smaller than the prototype bouncing bomb, than the Upkeep, which was considerably bigger. He worried that as the revolutions per minute were increased, so the vast sphere would simply spin out of its caliper arms – the spigots that kept it in place were really quite small compared with the overall size of the bomb. On Saturday, 3 April, the Upkeep was spun from a static rig for the first time. 'Run up to 150 rpm,' noted Wallis in his diary. 'All OK.'

Two days later there were further trials and at higher speeds, but not before Wallis had to examine seizure problems with the Mosquito 'ball-race' followed by urgent work on the B.3/42 Windsor's fabric rails. Not until the afternoon was the Upkeep spun again, this time at 400 rpm for thirty minutes, which again worked with no obvious problems. This was a great relief to Wallis, but 400 rpm, the limit of the static rig, was still some way short of the 500 rpm Wallis had calculated would be necessary on the raid itself. This meant the live trials would begin without the Upkeep having been tested at the correct spinning speed. It could not be helped. The same afternoon, the smaller Highball was spun at 800 rpm, also for half an hour. 'Notified CRD all OK,' noted Wallis. Air Vice-Marshall Linnell, like Harris, was now giving the project his full attention and support, regardless of what he thought of its likely chances of success.

On Wednesday, 7 April, Roy Chadwick arrived at Burhill from A. V. Roe's offices in Manchester and after a conference that morning he and Wallis drove to Farnborough to the Royal Aircraft Establishment. This was the RAF's principal aircraft research centre and where the first Type 464 had flown into the previous day. There were more spinning tests, this time at 320 rpm, 'witnessed by Chadwick', and a further conference the following morning to discuss issues over the hydraulic system in the Type 464. Finally, on Saturday, 10 April, everything was ready for the trials. The Vickers works at Barrow in Cumbria had told Wallis that it had completed its batch of fifty Upkeeps, complete with wooden spherical casings. Test Upkeeps and Highballs had already reached Manston, the airfield on the north Kent coast that would be acting as the base for the trials. In the afternoon, Wallis drove with Mutt Summers to Farnborough and there boarded the waiting Type 464, with its cutaway bomb bay and smooth upper fuselage shorn of a dorsal turret. At four o'clock, the great machine took off.

This was a big moment. During the short trip to Manston, Wallis would have looked down over the patchwork of fields, the villages and towns of England spread out beneath him, as the Lancaster roared towards the north Kent coast. South-east England looks a gentle, sleepy place, from just a few thousand feet. No one who saw the Lancaster thunder overhead would have had the faintest inkling as to where it was heading or why, yet in the fortnight ahead, Wallis would discover whether his predictions about the Upkeep had been right – or wrong. He had been given the most extraordinary, unprecedented, support for this weapon, and by the most senior air officer in the land. Yet theory and reality are different things, which was why trials were so essential. It was all very well running up the spinning Upkeep on the ground, but whether it would work when dropped from a moving Lancaster was anyone's guess. During these live trials, they would discover whether Portal's support had been justified.

Not for the first time, the entire project hung very much in the balance.

Sunday, 11 April 1943. A day of preparation. At 10 a.m., there was a general briefing for all those working on the trials in Hut 28 at RAF Manston. Everyone present had been issued with special security passes; security, it had been stressed yet again, was paramount. It had originally been decreed at the previous Ad Hoc Committee meeting that the Highball trials should go first, then those for the Upkeep, but now that everyone was together with the test Lancaster and Mosquito and the two different types of bomb – or 'store', as the trial bombs were called – it made more sense to run the two more or less together. The range was to be off the coast between Margate and Herne Bay, and just a few miles from Manston. It was a deliberately quiet stretch of the coast, and those watching from the shore would be doing so with gently sloping farmland behind them and little else, although police had sealed off the entire area beforehand. Away to their left lay a small scattering of farmhouses – all that remained of the village of Reculver, once a much bigger community, but which, over the years, had been largely lost to the sea. Overlooking them from a small promontory were the twin towers of the ruined St Mary's church, an emblem of Reculver's more prosperous past and long held as a landmark for sailors.

The Upkeep itself was designed around the steel cylindrical core, sixty inches long and fifty-one inches wide. The flattened side of the mine held the access for the standard naval Mk XIV hydrostatic pistol, which could be easily dropped into place. This was the detonator and, when live, would be inserted and fitted shortly before loading. The hydrostatic pistol being used was designed to withstand impact with water as well as underwater pressure. Crucially, the flattened ends also contained the inner support, or retaining, ring, into which the arms that held the bomb in place would fit. In other words, it would be possible to remove the outer spherical casing without radically altering the cylindrical core. This outer casing was made of wooden staves, held in place by strips of metal bindings, rather like a beer barrel. Wallis believed this outer casing, which gave the bomb its spherical shape, was essential to ensure maximum skipping distance; a sphere ensured less surface area made contact with the water at each bounce and would thus run truer than a cylinder.

The modifications to the Lancaster were reasonably straightforward and required little alteration to its Packard-built Merlin engines or its airframe. The mid-upper – or dorsal – turret was removed, as were the bomb-bay doors, which gave it an odd, slightly ungainly look about its underside, as though a large slice of meat had been cut out from a thick joint. Caliper arms were added – V-shaped metal struts on hinges attached to metal brackets that were fixed to the fuselage sides. At the end of each caliper were two free-turn discs, which slotted into the support rings on the Upkeep. On the right-hand disc was a pulley for the drive belt from the hydraulic motor. Wallis had designed such a motor, but it was then discovered that the Vickers variable speed gear used in S-Class British submarines was very similar so these were used instead. Power came from the hydraulic connection that usually would have operated the bomb-bay doors. The motor speed was controlled by the wireless operator using a valve and rev counter from a motorcycle. An ordinary Type F bomb slip, used normally for a 4,000lb 'Cookie' high-explosive bomb, was used to secure tension on the springs that enabled the release of the caliper arms. For all the enormous work this still required on the part of A. V. Roe and Vickers, the Type 464 was a classic case of making do with butchered pieces of existing equipment. It seemed to work.

In the afternoon, the huge Upkeep was hoisted into the Type 464 Lancaster and spun up using the aircraft's installed rotation gear. No broken calipers, no spinning gear failure. So far, so good.

On Monday, 12 April, Satterly rang up Gibson and told him and his Bomber Leader, Flight Lieutenant Bob Hay, the bomb-aimer on Mick Martin's crew, that they were to head down to Kent to witness the first trials of the weapon they would be carrying on Operation CHASTISE. They drove down, and after a long, 200-mile journey, reached Manston early in the afternoon. There they were told things were not quite ready – Wallis and his team were working on the Highball and Upkeep 'stores' all day, and running further spinning tests in both the Lancaster and the Mosquito. There were problems with the Lancaster's rev counters; adjustments were made.

It was a pleasant, warm, sunny spring day, and for once Gibson had nothing to do. He and Hay took a car and drove around Margate, intrigued by what a popular seaside holiday town looked like during wartime. The hotels were all closed, 'Dreamland' holiday resort had become an army barracks, there were thick tangles of barbed wire all along the beach, and the place was pullulating with soldiers. The fish and chip shops seemed to be just about the only pre-war feature of the town still open, so the two men stuffed themselves and sat in the sunshine and made the most of a few precious undemanding hours.

Later that evening, with finally a brief moment to himself, Wallis wrote to Molly. 'My Own Sweetheart Darling,' he began. 'Just a brief line to tell that I am all alive and well.' He had had great difficulty in finding a room, and like Gibson and Hay had been struck by how deserted the coast seemed, with many of the shops in the town boarded up. Now, however, he was in a simple but more comfortable guest house – a modern 1930s house in a quiet street in Beltinge called the Miramar. 'Ever your adoring husband, Barnes,' he had signed off after just a few lines. The letter was written on a single sheet of paper with details of stationery accounts on the other side, while the envelope was made from a recycled Tate & Lyle sugar packet. On the back he wrote a short ditty:

> Oh Censor! Should thy steely Eye
> Upon this missive chance to pry,
> Then prithee for the Writer weep,
> His feet are COLD; he cannot SLEEP.
> Spokeshave-on-Spurn

*

9 a.m., Tuesday, 13 April. Cloud had moved in the previous evening and still covered the sky that morning, but there was barely a breath of wind. Earlier, two Highballs had been dropped by a 618 Squadron Mosquito, but as Gibson and Hay now arrived at the ruin of St Mary's church, the base camp for the trials, they looked out onto becalmed sea with hardly a ripple on the water. It was cold, and Gibson and Hay, in their blue RAF greatcoats, turned their collars up, but the conditions were ideal, the tide just right. There were a number of people there – Barnes Wallis, Lockspeiser and Air Vice-Marshal Linnell, among others – while behind them, the distant figures of policemen could be seen patrolling the barbed-wire perimeter. Two cameras were set up ready – a high-speed theodolite camera on the shingly shore between the dark wooden groynes, and a second on the bluff by the church. The cameramen panned their lenses towards the east, waiting. Out on the sea, two white aiming marker buoys bobbed gently. On the beach, a naval lieutenant waited in his dinghy. An air of expectation hung heavily.

At 0920, the sound of aero engines interrupted the still calm away to their right. A twin-engine Wellington, rather than the Lancaster, was first up, and was now diving down to gain speed, then it levelled to around eighty feet and, at just under 290 mph, dropped its Upkeep.

The observers on the bluff watched the huge ball speed towards the water, turning at 520 rpm. As it hit the water, the wooden outer casing shattered, but the metal cylindrical core – the part of the bomb that would hold the explosive on the live version – continued to spin and bounce. Wallis was pleased.

The Wellington flew on and disappeared and there was then a wait as fragments were retrieved. On the bluff by the church ruins, Gibson and Hay waited, until, at 1108, the Type 464 Lancaster finally hove into view, flown by Squadron Leader 'Shorty' Longbottom, attached to Vickers as one of their test pilots. Gibson heard the four engines, in fine pitch, making a heavy growl across the still morning air. In the cutaway bomb bay, he could see the spinning Upkeep, painted black and white, and looking huge even against the giant aircraft. Gibson watched Longbottom level out and then approach at around 250 feet. Beside him on the bluff, Wallis was crouching on the ground, staring intently. The camera began to whirr, and Gibson put a pair of binoculars to his eyes. Then the mine was released. It seemed to hang in the air, but was slowly falling towards the water. A huge spray of white seawater erupted as it struck, then, through the spume, dark bits of the bomb were flung into the air as the bomb shattered.

Gibson said nothing. He felt bad for Wallis; he knew the vast amount of work that had been put into the mine and, since there was nothing he could say to make the situation better, kept quiet. But Wallis was not as disconsolate as Gibson had thought. The whole point of the trials was to test dropping heights and strength of casing; he had not been expecting to get everything right at the first attempt. At Manston there were a number of practice Upkeeps, and the staff, manpower and equipment to sustain a number of days of trials on both the Upkeep and Highball.

Gibson and Hay followed Wallis and his party back to Manston, where an Upkeep was further strengthened for another drop later that evening. In the meantime, Gibson managed to borrow a Miles Magister – an open-cockpit, two-seater monoplane trainer – from 137 Squadron and, with Hay, took it up to fly over the Reculver range and dropping area.

They had only climbed to around 300 feet and were over

Margate, when the engine cut. 'When an engine stops in a four-engine aircraft,' noted Gibson, 'you do not have to worry much about it – you have always got three others, but when it happens in a single-engine aircraft then the long finger of gravity points towards mother earth.' This was, of course, something of an under-statement. The Magister could stall viciously if the air speed dropped too savagely, in which case it would plummet in a spin. Even so, with a cool head, it was quite possible to glide and crash-land reasonably safely, but along this corner of Kent there were numerous anti-glider obstacles covering the fields to ensure no enemy airborne troops landed. His only option was to try and make the best crash-landing he possibly could, and although he managed to touch down safely in a field, they were unable to avoid the obstacles and rolled the Magister 'into a ball'.

Despite wrecking the plane, both men clambered free without a scratch only to find themselves accosted by a local man who had hurried over to check they were all right.

'I think they teach you young fellows to fly too early,' he told them. A policeman now appeared and took a statement from both of them.

'I'm glad to see our anti-aircraft landing devices work,' he said.

Gibson and Hay stumbled back to Manston, picked up their car, and drove back to Scampton, without waiting for the next trial, planned for that evening. They were lucky to still be alive.

Just after seven o'clock that evening, with the observers and cameras once more assembled on the bluff and shingle shore, the Lancaster flew across the makeshift range at Reculver, from east to west. It was the height, Wallis was convinced, that had been the problem, and this time, he asked the pilot to drop the Upkeep at just fifty feet.

Over the white buoys, the bomb fell towards the sea. Once more, a plume of spray shot into the air and, once again, bits of shattered casing spat into the sky.

But beyond, free of its casing, the cylindrical core sped on, bouncing, skipping across the sea.

17

A Matter of Height and Speed

BACK AT SCAMPTON, there were still arrivals of new crew members, but departures too. Gibson had been worried about one of his crews in particular, and by the end of the first week in April they had been posted back to 57 Squadron – no small humiliation since they were based at Scampton too. In the weekly training report, Flight Lieutenant Humphries, writing in Gibson's absence, had noted tersely, 'Flight Sergeant Lovell, from 57 Squadron, did not come up to the standard necessary for this squadron.' Lovell and crew were replaced by another from 57 Squadron, Sergeant Bill Divall. 'Divall is, of course, behind on his flying,' added Humphries, 'but should catch up by the end of next week.' On the other hand, the new crew, under Warner Ottley, had already caught up with the others, Humphries reported.

A couple of weeks later, a further crew left, that of Flight Sergeant Lancaster. It wasn't Lancaster who was the problem, but his navigator, Flying Officer Cleveland. Since Gibson was away, it must have been reported to him by Dinghy Young that Lancaster's crew were not up to speed with their navigation. This was a shame, because their bomb-aimer, Flight Sergeant Clifford, had been proving the ace among them during bombing practice. However, when Cleveland was sacked, Lancaster strongly objected and said that if he went, the whole crew would follow. Gibson was not one to back down on such a matter. He had repeatedly made it clear just how high the standards were he expected, so Lancaster and his crew left the squadron. Despite their departure, that still left a surplus of one. Twenty Type 464 Lancasters were being prepared, so only twenty would fly the raid.

Despite this surplus, there were still some incomplete crews, even by the third week of April. Another late joiner was John Fraser, who came to 617 Squadron on 21 April. It was true that he had requested to go back on ops right away after his first tour, but that had not meant during his seven days of leave – and especially not when he and Doris had planned to get married.

There was considerable inconsistency over how crews were brought across – most volunteered, but a number seem to have been ordered to do so, such as 'C' Flight from 57 Squadron, and men like John Fraser. In his case it was because he was a bomb-aimer, and Hoppy Hopgood needed a bomb-aimer. Most likely, Whitworth had rung up the Station Commander at neighbouring Skellingthorpe and asked if there were any navigators he might spare. No, would have come the answer, but there's one who has just finished a tour and wants to go back on ops. And so Fraser had been summoned. Immediately. After all, 617 were now more than three weeks into training. As far as Hopgood was concerned, Fraser could not get there quickly enough.

'This was the day,' Fraser wrote to his fiancée, Doris, on his arrival at Scampton, 'the day when a man loses his rights as a citizen and becomes a husband – to obey not the laws of the country, but to serve a lady. Just a simple little telegram with those few words (Return to Unit Immediately) spoiled everything as a dusty footprint on a shiny waxed floor.'

The Australian, Charlie Williams, was also hoping he would soon be getting married. He was thirty-two, and although he had been engaged to a girl back home, in Gwen Parfitt, 'Bobbie' as he called her, he had now become convinced he had found the woman with whom he wanted to spend the rest of his life. On 16 April, a Friday, he had been stood down and had driven to Nottingham with Phil Burgess, the navigator with his crew, for a party. There he had held Bobbie tightly in his arms as he led her around the dance floor, and proposed. It was a huge decision for her, because he meant for her to come back to Australia with him once he had finished his war service. It was the other side of the world, up to six weeks' sailing time away, and Bobbie was an only daughter and close to her parents. Nor did Charlie live in a city – he was an outback boy from northern Queensland.

They had made the most of a rare night together, however. When Charlie finally bade her goodbye, it was well after midnight and Phil was waiting for him in the car, in a 'rather beery state' and almost asleep. By the time they had driven the forty-five-mile trip back to Scampton, it was 1.30 a.m. The following evening, having been on a low-level bombing practice flight earlier that morning for nearly two hours, in warm, sunny conditions, he was back in his room and writing another long letter. The organization of the squadron had still not been entirely ironed out. Williams had been extremely put out by the temporary room he had been given on his arrival, and ten days later he was still there, his bags yet to be properly unpacked, although he had been assured he would be given proper digs of his own in the coming week.

His thoughts, though, were occupied by his proposal. He knew what an enormous step he was asking her to take into the unknown. He had tried to be straight with her, and hoped she would consider very carefully everything he had told her. 'I have not enlarged or boasted about my position at home in any way,' he wrote, 'so you know just how things are with me, and what to expect, you know that I do love you, so it is up to you to weigh up everything and think about it carefully.'

Had Gibson known that some of his men were not getting back from parties until late and thinking more about their sweethearts than the task before them, he would have probably given Williams a stiff talking-to. He had a deserved reputation as a disciplinarian, and did not think twice about making his views very clearly known. As Sid Hobday points out, 'He'd do it in front of the squadron. And that made you feel about two inches high.'

Harry Humphries, the Squadron Adjutant, thought Gibson could be a bit tactless at times and too quick to give a tongue-lashing.

There was a runner at the Squadron Offices called Turner, who ran errands and carried out any number of menial tasks.

'George, I want you,' Gibson called out to him on one occasion just as Turner was leaving the CO's office. Turner continued on his way, so Gibson called out, 'George!' again. Still Turner walked on down the corridor. Suddenly, Gibson sprang out from behind his desk, ran after Turner and, grabbing him by the arm, swung him around. 'You bloody fool,' he shouted. 'When I call you it's an order. I've a damn good mind to put you on a charge. Take this envelope to "A" Flight Commander.'

Gibson was still muttering as he passed back through Humphries' office. A little while later, Turner approached the Adjutant. He was a bit upset about being torn off a strip by the Wingco.

'Well, why didn't you stop when he called you?' Humphries asked him.

'My name isn't George, sir, that's why I didn't stop. I thought the CO was calling somebody else.'

Later, Humphries mentioned this to Gibson, who promptly rang for Turner to come to his office immediately.

'Turner,' said Gibson when the hapless runner appeared, 'I understand your name is not George.'

'No, sir,' said Turner.

Gibson then jumped up and banged the table. 'If I call you George and you have no further intelligence than to think I am talking to a brick wall, then I am sorry for you.' Then in a calmer voice he added, 'Now, in future, George, you are George. Understand, George?'

Les Munro had never even heard of Gibson before he joined 617, so his opinions were not at all influenced by reputation. 'My impression was that he was a typical peacetime officer,' he says, 'that was used to peacetime discipline.' But Munro also found him a hard person to describe. 'I never had occasion to dislike him or anything like that,' he says. 'I didn't have much to do with him at all on the whole.'

This was the difficulty Gibson faced. He wanted to gel his squadron, create a band of brothers that had his very distinct and personal stamp, just like he had in 106 Squadron, but in truth he did not have the time to give his men the attention this required. It took time, even when operating under normal conditions, but there was nothing normal about this operation at all. Precedents were being broken at every turn while the pressures on him to ensure his men could master the alien and extremely difficult skills in a short space of time were enormous, and compounded by the fact that he repeatedly needed to find new methods and new pieces of equipment to help them achieve this. In addition, there was the extra burden of secrecy – that he, and he alone within the squadron, knew what the mission was to be – and the endless trips south for meetings either at Grantham or in London or the Kent coast. There were others helping plan the operation – especially Cochrane and Satterly at 5 Group HQ – but his involvement was paramount. He was the commander, the leader, the man with the practical experience, but because of the secrecy this was not a burden he could readily share with Young and Maudslay, his flight commanders, or with friends from 106 days such as Hopgood and Shannon.

Many of the NCOs never really met him at all. Johnny Johnson spoke to him just once, and that was when Joe McCarthy had brought his crew with him to Gibson's office to demand some leave. 'He seemed to have great difficulty in getting down to talk to people below his rank,' says Johnson. Len Sumpter, David Shannon's bomb-aimer, rather agreed. 'I only spoke to him once or twice,' he says. 'He wasn't a mixer down on the floor, as far as we NCOs were concerned. He had just a little bit of side. He was number one and he knew it.' Grant McDonald barely saw him at all. 'You didn't see much of him,' he says. 'You know, just in the briefings and meetings we had, but other than that, no.'

Gibson's reputation as a disciplinarian had been well-founded at Syerston, but not his unwillingness to talk to non-officers. If it appeared to some that there was a bit of discrimination on his part, that was quite understandable, but in fairness to Gibson such were the pressures on his time, combined with the very short period they had all been together, it was hardly surprising if he seemed a little aloof. With the crews operating in two different flights, and more often than not independently anyway, and with two different Messes for officers and NCOs, it's hard to see how he could possibly have got to know each and every one of the 160 aircrew in his squadron. There simply wasn't the time or opportunity.

On the rare occasions Gibson was actually around to socialize in any way, he did, however, make sure, as he had always done, that he was seen in the Officers' Mess and that he had a few beers with the chaps. Most found him to be easy-going enough and appreciated the fact that although he was the Boss, he was also willing to join in the fun. And never far away, Nigger, his dog, helped him achieve an air of informality – particularly by drinking beer and getting slightly drunk. Everyone thought that a great laugh. Sid Hobday's first impressions were good. He thought Gibson seemed to be the 'life and soul of the party'. There was often a bit of rivalry between pilots and navigators – one flew, the other told the pilot where to go – but on his first night in the Mess Hobday saw Gibson come over to him.

'You're a navigator, are you?' said Gibson, noticing the half-wing and 'N' above his right breast pocket. 'I'll swap jackets with you.' Hobday did so happily. He thought it a nice touch – it showed that he was friendly and approachable. David Shannon, who thought of Gibson as a good friend, thought he got the balance about right. 'He was very strict on duty,' he says, 'but one of the boys off duty, and he managed to carry that off to perfection.'

Meanwhile, the reports from the first Upkeep trials at Reculver had filtered through to both 5 Group and Bomber Command Headquarters. At Grantham, AVM Cochrane could barely contain his despair in a letter to Benjamin Lockspeiser. From what he had heard from Gibson and others, it did not sound at all promising. The operation was probably just a month away and still the weapon did not work. A weapon with a casing that kept shattering on impact seemed very unlikely to destroy the mighty German dams, in which case the diversion of resources and enormous effort currently being put into the operation looked as though it was all for nothing.

'I would be glad if you could find the time to drop me a note giving your views on the chances of having the matter successfully adjusted in time for the target date,' wrote Cochrane. 'A lot depends on this in connection with our training.' He was also concerned to learn that on the trials the Lancaster had been flown with an inert Upkeep that had meant an all-up weight of 55,000lb. This was 8,000lb – or just under four tons – less than the 63,000lb expected on the raid itself. He was also concerned that the range finder suggested by Wing Commander Dann was hardly sufficient, and that the new spotlight altimeter was also unreliable. An entire squadron had been assembled for this project and, with time rapidly slipping away, some of the fundamentals had yet to be worked out. No wonder he was feeling twitchy.

Cochrane received a reply four days later and from Lockspeiser's deputy, W. J. Richards. 'On the point of chances of success in time for target date,' he wrote, 'I think it is impossible to make any definite statement at the moment.' All they could do was carry out the strengthening work and await the next set of trials, although he promised that Wing Commander Dann would be back at Scampton to supervise adjustment of the hand-held range finder. It was hardly a note to inspire much confidence.

Meanwhile, at Bomber Command Headquarters in High Wycombe, the results of the first trials at Reculver had not prompted despair but, rather, withering contempt. Group Captain Nigel Marwood-Elton, Operations Officer at High Wycombe, had produced a memorandum for Sandy Saundby, the Deputy C-in-C, which had then been passed on to Harris. 'From the Lancaster trials,' wrote Marwood-Elton, 'it would appear that very little latitude can be allowed in the height and speed factors at the time of release.' The spotlights, he wrote, apparently ignorant of Harris's earlier dismissive claims about these special altimeters, were being fixed at Scampton, but he suggested that, on the advice of 5 Group, the practical dropping speed should be between 205 and 210 mph. 'This point, together with the great height of the splash,' he suggested, '. . . may considerably limit the tactical use of this weapon.'

Saundby thought this speed limit was nonsense. 'I feel sure,' he added in a footnote for Harris, 'that experienced crews can drop at 250 mph under good moonlight conditions.'

Harris neither agreed nor disagreed on this point. He had accepted that he had no choice but to let preparations for Operation CHASTISE go ahead, but that did not mean he had to like it. 'As I always thought,' he noted in thick ink, 'the weapon is barmy. I will not have aircraft flying about with spotlights on in undefended areas . . . Get some of these lunatics castrated and if possible, locked up.'

Fortunately, it was a footnote to a memo that never reached either the crews still training at Scampton or those working hard to make the Upkeep work. Meanwhile, on the north Kent coast, the trials continued. Although the wooden casing had once again smashed on the Lancaster's second run on 13 April, Wallis had been encouraged rather than downhearted. No one had expected the trials to be perfect from the first run. In fact, when Air Vice-Marshal Bottomley had offered a pass to Portal, he had suggested the CAS not head down to Reculver right away, but take the D/CRD's advice and 'wait a day or two when he hopes to be able to give you a more interesting demonstration'.

The point was that on the first day of trials, the cylinder – the key part of the Upkeep – had continued to bounce and spin across the water. Even so, Wallis still believed he could get the spherical outer casing to work. The spherical shape was also much more aerodynamic than the plain cylinder. What's more, if the sphere wobbled on its axis, it mattered less than it would if it was cylindrical; a cylinder landing at an angle was less likely to bounce effectively and, crucially, in a straight line. This made the spherical casing worth persevering with. At Manston, the trial Upkeeps were therefore strengthened, with more, tighter, metal hoops around the wooden casing, which Wallis hoped would prevent further fragmentation.

The next set of trials were planned for Saturday, and Wallis, having spent the previous afternoon at Foxwarren and then the night at home, drove down to Manston, then on to Reculver for 12.30 p.m. Among those also there to watch were Linnell and Norbert Rowe, the Director of Technical Development at the MAP.

It was a calm enough day, but overcast with low, misty cloud, and at the appointed hour, 12.45 p.m., it was agreed that visibility was not good enough and the trial postponed. Such were the frustrations of trying to perfect a weapon in such a short time-frame. Wallis, however, ever an optimist, decided to make the best of a wasted trip and with Norbert Rowe stripped off and went for a swim in the icy grey waters, later drying themselves with hand-kerchiefs, much to the amusement of the others.

Wallis spent the evening at the Miramar, having a long chat with Professor Taylor, one of the original AAD Committee Members, about the trials so far, which continued until eleven o'clock at night. The following morning, however, the weather had improved once more, and at 11 a.m. Mutt Summers flew the Lancaster over the range and dropped the first Upkeep of the day. This had been varnished, and bounced once and then disappeared, sinking without trace. On the second run, the Upkeep was untreated and, much to Wallis's disappointment, once again smashed. A third run was made at 1.30 p.m., once again with a varnished casing, but yet again it disintegrated, although, as had happened five days earlier, the cylindrical core had sped on, boun-cing some 700 yards – more than a third of a mile. This was probably a big enough distance for a bomb dropped on the German dams. 'Lunch on sandwiches with Taylor,' noted Wallis in his diary, adding that he also paid the Professor's three-shilling travelling expenses; Wallis was always scrupulous where money was concerned.

This was presumably a worthwhile outlay, however, because as a result of his lengthy discussion at the Miramar the previous evening, and subsequent chat over their sandwiches, Wallis was persuaded that the troublesome outer casing should be abandoned. The trials would continue, but the Upkeep had, almost by accident, found its final form.

At Scampton, crews had mastered daytime low-level flying and navigation, but the problem was how to train for night flying. Dinghy Young had pointed out his concerns about night-flying training from the outset, when he and Maudslay had first sat down with Gibson to discuss the training programme. 'You know the difficulties in this country,' he had pointed out, 'there's not much moon.' This was true enough. He had suggested getting some form of synthetic night-flying equipment so that they could train by day. Tinted goggles were not enough, but he had heard that the US Army Air Force had developed such equipment, which involved wearing amber-tinted goggles and covering the Perspex in the Lancaster with blue celluloid. After ringing through to Satterly at 5 Group HQ, Young reported back to Gibson that it would be sent to Scampton as a top priority.

Four Lancasters – two for each flight – were duly kitted out with this American night simulation kit. Those who were struggling more than others tended to use the night simulator Lancasters more; Les Munro and David Shannon, both of whom were progressing well, had just a couple of flights each. David Shannon thought it worked well enough, although he found it quite hairy to begin with, especially taking off before properly used to it. Overall, however, it seemed to be a useful substitute. 'There is little doubt,' wrote Flight Lieutenant Humphries, the Squadron Adjutant, 'that this is the answer to all night map-reading problems.'

He was possibly overstating the case, however. Two aircraft between twenty-one crews was hardly enough. The alternative was to fly at dusk or first light, but it wasn't quite the same as flying in the milky monochrome of a moonlit night.

Fortunately, the weather remained reasonably good, although the full moon was not due until 28 April, so night flying during the moon period was not really possible until after the 20th. The crews, however, could not wait until then, so had to depend on clear starlit nights as far as possible. So it was that by the end of the third week of training Les Munro had managed only two night low-level cross-country training exercises – there were simply not enough aircraft available for him to carry out any more. It was the same for most of the crews. Norm Barlow's crew had carried out a long low-level cross-country flight on 14 April, and another on the night of the 18th, even though the weather was bad and earlier in the after-noon Barlow's wireless operator, Charlie Williams, had not thought there was much chance of them getting up. They did, though, for a long flight of nearly four and a half hours. They did not land until 12.30 a.m., and then, with the debrief and with something to eat and drink afterwards, did not finally get to bed until 2.30 a.m.

The new Type 464s did not arrive in any numbers until 22 April, and in any case would need a number of modifications at Scampton, which took time. Of the ordinary Lancasters, there had only ever been five per flight, and by the third week of training – which coincided with the moon period – were reaching the maximum hours before inspection and major maintenance were due. They were also getting damaged by endless low-flying and bomb practice. Aircraft regularly returned with scrapes and dents and bits of foliage stuck to their undersides, all of which had to be hastily repaired.

Les Munro nearly lost his Lancaster and worse during one of his two night-flying exercises. Flying back south down the North Sea on a moonlit night, they hit hazy conditions. Flying little more than fifty feet off the sea, out of the murk he suddenly saw a naval convoy ahead of him – just a brief outline of ships was visible. Munro yelled at Percy Pigeon, his wireless operator, to fire off the colours of the day, and as they burst, he saw to his horror that, directly ahead of him, barrage balloons were floating above the ships, attached to their decks by cable. Pulling hard on the control column, the Lancaster quickly climbed, and although fearing he was about to shear off the wings on the balloon cables, he somehow managed to hurtle past between both to safety. 'Lady Luck was on my side,' he says. 'There was not a peep out of the ships. We left them with a ghostlike appearance in the conditions of the night.'

Despite this hair-raising experience, he and the other crews had found it comparatively easy to fly at 150 feet at night, and, provided that navigation was from pin-point to pin-point, had had no major difficulty in keeping to their course. Jim Clay, Munro's bomb-aimer, had discovered that obtaining a fix on a feature immediately below them was nigh-on impossible. The trick, he worked out, was to keep maps orientated and to pick out any key features ahead or to the side. Since he had the best view in the aircraft, he would then pass a pin-point, or fix, to Munro and to Jock Rumbles, the navigator, then mark his own map. It was part of the new collaborative method of navigation. The rear gunner – in Munro's crew, Harry Weeks – was expected to play his part too.

By the end of the third week of training, the Squadron Adjutant was reporting that crews were proficient at map-reading at night and could fly at 150 feet over water, even though, once again, there had been a shortage of aircraft rigged up with spotlights. Only half a dozen Lancasters had been set up with these special altimeters – the complete set of twenty were due to arrive by the 24th and be fixed to the aircraft by the 26th – so it had meant even more sharing of aircraft than usual.

The net result was that bombing accuracy remained patchy, to say the least. The average error distance was coming down, to mostly between thirty and fifty yards, but it needed to be better than that. Despite Humphries' optimistic tone to his weekly training report, with under a month to go there was still plenty of work for all the crews to do if they were to reach the kind of flying standard needed for such a difficult and arduous operation.

Meanwhile, tensions were mounting between the Air Ministry and Admiralty. It was becoming increasingly clear that the Admiralty, who had initially backed Wallis's bouncing bomb so whole-heartedly and who were, in many ways, responsible for the current twin operations for which it was being prepared, were singing from a different hymn sheet from their fellow service senior staff. Still championed by Admiral Renouf but with ongoing and highly enthusiastic support from the First Sea Lord and others, there was a clear impression that Highball was far more widely supported by senior officers within the Navy than Upkeep was within the RAF.

Key to this support was the growing scale of their plans for Highball. Whereas the Air Ministry had not thought to look beyond the one mission to try and smash the German dams, the Navy were now thinking that it seemed a waste of a brilliant surprise weapon to use it on just one target. They had already ear-marked thirty Mosquitoes for modification and by the beginning of April had started talking about the possibility of getting even more and launching a separate strike on the Italian fleet in the

Mediterranean at or about the same time as Operation SERVANT against the *Tirpitz* and other German capital ships in Norway. There were, of course, risks with such an ambitious additional operation, but surely it was worth considering? The major stumbling block, as far as the Admiralty was concerned, was the impact this would have on Operation CHASTISE, because, as Admiral Renouf pointed out at an Admiralty meeting about Highball on 4 April, no attack on the Italian fleet could be carried out in the short timeframe allotted without a Mosquito force flying direct to the target via Gibraltar and North Africa. This in turn would dramatically increase the chances of a major security breach, jeopardizing both operations. The best solution would be if CHASTISE could be postponed for about a month. As it was, Operation SERVANT was lagging behind CHASTISE, not least because more modified Mosquitoes were needed than Lancasters and were taking longer to prepare. A month's delay and they could think about carrying out a triple-pronged surprise attack: against the dams, against the *Tirpitz* and against the Italian fleet.

Witness to this meeting was Group Captain Dicken, a planning officer at Headquarters, Coastal Command, who immediately wrote a memo for his boss, AVM Slessor, which was promptly forwarded on to AVM Bottomley at the Air Ministry. Bottomley in turn forwarded it to Portal. 'You will wish to see at once the attached account,' scribbled Bottomley, 'of extraordinary procedure adopted by the Admiralty in regard to the development of Highball aircraft!' Portal wasted no time in getting on to Admiral Pound and getting his agreement to stop all further talk of any attack on the Italian fleet. Portentously, however, there was no further discussion about the Admiralty's wish to postpone CHASTISE. This lay unresolved.

The truth was that although CHASTISE and SERVANT had been given equal billing, those in the Air Ministry believed the attack on the dams was the priority. The *Tirpitz* was a naval prize and did not seem as big a one as the dams. More to the point, the increasingly suicidal nature of such an attack in the Norwegian fjords was deeply off-putting. And the fact remained that although an Admiralty project, it was Coastal Command aircraft – from the

RAF – that would be carrying out the attack. Thus began a careful undermining of the Admiralty plans by the RAF, which was in many ways entirely understandable, but nonetheless rather hard on those within the Admiralty who had supported Wallis's weapon when their counterparts in the Air Ministry had been rather more dismissive.

This had begun with the appointment of Bottomley over Renouf as chair of the Ad Hoc Committee and had continued with his progress report to the Chiefs of Staff Committee at the end of March. The Chiefs of Staff – who admittedly included Admiral Pound – had at that point reserved the right to authorize when and how Highball and Upkeep should be used, but had asked Bottomley three questions: first, what was the maximum number of aircraft that could be equipped with these weapons week by week? Second, by what date would there be enough Mosquitoes to attack the German capital ships in Norway and the Italian fleet in the Mediterranean, and also to carry out a further plan to attack the Graf Zeppelin airship? And third, what might be the loss to other operations caused by these plans? In other words, the question marks were all over the use of Highball, rather than Upkeep.

Replying on 1 April, Bottomley methodically and thoroughly answered each question. At current rates, the thirty Mosquitoes needed for an attack on the German capital ships would not be ready until the end of May, after the last date for an attack on the dams. Another thirty, which would be needed for any additional attack, could possibly be ready by mid-July. This would require the highest priority and would have a detrimental effect on Vickers' output of existing aircraft, as well as de Havilland's normal production of Mosquitoes, and would further set back the production date of the Windsor bomber. Bomber Command, he stated baldly, would have to bear the brunt of these thirty Highball Mosquitoes. 'This would undoubtedly cripple the two Day Bomber Mosquito Squadrons and render them virtually operationally ineffective,' he noted. 'In addition, certain crews would have to be withdrawn from Coastal Command Beaufighter squadrons as was done for the first Highball squadron. This withdrawal of skilled Beaufighter

crews would entail a weakening of Coastal Command squadrons.'
Bottomley could not have made his views any clearer.

On 24 April, Shorty Longbottom flew into Scampton in a
Mosquito. He had come to collect Gibson for an urgent meeting
with Wallis down at Vickers' sheds at Brooklands, so once again the
Squadron CO was away from base for another day. Longbottom
may have been a hugely experienced aviator, but most pilots are not
good passengers and Gibson found weaving through the barrage
balloons at Brooklands quite terrifying. Safely landed, however, he
followed Longbottom to the Vickers red-brick office block where
Wallis, looking rather exhausted, was waiting with Admiral Renouf
and Mutt Summers.

It had been a frustrating few days for Wallis. Having decided on
the cylindrical shape, there had been a further trial on the 21st,
but the cylinder had sunk. Wallis had missed this run, having been
held up with Highball work and a rush of meetings, including one
with Fred Winterbotham. The following day, he had made it to
Reculver and had watched Vickers' test pilot, Richard Handasyde,
drop a further cylinder from 185 feet at 260 mph. It shattered and
sank. 'Failure,' recorded Wallis.

By the time Longbottom arrived at Brooklands at around
3 p.m. on the 24th, Wallis had worked out and plotted a number of
range and time charts. He had begun to have doubts about the
cylinder version and was wondering whether a return to the
spherical Upkeep might not be better. The real issue, though, was
the height and speed at which the Upkeep was dropped, not the
shape.

This he explained to Gibson. The bombs would not break up at
150 feet if travelling very slowly, but at much faster speeds had to
be dropped at forty feet to ensure they did not smash and that
meant the plume of water thrown up was dangerously close to the
Lancaster; on the evening trial on the 13th, when Longbottom had
dropped the Upkeep from fifty feet, one of the elevators on the aircraft had been shattered, making landing back at Manston difficult.

'The best height to suit your aircraft,' Wallis told Gibson, 'is
here – at the 60 feet level at 232 miles an hour.' He accepted that was

very low, very low, which was why he had called him down to urgently discuss it. 'Can you fly at 60 feet above water?' he asked him. 'If you can't, the whole thing will have to be called off.'

Gibson thought for a moment. Sixty feet was nothing in a plane of that size – after all, the wingspan of a Lancaster was more than a hundred feet. Sixty feet was ten men head to toe, not much more. 'At that height,' noted Gibson, 'you would only have to hiccough and you would be in the drink.' And they would be operating at that height at night. *In the dark.* Thirty tons of Lancaster, built to operate at upwards of 10,000 feet, would now be hurtling across the water at nearly 250 mph no higher than a medium-sized tree. But what could he say? No?

Of course he couldn't.

'We will have a crack tonight,' he told Wallis.

18

Scampton and Reculver

GUY GIBSON HAD returned from Brooklands on 24 April and, true to his word, had ensured test flights were carried out without delay with the spotlights altered to converge at sixty feet. First up had been David Maltby, formerly of 97 Squadron along with Les Munro and Joe McCarthy. He managed a dummy run but confessed sixty feet did seem frighteningly low. Next up was Gibson himself, ever the leader. Flying over Uppingham Lake in Northamptonshire, he noticed they were no higher than the trees along the banks of the reservoir. Crucially, though, the spotlights did seem to work. As they were dropping height, Terry Taerum, the navigator, would call, 'Go down, go down', until the spots made their perfect figure of eight, then yell, 'Go up!' with rather more urgency if Gibson fell below that height.

Harris had been concerned that on dead calm water the spots would converge below the surface, but Gibson did not think this was the case. Over the next few days, the rest of the crews practised at this new height, experimenting along the many canals and waterways of Lincolnshire and frightening the wits out of those they flew over. It was, David Shannon thought, quite a major adjustment. 'Flying at sixty feet in daylight or thereabouts,' he says, 'is a very different kettle of fish from flying at sixty feet at night.' Even so, he and his fellow pilots seemed to manage it; at any rate, no one had killed themselves after a few days of flying at this extreme low height. In any case, Gibson was able to ring Wallis and report back that it would, indeed, be possible to drop the bomb at such a height. With this confirmed, a further set of trials could be carried out at Reculver.

As 617 Squadron trained, the rest of Bomber Command continued to fly over Europe, dropping bombs and being blasted and shot out of the sky in return. On the night of 16 April, for example, there had been two targets: the Skoda Works at Pilsen and the Mannheim, between Berlin and the Ruhr. Fifty-four aircraft had been lost – 378 men – a huge number for one night, and the worst night for Bomber Command so far in the war. The attack on Pilsen had not been successful either – an asylum had been hit, not the Skoda factory. Losses such as these reverberated around the entire Command, and not least Scampton, now home to 49 Squadron as well as 57 and 617. 57 Squadron had sent thirteen Lancasters to Pilsen, 49 Squadron seven. Both squadrons had lost two aircraft and crews on the raid. 'What price the last big raid,' wrote Charlie Williams a day later. 'The losses were rather staggering, but I think they must have pranged the place well and truly.' It was also no wonder there were tensions between 617 and 57 Squadron, who had flown on the Pilsen operation. As they continued to fly most nights, the crews of the special squadron appeared to be larking about flying endless low-level training exercises and having a thoroughly good time.

Certainly, despite the urgency of the training programme and the intensity of the flying, crews were well looked after at Scampton. The only one trying to fit too much into twenty-four hours was Gibson. The Sergeants' and Officers' Messes were open most of the time. In the Officers' Mess there was a games room with a billiards table, and a reading room with comfortable chairs, newspapers and magazines. 'The Mess is quite comfortable,' wrote the newly arrived John Fraser, 'four to a table, sugar, milk and butter – one just helps himself – good service too and the grub is passable!' This was better than a lot of people in Britain were getting in the fourth year of the war, but entirely justified considering what the men of Bomber Command were expected to put themselves through. Hobby Hobday used to like a game of snooker and enjoyed his leisure time. He never got bored. Nor did Les Munro, although he was quieter than some and tended to stay on the station rather than head out. 'I was a peculiar bloke,' he admits. 'I was quite happy to stay in the Mess. There was always beer and whisky in the bar, although for two nights at the beginning of April it was banned – two officers had come back late and very much worse for wear.' The banning of drink for two nights was a punishment and warning to them all. 'We have been drinking grapefruit juice,' noted Charlie Williams, 'which is bad for the system.' John Fraser was also happy to stay on base. 'I intend to lead a very quiet life on this station,' he told his mother and sisters, 'and save a little money.' This was partly because he had just come from Skellingthorpe, where he had known everyone on the squadron, to Scampton, where he was very much the new boy once again and lacking bosom pals. The other reason was that although he had missed his wedding, he and Doris now hoped to tie the knot the moment he was next given any leave. He had his future married life to think about now.

Nor were the crews expected to slum it. Charlie Williams may have been taken aback by the barely controlled chaos of a squadron only two weeks old, and put out by the makeshift room he had been given, but on 18 April he was finally given a room of his own, complete with table and chair where he could write letters, and a wooden cupboard which contained a hanging area and drawers. He took great delight in finally unpacking his trunk and hanging up all his clothes properly. And although that night he was out on a long night-training exercise, he was able to sleep until well into the following morning, then had a hot bath, by which time he was feeling quite himself again.

The chaos Williams had witnessed on his arrival had also calmed by the time John Fraser arrived on 21 April. He was quite impressed by what he found at Scampton. He'd been allocated married quarters, with a room to himself, and hot water for a bath if they lit a fire downstairs. About the station, he was pleasantly surprised to see plenty of little gardens, with tulips, wallflowers and daffodils cheering the place up. 'All the lawns neatly mowed,' he noted, 'although the lawn in front of our billet is covered with dandelions – the hedge was trimmed sometime last year – everything else is OK, though.'

In any case, there was plenty for him and Les Munro and others to do on base. There were squash courts and films were shown most nights. Charlie Williams would often watch these to pass away an evening when he could not get to Nottingham to see his fiancée, Bobbie. One evening, he planned to see *The Female Touch*. 'Do you think I might learn something from it?' he wrote to Bobbie. Also laid on were ENSA shows. The Entertainments National Service Association had been set up in 1939 to provide shows and revues for troops and personnel from all three services. While there were some stellar names who had performed with ENSA – such as George Formby, Gracie Fields and Joyce Grenfell to name but three – the shows were more often a bit hit and miss. There was an ENSA concert party at Scampton on 13 April, which Charlie Williams went to, although he was half an hour late. He reckoned he hadn't missed a great deal. 'I did not enjoy it much,' he reported to Bobbie. 'It was very weak.'

There were also opportunities to go into Lincoln, home to one of the finest cathedrals in England and which dominated the landscape round about. With its winding cobbled streets, old stone gateways and numerous historic buildings, it was a lovely old city, although this was, for the most part, lost on the glut of late teenagers and twenty-somethings who filled the many airfields in the area, of which Scampton was just one. Towns were of interest not for their aesthetic values, but for the pubs, cinemas, dances and opportunities to meet girls. Fortunately, Lincoln offered all of these. A favourite haunt was the Saracen's Head at the bottom of the town right by the Clasketgate, while the White Hart Hotel, just beside the cathedral, was more upmarket and considered officers only; it was where John Nettleton, of 44 Squadron, had held his wedding reception. Hobby Hobday used to go with mates into Lincoln a fair amount, to pubs and to dances, as did Len Sumpter, bomb-aimer in Shannon's crew. 'There was a big joke,' says Sumpter, 'that if you went in for a drink at the Saracen's Head at lunchtime, the barmaid would tell you what target you were on that night.' She would have been struggling to predict much for the 617 Squadron boys, however, although it was hard to conceal that some special operation was up, as Lancasters from Scampton continued to roar over at rooftop height.

Johnny Johnson's wife, Gwen, was a WAAF and at the time of their wedding had been a telephone operator at Middle Wallop, down south between Salisbury and Andover. However, she had now been posted to RAF Ingham, just up the road from Scampton, on compassionate grounds, which meant they did get to see something of each other, meeting in Lincoln whenever they could coincide an evening off. The last bus back was around 9 p.m., so Johnny would accompany her and then walk the several miles back to Scampton. 'The things one did for love,' he says.

What Charlie Williams was doing for love was driving all the way to Nottingham whenever he could. Because of the shortage of aircraft and the less clement weather in recent days, he and his crew had been given a day off on 20 April, but fortunately for him they had been stood down the evening before, so he had sped off to see the girl who was occupying so much of his thoughts, booking himself into a hotel. Although Bobbie was in her twenties, the mores of the day made it very difficult for girls to either bring men back to their boarding houses or to spend a night away without causing major embarrassment. In his letters beforehand, Williams had hoped she would be able to stay the night with him, and so she did, no matter what others might think. 'I enjoyed every minute with you,' he wrote to her on his return to Scampton. Nor was it the first time they had spent the night together. Before joining 617, they had gone to Blackpool for a couple of days; he was thinking about it a few days later. 'Wish we were there again now, don't you, darling?' he wrote.

They would, however, soon be man and wife. Bobbie had by now agreed to marry him, although she was understandably worried about her parents, who had not taken the news well. It was understandable; they had not met Charlie and the thought of their only daughter starting a new life on the other side of the world had filled them with despair. 'I am anxious to know how things are at home,' he wrote to her, 'and if the storm has abated.' How the war was changing everyone's lives.

On Wednesday, 28 April, Wallis said goodbye to his three older children and two nephews. The Easter holidays were over; it was a year since he had first dreamed up the bouncing bomb with Elizabeth's, his youngest daughter's, marbles. Farewells over, he drove to Dorking to pick up Admiral Renouf from his house there, then motored on to Manston and Reculver for two days of Highball and Upkeep trials. Wallis was a man who viewed life through a glass half full. He may have been exhausted, juggling more than could be reasonably expected of one man in his fifties, but there was no crisis of confidence. Time was rapidly running out, but it had not run out yet, and he was sure these coming trials would prove the success of both Upkeep and Highball.

Gibson once again made the long trip south, and was there to see Shorty Longbottom drop a cylindrical Upkeep at 9.15 a.m. on Thursday the 29th. 'Ht 60', rpm 500, speed 258 ASI, less about 5mph headwind,' noted Wallis. Bouncing six times, it covered 670 yards, but did veer about thirty feet to the left – this had always been Wallis's concern about the cylinder rather than a sphere.

And it was a problem. As ever, Wallis believed it solvable, but it was now just two weeks until the critical May moon period began, and Upkeep still did not work – not well enough to justify the risk of launching the operation, at any rate. That afternoon, he drove up to London with Renouf and at three o'clock met with Air Commodore McEntegart, Linnell's deputy at the MAP, to report on the progress of both Upkeep and Highball and to discuss what they might do next. Highball was going well – very well – and would continue to perform consistently over the next two days; it was Upkeep that was the concern. On the raid, the bomb needed to bounce in a straight line at ninety degrees to the dam wall if it were to have the best chance of causing a breach. The following day, Upkeep was trialled again, and once more it veered badly. Next day was May Day, although the weather hardly heralded the start of summer. In rough seas, the Upkeep barely ran at all.

That was it for this particular set of trials. Wallis remained bullish that the bomb could work against the dams, but the problems of veering had not gone away. True, the seas had been rougher than anyone would have liked, and the reservoirs before the German dams were not the open sea and would only be attacked in fine, calm weather, but there were still question marks over its performance that had not been put to bed. On Sunday, 2 May, as they watched the last of the Highball trials, McEntegart and Group Captain Wynter-Morgan, the Deputy Director of Armaments at the MAP, agreed there should be one further set of five trials in a few days' time. That would make it just a week before the moon period.

It would be the absolute last chance to get it right.

In Lincolnshire, that Thursday, 29 April, had begun with a crisp frost and had remained cold – the warm, bright spring weather of earlier in the month seemed to have gone for the time being. For 617 Squadron, the first month of training was now over and Gibson was able to report to Cochrane and Satterly that all crews in the squadron were progressing well, with night-time navigation, accurate use of range-finder techniques and low-level night flying over water all mastered. Most crews had now amassed between twenty-five and forty hours of daylight flying – although Vernon Byers and his crew had managed over fifty – and between ten and fifteen hours' night flying. Les Munro had chalked up 35.30 hours daylight and 15.35 night; Joe McCarthy had 36.45 daylight and 12.30 night to his name; Barlow's crew 27.35 and 12.20; David Shannon, 27.10 daylight and 11.20 night. Inevitably, the one pilot nowhere near these figures was Gibson himself. He and his crew had managed less than twenty hours' daylight and four and a half hours of night training. Despite this, he was planning to lead the squadron on the raid.

With a month of training gone, and with the amount of training limited due to the shortage of synthetic night-flying Lancasters, it was decided to give crews forty-eight-hour passes. Credit is due to Gibson for this. Yes, the crews were well looked after, and certainly flying low had been a novelty and a thrill to begin with, but it was also exhausting. Lancasters were designed for altitude flying. The controls were connected to the ailerons, flaps and rudders by chains, rods and cables, which required careful and concentrated handling. It was easy to be buffeted by turbulence and drop ten feet or more, which at extreme low height was a problem. Simply turning such a huge thirty-ton beast was difficult. Normally, an aircraft would bank as it turned – and in so doing tilt, or drop a wing. But with wings that were fifty feet long there was an obvious danger of the one tilting downwards in the turn hitting the ground. Therefore a pilot had to turn very gently. But doing so increased the phenomenon of inertia, in which the force of the aircraft was still wanting to go in its previous direction as the pilot wanted to turn in another. Any turn involved considerable anticipation because the turning arc of a Lancaster was pretty wide, and at low altitude had necessarily to be even wider.

Everyone in the crew had to help and to scan the skies and the countryside around them as they hurtled past. This required concentration – considerable concentration. And concentration is draining, physically and mentally.

Recognizing that his men were getting tired, Gibson now gave his crews a couple of days' leave and a chance to refresh, but on the strict understanding not to breathe a word to anyone about what they were doing. It was a brave move, because it must have been very tempting to just keep going, to push them harder. Time was so short, after all.

John Fraser was glad of this decision, even though he had only been with the squadron a week. Hopgood's entire crew were packed off for forty-eight hours on 28 April and so, the next day, Fraser made the most of the opportunity to finally get married to Doris. 'No longer single – all our love,' he put on a telegram to his mother and sisters on Vancouver Island. 'In a quiet country church last Thursday,' he wrote a few days later, 'the deed was done. Very quiet – no rustle of silk dresses.' He was just twenty years old, his bride nineteen. They had one night together and then he had to return to base. As Johnny Johnson had discovered a month earlier, wartime weddings were often perfunctory affairs – a chance to say the vows, sign the register, raise a couple of glasses, and that was all.

Charlie Williams was given a half-day pass on 1 May. He could hardly wait to see Bobbie, although he was not looking forward to meeting her parents that Saturday and the 'commencement of hostilities'. He reckoned he would be able to stand up to the barrage all right, but was worried about her having to carry on the battle alone after he had gone. 'Never mind, my dear,' he wrote that frosty Thursday before his leave, 'they may see things in a different light when they have met me.'

It did not go well. Bobbie's parents were still dead set against the marriage. He returned to Scampton disconsolate, but then spent his forty-eight-hour leave with her in Nottingham on the following Monday and Tuesday, only to return feeling lonely and depressed. 'I miss you an awful lot,' he wrote, 'and only seem to run on two cylinders.' Both were feeling miserable. Bobbie wished she could run away from her job, from her billet, from her parents; she wished she was closer to Charlie. For his part, he was struggling to focus on the job he had to do; he was sick of having to find dark corners in which to steal a kiss, and of spending an age on the telephone waiting for the exchange to put a line through to her so that he could hear her voice for a few brief moments. And he desperately wanted the war to end so he could stop flying, settle down with her and live the rest of his life. There were moments, too, when feelings of distrust awoke in him. 'Why darling, should I feel deep, dark, depressed?' This was the agony suffered by so many when desperately in love yet forced to be apart, the separation made worse because the world seemed against them. He had no idea when he would next see her, but it was clear that after the round of forty-eight-hour leaves, the training would intensify. No one had said anything about when the operation might be, but it was clear it was likely to be soon. His chances of seeing much – if anything – of Bobbie during the next week or so were slim.

His instincts were right. As April made way for May, the count-down to the raid was now on. There was much, however, still to do.

19

Bottomley Sets the Date

11.30 A.M., WEDNESDAY, 5 May 1943. In Bottomley's office at the Air Ministry in King Charles Street, Whitehall, a meeting had been convened, not of the Ad Hoc Committee, but of those directly involved with Upkeep and Operation CHASTISE. Wallis had been invited, as had Sandy Saundby, Harris's Deputy at Bomber Command, and Cochrane, CO of 5 Group. Also sitting around the table were Air Commodore McEntegart, Deputy CRD at the MAP, Dr Glanville, and Air Commodore Sid Bufton, recently promoted to Director of Bomber Operations. AVM Linnell, who had been CRD throughout the development of Upkeep, was posted overseas the following day as the new Deputy C-in-C of RAF Mediterranean and Middle East.

First on the agenda was security. This remained absolutely paramount, but as work on Upkeep progressed and the prospect of Operation CHASTISE actually taking place seemed more likely, so the concerns about security increased. Wallis, in particular, had become quite edgy about the matter. What had been troubling him was that a couple of years earlier, when he had written his *Note*, he had sent a number of copies to colleagues and interested parties in the United States. Although the *Note* had made no mention of any bouncing bomb – that had lain in the future – it had included detailed diagrams of the Möhne Dam and had outlined the value of an Allied attack on this and other Axis dams. What if this paper had been passed on to a German? It seemed perfectly possible and the idea began to gnaw away at him to such an extent that on 21 April, after meetings with Wynter-Morgan and others, he had called on his friend Fred Winterbotham, his one confidant in British secret intelligence, to discuss his concerns. Winterbotham, who would shortly be heading overseas to North Africa, reassured him that he had nothing to worry about and stressed to Wallis that he was certain the Germans had no knowledge whatsoever of what was afoot. Wallis asked him how long it would take, should someone in America leak news of the operation, for the Germans to act on it. At least one month, Winterbotham told him. Wallis had been placated.

But, soon after, a very real breach of security did take place, albeit in England, and right under the noses of those carrying out the trials in Kent. On 2 May, following the most recent Upkeep trials the day before, one of 617's Armaments Officers, Pilot Officer Watson, returned to Scampton having spent the past three weeks based at Manston working on and observing the development of Upkeep. On his return, he was immediately called for an interview with Gibson and told his CO that within three days of arriving at Manston he had been shown a file which included sectional diagrams of 'certain objectives', a map of the Ruhr, and various other top-secret details about the operation. Watson confessed that he read this file along with Squadron Leader Rose from 618 Squadron.

Gibson was furious. Only two people at Scampton knew the targets – he and Whitworth, the Station Commander. No one else had been told a word. Gibson had even hidden the truth by using a series of white lies to make his men think it was a ship or U-boat pens that were the target, so to discover his Armaments Officer had been put in the know with quite such disregard for the secret was maddening, even though Gibson was satisfied that Watson understood the vital importance of not breathing a word to a soul.

Gibson acted immediately, complaining vociferously to Cochrane, who in turn wrote straight away to HQ, Bomber Command. Sandy Saundby in turn wrote to Bottomley. 'Incidents such as this,' noted Saundby, 'let down those of us who are trying to "play the game" by drastically restricting the number of people in the know and make our precautions look absurd.'

Fortunately, in this case, it seemed that no harm had been done. As it was, the offending file was quickly impounded and both Watson and Flying Officer Rose were told in no uncertain terms that none of the information they had gleaned was to be divulged to anyone under any circumstances – and that was the end of the matter. Even so, if those running Operation CHASTISE were feeling a little twitchy, it was entirely understandable.

The main point of the meeting, however, was to discuss the state of technical readiness and, if so, when it should be mounted. Wallis had been keeping in touch with Dr Glanville, head of the Road Research Laboratory, over water levels in the German dams, which was why he had been invited along. Glanville's team had been continuing their experiments on dams and had discovered that the impulse of the detonating bomb underwater fell off rapidly with a decrease in the level of the water. Glanville explained that the optimum detonation position was thirty feet below the sill of the dam, but with the water level five feet below the sill, there would be a decrease in effectiveness by 5 per cent. If the water was ten feet below the sill, the effectiveness of the blast would then be diminished by 20 per cent. 'While an attack with the level five feet below maximum would probably be sufficient to destroy the dam,' Glanville told them, 'the prospects of success would be most seriously diminished if the level was as much as ten feet below. In the latter case, it would be unlikely that a breach could be effected.'

Clearly, then, the water level of the dams was every bit as critical as Wallis had always claimed. Bottomley wanted confirmation that the hydrostatic pistol fuses being used were accurate, and that they would detonate at precisely thirty feet if that was the level they had been set at; Wallis confirmed that tests showed they were precise within one or two feet. That was good enough.

A further question was whether more than one explosion would be cumulative. Wallis told them this might be the case to a degree, although pointed out – and Glanville agreed – that to what extent was impossible to calculate. In other words, they had to assume that a breach would have to be achieved by just one Upkeep placed at precisely the right point at the right depth, and with the water level no lower than five feet below the sill.

'Must the attack be delivered in the May moon period?' Bottomley now asked. 'In other words, between the 14th and 26th May, or would it be possible to defer it until the June moon period?'

Both Glanville and Wallis stressed that it was impossible to determine what the level would be by June, other than by regularly taking photographs by reconnaissance aircraft. The maximum flow in the River Ruhr was March, and after that, water would begin to be withdrawn from the reservoirs. In the case of the Möhne, direct observation was the only sure guide to its water levels. However, they could expect the lowest water levels between June and October, and once levels began to fall, they would probably do so at the rate of about ten feet per month. Reconnaissance photographs from the first week of April showed the levels were about two feet below the sill in the Möhne. Wallis now requested a further reconnaissance as soon as possible. This was agreed, and it was accepted that should any emergency occur while this was being carried out, pilots should be ordered to bale out rather than try and land, so that the aircraft would crash and be destroyed, and with it any incriminating photo film.

Wallis now reported on the Upkeep trials. It was good that Cochrane was there to hear the latest technical update from the horse's mouth, rather than second hand. And Wallis being Wallis, his report was decidedly more upbeat than that of the more lugubrious Mr Richards at the MAP. The cylinder, he reported, was travelling 400–500 yards at around 220 mph flying speed, which should, he thought, be far enough. The weather had worsened in recent days, but as soon as it improved, there were more trials planned at Reculver, in which he would be experimenting with the rate of revolutions on the Upkeep; Highball trials suggested it might not be necessary to spin the larger bomb at more than 500 rpm after all, which might have an effect on the balancing of the Upkeep – that is, it might be possible to spin the Upkeep at lower revs without having to dynamically balance it. This was because, rather like a car wheel, any slight imbalance would have less effect at lower revolutions than higher. Balancing the weapon was quite an undertaking – and had to be done twice, once without the explosive and fuse in place and then again with, and meant altering the Upkeep to make it spin perfectly without any vibration. At any rate, if these trials were successful, Wallis reckoned his weapon would be ready for use on the night of 14/15 May or very shortly afterwards.

It was now Cochrane's turn to speak. Reporting on the state of training, he asserted the crews were approaching their peak, were keyed up for the job and almost ready to go. As far as he was concerned, he would like them to go as close to 14/15 May as possible. Bottomley agreed – and from the security point of view as well it would be good to get going as soon as feasible.

No one had mentioned the Admiralty's operation, which was still, officially, supposed to be given equal priority. Coastal Command still had 618 Squadron training for its operation every bit as hard as 617 Squadron was training for CHASTISE. Trials on Highball had been more successful to date than those on Upkeep, yet there was no question that anyone around that table was going to let the Navy's operation get in the way of their own. Only then, as the meeting was drawing to an end, did Sandy Saundby raise the matter, pointing out that since Upkeep was now a cylinder and Highball still a sphere, there was less chance of CHASTISE affecting the security around SERVANT. Furthermore, he suggested that any observers of 617's attack would be unlikely to get a clear impression of what the weapon was or quite how it was delivered. In other words, they should stop worrying about Highball and get on with their own project without any concerns about letting down the Navy.

Bottomley now announced his conclusions. The primary objective was the Möhne, codenamed Target 'X'. The aircraft were to be given local VHF radios so that aircraft could be co-ordinated into attack and that, if success was achieved early, they might be easily diverted to the next target, the Eder Dam, to be known as 'Y'. At the same time, he suggested those crews who had not achieved quite the highest standard of bombing accuracy should be sent to attack a third target, 'Z', the Sorpe Dam, which he believed was a more straightforward target to bomb. Wallis agreed that by dropping a number of Upkeeps directly onto the dam wall of the Sorpe, it would offer a good chance of damaging it to such an extent that it would bring about its destruction, although this would come about by seepage through the water-tight wall which formed its central core and would take a little time to develop.

So now there was both a date and a plan: three priority targets to be hit in one operation as close to the night of 14 May as possible.

That was less than ten days away.

Since the start of the new month, Gibson had been trying to catch up on his flying. He flew his whole crew down to Manston on the 1st, then flew a low-level cross-country training mission the following day, practised bombing from sixty feet on the 3rd and flew to Manston again on the 4th, even though there were no trials going on because of poor weather. On the 5th, he flew three times, including a night-time flight to practise using the spotlight altimeters. He had also been to Tempsford, to see Wing Commander Charlie Pickard, who was commanding 161 Squadron. Pickard was known throughout Britain as the star of a propaganda film made in 1941 called *Target for Tonight*, in which he had played the skipper of a fictional Wellington bomber called 'F for Freddie'. Quite apart from his screen role, however, he was also an exceptional bomber pilot and leader of men, and had earned an unprecedented three DSOs, a medal second only to the Victoria Cross. Tempsford was home to the Special Duties squadrons, who were given all kinds of covert roles to perform, not least dropping agents into enemy-occupied territory. They had produced a paper plus maps on low-level navigation in moonlight, including identification of ground features and methods of crossing the coast away from known defended areas. This kind of information, not to say know-how, was obviously vital to Gibson and Satterly as they began detailed planning of the operation. Pickard – and others at Tempsford – were clearly people whose brains were most definitely worth picking.

But as April now turned to May, and with the squadron having amassed over a thousand hours of flying time, it was time to implement the final phase of training. 'The time has now come,' wrote Gibson, 'when this standard of training will have to be co-ordinated into one tactical operation.' With this in mind, he and his flight commanders had begun preparing a simulation of the actual operation, which would include a long low-level cross-country route, plus a stretch over the sea, and a lake to stand in for the Möhnesee. This was the Eyebrook Reservoir, just south of Uppingham in Northamptonshire. A further reservoir, the Abberton near Colchester, was to simulate the Eder Dam, while the Derwent Reservoir would also continue to be used. It was an odd decision, to say the least, because around Colchester it was even flatter than it was in Northamptonshire, while in the Peak District, the hills far more closely resembled the topography around the Eder.

At any rate, final training was being interrupted by a succession of VIP visits to Scampton. On the very same day that critical decisions were being made about the timing and targets for CHASTISE at the Air Ministry in Whitehall, 617 Squadron was being visited by the Marshal of the Royal Air Force, Lord Trenchard, known universally as 'Boom'. Trenchard had founded the RAF in 1918 and, although long retired, remained a figure of influence and very much the grand old man of the RAF. He was also very much a bomber man, and thoroughly approved of Harris and what he was trying to do with his area-bombing campaign. Apart from Churchill and the Royal Family, there could be no greater VIP visiting Scampton, so despite the sudden proximity of the mission and despite the need to keep training, this had to be put on hold while Trenchard paid his visit. Nonetheless, Charlie Williams, for one, was quite impressed, not least by the four rows of medal ribbons on his chest. 'He spoke to us for about fifteen minutes and was very interesting,' noted Williams, 'and gave us the usual "pat on the back".' The following day, it was Harris's turn. This was indeed an honour, because the C-in-C was not known for getting out and about and visiting his men, and it was even more significant considering the considerable reservations he still held about the entire project.

With the inspections over and Harris on his way, Gibson held a training conference with his senior pilots and the Engineer Officer, Flight Lieutenant Capel, known as 'Capable', and Flight Lieutenant Watson, the Armament Officer now back from Manston. They crammed in, perched on chairs specially brought in. Gibson's own chair was occupied by his dog, Nigger, who watched them all with apparent interest. Gibson himself perched on the windowsill, the vast grass airfield beyond.

Gibson was suddenly feeling a whole lot more confident – about his squadron's state of training, but also the chances of the operation's success. No doubt, his own recent spurt of flying had given him personal confidence, but over the past month the considerable obstacles thrown at them had been, one by one, largely overcome: by their hard training, by the synthetic night-flying kit, by the spotlight altimeters, by the techniques adopted and crew co-operation that made low-level navigation possible, by the priority treatment the squadron had been given, and by the incredible support offered by the headquarters staff of both 5 Group and Bomber Command at a time when they were fully occupied with the ongoing Battle of the Ruhr. The operation was still a massively tall order, but it was, Gibson reckoned, *possible*, rather than the non-starter it had seemed at first, and the suicide mission it had looked sure to become.

As he looked around at his captains, most smoking and chatting, he wondered whether any of them had started to twig about the targets. He had said nothing and nor was he about to let them in on the secret, but there were a number of obvious pointers, not least the precision bombing training over various reservoirs. They would all know soon enough.

'Well, chaps,' he began once they were ready, 'you know as well as I do it has been absolute hell getting this right in the last few weeks, but now I think we are more or less set.' The reason to call them together was to plan the final phase of training so that he could quickly put together an operational plan when the time came for it. This was where the route around the Eyebrook Reservoir came in.

'When will that be?' asked Dinghy Young.

Within a fortnight, Gibson replied, then, having once again stressed the importance of security, outlined his ideas for carrying out some night-time simulations of the actual raid, which would begin that night and would follow the conditions of the operation as closely as possible.

This was the chance for everyone assembled to say their piece. Clearly, all serviceable aircraft would be needed if both flights were to be expected to fly on the same night, and this worried Capable Capel, who had been short of groundcrew since the outset. In any case, not all the modified Type 464 Lancasters had yet reached Scampton and when they did they took at least twenty-four further hours to get ready. Gibson promised Capel he would ask Satterly to send him some more men but stressed that groundcrews would simply have to work around the clock until the operation.

Gibson also insisted they fly at an all-up weight of 63,000lb – in other words, as though they were loaded with maximum fuel and the weapon itself.

Dinghy Young was worried about the front turret. Since the dorsal turret had been removed, the mid-upper gunner had been relocated to the nose turret, but on the raid itself might then get in the way of the bomb-aimer at the crucial moment. 'It would be a good idea,' he suggested, 'to fix up some stirrups for his legs because he would be more comfortable himself and the wretched bomb-aimer wouldn't have to put up with the smell of his feet.'

Gibson reckoned this was a good idea. Another task for Capel to sort out.

Someone else suggested fixing a second altimeter in front of the pilot's face and attached to the windscreen so he wouldn't have to look down at the control panel when flying at treetop height. This was another good idea.

'How about radio telephony?' asked David Shannon. 'I'm pretty hazy about this, not ever having been a fighter boy.'

Gibson had already thought about this. He suggested they communicate with each other in the plain – that is, speaking English – but using simple code words. If the radio failed, they could use their existing wireless telegraphy sets. Gibson had prepared a sheet of code words. For example, 'Dinghy' meant the Target Y had been destroyed – the Eder – while 'Nigger' meant that Target X – the Möhne – had been successfully breached. There were a number of others, and it was, of course, imperative that everyone knew them all and had them learned off by heart. In the crew room, twenty dummy headsets had been fitted up, which would be used for practising R/T. As soon as the meeting had ended, Gibson led them all down for a trial run on the headsets. The drill would be practised over the ensuing days until everyone had learned it by heart.

That night, as Gibson had planned, the squadron began these simulated rehearsals of the operation, although in threes to begin with rather than as a squadron. It had also become apparent that Gibson's new radio communication system was not going to work with the existing radio sets. The Type 464s had been equipped with a TR 1196, which worked fine so long as it was being used between the air and ground controllers down below, but was hopeless air-to-air between aircraft. Once again, Gibson kicked up a fuss. He had been promised top priority for his squadron and was getting it; a quick phone call to Cochrane and Satterly, usually accompanied by the threat of mission failure unless something was done immediately, tended to do the trick.

So it was with the problems with the TR 1196. Calls were made to RAE Farnborough, who suggested equipping all the Lancasters with the very latest VHF sets, as were used in fighters. On 7 May, twenty sets duly arrived accompanied by thirty-five men to install them. By 9 May this had been done. That same night, the two flight commanders, Maudslay and Young, tested the new VHF sets and found they were a massive improvement. A few more tweaks and modifications were made and then they were all ready. Operation CHASTISE was repeatedly proving what could be achieved in a very short space of time when the right people put their minds to it.

Early in May, Gibson somehow found the time to slip away from Scampton and his many other commitments, and meet up with Maggie, now married and called Mrs Margaret Figgins. It was he that instigated the meeting, even though they had not met since February, the week before her wedding. He had recognized that his men had needed a breather at the end of April, and perhaps that had been prompted by the realization that he needed a break himself. Perhaps, too, the imminence of the mission had prompted him; more likely, he was suffering from loneliness and the despair that plagued his private thoughts. Certainly, he was struggling – from the immense pressure, from the many and often conflicting demands on his time, from the responsibility resting on his still very young shoulders, from the strain of having to always appear the bullish, determined, super-confident squadron commander. From having to fly late in the evening because that was the only time he could, and from now, suddenly, having to catch up because he was supposed to be leading the squadron on the operation and was behind everyone else. He had never been one of the force's great natural pilots; he had to train hard for this completely new type of flying just like everyone else.

Quite simply, he was not getting enough sleep or rest, and the strain was beginning to show; he was becoming irritable and bad-tempered. Gibson recorded that a boil developed on his face, an affliction often prompted by stress and fatigue, but Flying Officer Alan Upton, the Scampton Medical Officer, remembered seeing Gibson about pains in his feet. Upton diagnosed gout, which was caused by excessively high levels of uric acid in the blood and led to inflammatory arthritis, and was, more often than not, a hereditary disorder but could be brought on by stress and fatigue. It was extremely painful, and no doubt exacerbated by the amount of regular flying Gibson was now putting himself through. Flying a Lancaster required plenty of footwork, as the feet controlled the rudders.

Upton recommended that he take two weeks off; Gibson laughed in his face. It was out of the question. He would just have to somehow put up with it and keep going. Even so, the flashes of temper and irritability were increasing. Command could be lonely; sometimes the urge to be able to talk to someone without fear of revealing his inner thoughts must have been overwhelming. Eve was still in London, and although she had visited Scampton one or

One of the Second Wave Lancasters takes off on the night of 16 May.

Below left: British weather forecasts were plentiful and detailed, but on the night of the Raid, those compiling them misread the strength of the winds and delivered an inaccurate assessment.

Above and above right: The wreckage of Hopgood's Lancaster, *M-Mother*, blasted into a million pieces, on the hills north of the Möhne Dam.

Left: 'Terry' Taerum, navigator, seated in cap, at the debriefing of Gibson's crew following the Raid. Behind, Harris and Cochrane look on. 'Spam' Spafford sits next to Taerum, with 'Trev' Trevor-Roper opposite.

Mass devastation in the aftermath of the tidal waves that thundered down the Eder and Möhne valleys. The force of water hurtling out of both dams was immense, like a tsunami destroying much in its wake.

Top: The Möhne breached.

Left and below: The Möhne and damage downstream, photographed by RAF Photo Reconnaissance.

Destruction at Neheim, six miles downstream from the Möhne.

Above: Flooding at Kassel, thirty miles from the Eder Dam.

Below: The Eder, breached as a result of one of the most extraordinary pieces of flying imaginable.

After the flood. Devastation in the Möhne Valley. No wonder the Germans still refer to it as the *Möhnekatastrophe*.

The massive reconstruction work at the Möhne – a feat of engineering that was repeated at the Eder and, to a lesser extent, at the Sorpe, too. The cost was phenomenal, and with far-reaching knock-on effects, at a time when Nazi Germany could ill-afford such a huge diversion of resources.

Top: After the Raid came the celebrations. The King and Queen visited Scampton, then the Squadron went to London for the presentations of medals. Gibson, in the front row, third from the right, was given a VC, and deservedly so.

Above: Les Munro's menu card from the dinner that followed.

Below: Many of the pilots, Les Munro, David Shannon and Joe McCarthy included, became the backbone of the Dam Buster Squadron that developed into an elite precision unit. And in the following year, it was 617 Squadron who sank the *Tirpitz* (**right**), using Tallboys. These, together with the even bigger Grand Slams, were the huge earthquake bombs Wallis had envisaged using in his *Note* back in 1941.

two times, these occasions had not been a success. 'Gibson was always worrying about her,' says Fay Gillon, the Intelligence Officer, 'but when she visited she was always very off-hand.' Eve frustrated Gibson by refusing to stay. Whatever Gibson saw in Eve, his wife could not fulfil his emotional needs, that much was plain. In fact, the only person he could still really talk to – who understood – was Maggie.

They met in the same pub they used to frequent, the conversation stilted and awkward to begin with. Both asked after the other's spouse, but gave the same unenthusiastic answer, before suddenly they both burst out laughing. The ice broken, they went on into Grantham to watch *Casablanca* at the Picture House. Gibson enjoyed it, and afterwards whistled 'As Time Goes By'. At no point did he give any indication of what was to come or begin to explain his feelings for Maggie.

In contrast, neither Charlie Williams nor his fiancée, Bobbie, were in any doubt about how each felt for the other. On 7 May, Williams flew with Norm Barlow down to Manston. They had by now received their own Type 464, codenamed *E-Easy*, but on this occasion were flying one of the ordinary training Lancasters, presumably to pick up something from the workshops there; Upkeep trials had begun again. They were delayed getting going and were held up at Manston before the return leg, which meant Williams was unable to put a call through to Bobbie as he had planned that lunchtime. Telephone calls were, he knew, his only realistic chance of hearing her voice as training now intensified with the countdown to the raid, but even a simple phone call was no easy undertaking. A line had to be booked through the exchange, and could involve a lengthy wait. If and when he did finally get through, there was then no guarantee that she would be there, in which case the entire palaver would have been for nothing. It was a constant source of frustration to him.

Instead he had to make do with letter writing, and working on a scrapbook they had bought together and which he was filling with photographs, jottings and other bits and pieces; it was something she had urged him to do and in between lengthy letters was clearly proving a good diversion for him.

Even so, he was still desperately worried about her parents' reaction to their planned wedding. Her mother was, according to Bobbie, having 'hysterics' about it. 'The news must have shaken her as much as the Berlin searchlights shook me,' he wrote to her. 'In time, when she realizes that you are serious she may take a different view.' There was not much optimism in his tone, however.

But then, good news at last. The following day, Saturday, 8 May, he managed to speak to her for three allotted minutes on the phone and heard that her parents were at last coming round to the idea. 'What wonderful news,' he wrote to her just a short while after speaking to her. 'I cannot yet make myself believe it.' He wondered how such a change of heart had taken place. His relief was enormous. 'I was rather worried about it all,' he scribbled, 'and felt that I was not doing the right thing by them.'

Meanwhile at Manston there was better news too. A change of approach had been set up for these latest trials, with two large screens put up east of the ruined church which were to act as substitute dam towers. Rather than running parallel to the coast, the pilots were now going to drop their Upkeeps towards it, as though making an attack on one of the dams; there was a sloping beach and a shallow bluff between beach and the mined fields beyond.

On Thursday, 6 May, Barnes Wallis had worked on the B.3/42 Windsor bomber petrol tanks in the morning, then after a brief lunch with Mollie at home had travelled on to Manston with Mutt Summers and from there had watched Shorty Longbottom drop the second of two Upkeeps. It bounced short.

Back at Manston, it was clear the Lancaster's caliper arms had become badly aligned, presumably through so much use, and this was most likely the reason for the less than satisfactory drop. At any rate, the following day, he was able to oversee the realignment of the caliper arms and then hurried back to Reculver to watch Shorty Longbottom carry out two further drops.

And these not only ran well, they were also direct hits. With the aircraft level at the point of release, and with the Upkeep properly balanced, there was little if no deviation at all. A live bomb had yet to be trialled, but with a week to go to the raid, it seemed that Wallis's weapon was finally beginning to work.

20

Air Ministry versus the Admiralty

MONDAY, 10 MAY 1943. At his office at Burhill, Barnes Wallis was beginning to feel impatient. Pressure was mounting to launch the raid in just four or five days' time, but more trials were needed at Reculver. True, Longbottom had now delivered two accurate drops, but this was hardly enough to convince all those backing CHASTISE that the Upkeep was now ready to be launched at the German dams; further accurate drops had to be done again. More to the point, a *live* Upkeep needed to be successfully dropped. It was even more inconceivable that some 140 men should be sent low over enemy territory carrying a weapon that had not even once been detonated. Yet the fine weather that had blessed them during much of April and early May seemed to have deserted them. Rain had lashed down, winds had blown. 'Weather still unsuitable,' Wallis had lamented that Monday.

He was also fretting about the water levels in the dams. If the water began to drop more than five feet from the sill ... He had rung Sid Bufton at the Air Ministry to see whether 542 Squadron's photo reconnaissance pictures had come through, but they hadn't – not yet.

The latest reconnaissance photographs might not have come through yet, but that same day Squadron Leader Fred Fawssett, an intelligence officer at Bomber Command Headquarters, sent

Satterly copies of information about the targets, which included the width between the towers at the Eder – 750 feet – as well as details of the defences at the Möhne. According to their latest intelligence, the Möhne was the only one of the three primary targets to be defended at all.

Analysis of earlier aerial photographs showed two single 20mm flak guns on the roofs of each of the Möhne's towers and a further gun beyond the northern tower. Below the dam lay a small lake – the compensating basin – and there were signs of a further three light flak guns on raised platforms on the northern bank, each surrounded with sandbags. In front of the dam itself, there was a double line of anti-torpedo nets, which appeared to be between ten and twenty feet apart. In other words, seven guns defended the Möhne. This was not a heavy defence by any means, but the battery there still represented a major threat. As all the crews were keenly aware, there was simply so little margin for error when operating at such extreme low heights. If a Lancaster was hit by a cannon shell at several thousand feet, there was room to do something about it more often than not. At sixty feet, there was no such luxury. Make no mistake, seven flak guns would be a problem for those attacking the Möhne. A very major problem.

As Fawssett's information was reaching St Vincent's, the 5 Group Headquarters, so Satterly was completing his first draft of the Operation CHASTISE Operation Order and sending it up to Whitworth at Scampton. 'Will you please get down to it right away with Gibson,' he jotted, 'and either re-write it completely to suit yourselves or pin on it slips of paper giving amendments you want to suggest.' He asked Whitworth to get their comments back to him by no later than four o'clock in the afternoon in two days' time – that is, Wednesday, 12 May.

Fortunately, Gibson was at Scampton on that Monday, and did make a number of points, beginning by suggesting using different code letters for the targets. 'Let us call targets, A, B and C instead of X, Y and Z,' he wrote, 'as all our training has been done in this way.' Here he was referring to the Eyebrook, Abberton and Derwent reservoirs, which had been called A, B and C, respectively, during recent training. He suggested attacking the Möhne first and, once it was destroyed, aircraft would be sent to the Eder and Sorpe in turn, but that five aircraft would be sent direct to the Sorpe so as to avoid any congestion of aircraft over the Möhne and Eder. However, although he intended that all twenty crews should take part in the operation, it was clear that he was thinking it would be the first nine aircraft that would do most of the work. Having given each pilot a number, he placed numbers one to nine into groups of three, which would take off at ten-minute intervals. Once these nine had departed, the remainder would set off, not in formation, and at three-minute intervals. The First Wave of nine would fly over the North Sea at sixty feet and would stay at extreme low level throughout the journey to the dams and on the return leg too, although a formation leader should occasionally climb to check fixes.

The First Wave was listed as follows:

1 Gibson
2 Hopgood
3 Martin
4 Young
5 Maltby
6 Shannon
7 Maudslay
8 Munro
9 McCarthy

Gibson also made clear his preferred chain of command. 'Should the leader's R/T fail at any time,' he noted, 'he will inform either No. 2 or No. 4 by W/T and will hand the control over.' This meant that Hopgood and Young, rather than his other Flight Commander, Henry Maudslay, would act as deputy leaders on the raid. He also included fail-safe instructions about what would happen should all three lose wireless and radio contact – various flares would be fired – and details about signals procedure as they had been training to use on the practice headsets in the crew room at Scampton.

Satterly had written that 'it is strongly urged that a dusk raid' by Mosquitoes should be made on Soest, an hour ahead of 617's attack. Gibson added his own notes to this, then put a line through the whole idea, as though he had changed his mind. Since the town was only ten miles north of the Möhne, they would be able to check the lie of the land around the dam and particularly gauge visibility. Gibson ran a line through this suggestion as well.

Satterly's draft had been just that, but between him, Gibson and Whitworth a detailed and sensible operational plan was emerging. With Gibson's notes duly returned by the 12th, as requested, Satterly now set to typing up a further draft of the Operation Order. Little did he – or Gibson or Satterly for that matter – realize, however, that although CHASTISE was due to take place in just a few days' time, it was still by no means certain that it would be authorized – not if the delays to SERVANT could not be resolved. Way to the north, in Scotland, live trials were taking place, with Highball-carrying Mosquitoes of 618 Squadron attacking a moored old French battleship, the *Courbet*. And the trials were not going well. Not well at all.

Although the Highball trials at the end of April had gone seemingly much better than those of Upkeep, there were still certain question marks hanging over it. The wooden casing had proved almost as problematic as it had with the Upkeep, and at a meeting specially convened by Group Captain Wynter-Morgan in his office at the MAP on 5 May, at which Wallis, Renouf and Squadron Leader Rose, CO of 618 Squadron – among others – were all present, it had been agreed that the wooden sphere should be covered in steel plating. Four were to be prepared immediately for the forthcoming live trials at Loch Striven on the western side of Scotland.

The second question mark was over how the Highball would perform when it struck the target. Highball was substantially smaller than Upkeep, and lighter and expected to travel further. The April trials had been extremely promising, but just as there were still unanswered questions over how Upkeep might detonate, the same was true of Highball – only perhaps more so. A key objective of the Loch Striven trials was to discover the Highball's ability to withstand impact against the side of a battleship like the *Courbet*, so it was agreed that the first four, all to be dropped by

Squadron Leader Rose, should be done so under attack conditions: at ninety degrees to the side of the ship, at a height of fifty to sixty feet, with the aircraft flying at 360 mph, the Highball spinning at 700 rpm, and dropping at a range of 1,200 yards.

Using Turnberry on the Ayrshire coast as their equivalent base to Manston, the trials began on that same Monday, 10 May. The weather was not as bad as it was on the south coast, but it was a nonetheless monochrome day of grey: grey sky, grey sea, and camouflaged grey Free French battleship. Crucially, however, the waters in the loch – chosen to simulate the Norwegian fjords where the *Tirpitz* skulked – were calm. Conditions were good.

On cue, Squadron Leader Rose appeared, at the right height, right speed and right alignment – but instead of dropping the bomb at the right distance, something went wrong with the release mechanism and the first fell abortively. Rose disappeared back to Turnberry, loaded up again, and reappeared for a second run. Again, the drop was defective. Both Highballs had disappeared into the dark waters of the loch, never to be seen again. That left just two specially plated Highballs.

Finally, on the third attempt, the bouncing bomb was success-fully released, and ran on perfectly, skipping gleefully, and smacking into the side of the *Courbet* more than eleven feet above the waterline and at very high velocity. Caught in the net that had been suspended under the water, it was hauled up and taken off for examination. Everyone could see as clear as day, however, that the force of impact had damaged it severely. This did not auger well.

Rose completed a second successful drop. This time, the Highball crashed into the side of the battleship just five and a half feet above the waterline, and then sank without trace. The trial bombs had been inert, but had been filled, and carried the hydro-static pistols that would be used on the live versions. Hydrophones – the marine equivalent of a microphone – had been set up on the ship to determine whether the pistols in the Highballs had worked, but nothing was detected from either of the drops, and the obvious conclusion was that they had been too damaged by the impact to work.

To add to their woes, it was later discovered that the marker buoys for Rose's drops had been set at 800 yards, not 1,200; perhaps, had the Highballs been dropped from the correct distance, they would have been less severely damaged and the hydrophones might have detected a sound from the hydrostatic pistols, but, as it was, the four specially plated Highballs had been used with no detectable results. More trials were to be arranged, but not for another week. That meant there was now categorically no way Operations SERVANT and CHASTISE could be mounted together. That was of no great concern to those in the Air Ministry and Bomber Command about to mount the attack on the dams, but it certainly was as far as the Admiralty was concerned.

Trouble was brewing – a conflict of interests that now threatened to wreck both operations at the tenth hour.

Even before the Loch Striven trials, Air Vice-Marshal Bottomley and Sid Bufton at the Air Ministry had been anticipating trouble over the conflicting aims of their bouncing-bomb projects. The last time the Chiefs of Staff had considered both Upkeep and Highball, towards the end of April, Admiral Pound, the First Sea Lord, had asked for a further thirty modified Mosquitoes. The Chiefs of Staff Committee had agreed to await the trials against the *Courbet*. On that fateful Monday, 10 May, and aware of what was taking place in Scotland, Bottomley began preparing for a confrontation with the Admiralty. He was sure Pound would repeat his request for more Mosquitoes. What was particularly concerning them was that the next progress report to the Chiefs of Staff Committee was not due until Sunday, 16 May – but they were hoping to launch CHASTISE before that date. The Chiefs of Staff had insisted on authorizing both CHASTISE and SERVANT themselves, but they were now all in Washington for the Trident Conference to discuss joint Anglo-American planning for the next stage of the war. It was clear to Bottomley that, if they weren't careful, precious days could be frittered away in a huge policy bust-up with the Admiralty, made worse by the toing and froing of cables and messages across the Atlantic. This meant that if and when the First Sea Lord made his request for more Mosquitoes, they needed to be ready.

With this in mind, Bottomley drafted a memo for Air Marshal

Sir Douglas Evill, who had taken over from Sir Wilfrid Freeman as Vice-Chief of the Air Staff in March. 'There is considerable divergence between the needs of Bomber Command and Coastal Command,' claimed Bottomley. 'The Admiralty are of the opinion that we should defer the initiation of these operations until we have adequate force to achieve the greatest measure of success by surprise. They have in mind some date in June and are now contemplating operations in the Mediterranean at the sacrifice of operations in Norway.' In fact, in light of the failure of the Loch Striven trials, what was being contemplated was about to become a firm decision: Operation SERVANT, the planned attack on the *Tirpitz*, was about to be axed. The squadron was not ready, the necessary auxiliary fuel tanks needed to get them all the way to the Arctic Circle had not been prepared, and there was a realization at last that the distances involved and the enemy defences in the fjord were insurmountable obstacles. However, the Admiralty had no intention of letting its massive investment in Highball fail, and had become set on a strike on the Italian fleet instead.

This was mission creep, as Bottomley was well aware. The Admiralty was estimating a strike in June, but Vickers, who would be modifying the extra thirty Mosquitoes, reckoned it would be more like July at the earliest before they were ready. If the Admiralty got its way, and ensured that CHASTISE was postponed, there would almost certainly be no attack on the dams until 1944. A more likely scenario was that neither operation would ever be mounted. On the other hand, 617 Squadron was almost ready to go. Gibson was heading down to Reculver the next day, and it was planned that more pilots from his proposed First Wave – his main strike force – would have a practice run with an Upkeep the day after. Wallis and Vickers were also proposing to drop a live Upkeep within the next day or so. Assuming these tests went well – and Wallis was certainly confident they would – then there was nothing to stop the operation from going ahead other than inter-service rivalry.

In three days' time, the Vice-Chiefs of Staff were due to meet, and Sir Douglas Evill would have to fight hard for the RAF's corner in this debate. Ever since the greenlight of Upkeep back in

February, the Air Ministry staff had rather thrown their weight around over the obvious priority *they* were according to an attack on the dams over the Admiralty's plans. Now, as the decisive moment rapidly approached, they were in severe danger of being hoist by their own petard.

At Scampton, training was continuing and going well. Inevitably, some had proved more adept than others at overcoming the operational challenges thrown at them. These were the men whom Gibson was intending to take with him in the First Wave, his main strike force.

By and large, spirits were good too. Gibson had forged a very strong *esprit de corps* at 106 Squadron, but this had been impossible to re-create in the short time 617 Squadron had been in existence, not least because for so much of the time he had not been around. 'I found that with all your training,' says Les Sumpter, 'you didn't know anybody else, you didn't get friendly with other crews. You were your own band of seven and that was it, you just kept yourselves to yourselves.' This was no slight on Gibson or anyone else in 617 Squadron; it was just the way it was. The intensity of the training and the short timeframe largely precluded it.

However remote Gibson may have seemed to some, he was still the boss, as everyone was keenly aware. Nonetheless, if there was anyone who represented the fledgling spirit of the squadron, it was probably Dinghy Young, who was clever and worldly-wise, had served overseas and was, above all, good fun – particularly in the Mess, where his drinking tricks were already legendary. That he was older than most – albeit still very young – and possessed an air of calm self-assurance also helped lift him up in the minds of many. As 'A' Flight Commander in a new squadron, he was also very obviously Gibson's number two, rather than Maudslay, who despite being an old Etonian was rather self-effacing and reserved. During Gibson's many absences, it was Young who naturally and unobtrusively took on the mantle of deputy commander. In many ways, he was a natural leader. The nickname testified to a sense of humour and a willingness not to take himself too seriously; his management and administrative skills also helped ensure things got done; yet he also knew the value of discipline too, as Charlie Williams discovered.

Williams had been late getting up one morning and did not have time to shave. He decided he would try and get back to his room and shave at lunchtime, but did not get the chance. Around three in the afternoon, Young was standing beside him.

'Did you shave this morning?' he asked Williams.

'Yes, sir!' Williams lied. 'I was late and had a very hurried one.'

'Yes, I think you must have done.' A short while later, he said, 'My word, you must have had a rough shave! See that you use a new blade tomorrow.'

It was hardly a major reprimand, but the tone had been sufficient to ensure Williams never failed to shave again.

For the most part, the men of 617 Squadron accepted their lot. Most had enjoyed the training and the break from operations. And while some, like Johnny Johnson, tended to keep to themselves during time off from flying, others were inevitably more extrovert – men like Joe McCarthy, Dinghy Young and Mick Martin; David Shannon, too, who was busy wooing Section Officer Ann Fowler, a WAAF at Scampton.

Others – those who had joined late – had had even less chance to integrate. No one, however, had been at Scampton less than John Fraser, who had barely been there at all. Since joining, he'd had his forty-eight-hour leave and then had returned only to be struck down with impetigo, which had ensured he had been packed off to hospital. He did not rejoin his crew until 8 May, which meant he had so far had just one week of training. One week! It was not enough. Yet, despite the shortage of training on Hopgood's crew, on Gibson's current pecking order his friend, John Hopgood, was due to be number two on the raid. Fraser was a very experienced and proven bomb-aimer, but this raid required a number of very different skills. There was a reason why the squadron as a whole had been given at least six weeks to prepare.

Fatigue levels were also on the rise once more, the forty-eight-hour leaves already a distant memory. Charlie Williams was feeling exhausted, partly from the intensity of the training and partly from the accumulated strain of many long months of action. It did not help, of course, that he was lovesick as well, or that news from home was not good. On that Monday, 10 May, he received a telegram from his family to say that his father was now seriously ill in hospital. He had terminal cancer, and had been unwell for some time, but it sounded as though this time the end was near. They were a close family, and with his older brother and father they had together worked hard – very hard – to bring themselves back up out of the depression of the early thirties that had so nearly ruined the family for good. 'I am expecting to hear the worst any day,' he wrote to Bobbie.

His day had got worse, however. Unexpectedly stood down at 4.20 p.m., he hastily changed and then hurried to his car and with Philip Burgess and Harvey Glinz, two of his crew members, he drove the forty-five-mile journey to Nottingham. Heading straight to Bobbie's office, he was dismayed to find no sign of her, so he went to the Nag's Head on the Mansfield Road instead. It was their local, the pub they always went to and where Bobbie would go with her friends after work. But there was no sign of her there either. He phoned the office just in case she had been there all along, but there was no answer. Perhaps she had gone home, but he did not want to go there in case his unexpected arrival upset her parents – which, considering they were only just coming round to the idea of him marrying their daughter, he thought might be pushing his luck.

So he stayed in the Nag's Head, hoping that every time the door swung open, it would be his Bobbie. At half-past eight, after he had a couple of beers, there was still no sign of her. Another hour passed. Nothing. Tired and fed up, he went outside to his car and dozed. At eleven, Philip and Harry turned up again and, disconsolate, he drove them all back to Scampton. Back in his room, he could not get to sleep, even though he felt tired; he could not stop thinking about his wasted evening, and about how excited he'd been when he had left Scampton and how deflated just a few hours later. 'I was so certain that I would find you there,' he wrote the following day, 'however, I have learnt my lesson and will not do that again. The worst of it is that I may not have the same chance again for some little time, and I did so much want to see you.'

*

Tuesday, 11 May 1943. It was now time for some of the 617 Squadron pilots to try dropping inert Upkeeps at Reculver. The first were Gibson, Hopgood and Martin, numbers one, two and three in Gibson's strike force. They took off in the afternoon, flying low level and in formation and headed straight to Manston, where they were loaded up with an inert Upkeep for the first time.

Wallis was at Reculver to watch these practice runs. Earlier in the day, he had been at Weybridge to receive defective Mosquitoes from Turnberry, then had headed into London for a meeting with Wynter-Morgan, before returning to Weybridge for a quick lunch and then driving on to Reculver. By 6 p.m., he was on the bluff by the ruined church watching Gibson fly over. It was a good run: dropped at sixty feet, the Upkeep bounced over the water for 600 yards, hitting the shore between the screens. The raid leader, despite fewer training hours than the rest of his squadron, had delivered his inert bomb almost perfectly. Barlow, on his turn, also dropped successfully, at sixty feet and at 220 mph.

Wallis declared the runs '100% successful'. What a contrast from Loch Striven! It was strange how quickly plans for Highball had unravelled, when less than two weeks earlier it had been Upkeep that looked as though it would never work satisfactorily.

Afterwards, Wallis drove over to Manston to meet the three crews – it was the first time he had been face to face with some of the young men who would be delivering his weapon to the dams. It was not a long meeting – the crews were about to fly back to Scampton, and in any case Wallis was to have dinner that night with Sid Bufton. Over supper at Reculver, Bufton discussed with him the planned method of attack as devised by Satterly and Gibson. Wallis had been thinking about how to attack the German dams ever since the start of the war. For three long years this had seemed an ambition that was frustratingly out of reach. That early summer's evening on a quiet part of the north Kent coast, however, as three 617 Squadron Lancasters had roared over and dropped their Upkeeps with calm precision at the required height and required speed, that goal was now within touching distance. Really, it was nothing short of a miracle.

The following day, more 617 crews headed to Reculver. Among

them was David Shannon, now flying *L-Leather*. Each of the crews
had been allocated their own Type 464 by now, with their own
groundcrew to look after them. Len Sumpter, Shannon's
bomb-aimer, was relieved. 'We didn't like borrowing planes,' he
says. 'It was like when you go home, you walk into your own house.
You could always tell when you were in your own plane.' Gibson
had also noticed the pride and care taken by each of the crews as
they had been allotted their brand-new Type 464; he had heard one
pilot swear at his bomb-aimer for boarding their new aircraft with
muddy boots on.

There had been speculation about the modified Lancasters as
they had first arrived with their bomb bays off and with no dorsal
turret, but there was even more surprise when they first saw the
Upkeeps. 'They looked rather like a huge oil drum,' says Shannon.
'A most cumbersome looking thing.' As with the previous day, they
flew down to Manston in formation, the inert bombs already fixed
into place to make the flying as realistic as possible, and then took
off again to make their runs. Most found the handling of the Type
464s, even when they were fully loaded, was not significantly
affected; it was much the same as carrying a normal heavy bomb
load. 'When the rotor was on it made a difference,' says Les Munro.
'Nine thousand pounds of bomb spinning at 500 rpm meant there
was a juddering effect, but not unduly so.'

However, the gyro effect on the aircraft of a four-ton bomb
spinning at 500 revs was considerable the moment the pilot tried to
turn or in any way manoeuvre the aircraft. This was because it
created resistance to anything other than level forward movement
and made the controls heavy, sluggish and slow to respond. The
trials at Reculver involved flying straight and level. Over the Eder
Dam in particular, where they would have to make a ninety-degree
turn, the effect of a rotating four-ton bomb was going to make an
already difficult piece of flying even harder.

On the bomb run itself, Shannon managed to get the aircraft
down to about the right height and speed and then it was up to Len
Sumpter to drop the Upkeep at the right spot. Unfortunately, he
misjudged it slightly and dropped too soon – by about forty yards.
The bomb skipped across the sea perfectly, but did not reach the

shore. Had it been for real, Shannon's crew would have failed to hit the dam. Even so, Sumpter thought the bomb was incredible. 'It was hard to think,' he says, 'when you first see it, that when about five tons of metal hits the water that it's spinning . . . you think that it will go straight in. But it didn't.'

Les Munro also had an incident as he flew over. As their practice run was done in broad daylight, they did not have the benefit of the Aldis spotlights to anchor them at sixty feet precisely. Munro flew about ten feet too low – at around fifty feet – and as the Upkeep landed, the spume of spray hurled into the air hit his plane, knocking a piece of fairing off the bomb bay. The damage was minor, and the bomb ran on perfectly, but it was a stark warning about how important it was to get the height exactly right. Pilots also needed to make sure they pulled up immediately the bomb was released. Even a few feet of extra height could make all the difference.

The following day, the 13th, Gibson called Len Sumpter into his office. Sumpter had Shannon with him. It was the only time Gibson had ever directly spoken to him and it was to give him a talking-to for dropping his Upkeep too early the day before. Sumpter did not resent the reprimand; Gibson had been right – it had been due to a lapse in concentration, but this was something that no bomb-aimer could afford and with just one practice run Gibson clearly felt he needed to drive the point home. The next time Sumpter dropped an Upkeep, it would be over the German dams.

That same day, more crews flew down to Reculver, among them the 'B' Flight Commander, Henry Maudslay. His aircraft suffered even more than Les Munro's. So bad was the damage, groundcrews back at Scampton were ordered to work around the clock to get it ready in time for the operation itself.

Thursday, 13 May 1943. At 1.16 p.m., Field Marshal Alexander, commanding the combined Anglo-American 18 Army Group in Tunisia, signalled to the Prime Minister in Washington. 'Sir, it is my duty to report that the Tunisian campaign is over. All enemy resistance has ceased. We are masters of the North African shores.' This was an enormous victory. Over 250,000 Axis troops had been captured, more than had surrendered at Stalingrad three months earlier. In addition to the large numbers of troops, the Axis had also lost crippling numbers of vehicles, tanks and especially aircraft, which Hitler had insisted on pumping into the Tunisian bridge-head. The loss of North Africa, fought over in a see-saw conflict that had battered Britain and Italy especially, and in which so many had been lost, marked the death knell of Italy's part in the war. The Allied Combined Chiefs had already decided on an invasion of Sicily next. Assuming the island was taken – and confidence was now high that it would be – it was hard to see how Italy could fight on. That in turn would make it even harder for Germany. After years of success, the blows were coming hard and fast now.

Axis vulnerability in the Mediterranean lay behind the Admiralty's desire to play a decisive role in ensuring Italy's demise was a swift one. There were emotional ties to the Mediterranean, too. The Royal Navy had maintained a strong presence there ever since Nelson's day; there was barely a single member of the Board of the Admiralty that had not served there at some point in his career.

Equally, though, there were now very good reasons to launch the attack on the dams as soon as possible. Italy was the junior partner in the Axis, and probably finished regardless of a Highball attack on the Italian fleet – a navy that had consistently proved reluctant to engage and which now posed only a limited threat to an Allied invasion force assaulting Sicily. Germany was the country they needed to beat, and destruction of the dams, of crucial material and psychological importance to the Reich, would be a major body blow – a strike when the enemy was already crippled. Most involved in CHASTISE had now come to believe it was possible to hit them. Therefore there should be no delay. They should strike while the iron was hot.

As news of the great Allied victory in North Africa was filtering through, the Vice-Chiefs of Staff were meeting, and among the subjects to be discussed was the highly charged issue of whether Upkeep and Highball should continue side by side, or whether they should separate and be operated entirely independently.

Predictably, Air Marshal Sir Douglas Evill and his counterpart, Admiral Sir Charles Kennedy-Purvis, disagreed over future policy on these two bouncing bombs. Evill, for his part, repeated the arguments that Bottomley, Saundby, and others with the Air Ministry and Bomber Command had been reciting for the past couple of weeks. Specific scientific advice had warned of the pitfalls of leaving the operation until June and had advised an attack on the dams in the May moon period. Upkeep and Highball now looked completely different: one was a cylinder, the other a sphere. The earlier argument that they were too similar to be launched independently was no longer valid. In any case, by their attacking at night, the enemy was hardly likely to know precisely what had hit them. Even if the enemy did come into possession of an Upkeep, Evill argued, it was highly improbable that the Germans would associate it with the principle of a spherical surface bomb employed against ships. Furthermore, 617 Squadron was now at a heightened state of readiness; training was complete. The men were keyed up to go. If they waited until June, it would mean an entire squadron would have to wait, doing nothing but further and unnecessary training, when they could be put to use on further operations not related to Upkeep.

These were all perfectly reasonable arguments, but, needless to say, they did not wash with Admiral Kennedy-Purvis, who had been given strict instructions by the First Sea Lord before he set off for Washington not to budge an inch on this matter. With the matter unresolved, the only agreement they came to was to signal to Washington and to ask the Chiefs of Staff to make a decision one way or the other.

While these political machinations were going on, not far away from Whitehall, on the north Kent coast, Shorty Longbottom was about to test a live Upkeep for the first time. For the previous two days, the Vickers pilots had continued carrying out trials in between the practice runs made by 617 Squadron members. Wallis's pledge to attempt drops at lower revolutions had been abandoned, not least because the Upkeeps were running so well at the agreed 500 rpm. Two good runs had been carried out on the 11th without any deviation from track at all; the calm seas had been the key ingredient, but then the waters on the German reservoirs would be calm too.

Now, on this Thursday, 13 May, Shorty Longbottom flew out to sea, away from prying eyes on the coast, although there were several observers along for the ride: in the tail turret was Group Captain Wynter-Morgan from the MAP, while flying alongside in a second Lancaster was Handasyde with Gibson beside him. The 617 Squadron CO felt quite tense as the spinning bomb was finally released. Dropped in attack conditions, it bounced seven times, for about 800 yards, then sank and disappeared. A moment later there was a massive eruption. Gibson thought it seemed like the whole surface of the sea had been shaken by a mighty earthquake. A few seconds later, a huge column of bright white water slowly rose into the air, 'beautiful to watch', and rising to some 1,000 feet above them, before slowly subsiding into the May sunshine.

At five minutes to seven later that evening, Brigadier Leslie Hollis, Secretary to the Chiefs of Staff, sent a coded signal to his bosses in Washington, outlining the arguments Bottomley had drafted and which Evill had used earlier in the day. The following morning, with still no response, Evill sent his own 'most immediate and personal' signal to Portal. 'Much regret having been forced to refer this matter to you,' wrote Evill, 'but VCNS states that he is unable to discuss here. We are fully convinced that balance of factors is strongly in favour of disassociating the two operations and getting on with the heavy.' He added that the Admiralty representative on the Ad Hoc Committee – Renouf – also agreed. Furthermore, good weather was forecast but might not last. He pointed out that the final trials had proved that the weapon worked, both technically and tactically.

Whether this message was ever read by Portal is not known; it arrived in the middle of the night, after all. However, at 2.40 p.m. in the afternoon, Friday, 14 May, the reply came back from Washington. A little over an hour later, at five minutes to four, it had been decoded. 'Chiefs of Staff agree to immediate use of Upkeep without waiting for Highball.'

Operation CHASTISE was on.

21

Countdown

FRIDAY, 14 MAY 1943. The second day in a row of warm, sunny weather. After dark days of rain and wind, summer was now in the air. Certainly, the spell of high pressure hovering over Britain and the Continent was an incredible stroke of luck, and further reason to launch the operation without delay.

The pace was now galloping as the Raid itself drew ever nearer. Gibson was feeling bullish and confident that his men were now, broadly speaking, up to scratch, but even so, the final days of preparation were falling short of what most organizing an operation of this magnitude might expect. More than half the squadron had not had a chance to practise at Reculver; really, considering the enormous time constraints placed upon Wallis and all involved, it was amazing they had had any practice bombs to drop at all. However, there was no avoiding the fact that half the squadron would be flying to the dams having never before flown with one, let alone actually dropped it.

Training had continued at an increased pace. On 13 May, several more had flown down to Reculver, while others carried out other training exercises. Charlie Williams and his crew had been out on an R/T and bombing practice; Les Munro had carried out bombing practice with Bob Hay, the Squadron Bombing Leader, on board. Later in the evening, at dusk, John Fraser was in the air with John Hopgood and crew for a night-flying test.

The focus of the day, however, was to be the dress rehearsal for the raid itself – a 'tactical exercise'.

Gibson's idea had been to use the simulated routes to the Eyebrook and Abberton reservoirs and adopt, as far as possible, the radio signals, codes and tactics that they would use on the actual operation. In fact, it was precisely the dry-run operation he had outlined in his training report of 29 April, when he had suggested such simulated flights would begin on 5 May. That date had come and gone, and it had not been until 6 May that he'd held his training conference and outlined such ideas and the need to start practising the operation right away. Since then, aircraft had been flying in vics of three and sometimes more, but there had been no single combined training exercise involving every crew in the squadron. And even this latest 'dress rehearsal' would not involve the entire squadron. David Maltby could not fly – he was over at Woodford with his Type 464, *J-Johnny*. Henry Maudslay, the 'B' Flight Commander, had to fly one of the original Lancasters because his Type 464 was still being furiously repaired after the damage suffered at Reculver. Mick Martin did not fly either. Others would not be using their Type 464s as well, which meant not everyone could fly under operational conditions because the ordinary Lancasters did not have the VHF sets so key to the command and control of the squadron during the attacks on the dams. While all the Type 464s had now arrived, that did not mean they were operationally ready. Spotlights had to be fixed, fine-tuning had to be done on the bomb-holding gear, radios needed to be adjusted, Perspex in the bomb-aimer's nose marked up. In addition, there were all the mechanical checks that were necessary – Lancasters were not designed to be flown as hard and intensively as they were currently being flown. Merlin engines were complicated pieces of machinery and required considerable maintenance. It all took time, even when the poor groundcrew were working around the clock as they were.

Despite whatever shortcomings there might have been, the dress rehearsal went as well as could be expected. Crews reached their targets, carried out their dummy runs, and then headed back to base. 'Full dress rehearsal on Uppingham Lake and Colchester Reservoir,' wrote Gibson in his logbook. 'Completely successful.'

Saturday, 15 May, and another fine day. At 9 a.m., Bottomley's office at the Air Ministry sent a brisk cipher to Bomber Command Headquarters: 'Operation CHASTISE. Immediate attack of targets "X", "Y" and "Z" approved. Execute at first suitable opportunity.'

As soon as this was received at High Wycombe, its order was passed on to 5 Group Headquarters at St Vincent's in Grantham. Operation CHASTISE was just thirty hours away.

At St Vincent's, Satterly set to work drafting the Operation Order that he had begun five days earlier. He had received Gibson's notes and, having continued to think matters through, was now ready to commit the plan to paper. Most of Gibson's comments were taken on board; there would be no Mosquito attack on Soest, although he did suggest Bomber Command mount a number of diversionary raids. The running order, with the main strike force attacking the Möhne first and supported by two further waves, was also much as Gibson had planned. There were to be two routes. The first was southerly, down across East Anglia, out over the Channel to the Dutch coast, crossing the East Scheldt between the islands of Walcheren and Schouwen, and avoiding the known enemy night-fighter bases at Gilze-Rijen and Eindhoven.

The other route would cross the Dutch coast some 130 miles further north at the undefended and narrow island of Vlieland, and would involve a much longer, and therefore more problematic, flight over the North Sea. The First Wave would use the southerly route and would attack the Möhne and then the Eder, Targets X and Y. For some reason, however, Satterly downgraded the Sorpe – Target Z. '2nd Wave,' he wrote, 'is to consist of five aircraft manned by less experienced crews who are to take the Northern route to the target, but are to cross the enemy coast at the same time as the leading section of the 1st wave. This 2nd wave are to attack Target Z.'

All the reports by Wallis, by the Ministry of Economic Warfare and by the Prime Minister's Office had consistently pointed out that the Eder was the least important of the three primary targets, but this had not been registered by Satterly. It was true that the

Upkeep had been developed with attacking gravity dams such as the Möhne and Eder in mind, rather than earthen dams like the Sorpe, but this did not mean the latter could not be breached with the bomb. Rather, it would take, Wallis had reckoned, at least six Upkeeps accurately dropped directly onto the sloping wall to cause the fissure in the concrete core, which would then expand and eventually cause complete collapse. Wallis never thought there would be a dramatic punch through the wall from just one precisely placed Upkeep, as he hoped would be the case with the other two dams.

However, although effecting a breach at the Sorpe was, on the face of it, more problematic, there was no reason to downgrade it as a target. On the contrary, greater effort needed to be made to ensure it was breached. As the earlier intelligence reports had made clear, destroying both the Möhne and the Sorpe together was worth more than the sum of their individual parts.

Nor had Satterly adopted Gibson's suggestion of changing the target code letters to A, B and C. He also listed four further 'last resort targets': the Lister, Ennepe and Henne dams, all in the Ruhr area, and the Diemel, which was nearer the Eder. They were much, much smaller than the primary targets, but would be certainly worth destroying if possible. However, they were only to be attacked if all the others had been destroyed and there were aircraft and Upkeeps to spare – and would most likely be targeted by the third wave, the Reserve Wave. These would leave well after the First and Second Waves and would be under the control of 5 Group Headquarters.

While Satterly was drawing up this first operation order and consulting with Wing Commander Wally Dunn, the 5 Group Chief Signals Officer, Cochrane headed up to Scampton to see Whitworth and Gibson in person to give them the news that the operation would be launched the following evening, Sunday, 16 May.

There was still much to be done.

There was little activity from the 617 crews that day. After the tactical exercise of the night before, they were not expected to get up in a hurry, while most of the Type 464s were grounded as they underwent thorough maintenance checks.

For Charlie Williams, when not flying his thoughts were rarely too far from his fiancée, Bobbie. There had been two long, breathless letters from her in the post that day, which he had devoured eagerly. There was a bus drivers' strike, which, considering there was a war on, disgusted Charlie, and it was clearly making getting about difficult for Bobbie. Mostly, though, her letters were about the future. Williams had told her that a grandfather of his had gone to America, and, like many young women in Britain, Bobbie believed the United States was a golden land of plenty. Perhaps they could settle there instead of Australia? She was also going to try and start saving for their married life together. There were also their future children to consider. 'You certainly make me out a wonderful racial mixture,' Williams wrote back to her later that afternoon, 'but I think it is quite a good one and the result of combined bloods should produce something extraordinary.'

After the two letters had come the telephone call. She'd been lucky to catch him – he had just been about to head out when she rang. Unbeknown to him at the time, she had been at a party the previous evening in Lincoln – despite the bus strike – and had seen them all leave and then come back again.

'I am very glad, darling, that you were there for the take off and the return,' he wrote. He'd spoken to her just a little while earlier, but the three allowed minutes on a muffled, static-filled line went in a flash. There was always more to say in a considered letter. 'And now you will fully realize what a strain we are under the whole time, without the actual operations, and you will not now wonder why our nerves are bad at times. You will have an idea what we feel like every time some of our pals or even just aircrew acquaintances fail to return. We get hardened to it to a certain extent, but cannot help feeling depressed every time some of them fail to return. Many of the chaps I know well who did not return were some of the finest chaps I have ever met, and there are many more of them on every RAF station in England.'

As ever, he was missing her, and frustrated at being kept on base and at being unable to tell her what he was doing. The operation was due any moment; he would see her after. He had to focus his thoughts on that. He was also enjoying the sunny weather and spending as much time as he could outside. It reminded him of home. 'I want to see you, darling, and I want some leave,' he scribbled. 'All this hard work is making me rather tired and I feel like a rest. I seem to want so many things but as I cannot get them just yet, will have to make the best of it, and hope for the future.'

Charlie Williams wrote his letter to Bobbie at 5.30 p.m. Earlier in the afternoon, his pilot, Norm Barlow, had signed an authorization form for a flight with Vernon Byers and his crew to Wainfleet, but it seems they never flew it after all; perhaps it was because suddenly the Type 464s were beginning to be loaded with the live Upkeeps that had arrived a few days earlier. It was a big job – each bomb took around half an hour to load into their calipers hanging down from the bomb bay and to have the rotor belt fitted. Maudslay's aircraft was still being repaired, but there were nineteen others which now all needed loading.

Not that any of the aircrew had yet been told about the operation. That was still secret. 'Secrecy is VITAL,' Satterly had written that morning in his drafted operation order. 'Knowledge of this operation is to be confined to the Station Commander, OC 617 Squadron and his two Flight Commanders until receipt of the EXECUTIVE signal.' Even once crews *had* been briefed – which would not be until the following day – they were to be reminded of the urgent need to say nothing to anyone.

Satterly's Operation Order was a vastly more complete document than it had been five days earlier, but it was still not the finished article. While he had been consulting with Wally Dunn about the signals procedure, the AOC 5 Group, Air Vice-Marshal Cochrane, had headed up to Scampton where he had told both Whitworth and Gibson, man-to-man, that the operation would be on the following night. Clearly, some further consultation with both Satterly and Dunn was needed, so Cochrane took him back with him to St Vincent's, where they thrashed out the finer details of the Operation Order, which was then sent to Bomber Command HQ for approval.

While Gibson was in Grantham, Barnes Wallis flew up to

Scampton in a Wellington piloted by Mutt Summers. Wallis had been asked up to help with the briefing of the aircrews. Touching down on the grass at around 4 p.m., Summers then taxied around the perimeter, coming to a halt in front of No. 2 Hangar. Stepping out, Wallis and Summers wandered around in the sunshine. Soon after, Gibson arrived back again and showed them around some of the waiting Lancasters, a number of which already had their live Upkeeps winched up beneath their bellies.

Pleasant though it was inspecting aircraft in the early evening sun, there was work to be done. Gibson led Wallis to Whitworth's house, a large yellow-brick purpose-built home on the edge of the Station. Dinghy Young and Henry Maudslay had also been invited along, as had John Hopgood and Bob Hay, the Squadron Bombing Leader. These men, and these alone on that Saturday before the Raid, would be told of the targets.

In the Officers' Mess that evening, there was an air of nervous expectation. Harry Humphries, the Squadron Adjutant, noticed that there were many more men than usual for a non-operation night. Everyone knew the operation was imminent – a day, maybe two, away. They had all seen the Upkeeps being loaded. It didn't take a genius to work out this was unlikely to be for an exercise. Few were drinking beer, preferring something soft instead in case the following day was the day. 'The boys were taking no chances,' noted Humphries, 'and were keeping off the liquor.' The only creature drinking beer was Gibson's Labrador, Nigger.

Humphries was standing with Pilot Officer Gregory, rear gunner on Hopgood's crew. Greg's wife had been in Lincoln for a few days, but had since gone back home to Scotland. He was missing her and feeling on edge now that the operation was so close, yet still unconfirmed. Humphries noticed Gregory did not know what to do with himself – whether to play snooker and have another drink, or go back to the digs he shared with Humphries. Eventually, Humphries suggested they head out for a stroll around the Mess; Gregory agreed.

Outside, it was a beautiful summer's evening. The birds were twittering away in the trees as they always did in May, while in the many flower beds around the Station, tulips and daffodils were in full bloom. On the nearby tennis courts, a couple of officers were playing. It seemed incredibly peaceful. Humphries and Greg ambled back to their digs – one of the married quarters across the road from the Mess that they had been allocated, where they found their batman playing with Gregory's dog who had recently had a litter of puppies – possibly thanks to Whitworth's spaniel. The batman made them sugary tea, then Gregory, calming down at last, announced he was going to bed. 'May be working tomorrow,' he explained.

Humphries, who would not be flying, but who felt the tension every bit as keenly, was too restless to turn in. Tea drunk, and with Gregory headed to bed, he wandered back to the Mess.

Not far from the married quarters was the Station Commander's house, where Wallis and the senior officers were in the depths of discussion. In his usual calm, assured and extremely cogent manner, Wallis had told the new initiates about the bomb and how and why it worked, and why the dams were such an important target – and that included the Sorpe. He answered their questions much as he had done during his second meeting with Gibson back in March.

They then turned to the practicalities. Satterly's now typed-up Operation Order had been given to Whitworth and Gibson, and to Bomber Command HQ, who were considering it overnight. Gibson was broadly happy with the outline, but it was, of course, important now to have the input of the others, and even Wallis too, who knew more than anyone in the room about the targets themselves.

They were also armed with more information than Satterly had had that morning. In his draft he had listed the defences at the Möhne, but had still not had the photographs back from the Photo Reconnaissance Unit about the defences – if any – at the Eder and Sorpe. The 'last resort targets' – the four other dams listed – were, Satterly had noted, 'unlikely to be defended'. These photographs had now come through at long last. Furthermore, that morning, Flight Lieutenant Gerry Fray of 542 Squadron had once again been over the dams in his high-altitude Spitfire IX, covering a larger area that included Soest, Dortmund, Duisburg and Borkum, and with the brief to let his cameras run over the Möhnesee, the reservoir behind the dam. This he duly did on a day that was every bit as fine and clear as it was over England.

After he had safely made it back to RAF Benson, the film was hastily taken from him and immediately developed and then, soon after and much to his surprise, Fray had been ordered to fly straight on up to Grantham to deliver the developed photographs of the Möhne to 5 Group HQ. Driven from the airfield, he was ushered into Cochrane's office, alongside an intelligence officer, who eagerly took the photographs from him. He seemed pleased; water levels were still high. Conditions for an attack were perfect.

At Whitworth's house, the planning continued. Gibson was soon to be very glad he had brought Hopgood along. Both the northerly and southerly route eventually took them over Hüls, a small town on the western edge of the Ruhr and chosen because it neatly bisected Duisburg and Mülheim to the north and Kreveld and Düsseldorf to the south, all of which were heavily defended, and because, according to their flak map, it was largely undefended.

'That night,' noted Gibson, 'Hoppy saved our lives.' It seemed that Hopgood knew that there was a well-defended factory at Hüls and so suggested they fly north of it. 'If Hoppy hadn't known,' added Gibson, 'we would have gone over that factory and it would have been too bad.' In fact, the new route would take them quite a distance further north, around the top of Dortmund and Essen, and clear of the Ruhr industrial heart altogether.

One of the key issues to finalize was the order of attack. Gibson had had some new thoughts since jotting down his strike force a few days earlier. It was a tough call, but as leader he needed to have confidence that he had the best nine crews in his strike force. An unofficial bombing competition had taken place during training with those achieving the most accurate drops at the top. All other skills had been taken into account as well, as had Gibson's own personal assessment of his pilots. He could be quick to judge, and was not always necessarily fair, but he was decisive and, as commander, this was an important and necessary attribute.

A further issue was that the Sorpe was by no means to be seen as a secondary target. Satterly may have suggested that less experienced crews should be sent there, but this was a mistake that Wallis would certainly have highlighted during that long discussion at Whitworth's house. At any rate, Gibson now rearranged the squadron order of battle. Les Munro and Joe McCarthy were pulled out of the First Wave and put into the Second Wave, replaced by Les Knight and Bill Astell. Les Munro wondered whether this was some kind of demotion for causing damage to his Lancaster over Reculver, but this seems unlikely. Maudslay suffered considerably more damage during his run, and he was still in the First Wave. Gibson rated Munro – he had done well during training and was pretty high up on the bomber leader board, as was Joe McCarthy.

Rather than a demotion, Munro and McCarthy's move to the Second Wave was a recognition that the Sorpe needed senior squadron crews. The order of the First Wave supports this. Gibson knew from everything that Wallis had told him that just one Upkeep, placed in the right place, *should* be enough to destroy the Möhne. He was confident this would be achieved by the first three aircraft to attack; no doubt, he hoped his crew would smash it with the first drop. Therefore he would lead the first attack of three aircraft. Deputy Leader on the Möhne was to be John Hopgood, his closest friend in the squadron and the man he wanted right beside him. This was understandable – the two had been close friends and colleagues since 106 Squadron days – but was perhaps the least sensible of all Gibson's decisions over the running order. No one could doubt Hopgood's undoubted experience and skill, and yet his crew was about the least settled in the entire squadron. His bomb-aimer, John Fraser, had not joined until 21 April and, having then been hospitalized for a week with impetigo, had had the least training of anyone in the entire squadron. He had done very well in the short time given him but, even so, a huge amount was being expected of him. Fraser was still just twenty years old. The only person who had perhaps had even less training than John Fraser was Ken Earnshaw, the navigator on Hopgood's plane – and thus another key role – who did not join from 50 Squadron until 29 April. Both men were experienced and proven to be good at their jobs, but this operation required some entirely new skills – and a level of crew co-operation that had taken most of the others some six weeks to perfect. Was it therefore fair to expect so much of them? Or to make Hopgood deputy leader on the number one primary target?

Number 3 was Mick Martin, who was unquestionably the finest low-level flyer in the squadron and had the Squadron Bombing Leader and Squadron Navigation Leader in his crew. The choice was an obvious and undoubtedly correct one.

Numbers 4, 5 and 6 were Young, Maltby and Shannon. Young, as senior Flight Commander, was also the obvious choice to lead the next attack of three, which, in Gibson's mind, he assumed would be directed at the Eder Dam. Maltby and Shannon had also proved themselves to be among the best in the squadron and were natural choices for the next in line, even though Shannon's bomb-aimer, Len Sumpter, had fluffed his drop at Reculver. Gibson clearly felt that was an exception; the bombing practice results certainly suggested so.

Maudslay, as 'B' Flight Commander, commanded the third trio with Astell and Knight. He was not as ebullient as Dinghy Young, but had demonstrated a quiet confidence and self-assurance. He was repeatedly described as a 'perfect gentleman'. The mishap at Reculver does not appear to have been held against him; David Maltby also damaged his Type 464, and it was recognized that finding the exact dropping height without any form of altimeter was problematic, to say the least. That he was leader of the third trio in the First Wave was the correct position for him, although in his mind Gibson would have hoped that both the Möhne and Eder would have been breached before Maudslay's three had to attack, although there is no question that he would still have had every confidence in all three.

The Second Wave now looked a lot more solid, too. Byers and Rice were very under-experienced, but had done well enough during training. Barlow was highly experienced, had just been awarded the DFC, and had a good crew, as did Munro and McCarthy. The Second Wave was no longer the afterthought it had been five days earlier. The rest of the squadron would be in the Reserve Wave, although because there were only twenty Type 464s, that meant one crew would be left out. As things stood at midnight on 15 May, that was going to be Ken Brown and his crew.

The meeting in the Station Commander's house did not break up until after midnight, but, just as they were leaving, Whitworth appeared, his face ashen.

'Look here, Guy,' he said, 'I'm awfully sorry, Nigger's had it. He has just been run over by a car outside the camp. He was killed instantaneously.'

Perhaps his dog had drunk too much beer that night; it was certainly usual for him to go for a quick run-around before bed, but with the comparatively small number of cars on the road by 1943, it was very bad luck that the dog had been hit. Gibson put on a brave face, but he was greatly shaken by the news. Most dogs love their masters unconditionally, and Nigger had been a loyal and faithful companion during the many lonely moments of command. He had also become a feature about the place. The men liked to see a dog about – it was a link to normal life. Gibson held little store in omens or rituals, but he was worried that the death of his dog might be seen as a bad sign by the men.

Back at the Mess, Upton, the MO, was handing out sleeping pills. Gibson went back to his digs. 'Then I was alone in my room,' he noted, 'looking at the scratch marks on the door Nigger used to make when he wanted to go out, and feeling very depressed.'

LANCASTER I II III
★ AS ILLUSTRATED

Part III

THE RAID

ilot's Controls

22

Final Day

SUNDAY, 16 MAY 1943. Another fine day, the dawn chorus bursting with life, the sun beating down; that ridge of high pressure was still there. In the Met Office, the first weather charts of the day were already being marked up, ready for interpretation and then to be issued to the various Command headquarters. All looked good. No one was anticipating anything other than the continuation of the fine weather throughout the day and into the night.

Breakfast in the Scampton Messes was just like any other. Porridge or cereal, then sausage and potatoes. Toast and marmalade. Harry Humphries, who had been woken with a mug of sugary tea at seven, had then eaten a full breakfast before heading over to his office at No. 2 Hangar early.

By nine, Gibson had appeared too. Unbeknown to Humphries, Gibson had been up since 5.30 a.m. – he had had no more than five hours' sleep. His gout was causing him extreme pain and he went to see Upton. Gibson told him he would have to fly that day. This, Upton guessed, meant they would be operating that night. Yes, Gibson had replied, but then had warned him that if he breathed a word, he would be shot.

'Flying programme, Adj,' he said to Humphries.

'Training programme, sir?' Humphries now replied.

'No, um, that is yes, to the rest of the Station.' Seeing

Humphries' look of puzzlement, he added, 'We are going to war at last, but I don't want the world to know about it so do not mention the words "Battle Order", just make out a night-flying programme. All who should know will receive their orders verbally.'

He stayed with Humphries until the Adjutant had all the necessary details, then left him. 'Well, I'm off now, Adj,' said Gibson. 'God knows when the flak will die down, but I'll try to give you mealtimes and take-off details later.'

For Gibson, there would barely be a moment's rest that day. In the morning, Satterly's final Operation Order came through, delivered personally by Wing Commander Wally Dunn at around 11 a.m. The final version arrived complete with appendices that listed the routes and timings, the signals procedure, and light and moon tables. The plan had, at last, been finalized. Following the long discussion at Whitworth's house the previous evening, the Second Wave had now been upgraded. Instead of consisting of less-experienced crews, it was to be made up of five aircraft manned by 'specially trained crews'. The routes had also been modified to avoid Hüls, and the Henne Dam taken off the four 'last resort' targets. Now there would be three primary targets and three last resort targets: the Lister, Ennepe and Diemel. The largest of these three, the Lister, with 22 million cubic metres of water behind it, was almost ten times smaller than the Eder.

At Scampton, the activity around the airfield and in No. 2 Hangar was feverish. The crews had still not been told they would be flying the mission that night, but it was hard not to realize it must surely now be that night. Belts of bullets were being loaded, if anyone cared to notice, as too were all the Upkeeps. And work continued on Maudslay's battered Type 464.

At one point, Mick Martin clambered into his Lancaster, *P-Popsie*, with his crew for some pre-flight checks. All of a sudden, the Upkeep fell from its calipers onto the ground. Hurriedly, the crew scrambled out of the aircraft and Martin ran as fast as he could to get the Armament Officer, 'Doc' Watson. Fortunately, on arrival, Watson was able to announce the weapon completely safe. Once more, it was carefully hoisted back into place, and Martin and his crew had to pray that it would not fall out prematurely again.

Satterly had listed other details. All machine guns mounted in the Lancasters were to use 100 per cent daylight tracer to give the impression of a heavier weight of fire than was the reality. Watches were to be synchronized to the BBC's clock. The Eastern Chain GEE radar stations were to be switched on at Z −20 (zero hour minus twenty minutes, zero hour being take-off time) and kept on for the entire operation.

At around noon, the briefings began. Barnes Wallis had risen late, at around ten, but was on hand with Gibson to brief all the pilots and navigators while Wally Dunn briefed the wireless operators. They were all surprised to see the targets when they entered the room. The scale models of the Sorpe and Möhne, which Gibson had seen when he'd first been summoned by Cochrane back in March, were there, as were large maps and plenty of aerial photographs of all the targets. 'None of us had any idea it was a dam,' admits Joe McCarthy. 'None of us that I know of had said, "I'd thought of that."' For Les Munro it was not the dams themselves that caused him any undue concern. 'The main concern,' he says, 'was the routes in and out of the target – through the heavily defended area of the Ruhr Valley.' They were not going to fly over them, but near enough.

Gibson stressed the importance of succeeding – no one wanted to go back a second time once the enemy were alerted and primed for them to come. He ran through the battle order, announcing who would be in which wave. Both Divall and Wilson, the later arrivals as pilots, were 'sick' – either a curious piece of bad luck or a euphemism for Gibson's belief that, as crews, they were not quite up to scratch. At any rate, they would not be flying; it was a blow for them and their crews after all the work they had done, but could not be helped; the only unfit pilot to fly would be Gibson. Ken Brown and his crew were back on the flying list after all, added to the Reserve Wave.

The routes, so carefully prepared, were also issued. There were specific way-points and fixes worked out that avoided the most hazardous obstacles and enemy defences. Pilots and navigators were then told to study the maps and models and memorize them as much as possible. After a couple of hours, both groups broke for some food and drink – all still sworn to secrecy – and then at 2.30 p.m. they were joined by the bomb-aimers and gunners.

Discussions and study of the mass of information now before them continued for much of the afternoon. Briefings before any operation were thorough, but they were not used to this level of detail or micro-management, which was, of course, absolutely necessary for such a precise operation as this. Individual crews got together, navigators drawing tracks and working out their flight plan, and marking up maps. Len Sumpter, bomb-aimer on Shannon's crew, made sure all the power cables that were likely to cross their tracks were marked up in red on his maps. 'They were very high, the Dutch pylons,' he says. 'They were about one hundred feet. You had to watch out for those. You either had to go over or under them.'

Johnny Johnson was a bit disappointed when he learned they would be going to the Sorpe. 'It had no towers and there was nothing to sight on,' he says. 'It was in a very hilly area and it was a much more difficult proposition than the Möhne.' Joe McCarthy was of much the same opinion. 'We studied the models of the dams,' he says, 'and I could see I was going to have a problem with mine.' They were to fly along the top of the dam, parallel, and drop the bomb without it rotating or bouncing. 'We hadn't practised that,' says Johnson. 'We weren't particularly happy about it but that was the job we had to do.'

Those heading to the Eder also faced a particularly tough proposition. There was no scale model of this dam – only two-dimensional maps and photographs which did not really convey just how steep-sided the hills were that surrounded it. What they could see was a curving spit arcing out into the reservoir just in front of the dam itself. How a thirty-ton Lancaster carrying a four-ton bomb was going to get around that and straighten up in time to drop the Upkeep ahead of the dam wall was not clear. It was also odd that the crews had not practised flying this technique. It was all very well maintaining secrecy, but the Sorpe was a priority target. Ullswater, for example, in the Lake District, would have made an ideal training lake.

*

Meanwhile, preparations were being put in place at High Wycombe and at the Air Ministry in London. At 1.15 p.m., Bomber Command asked Fighter Command to carry out some intruder operations over the Continent between 11.30 p.m. and 12.30 the following morning. At 2 p.m., a signal was sent to Fighter Command, Coastal Command and the US 8th Air Force in Britain warning them that a special operation was being carried out that night. Instructions were also issued to ensure the GEE Eastern Chain radar stations were switched on at 'Stud 5' at Z –20, and zero hour was to be at 2248 – twelve minutes before 11 p.m. A little after 4 p.m., a signal was sent to Scampton from St Vincent's informing them that the codename for the operation, agreed back in March, but until that moment never shared with Whitworth or Gibson, was Operation CHASTISE.

With these necessary arrangements squared away, and with the weather charts continuing to look promising for the entire night, Cochrane was finally able to give the 'executive' order for Operation CHASTISE – the final authorization – at 4.45 p.m. By the time this cypher message came through, all the crews knew they would be operating that night, but the final countdown was now on.

The operation was just a few hours away.

For the Adjutant, Harry Humphries, the entire day was proving to be a battle against time. After his meeting with Gibson earlier that morning, he had anxiously awaited the take-off and estimated return times. These had eventually been delivered to him via a runner rather than from the CO himself, handed over in a sealed envelope addressed to him in Gibson's handwriting. Take-off was to begin at 2100 hours – 9 p.m. – with the first of the Second Wave, who had a longer journey and therefore would be departing before Gibson and the rest of the First Wave. Return was given as being around 0300 the following morning. Armed with these timings, Humphries now had to work out when buses should arrive at No. 2 Hangar to take crews to their waiting Lancasters, but giving them enough time to complete pre-flight drills without hurry.

There were mealtimes to sort out as well as flying rations and coffee which the crews could take with them if they chose. He also had to be on hand to accept any wills, cash, letters for next of kin, or any precious items that members of the aircrew might want him to keep safe for them. Then there were the buses to collect them at the end of the mission, plus the traditional bacon and eggs in the Messes upon their return. He had some trouble with this because, in keeping with the security brief, he did not want to let on that the squadron were going on ops that night. Unfortunately, the WAAF Sergeant who ran the kitchens refused to lay on any late food for what Humphries said was merely a training flight. Only when he implied that it was not really a training flight did she concede.

On top of all that, Humphries had a number of other tasks, such as issuing Bomber Command Codes, and even making sure the various dogs that belonged to aircrew were fed and looked after. The men expected their Adjutant to be a maid of all work; Humphries liked to make sure he was.

Meanwhile, the mechanics working on Maudslay's aircraft had to admit defeat. His aircraft would not be ready. Fortunately, with Divall and Wilson ill, there was now one spare aircraft. It was not the Type 464 Maudslay's crew had trained on, but it was in perfect working order. It would do. As a back-up, a further Type 464 was flown up from Boscombe Down in Wiltshire, where it had been carrying out weight and fuel tests. It arrived safely later in the afternoon, but after many long flying hours carrying out various tests it was in need of maintenance. The pilot ferrying it to Scampton had noticed the No. 3 engine was not running properly – it would only run smoothly with the fuel booster off. As it was, he landed safely at around 3.30 p.m., and within moments of his arrival groundcrew were swarming all over it. They quickly discovered that a crucial cable that fitted to the GEE box was missing and there was no spare. Ingenuity and a good old-fashioned make-do-and-mend attitude ensured that a makeshift cable was quickly acquired and made to work. As matters stood, the aircraft would not be needed, but having been got to Scampton, it needed to be ready for use should it be called upon. It was – but only just. Another day, and in different circumstances, these problems would have been enough to have the aircraft declared unserviceable. But not today.

6 p.m. An announcement made over the Station public address system: 'All crews of No. 617 Squadron report to the Briefing Room immediately.' All the crews made their way to the Operations Room, noisily climbing the staircase, then settling down with a loud scrape of chairs. Sentries were placed outside. Security, even now – or perhaps especially now – was to remain as tight as ever.

'My God, that was a briefing,' says Johnny Johnson, who was impressed by the number of key figures there waiting for them on the raised dais, and the air of nervous expectancy in the room. Many of them were smoking – both pipes and cigarettes – the smoke rising into the still, fetid air. On the wall were enlarged reconnaissance photographs and a huge map of Europe with red tape pinned to it marking the two different routes. Sitting below were Gibson, Whitworth and AVM Cochrane, as well as Barnes Wallis, the Met Officer and Wing Commander Wally Dunn.

Gibson, who began the briefing, was rather of the same mind as Johnny Johnson. 'I will never forget that briefing,' he wrote. The heat of the day had only just begun to cool down, as he announced the target and introduced Wallis, who was now briefing the rest of the crews for the first time. He again stressed the economic importance of the dams before describing the development of the bomb and then talking through the importance of the attack and why it needed to run at 500 rpm and be dropped at sixty feet and at 220 mph. Most were struck by his lucid explanations, and by the gentleness with which he spoke. 'He was a lovely gentleman,' recalls Joe McCarthy. 'He was a very kindly man,' agrees Sid Hobday, 'obviously very dedicated . . . we were very impressed with him. We thought he was a marvellous man. Everyone did.'

Wallis was followed by Cochrane. 'Now, you are off on a raid which will do a tremendous amount of damage,' he told them, in his polished, clipped voice. 'It will become historic. Everyone will want to know how you did it, and it will be very difficult not to tell them. You must not do so because we have other uses for the weapon. I am giving you this warning now because, having watched your training from the beginning, I know that the attack will succeed.'

Gibson then ran through the running order again, reiterated the need for strict wireless and radio silence until Z +30 minutes for the First and Second Waves and Z +three hours for the Third/Reserve Wave. Even then, W/T and R/T were only to be used when absolutely necessary. He also briefed them on the enemy defences, warning them of known flak concentrations, night-fighter units and airfields. It was enough to make any man gulp.

Gibson reckoned he spoke for the best part of an hour, a tiring exercise in itself. He was struggling with his gout, yet stood throughout. He had been up since 5.30 a.m., and had barely stopped since. In little more than a couple of hours, he would be leading his squadron on what was unquestionably an extremely difficult and arduous operation deep into some of the most heavily defended territory in the entire world.

He was followed by the Met Officer and then by Wally Dunn. The weather was due to be about as good as they could possibly hope, the met man told them. The sky would be clear, the moon full and winds minimal – there would be calm winds over the sea, gently rising as they pushed inland. Over the target, they might be between 15 and 20 mph north-easterlies, but this was no great concern because by that stage they would have enough visual markers to easily correct any effects of wind.

Each navigator had his own Navigation Log, in which the various legs and courses they would be taking, and the planned distance and speed on each, were all noted. On the right-hand side of the log sheet was a place to mark up the 'Forecast Winds' and the 'Weather Forecast'. The first stage would take them out across the east coast of England and then over the North Sea and the Channel. West of three degrees east was the first area to be covered in the forecast winds – in other words until they reached the enemy coast. In this column Jack Leggo, the Squadron Navigation Officer, wrote 'calm'. Joe McCarthy's navigator neatly wrote three zeroes in pencil – no wind at all. This was ideal. Navigating over sea was the hardest task of all because there were no visual markers. With no wind, the job would be that much easier. Sergeant Nicolson, David Maltby's navigator, did not even fill out the wind and weather forecast sections at all. The weather was predicted to be so good, he presumably felt there was no need.

It was now around 7.30 p.m. Watches had been synchronized to BBC time, but until take-off the crews now had an hour or so to get something to eat, to have a moment to themselves, and to collect their thoughts. The waiting was often the hardest part. In the Officers' Mess, as they sat down to a pre-flight meal of bacon and eggs, Dinghy Young said to Gibson, 'Can I have your egg if you don't come back?' He meant the post-flight meal. It was an old line, a touch of black humour to ease the tension. Gibson swore at him and 'told him to do something very difficult to himself'.

Charlie Williams went back to his room, where he wrote a letter to Bobbie. He apologized for not getting down to Nottingham to see her that night. It had been nearly a fortnight since they had last been together; if only he had found her the previous Monday, when he had unexpectedly driven over. When he did next see her – and he wished it would be very soon now – he hoped he could explain why it had been so difficult for him to get away. He thought there was a good chance of a few days' leave very soon. 'And when I do get that leave,' he wrote, 'I hope you are able to get leave also, so that we can be married.' He apologized for the short letter, but he had little time and work to do. As soon as he had signed and sealed it, he would be back down to No. 2 Hangar, to the Crew Room and to wait for the off. His crew were to be the first to take off on Operation CHASTISE, at 2100 hours.

'Cheerio for now darling,' he finished off his letter, 'and believe me when I say I love you very dearly and always will.'

Around 8 p.m. At No. 2 Hangar, the men were arriving, some on foot, others on bicycles. Harry Humphries paced around, running through his check list. The buses were ready, flying rations were there, waiting to be collected, coffee was available. In the Crew Room, the young men of the squadron were busily getting ready, grabbing flying jackets, fur-lined boots, gloves, and helmets, goggles and parachutes. Few spoke. Many were still in shirt sleeves, or just their blue battle-dress; it was too warm to wear sheepskin Irvins. They might be worn later. Outside, on the expanse of open grass, the Lancasters were lined up around the perimeter, dark and brooding. Still.

Most came out of the Crew Room and sat on the grass. Les Munro was sprawled in a deckchair, reading the RAF magazine, *Tee Emm*, looking as imperturbable as ever – the fatalist's attitude to the impending operation. Others were talking in low voices. David Shannon, still in the Crew Room, had a mixture of feelings: elation, excitement and relief that the training had come to an end. Overall, he was anxious to get going, to get on with the job in hand.

John Hopgood was feeling more subdued. For some reason he felt convinced he would not be coming back and had said as much to Shannon. Many people did have feelings of imminent death, but it did not necessarily follow that such premonitions would be fulfilled. Hopgood was not the only one feeling a sense of impending doom. Ken Earnshaw, his new navigator, confessed to John Fraser that he thought eight of them would not be returning that night. Eight was a lot. There were 133 men flying on the raid; if Earnshaw was right, fifty-six would not be coming home. It was a sobering thought. Fraser had to hope it was based on nothing but pre-op nerves.

Gibson arrived in his car, complete with his crew, who piled out. Inside, Gibson was feeling tense and not a little scared and apprehensive about the operation being a success. As usual, he hid his feelings well, chatting and smiling.

Humphries managed to catch his eye. 'Anything you want me to do, sir?'

'Always on the spot, Adj,' Gibson replied. 'I don't think there is anything at the moment. Oh, yes, there is though. Plenty of beer in the Mess when we return.' Gibson spoke to Hopgood. 'Hoppy, tonight's the night,' he said. 'Tomorrow we will get drunk.' They always said this, before a mission.

At 8.30 p.m., the buses arrived to take the First and Second Waves to their aircraft. The men clambered on, Mae Wests now around their necks and waists, clutching parachute packs and leather flying helmets. There was no sign of David Shannon. His crew began shouting for him and eventually he sauntered out, grinning as the others called out, 'Don't let us worry you!' and 'Have you cleaned your teeth?' He was last onto the waiting bus, which then trundled off around the perimeter track. As they reached the aircraft, the buses stopped and seven men stepped down and walked over to the waiting, looming Lancaster, its strange cylindrical bomb looking huge and cumbersome like a giant egg clutched beneath it. First to take off would be Joe McCarthy's *Q-Queenie*. Groundcrew fussed about their aircraft. Near the tailplane on the starboard side of the aircraft was the hatch. At *E-Easy*, Norm Barlow's Lanc, the hatch was already open, a small five-rung metal ladder propped up against it. First the bomb-aimer, Pilot Officer Alan Gillespie, climbed board, followed by Harvey Glinz, normally the mid-upper gunner, but for this operation the front gunner alongside Gillespie. Third to clamber aboard was Barlow, the purple and white ribbon of his DFC already stitched to his battledress. Then came Pilot Officer Sam Whillis, the flight engineer; then the navigator, Phil Burgess, and then Charlie Williams. Last aboard was the rear gunner, Jack Liddell, the only man to turn left inside the aircraft, into the narrow confines of the fuselage. It was dark and narrow and smelled of metal and rubber and oil. To reach his wireless operator's desk, Williams had to clamber over the two wing spars, which barred any easy access to the front centre section of the aircraft. It was incredibly cramped. By the hatch hung the main compass, surrounded by a protective metal cage. There were no frills, and few comforts; the Lancaster was designed for one thing, and one thing only: bombing.

Just beyond the second wing spar, on the left-hand side of the plane, was Williams's desk, which jutted out from a bulkhead that ran from the floor to the roof. On the other side was the navigator's desk, where Phil Burgess was now laying out his maps and logs. Williams's station was the warmest in the Lancaster as it was right next to the warm air outlet. On those long flights during the winter it had been a huge advantage. He had often been the only warm person aboard.

With everyone aboard, the engines were run up and the pre-flight checks begun. This completed, the Form 700 was signed by the pilot and passed back to one of the waiting NCOs on the ground.

A little way away, at *G-George*, everything seemed to be in order. Gibson and his crew had been accompanied to their aircraft by Cochrane and an official photographer. As they boarded – Gibson going first – the photographer asked them to pause to have their photograph taken, the moment captured for posterity. Gibson, his hair neatly parted, in just his shirt, with the sleeves buttoned and wearing tan leather gloves, still looked calm, a trace of a smile on his face.

9 p.m. With double British Summer Time, it was still light, although dusk was drawing in. A Very pistol was fired and a flare whooshed into the sky before bursting and crackling with a red glow as it slowly descended. This was the signal for the first two waves to start their engines for the run-up prior to take-off. Around the airfield, engines slowly coughed into life. First the starboard inner, then the starboard outer, then port inner and port outer. With each, the propeller would slowly begin to turn then with a lick of flame and smoke from the exhaust stubs would kick into life, until in moments the propellers were nothing but a whirr.

Aboard *W-Willie*, Les Munro was running up each of his engines. The airframe began to throb and rattle as each was run up to around 1,800 rpm and a magneto check carried out, first one magneto, then the other. If there was any appreciable drop in revs between the magnetos, then the aircraft would be considered unsafe to fly. But all was well. With the engines running well, he went through the check list with his flight engineer, Frank Appleby. Everything appeared to be in order, just as he expected it to be; earlier that afternoon they had carried out a brief night-flying test – a quick take-off and circuit – and had already completed and signed the standard Form 700 that every pilot filled out before each op. He now plugged his helmet leads into the intercom and asked each of the crew to call in. They did so, and then Munro sat back and waited.

Next to him, in *Q-Queenie*, Joe McCarthy and Bill Radcliffe, his flight engineer, were suddenly encountering difficulties. There was a pressure drop in the cooling system on his starboard outer engine. This was a problem because it would soon run out, then the temperature in that engine would rise and rise until the whole thing seized or worse.

In the bomb-aimer's compartment, Johnny Johnson now heard McCarthy tell them the bad news, then heard him add, 'For Christ's sake, get into that spare aircraft before some other bugger gets there and we don't get to go!'

Clambering out, they hurried over to *T-Tommy*, the spare aircraft that had been flown up that afternoon from Boscombe Down. It had been loaded with fuel, ammunition and its Upkeep, but nobody had given it an air test. Normally, compass swings were carried out before the weapons were loaded and then swung again so that the deviation factor from the magnetic field set up by the steel of the bomb could be taken into account; but this had not been done, and having hastily clambered aboard, McCarthy now discovered there was no compass deviation card on board, a victim of the last-minute nature of the aircraft's arrival earlier that afternoon.

Muttering and cursing, and conscious of the clock ticking and the thirteen other Lancasters around the airfield already running up their engines, McCarthy jumped into the nearest van and sped back towards No. 2 Hangar.

'What's the matter, sir?' asked Chiefy Powell, hurrying out towards him.

'My bloody aircraft is u/s,' he yelled. 'I've got to take the spare. There's no compass deviation card. Where are those lazy, idle incompetent compass adjusters?'

Harry Humphries tried to calm him down while Chiefy Powell hurried off to find one, but it was already too late for him to leave on time. The first deviation from the plan had already taken place, before a single plane was airborne.

The rest of the Second Wave were already on the move, led by Norm Barlow in *E-Easy* and followed by Les Munro in *W-Willie*. Behind Munro came Vernon Byers in *K-King* and Geoff Rice in *H-Harry*, slowly prowling around the perimeter, dark and brooding, to reach the end of the open grass runway.

It was now 9.28 p.m. From the control caravan out on the field, a green Aldis lamp flashed. *Q-Queenie* had been due to be first to get airborne, but now it was to be Norm Barlow in *E-Easy* instead.

With the throttles pushed forward, the Lancaster began

bumping down the grass, engines developing maximum power, the crews pushed back into their seats. Charlie Williams sat at his desk, flying helmet on and leads plugged into both the intercom and the radio and wireless sets in front of him. Fifty miles per hour, sixty, seventy, eighty, every bump across the grass exaggerated by the weight of the bomb. The crescendo of the four Merlin engines, the speed across the grass quickening. Tail up. Ninety miles per hour, then a hundred and then, at 105 mph, and fifty seconds after they had begun, the bouncing stopped and the great Lancaster, cylinder protruding beneath it, rose into the air.

Operation CHASTISE had begun.

23

Outward Journey

NOT EVERYONE WHO tried was able to master taking off in a Lancaster, which was why not every pilot made it through the Heavy Conversion Unit. It was straightforward enough once you knew how, but, especially in a laden Lancaster, it required resolute concentration, and a degree of strength in the hands and feet. It was a big beast, after all.

Yet for the nineteen pilots of 617 Squadron, the take-off, even with a four-ton bomb protruding underneath, was one of the lesser challenges they faced, and although, for those watching, the Lancasters looked worryingly slow and cumbersome as they gradually lifted from the ground and cleared the hedgerow at the far end of the field, the first two waves all managed it without hiccup.

In fact, the only hitch was the failure of McCarthy's aircraft. At 9.39 p.m., the control caravan once again flashed its green Aldis light and Gibson, with Hopgood and Martin either side of him, opened the throttles and gathered speed across the grass, and climbing into the air disappeared into the dusk. Standing beside No. 2 Hangar, clenching and unclenching his fists, McCarthy could only watch with mounting impatience and frustration. Soon after, Powell reappeared with the card, handed it to him, and McCarthy headed off back towards *T-Tommy*, although in his haste as he stepped back out of the van, he clutched the ripcord on his parachute rather than the handle, and suddenly white silk bloomed everywhere. Flinging it onto the ground in irritation, he jumped back on board.

He could still not get going, however – not yet. No matter how much the minutes were ticking by, he still had to run up his engines and go through the rest of his pre-flight checks. At 9.47, the next three of the First Wave, led by Dinghy Young, headed down the runway. Now Maudslay, Bill Astell and Les Knight were taxiing their aircraft to the far side of the field ready for take-off. As they waited for the signal, McCarthy finally moved off. *T-Tommy* did not have VHF or spotlights fixed – fortunately not needed for the Sorpe – but the engine problem encountered en route to Scampton had been solved. The Lancaster was ready to fly even if not quite ready for the operation. She would have to do.

At one minute to ten, the last three of the First Wave thundered down the runway, and barely had they begun their take-off than McCarthy was manoeuvring *T-Tommy* into position. Two minutes later, at 10.01 p.m., they were at last on their way, half an hour behind Geoff Rice, the fourth to take off in the Second Wave. Watching from the window of his office on the first floor of No. 2 Hangar was Harry Humphries. He worried about 'Mac' taking off in such a state. He hoped he wouldn't make a mess of the whole thing.

Gibson's trio had been due to cross the English coast over Southwold after thirty-eight and a half minutes, and so they did, having encountered nothing but the fine weather forecast and with by now familiar landmarks to guide them. In *G-George*, no one had spoken. Radio silence had been demanded and Gibson and his crew abided by it, although the skipper was busy with his own thoughts.

Crossing the sea was monotonous but required intense concentration because it was very important they crossed the Dutch coast precisely where they planned to do so. Danger was never lurking far away in Nazi-occupied Europe, but the enemy coast was particularly well defended with heavy and light anti-aircraft guns and also night-fighter airfields. There were five night-fighter units – or

Nachtjagdgeschwader – in the area 617 Squadron had to fly through, each of which was divided into three groups – or *Gruppen* – of three squadrons – *Staffeln* – which at full strength had twelve aircraft each. In other words, Nachtjagdgeschwader 1, based in the Scheldt estuary area, had just over a hundred aircraft, most of which were Messerschmitt 110s and Junker 88s, twin-engine aircraft that were both much faster than Lancasters and had fearsome firepower – a mixture of 20mm and 30mm cannons and machine guns. These were supported by a thorough system of two types of radar and ground controllers who were able to vector night fighters onto their targets. The huge advantage the Lancasters held was that the radar defence system was only really effective over 1,000 feet, and not at all under 500 feet – it had been designed to counteract the kind of high-level bomber streams that Bomber Command normally operated. Thus, so long as the nineteen Lancasters stayed below 500 feet, they were unlikely to be picked up by radar.

This, however, did not mean they were safe from enemy night fighters, which were based at a number of airfields horribly close to the planned route. In Holland, between the towns of Breda and Tilburg, lay the night-fighter base of Gilze-Rijen. The planned route of the First Wave took them only a few miles to the south, and then, a short distance further on, not far north of Eindhoven, another major night-fighter airfield. As those on the Augsburg Raid had discovered to their cost, low-flying Lancasters that strayed too close to enemy fighter airfields were far from immune; after all, several of those attacked on that raid had been shot down by fighters taking off after seeing them and catching them up soon after. It might be night time and not daylight, but the skies were clear and the moon was full. Even without radar to help them, German night fighters could still spot them and shoot them down.

A potentially far bigger danger, however, was from the vast numbers of anti-aircraft guns. The 10,000 and more flak guns that protected the Reich were, admittedly, spread wide, but were concentrated along the coast and over cities and the industrial heartland. Heavy guns were unlikely to cause too much of a problem with the Lancasters flying so low – they were capable of hurtling a shell vertically to some 24,000 feet, but could not easily be traversed quickly enough to shoot down an aircraft at only a hundred feet and travelling at over 200 mph.

Light anti-aircraft guns could, though. Most were 20mm guns, either the Flak 30 or the Flak 38. These latter weapons were either single-barrelled – as Leutnant Widmann commanded at the Möhne – or had four barrels. All three types were automatic, with a fairly rapid rate of fire. Single-barrelled guns had a practical rate of fire of 180–220 rounds per minute, but the Flakvierling 38, the four-barrelled beast, could pump out a terrifying 700–800 rounds per minute. There were also a number of bigger, 37mm varieties of light flak guns. A single cannon shell from any of this array of anti-aircraft guns had the potential to bring down a Lancaster.

So long as the Lancasters kept low and stuck religiously to the planned route, they *should* be all right. The higher they were, the easier it would be for enemy gunners to hit them; on the other hand, the lower they were, the less chance they would have of ever recovering if they were hit. They were vulnerable to small-arms fire as well. If, while trying to locate a fix, they climbed too high for too long, they might be picked up by flak and night fighters. Equally, if they slightly strayed off the planned track, they could find themselves flying over either a night-fighter airfield swarming with Messerschmitts and Junkers eager to chase after them, or concentrations of flak. Or a combination of both.

The difficulty was that if they flew at a hundred feet or less, their GEE would not work, because of the curvature of the earth. It was impossible to map-read over sea, which meant relying on the compass and taking regular drift readings, or climbing to take a GEE fix. Taking drifts for undetected wind variations was fine out at sea, but even that required a fair degree of skill. In short, arriving at the Dutch coast with the kind of precision the operation required was ridiculously difficult.

10.50 p.m. Both the first aircraft of the Second Wave and Gibson's trio were now approaching the Dutch coast, albeit some 130 miles apart. The Second Wave had been supposed to fly closely but not together – that is, not in formations of tight vics. Certainly, with under ten minutes until they reached the Dutch coast, Les

Munro could not see any of the others; normal visibility at night, even in moonlight, was little more than a mile. The route they had been following had been due east and was the longest straight leg on the journey by a big margin – most of the remaining legs to target were between ten and forty miles. Munro had flown low the whole way across the North Sea. Drifts had been fired out of the aircraft and had shown a stronger northerly wind than expected, but having made their first change of direction – a slight turn to north on a bearing of 085 – and with the Dutch coast now looming ahead of them, they turned again, this time on a bearing of 147, which took them south-east and should, if they had reached the coast where they thought they were, mean they passed over the narrow island of Vlieland at right angles to the shore and halfway along, at its narrowest point.

As Munro made his starboard turn for his second change of course, he could see the water below and ahead, the waves breaking on the shore. It was time to fuse the Upkeep, but off to his right, some distance away, Munro suddenly saw a flash of light – an explosion, a large burst of flames. He suspected it was one of his Wave, although he hoped he was mistaken; if he was right, however, the aircraft had drifted badly southwards over the island of Texel. It was much the same length as Vlieland, although wider and certainly defended with plenty of flak, which was why they had been warned to avoid it. The trouble was, if the stronger, northerly, winds had not been detected, they could have easily been blown off course. Approaching the islands at just a hundred feet, Vlieland and Texel would have looked very much the same – and especially so in moonlight.

Vlieland was a thin, narrow island, barely more than a low-lying collection of sand dunes, yet the dunes on the shore were high enough to make Munro pull back slightly on the stick and climb just a little to clear them. Between them, they had done astonishingly well: they were crossing the coast at 10.57 p.m., on time and almost perfectly on target. Unfortunately for them, however, they were not quite perfect enough. Unbeknown to the planners, there was one flak unit on Vlieland, the 3rd Battery of Marine Flak 246, and as *W-Willie* passed over the narrow strip of land, at its thickest little more than two miles wide, Munro saw a single line of tracer coming towards them and a moment later there was a crack from behind and his headphones went dead. No engine had been hit and Munro was able to fly the aircraft on out over the Waddenzee, but it was very quickly clear that the shell that had hit them had severed the intercom and VHF. Munro decided to circle for a moment over the water and spoke to his flight engineer, Frank Appleby. With the noise of the Merlins, and with their helmets on, the only way they could hear each other was by Appleby leaning next to Munro, undoing the strap of his helmet and lifting his helmet free from his ear and bellowing as close as he could. Munro told Appleby to send Percy Pigeon, the wireless operator, to go and check that his rear gunner, Harry Weeks, was OK and to have a look at the damage.

Several minutes passed, with Munro repeatedly circling in a wide arc over the Waddenzee, the moon crossing over them as they did so. Eventually, Pigeon reported back. There was a big hole in the rear fuselage and the master compass by the hatch had been smashed. Weeks was fine – all the crew were – but there was no hope of restoring communications. None at all.

If they were to have any chance of finding the target and successfully dropping the Upkeep, they *had* to be able to talk to one another. Clambering back and forth and yelling in each other's ears was not going to work. Even if they had managed to reach the Sorpe, there was no way they would be able to drop the Upkeep accurately – not without bomb-aimer and pilot being able to talk to one another freely; decisions needed to be made instantly, not at minute-long intervals. A mile further north or south – even half a mile – and they would have passed over Vlieland safely. To the north lay the very narrowest part of the island, containing a track and little else; to the south, the rest of the island was nothing but a sand bar. At least, though, they were alive to fight another day.

'I made the decision there and then,' says Munro, 'to return to base.' It was bitterly disappointing, but there was no other choice. Munro had made absolutely the right call.

Munro and his crew did not know it at the time, but the Second Wave was unravelling badly. The explosion Munro had seen had been a Lancaster – that of Vernon Byers's *K-King*, hit by flak over Texel. The burning inferno had plunged into the polder. Just a minute or so after Munro and Byers had been hit, disaster hit Geoff Rice's crew in *H-Harry*. They had also seen the explosion of Byers's Lancaster but were about to have their own troubles to contend with. They had been flying low over the North Sea – very low – and approached Vlieland without making the earlier slight change of course. Like Munro, Rice had climbed a fraction to clear the dunes of Vlieland, and then changed course, turning to the south-east. Immediately, with the moon ahead, Rice found it even more difficult than usual to judge height. The water was playing tricks, but Rice's flight engineer, Sergeant Ed Smith, realized the altimeter, for what it was worth, was showing they were flying at zero.

Before Smith could say anything, however, there was a violent jolt, Rice instinctively pulled up, and then there was an immediate second jolt, the big aircraft bucked and suddenly sea water was spraying the main cabin and showering the navigator and his charts.

There were expletives from the rear and then Sergeant Burns, his rear gunner, told them the Upkeep had gone. Incredibly, Rice had been flying so low, the protruding mine had actually hit the water. The force of impact had ripped it from the caliper arms and it had then hit the tail wheel as the Lancaster passed over it, ramming the gear through the tail, smashing the Elsan toilet, and giving Burns a drenching of both sea water and disinfectant. Amazingly, Rice was able to continue flying the aircraft, and so climbed and flew on towards the IJsselmeer. In the moonlight, they realized the Upkeep had definitely gone, and water began draining through the bomb bay. As with Munro, though, there was nothing for it but to turn and head back to Scampton. They, too, would live to fight another day, although how they avoided plunging into a watery grave was something of a miracle. Thirty-ton Lancasters that flew so low they actually took on water tended not to survive. Rice and his crew had had a very, very lucky escape.

At any rate, the bare facts were these: in the space of just a few minutes, three of the original five aircraft of the Second Wave were no longer part of the operation. The only aircraft of the five so far to safely cross the coast was Norm Barlow's *E-Easy*, which had made its turn and was now heading south-east over the large expanse of the IJsselmeer. However, the Sorpe, the second most important of the three primary targets, was not a structure that was likely to break from the careful dropping of a single bomb. As Barnes Wallis had made quite clear, it would require multiple Upkeeps to breach it. Already that was now looking unlikely. The initial stages of the raid were not going well. Not well at all.

As Munro and Rice were running into trouble, 130 or so miles to the south Gibson, Hopgood and Martin were approaching the Dutch coast, a little behind schedule. The two waves had been supposed to cross the Dutch coast at the same time; to be just a few minutes apart was not such bad going.

At around 10.55 p.m., in *G-George*, Gibson's navigator, 'Terry' Taerum, said, 'Five minutes to go to the Dutch coast, Skip.'

'Good,' Gibson replied and peered out ahead. Pulford briefly switched on the spotlights and suggested he go lower – they had crossed the Channel at around one hundred feet. Dropping a bit, they quickly turned the lights off again. In the front turret, George Deering began swinging his twin Brownings from side to side in anticipation of any enemy flak ships or gun positions below, while Trevor-Roper readied himself in the rear turret. Either side of him, Gibson saw Hopgood and Martin close in a little more tightly. Someone began whistling and someone else said, 'Shut up.'

A moment later, Spam Spafford, the bomb-aimer, called out, 'There's the coast.'

'No it's not,' answered Gibson, 'that's just low cloud and shadows on the sea from the moon.'

Spafford was right, however. There was land up ahead. Gibson thought the islands looked low and flat and evil in the moonlight.

Terry Taerum came up beside Gibson and Pulford. 'Can't see much,' he said, peering out of the canopy. He reckoned they ought to be on track, however.

He could not have been more wrong. The same northerly winds that had pushed Byers so badly off course had sent them further south too. As they had been crossing the Channel, Martin's aircraft at least had been climbing occasionally to take GEE fixes. Jack Leggo, who despite being Squadron Navigation Officer seemed to take a very casual approach to log-keeping, had taken two wind variation tests and had discovered northerlies of 19 and 12 mph. That was enough to blow anyone off course. Furthermore, their ground speed should have been something of a warning: it was lower than they had planned. They should have been entering the mouth of the East Scheldt, between the islands of Schouwen to the north and North Beveland to the south, but ahead of them was land, not the wide expanse of the Scheldt estuary. They had taken very few drifts during the crossing and were now about to cross Over Flakee, a large and heavily defended island between the East and West Scheldt estuaries.

'Stand by front gunner,' said Gibson. 'We're going over . . . No talking. Here we go.' It was now 11.02 p.m.

Roaring over the coast, Gibson made sure they flew low and straight. Speed was of the essence and evasive action slowed them down. But as they sped over, they lost Hopgood for a short while. Eventually, he reappeared, back on their wing. Fortunately, the first three seemed to have caught the enemy gunners by surprise; they had not been picked up by radar or any other means. Flying at the best part of 200 mph, and at almost zero feet, they were an admittedly difficult target, but as Gibson and his crew now realized, they were in the wrong place. They had been lucky – very lucky.

Clearing North Beveland and finally crossing over the East Scheldt, Gibson now decided to climb a little, to around 300 feet, so that Spam and Terry could get a better view and try to find a fix. Their first landmark over the Dutch mainland was a windmill and telegraph mast near Roosendaal, which Taerum spotted quickly enough. Giving Gibson a new course of 099 degrees they skirted around Roosendaal, heading almost due east, and soon after found themselves back on track, following the correct course and thundering over the Dutch countryside at a hundred feet or less. In the nose, the bomb-aimer Spam Spafford was also armed with a roll of maps, each joined together like a giant paper roll. So low were they flying that on more than one occasion Spafford yelled at Gibson to pull up over power cables that were strung out ahead of them.

Precisely ten minutes behind them were the second trio of Dinghy Young, David Maltby and Dave Shannon. Crossing the Channel, they had also been blown further south but had realized and managed to correct themselves by regularly climbing to take GEE fixes. As a result, they reached the East Scheldt where they were supposed to and headed on down the estuary, over the island of Tholen and towards Roosendaal. They should have remained over the water of the estuary, threading between the islands, but they chose to cross direct. It seemed the first three Lancasters had awakened the defences below, however, because as they approached Roosendaal they now came under flak attack, forcing them to take dramatic evasive action. It could also have been because they had climbed too high, thereby alerting German radar; at that point, Maltby's navigator, Sergeant Vivian Nicholson, recorded taking a fix, followed by 'evasive action'. In *L-Leather*, Shannon could see arcs of tracer rising up towards them and searchlights criss-crossing although the Lancasters were still flying too low to be caught in their beams. This flak had not been anticipated, however, not at this particular point. 'The information we had of the place-ment of night flak along the route,' says Shannon, 'was not entirely correct.'

They were confident they were on the right track, however. In the nose, Len Sumpter's preparations were paying off. He had a series of folded maps rather than the loo-roll Spam Spafford had adopted, but his bright markings were working a treat and he was able to give Shannon plenty of warning of upcoming hazards and support Danny Walker, their navigator. The teamwork they had been practising was paying off.

All three were also regularly climbing to take GEE fixes. In Maltby's *J-Johnny*, Nicholson was taking wind variation tests every ten minutes or so. Climbing higher, of course, had its risks, as they had discovered when they had reached the Dutch mainland. 'GEE jammed something chronic,' Nicholson noted a short while later as they had climbed to take another fix.

Up ahead, Gibson's trio had safely passed the night-fighter base of Gilze-Rijen and had picked up the Wilhelmina Canal south-west of Tilburg, where, for a short stretch, it ran due east before forming a highly visible T-junction south of the village of Beek and north of the town of Helmond. This was the fix they needed to make another turn, this time on a bearing of 061 degrees to the north-east towards the German border and their next way-point, a bend in the River Rhine near the town of Rees.

11.13 p.m. To the north, Joe McCarthy in *T-Tommy* had reached the Dutch coast, having shaved off the best part of ten minutes so that he was now only twenty minutes or so behind schedule. He had no idea that Munro and Rice had turned back or that Byers and his crew were already all dead. Their own journey had not been without incident. Although they had taken off without VHF, the aircraft did have a radio set, but half an hour out, that packed up too. They could no longer receive anything.

As they approached Vlieland, McCarthy ducked down even lower between dunes to the south of the island. The flak battery began firing at them but, unlike Munro's crew, they made it through unscathed.

Eight minutes later, at 11.21 p.m., the third trio of the First Wave – Maudslay, Astell and Knight – reached the East Scheldt, a little later, but again pretty much in the right place despite the unexpected winds. GEE had helped ensure they were on course, although Hobby Hobday, the navigator on Knight's plane, *N-Nuts*, had not taken any drifts at all. 'I was navigating all the time,' says Sid Hobday. 'I had my head bowed down over maps a lot of the time over the North Sea, to be sure, absolutely sure, that we were going to hit the coast at the right place.' They might have been part of a vic operating in close formation, but they still navigated as individual crews in case anything should happen. As they sped over the Dutch countryside, the full moon bathed the landscape in a milky monochrome glow. With their eyes fully adjusted to the light, villages, trees, canals and farmsteads were all clearly visible. So too were power cables. 'On one occasion,' says Hobday, 'we nearly hit some high-tension wires, but we managed to get over the top of those.' Others flew under them, but they remained one of the major hazards of the operation. It was all too easy to lose concentration for a split second, to be looking down at the dials or at a map and to miss those power lines up ahead.

At 11.50 p.m., Norm Barlow in *E-Easy* had been ahead of the rest of the pack, and having reached the way-point of Rees, on a bend in the Rhine, had turned slightly north-east on a heading of 078 degrees. A few miles on, they had crossed over the railway line and had immediately been confronted with a swathe of power lines. Perhaps Barlow had not been warned in time, or maybe he lost concentration for a brief moment. Maybe they failed to see them against a backdrop of trees and houses in Haldern, a mile to the south.

Whatever the reason, *E-Easy* hit the 100,000 volt electricity cables, became engulfed in flames and plunged towards the ground, ploughing through the soil until the burning wreck came to a halt in the field's corner. The Upkeep had incredibly rolled free without exploding, but there was no escape for the crew. All, Charlie Williams included, had been killed. Four hours earlier, he had been writing to Bobbie, looking forward to the leave they would surely get after the operation and the moment the two of them would be married. That would now never happen.

The loss of *E-Easy* meant the attacking force was already down to just fifteen aircraft; the group heading to the Sorpe was down to just one. The Second Wave had been all but entirely knocked out.

The First Wave, however, was still intact. As the first three flew over the border, Gibson was struck by how quiet Germany seemed. There was no sign of any movement at all as far as he could see. No flak, no night fighters – nothing. On they droned, skimming tree-tops, dodging power lines over a largely featureless part of Germany, until up ahead they spotted the mighty River Rhine, straightened all those years earlier to make it one of the most important shipping routes in Europe. Gibson thought it looked white and calm and sinister in the moonlight – perhaps more sinister because he knew only too well it marked the barrier to the Ruhr. Beyond lay the German industrial heart with its countless flak positions. Their progress would be noted – if not picked up by radar, then visually and audibly, and reported. Germans would be furiously phoning and sending messages warning each other that intruders were hurtling low over the Reich. As they crossed the

there, they turned on a course of 196 degrees south-south-west, with just nineteen miles and six minutes' flying to target. Away to starboard lay Hamm – home to the largest railway marshalling yards in Europe – and a familiar target to the men of Bomber Command. It was also very, very well defended and looked very different from a hundred feet and less. If they cleared Hamm, they would be almost at the dam.

At a quarter past midnight, and some twenty minutes behind Gibson, Maudslay's wave were pressing north of the Ruhr. In *N-Nuts*, the navigator, Hobby Hobday, was still finding he could get GEE so long as they climbed high enough. A careful and methodical navigator, he made sure he took as many fixes as he could to ensure he stayed on track. In his navigation bag, he had brought with him various navigational instruments to help: a large sextant, a drawing compass, extra maps and a ruler. On the whole, he felt sure he had navigated pretty accurately. 'We always knew exactly where the plane was located,' he says. Any kind of tight cohesion had gone and the three aircraft were strung out, minutes apart. Hobday now noticed that Astell in *B-Baker* had started falling some way behind. Certainly, *B-Baker* was in the wrong place; Hobday urged his pilot, Les Knight, to stick to the route he was giving him.

Not long after, Maudslay's aircraft crossed over some power lines that ran right across their path just a few miles south of Borken. A minute or so later, Knight in *N-Nuts* did the same, but Astell was still floundering some way behind.

A moment later, however, Astell's Lancaster was erupting into flame. For the second time that night, a set of high-tension electricity lines had brought down one of the attacking aircraft. Engulfed in flame, the stricken Lancaster seemed to climb. An eyewitness on the ground, Roswitha Reiming, a maid at a farm near Marbeck, saw the flaming aircraft fly on, over their farm, then crash in a field some 200 yards away. In the fire, the ammunition from the six machine guns began exploding, bullets fizzing and hissing across the field. Two minutes later, the Upkeep exploded, smashing the glass of every window in the farmhouse and leaving a vast crater. Needless to say, there were no survivors from the Lancaster, which now lay broken and burning. That meant there were now five lost, and still not one of the dams had been attacked.

That moment was not far off, however. As Astell and his crew were plunging in flames to the ground, Mick Martin and his crew in *P-Popsie* were the first to reach the Möhne, followed by Gibson and then Hopgood. They had made it.

'In that light,' he noted, 'it looked squat and heavy and un-conquerable; it looked grey and solid in the moonlight as though it were part of the countryside itself and just as immovable.'

24

Goner

As Astell's Lancaster was plunging into the ground and as the first three aircraft had reached the Möhne, so the last of the attacking aircraft took off from Scampton. The Reserve Wave had begun to take off at 12.09 a.m., Ottley in *C-Charlie* the first to take to the air and swiftly followed a couple of minutes later by Burpee in *S-Sugar* and then Ken Brown in *F-Freddie*. The last two to leave were Bill Townsend in *O-Orange* and finally Cyril Anderson in *Y-York*.

There was a strange, tense mood at Scampton. Harry Humphries had felt restless all evening. Normally, he might have taken himself off to bed but he felt he had to stay up. Earlier, he had written up his squadron diary. 'This is Der Tag for 617 Squadron,' he had scrawled. 'The Day.' Of course, he had to stay up on this their first operation; all those in the know did.

However, if it was an anxious time for those non-flyers in the squadron, it had been doubly so for the thirty-five men in the Reserve Wave.

'It was a lot of hanging around,' says Grant McDonald, tail gunner in Ken Brown's crew. 'But it was a very pleasant night.' He'd watched the First and Second Waves take off and been quite impressed; he'd not seen Lancasters taking off in daylight, in formation like that, before. For the next two hours, they had sat around on the grass outside No. 2 Hangar – talking, smoking, trying to take their minds off the job they had to do. Then, at around 11 p.m., the buses had come around and picked them up and taken them to their aircraft. There had still been an hour and more to wait, but at least now they had something to do: the running up of engines, all the pre-flight checks.

Finally, just after midnight, it was time to go, although there was none of the fanfair that had accompanied the first to depart. No AVM Cochrane, no Barnes Wallis – they had left Scampton at about 11 p.m., heading to St Vincent's, where, in the underground operations room, they would follow the unfolding events alongside the chief himself, Air Chief Marshal Sir Arthur Harris.

An hour later, at midnight, the remaining five aircraft trundled out and began creeping around the perimeter track, engines rumbling, noses pointing upwards, their huge shapes silhouetted against the clear moonlit sky. At nine minutes past midnight, the green Aldis light blinked, and suddenly *C-Charlie* was surging across the airfield and slowly, painfully lumberingly, getting airborne. Eight minutes later, the last of them was gone, the roar of their Merlins gradually dying away until all of Scampton was shrouded in an eerie calm.

Sunday, 16 May was Mother's Day in Germany, and on this fine sunny day people had been out and about. It wasn't quite like pre-war days, but it was certainly peaceful enough. Here at the Möhnesee, it was hard to think of the terrible destruction going on in Essen and Dortmund and in other cities of the Ruhr. The sun had shone down on the lake, still very full, while around its shores, the trees were just beginning to bud and burst into leaf. Summer was well on its way – this fourth since the war had begun.

A beautiful day had been replaced by a warm, bright, moonlit night. At his post at the North Tower on the dam wall, Unteroffizier Karl Schütte was feeling bored. It was a quiet night, with nothing stirring. Before midnight, however, the telephone suddenly rang at the Command Post. It was the area Luftwaffe Flak Headquarters at the Schloss Schwansbell in Lünen, not far away between Dorsten and Hamm. News of the low-flying Lancasters had reached them and Widmann's battery at the Möhne were to stand by. In quick time, they were all ready, guns loaded and primed. Schütte stood beside his Flak 38 on the North Tower watching, waiting. Nothing. He began feeling quite bored again; staring at the moon's reflection in the calm waters of the lake was all very well, but for night after night they had been manning this dam and absolutely nothing had happened. Nothing had happened at all – just the odd aircraft flew over once in a while, using the lake as a fix.

Suddenly, around a quarter past midnight, he heard the faint thrum of aircraft from the north, but he doubted it was the dam they were after. They grew nearer and nearer, however, and although he could not see anything, he ordered his crew to send up some defensive fire. And then he saw them – faint black shadows. 'Aircraft were circling around the lake,' he says, 'and our defences were firing in all directions.'

On *G-George*, Gibson and his crew had been rather taken aback by the ferocity of the flak. There was a mixture of colours – different tracer for different types of shell – but because they were reflected on the water it gave the impression there was twice as much as was actually the case. Gibson had been hoping the guns at the dam were manned by the German equivalent of the Home Guard and that they would already be in bed. Nor could he tell quite how many guns there were, although the intelligence they had been given seemed pretty accurate – certainly there were neither barrage balloons nor searchlights.

They circled, picking out landmarks. Whenever they strayed too near to the dam, the flak opened up again.

'Bit aggressive, aren't they?' said Taerum.

'God, this light flak gives me the creeps,' said Gibson. Each of the dams had its own unique difficulties for those attacking. At the Möhne, the approach was ideal: a good, clear run of more than a mile from the protruding headland, which allowed the attackers plenty of space to manoeuvre into precisely the required position. The problem here was not the geography but the flak. So far as they could tell, there were twelve guns, a number of which, including those on the sluice towers, would be able to fire almost horizontally at the Lancasters as they made their approach run. In fact, there were only six, but a single shell from one of those guns could bring any of the aircraft down.

The crew all began talking about how 'binding' light flak was, while Gibson called up Martin and Hopgood. They had lost formation on the last leg, but they were both there safely. The Möhnesee was like a big jagged 'C' – with the northern prong running from what had once been the River Möhne, and the shorter, southern prong, curling around a protruding headland. Beyond this southern prong was a valley and it was above here, a couple of miles back from the dam wall, that Gibson now ordered Hopgood and Shannon to orbit while he carried out a dummy run.

'Stand by, chaps,' he said over the VHF, 'I'm going to look the place over.'

Despite the flak, *G-George* passed over the dam safely, then climbed and banked around back towards the orbiting aircraft. The first three had now been joined by Young and Maltby, who had also arrived separately. Last of the second trio was David Shannon, who crested the ridge to the north almost directly over the dam. 'We came in over one of the towers,' says his bomb-aimer, Len Sumpter, 'and were sprayed with flak, which I didn't like very much.' There was a rattle as something hit them, but it did not seem to have caused very much damage so he climbed to around 600 feet and joined the circling aircraft orbiting a little way back.

'Well, boys,' said Gibson to his crew, 'I suppose we had better start the ball rolling.' He felt absolutely no enthusiasm for the task whatsoever. Despite his usual outward show of confidence, the fear was gnawing at him horribly.

'Hello, all Cooler aircraft,' he said over the VHF. 'I am going to attack. Stand by to come into attack in your order when I tell you.' He spoke directly to Hopgood's crew. 'Hello, *M-Mother*. Stand by to take over if anything happens.'

'OK, Leader,' Hopgood replied. 'Good luck.'

At almost precisely the same moment that Gibson reached the Möhne, Joe McCarthy and *T-Tommy* arrived over the Sorpe. Despite the lack of VHF, and despite ongoing compass problems, they had found it and in good time. In fact, they must have been slightly ahead of the First Wave, which was possibly why flak and searchlight defences between Rees and Ahlen were rather more alert than they might otherwise have been, having heard and even seen a low-flying Lancaster hurtle past in what unexpectedly turned out to be the vanguard of the entire operation.

They had done well – very well – to make up lost time and to reach the target in a reserve and under-prepared Type 464, but then again there was possibly an advantage to operating alone. Nor had the journey been entirely trouble-free. As they had crossed over Holland towards Rees, a light had inexplicably turned on in the nose, a marker for anyone who wanted to target them. And, above, McCarthy had seen enemy night fighters, silhouetted clear as anything against the moonlit sky. 'They must have been above at about a thousand feet,' he says, 'and with our light on, I figured we would be a good target.' They could not figure out how to turn off the light, however, until eventually Bill Radcliffe smashed it with a crash axe. That sorted it.

They managed to dodge the flak and searchlights without too much difficulty and were left alone by any night fighters circling overhead. South-east of Hamm, however, they flew over a railway line and below saw a train chugging along. Sitting above Johnny Johnson in the nose was the front gunner, Ron Batson.

'Can I have a go, Skip?'

'All right,' McCarthy replied, although Johnson thought a little reluctantly.

Batson began peppering the train with his machine guns, but although it looked like an innocent goods train, it quickly replied with what they all realized was something heavier than a .303 Browning, and a moment later there was a crack as a cannon shell hit them under one of the wings. 'We felt it and heard it,' says Johnny, 'but it didn't seem to affect the aircraft.'

They had flown on, a little chastened, but although they knew they were in the vicinity of the Sorpe, they struggled to find it. The surrounding area was of steeper hills than around the Möhne and there was a lot of mist in the valleys. But then there it was: dark, cut-glass water, twinkling in the moonlight, but although no one shot at them or shone a searchlight, as soon as they saw it, they realized what a difficult, formidable target the Sorpe really was.

Wallis had explained that the best way for them to hit it was to drop the Upkeep directly onto the dam wall. It would then roll down and explode. It did not need to be revolving for this, but extreme accuracy was paramount. The only way there was any chance at all of achieving this was to fly parallel to the dam's wall. The Sorpe Dam was long – at 700 metres the longest of the three primary targets – but travelling at 200 mph, that only gave them just a matter of seven seconds to cross it. The dropping of the bomb – Johnny Johnson's task – would be a split-second decision. A fraction early or late and it would not hit the centre of the dam.

A second problem was the angle of approach. Rising up at its western end was the village of Langschied, perched on the hill and with a church with a high steeple perched even higher and pretty much directly in the way. On the far side, steeply wooded slopes rose several hundred feet. The difficulty was that to drop the Upkeep with the kind of accuracy required meant getting in low – really low – but the church and the steep slopes either side suggested this would not be possible.

For a while, McCarthy flew around. They did not want to hang around, but at the same time he did not want to come all this way and make a mess of things. No, the Sorpe needed a little bit of working out.

12.28 a.m. Back at the Möhne, and circling in a wide anti-clockwise turn, Gibson took *G-George* around, down moon, over the low hills, over the headland, straightening up and diving down towards the lake. Through the windscreen, Gibson could see the dam silhouetted against the haze of the Ruhr Valley beyond, the two sluice towers clearly identifiable. As they came in low over the trees on the headland, Spafford, in the nose, said, 'You're going to hit them. You're going to hit those trees.'

'That's all right, Spam,' Gibson replied. 'I'm just getting my height.' He now spoke to Taerum. 'Check height, Terry – speed control, Flight Engineer – all guns ready, gunners – coming up, Spam.' Taerum turned on the spotlights as they cleared the shore and flew on over the water. Less than a mile to the dam.

'Down – down – down,' said Taerum. 'Steady – steady.' He saw the lights make their figure of eight. Sixty feet. Beside Gibson, Pulford began working the speed – adding a bit of flap to slow them, then opening up the throttles to get the air speed indicator against the red mark that had been put onto the ASI with a china-graph pen. In the nose, Spafford began lining up the towers. He had now turned the fusing switches to 'ON'. In the pilot's seat, Gibson concentrated hard, keeping the aircraft steady and level. Two hundred miles per hour. Sixty feet.

For Karl Schütte and the defenders at the dam, the spotlights suddenly gave them a visible target where before there had been just noise and shadows. Tracer hurtled towards *G-George*, some even bouncing off the water. This was a terrible moment for Gibson and his crew, like making a direct charge over clear open ground against a machine gun. Gibson felt he was being dragged towards the target, against his will. Fear gripped him. *In another minute we shall all be dead*, he thought to himself. *This is terrible – this feeling of fear.*

They were now just a few hundred yards from the dam. In a quiet voice he said to Pulford, 'Better leave the throttles open now and stand by to pull me out of the seat if I get hit.' Still they had not been hit, and although Gibson had flown through worse flak and survived, he had not done so at such a low height. Taerum was still watching their height, Spafford was clutching the bomb release and the front gunner began firing. Gibson was overwhelmed by the vast size of the dam. His Lancaster, normally such a beast, seemed suddenly very much smaller, and the dam wall so impregnable. Their own 100 per cent tracer rounds were pumping towards the towers while cannon shells hurtled past them.

'Left – little more left,' said Spafford, 'steady – steady – steady – coming up.'

The nose gunner continued to rattle as Pulford crouched beside him. Gibson could smell burned cordite. Tracers flashed past them. Another gun seemed to be firing in completely the wrong direction. The wall loomed towards them.

'Mine gone!' said Spafford and immediately Bob Hutchison, the wireless operator, fired a red flare, as pre-arranged, through the astrodome, partly as a signal to the others that the Upkeep had been released, and partly to blind the defenders. Both guns now chattered, peppering the defences as they hurtled over the wall and beyond. As they circled around there was a sudden huge explosion and a massive column of water towered some thousand feet into the sky.

On the dam wall, Schütte and the other defenders had been caught out by the speed with which the Lancaster had come at them – and by the low level of the approach. 'Suddenly,' says Schütte, 'the speeding black shape was thundering like a four-engined monster between the two towers and over the wall at a height of about twenty metres, spitting fire and almost ramming the defence post with its tail.'

Moments later, the Upkeep exploded, drenching them all. Waves as high as houses battered the crest of the wall, but, as the water subsided, it was clear the bomb had not breached the dam. For Gibson and his crew, it was a bitter disappointment.

Next up was Hopgood in *M-Mother*. In the nose of the Lancaster, John Fraser now heard Gibson assure them it was 'a piece of cake'. It was an interminable wait, but several minutes passed to allow the water to subside and become calm again, and then, at 12.33 a.m., Hopgood gave the signal: 'OK, attacking.'

Just as he began his run, Maudslay and Knight arrived and quickly joined the orbiting aircraft a few miles back. Hopgood was now approaching the water. On came the spotlights and as soon as they did so, the aircraft was met by a fury of tracer from the defenders, now very much alive to what was going on, and no doubt with their blood well and truly pumped up.

One can only imagine what was going through bomb-aimer John Fraser's mind. The nose gave him the best view in the house, but it must have made him feel incredibly vulnerable too. His job was not to look down towards the water, but dead ahead, towards those two towers, and to somehow, with his hand-made wooden Dann bombsight, line up his target. Precision was the key, and yet to hold that bombsight without shaking, as tracer pumped towards him, each shell enough to smash both the Perspex and his body, required nerves of steel.

On this first run, they now slightly overshot their mark. With tracer still arcing towards them, Fraser was just about to call 'dummy run' when the plane jolted as cannon shells struck.

On the dam wall, Karl Schütte stood behind his gun crew commander directing fire and shouting, 'Harder! Harder! You're getting to them.' Suddenly he saw the streams of tracer hammering into the aircraft and a moment later flame billowed out.

Circling behind, Dave Shannon, in *L-Leather*, also saw Hopgood's plane get hit, and he reckoned it was in the petrol tanks because one wing was quickly engulfed in flames.

'It's burning! It's burning!' yelled Karl Schütte from the north tower. On board *M-Mother*, Hopgood called to Fraser to drop the Upkeep. As the burning Lancaster hurtled over the wall trailing fire and smoke, so the Upkeep skipped on the water then right over the wall and plummeted some 200 feet onto the power station below and exploded sending a further sheet of angry flame into the sky. This time the dust and force of the explosion almost took the German defenders' breath away. Stones clattered around them. Karl Schütte was knocked to the ground. As he stumbled to his feet again, he looked down over the immensity of the dam wall and saw the power station had gone.

On *M-Mother*, somehow, a red flare was fired from the fuselage, but it was clear the aircraft was finished. Desperately, Hopgood tried to climb, and managed about 500 feet, turning to starboard to clear the wooded ridge to the north of the Möhne. On board, as Hopgood battled to control the badly burning aircraft, he said, 'For Christ's sake, get out of here.' In the bomb-aimer's nose, John Fraser now released the escape hatch and jumped. The trees, he thought to himself, *look awful damn close.* No sooner had his parachute opened than he was landing among them – and, incredibly, largely unhurt.

In the aircraft, Burcher, the tail gunner, was clambering out of his turret and saw Minchin, badly wounded, struggling back down through the fuselage. Burcher grabbed him, pulled the ripcord and pushed him out through the hatch, then opened his own parachute, held it in his hands and jumped himself. It was not a second too soon, because a moment later, *M-Mother* blew. Those still circling behind the dam saw it all – a mighty explosion and then bits of aircraft were sprayed over the ground beyond. Burcher, miraculously, survived, although with a badly damaged back, as did John Fraser. Minchin was not so fortunate, and nor were the rest of the crew. Hopgood's sense of foreboding had come horrifically, violently true.

It was now 12.36 a.m. Just after Hopgood's plane disintegrated, Les Munro and his crew in *W-Willie* were about to touch back down, the Upkeep still held in place beneath them. None of the pilots had been given any orders to jettison their bomb load should they encounter difficulties and be forced to turn back, and knowing the highly secret and sensitive nature of the weapon, Munro thought it best to keep hold of it. The trouble was that just as he was trying to land, so too was Geoff Rice in *H-Harry*, but with no means of communicating with the controller at Scampton, Munro had simply flown straight in. The chances of landing precisely the moment someone else was about to do the same was, on the face of it, extremely remote – after all, Munro had no idea that Rice had turned back too – but *W-Willie* went in straight underneath *H-Harry*. A tragedy was avoided by a whisker.

As it happened, Rice and his crew had been circling near Scampton for about twenty minutes already, because as they had been nearing the Station, Smith, the flight engineer, had been sent to check the hydraulic system for the undercarriage. He had soon reported back that most of the fluid had leaked, so Rice decided to lower the wheels using the emergency air bottle. However, he knew from experience that once the wheels were locked in place there was then not enough pressure to operate the flaps fully, which were needed to help brake and slow the aircraft. Furthermore, there was no tailwheel any more after the detached Upkeep had smashed it, so he had already ordered his crew into emergency crash positions and had circled Scampton burning off the last amounts of fuel. They were just coming into land when *W-Willie* had steamed in under them. 'I had the dubious honour,' says Les Munro, 'of being the first one to land back at Scampton – and with a live Upkeep.' His mission may have been cruelly cut short, but at least he and his crew were still alive.

*

At the Möhne, the tragic demise of *M-Mother* had underlined just how dangerous and difficult an operation this was. Next in was Mick Martin, one of the calmest, most cool-headed men in the squadron; even so, to follow Hopgood was no small task.

For Gibson, this was a particularly devastating moment. Hoppy had been his closest friend in the squadron. He'd lost many friends before, but this would hit him hard, and yet he had to somehow put this to one side, otherwise the operation was in danger of disintegrating as quickly as *M-Mother*. Four of the Second Wave, he had now learned, had gone, and two of his Strike Wave as well. Not one dam had been breached and the Möhne looked utterly impregnable.

At this moment, Bob Hutchison sent the first signal from the dam back to 5 Group HQ. A series of signals had been worked out, which would be relayed to Grantham after every drop. 'Goner' was the codeword for a released Upkeep, '6' then meant that it had exploded within five yards of the dam, '8' meant with no apparent breach, and 'A' referred to the Möhne. Gibson's signal, 'Goner 68A' was sent at 12.37 a.m.

It was also at this moment that Gibson somehow managed to dredge the depths of his very being and show the extraordinary raw courage and incredible leadership that proved why men like Cochrane and Harris reckoned he had been the right man to lead 617 Squadron. Adrenalin was keeping him going, but his feet were agony, he was feeling repeated bouts of intense fear, and yet, having faced two runs at the dam already, he now recognized that something drastic was needed if they were to have any chance of hitting the wall without being shot to pieces first.

On the dam wall, the gunners had used the gap between attacks to dust themselves down, replace overheated gun barrels and oil the breeches. Every man, apart from the gunner himself, was hurriedly rearming the guns, but then came news from the south tower that the gun there was finished. The attackers did not know it, but their task had just become a little bit easier.

At 12.38 a.m., Martin began his run and this time Gibson flew alongside, slightly ahead and to starboard in an effort to distract the gunners and draw some of the flak from Martin's Lancaster. It didn't stop *P-Popsie* from being hit, but this time the damage was not serious. Smoke from the explosion beyond the wall was obscuring part of the south tower, but Hay reckoned he had dropped his bomb dead-on. It was not precise enough, however, for it sheered away to the left. As Martin pulled away to the south, the third Upkeep exploded, again sending a giant spume of water high, high into the air.

But when the water subsided again, the dam was still intact.

Gibson had hoped that Young and his crew would not be needed at the Möhne, but now with three Upkeeps gone and one crew shot down, he called upon his senior Flight Commander. Again, Gibson drew the flak, now flying parallel to the dam on the northern side, but this time kept wider, hoping to draw the enemy fire further away, while Martin, having circled, joined Young on his port side.

As *A-Apple* switched on the spotlights and began its run, so Gibson ordered the identification lights on his own *G-George* to be flickered on and off as a further distraction. From *G-George*, machine-gun fire spat towards the defenders as Young lowered and settled, the figure of eight glowing on the surface of the lake. At precisely sixty feet and in perfect line with the aiming point at the centre of the dam wall, his bomb-aimer, Flying Officer Vincent MacCausland, dropped the fourth Upkeep. Three good bounces, the bomb hit the wall, sank, and a few moments later came a third giant column of water.

'I think I've done it!' Young called out. It was the perfect strike – no deviation, dead centre – surely it would break it.

As the water subsided, however, the great wall of the dam still looked worryingly solid. Gibson was sure another Upkeep would do it. Just one more. It had to go then. Surely . . .

12.46 a.m. At the Sorpe, the crew of *T-Tommy* were beginning to lose their patience with their Skipper and bomb-aimer. They had now made nine runs at the dam, and had been there half an hour. Any moment, enemy night fighters might swoop down on them; on the return leg, the journey might now be much, much worse.

On the ground, some troops might start taking a pop at them – they were certainly low enough. They were flying round and round over enemy-occupied territory, for God's sake. And another thing: where was everyone else? They had been last airborne. Where were the other four? They could not understand it. They had no idea that two entire crews had been killed and a further two had been forced to turn back.

The problem for Joe McCarthy was that he just couldn't quite get down low enough. 'I had trouble with that darn steeple,' he says. It even crossed his mind to try and shoot it down to clear the way. When they did attempt it neither McCarthy nor Johnson ever seemed satisfied.

'When I wasn't satisfied,' says Johnson, 'I called "Dummy run", and if Joe wasn't satisfied, he just pulled away and left me to call "Dummy run".' Eventually, a lone voice from the tail said, 'Won't someone get that bomb out of here?' Tail gunner Dave Rodger had had enough. They all had. Johnson was determined to get it right, however. They had all done so much training, made so much effort. There was no point in reaching the dam and not doing the job properly.

Now, at just gone a quarter to one in the morning, they began their tenth run. McCarthy managed to climb down spectacularly low so that as they reached the centre of the dam, they were just thirty feet off the top of the wall, the centre of the aircraft just fractionally to the starboard side of the crest of the dam. Perfect, and in that split second, Johnson knew it was as clear a shot as he was ever going to have. Pressing down on the release, he called out, 'Bombs gone.'

'Thank Christ,' muttered Dave Rodger from the back. Immediately the Lancaster lurched upwards at the release of the four-ton Upkeep and McCarthy pulled the control column towards him, *T-Tommy* climbing stomach-lurchingly steeply and banking to port to clear the wooded ridge beyond.

Suddenly, as they circled around, the bomb detonated, a massive fountain of water and debris erupting into the air. Wallis had told them that one bomb was unlikely to cause a breach, and even if it did it would not be not immediately. The explosion was certainly dramatic enough, however, and as McCarthy banked around and turned north-eastwards towards the Möhne, they all felt satisfied that they had done precisely what they had been asked to do.

At Grantham, Wallis, Cochrane and Harris were all down in the underground operations room, which had been dug a little way from the main entrance to the house and was connected to the main headquarters building by an underground passageway. On one side stood a raised dais, on which sat Wing Commander Wally Dunn, the Chief Signals Officer. On another wall was a huge map of Europe and a list of operational aircraft and their current state. WAAFs and headquarters personnel hovered with headsets, taking down signals, chalking up new pieces of information.

Wallis struggled to keep still and paced continually. Earlier in the day, at the main briefing at Scampton, he had leaned over to Gibson and said, 'I hope they all come back.' Gibson had replied, 'It won't be your fault if they don't.' It did not quite seem that way to Wallis, who was suddenly burdened by a huge sense of responsibility for having created a weapon that had to be delivered by young men in extremely dangerous circumstances. Up until then, it had just been a weapon and nothing more. Wallis had been concentrating on simply trying to make both Upkeep and Highball work.

It was also unprecedented for 5 Group HQ to be in direct wireless contact with a bomber force as they were operating. Wally Dunn received any incoming messages then repeated the translated code to those waiting below. The first from the dam, Gibson's 'Goner 68A' at 12.37 a.m., had caused mutters of despair from Wallis, because a contact five yards from the wall should have been enough. In fact, his bomb had not hit as perfectly as that, but at the time neither Wallis nor anyone in the operations room knew that. As far as Wallis was concerned, it looked horribly as though the weapon was a terrible failure.

Meanwhile, thirty miles away at Scampton, groundcrew had hurried over to Munro's aircraft. Overhead, Rice circled around, waiting for confirmation that the Upkeep on *W-Willie* was safe.

Then, at 12.47 a.m., and with the crew in emergency crash positions, he came into land, the wheel-less tail tearing across the grass. Despite his concerns about the flaps, the landing was without a hitch and Rice was able to switch off his engines. He clambered out feeling utterly wretched. A mixture of disappointment and humiliation consumed him as Whitworth drove out to meet him and take him and his crew to their debriefing. But as with Les Munro, no matter how bad he was feeling, he was unquestionably very lucky to still be alive. All his crew were.

12.49 a.m. On the dam wall, Karl Schütte and his men were close to despair. Gibson's idea to circle around and fire at the defenders had been inspired because now, amidst the smoke and water and confusion, they had no clear idea of what on earth was going on. It seemed they were being attacked from all sides. To make matters worse, his Flak 38s had jammed. 'We tried desperately to clear the jammed guns,' says Schütte, 'but all to no avail. We just despaired.'

By now it was David Maltby's turn in *J-Johnny*. Once again, Gibson and Martin stayed to draw the flak, circling closely around the dam rather than flying alongside. Maltby came in low, and again at the correct line and height. For Karl Schütte, it seemed as if the attacks were little more than child's play for the enemy bombers. As Maltby's plane roared past, it seemed so close he almost believed he could touch it. He was certain he saw the outline of Maltby's head in the cockpit. He and his men took pot shots with their rifles. 'It seemed almost laughable,' says Schütte, 'but we fired and it took our minds off the danger we were in.'

As the fifth Upkeep was released, however, Maltby's crew could see the dam already beginning to crumble – Young had been right. His bomb had done the trick after all. As Maltby's Upkeep landed and sank and then exploded, it sent up not just water but mud and stone as well, rising high and silhouetted spectacularly against the moon.

At the same time, David Shannon in *L-Leather* was preparing for his run. 'And then,' recalled Shannon, 'there was an excited yell over the R/T. "It's gone! It's gone!"'

Gibson ordered Shannon to pull away and not attack and then

said, 'Stand by until I make a recco.' As Gibson looked down he could barely believe his eyes. There was no doubt about it. Across the dam wall was a vast breach. Water was pouring through. Gibson thought it looked like stirred porridge in the moonlight. Most of the flak had now stopped firing, and one by one the others all came to have a closer look. 'I can hardly describe the atmosphere in the plane,' says Shannon. 'The yelling, the pure excitement.'

There was shouting and screaming in *G-George* too, the VHF ringing in their ears with over-excited delirium. It was, Gibson thought, a tremendous sight – and one no man was likely to ever see again.

On the remains of the dam wall, still at his station on the north tower, Karl Schütte and his men could hardly believe what had happened. The dam was broken, water pouring through. The air was so full of spray they could barely see a thing, but it was clear enough they needed to get away and get away quickly, before they too were consumed by the gushing torrent now thundering down the valley beyond.

Still circling overhead, Gibson ordered Hutchison to send the signal 'Nigger' – the codeword that the Möhne had been breached. Below, millions of cubic metres of water were now gushing down the valley like a tsunami and the steam and spray causing a fog that had quickly shrouded the deluge.

The main target had now, emphatically, been destroyed. That was one down. Forty-five miles away as the crow flies, however, lay the next target. It was now time to head to the Eder Dam.

At Grantham, the waiting had been interminable – long, drawn-out and excruciating minutes. Then, at 12.50 a.m., they had received another signal, this time from Young's aircraft. It had been sent just after the water had subsided on his run, when, despite Young's conviction that the dam was about to crumble, the blast appeared to have caused no damage at all. 'Goner 78A' was the signal. Exploded in contact with the dam but no breach. For Wallis, this was worse news than Gibson's signal. The weapon had not worked. It was a failure. All this time and effort, all these young men's lives, had been for nothing. He had buried his head in his hands.

Three minutes later, inexplicably, Martin's signal had come through. 'Goner 58A' – Upkeep exploded fifty yards from the dam, no breach.

But then, three minutes after that – at 0056 – a further signal had come through: 'Nigger' – meaning a breach in the Möhne. Dunn demanded confirmation and received it a minute later, then announced it to the room.

Immediately, Wallis jumped into the air and pumped both arms. Everyone was smiling now. Even Harris, who had once suggested that Wallis should have his testicles removed and be locked away, had the grace to shake him by the hand and congratulate him. 'Wallis,' he said, 'I didn't believe a word you said when you came to see me. But now you could sell me a pink elephant.'

From agony to ecstasy. The mighty Möhne had been smashed.

25

The Hardest Target

A<small>T THE</small> M<small>ÖHNE</small>, Gibson had sent Martin and Maltby on their way, and instructed the remainder to make for the Eder. He included Dinghy Young, who he had always planned would lead the assault on Target Y, and his own crew. As commander, he wanted to do all he could to assist the remaining three aircraft from the strike force who still had Upkeeps. These were David Shannon, Henry Maudslay and Les Knight.

No sooner had he left the scenes of mounting devastation at the Möhne than Joe McCarthy and his crew flew over. They had heard over their wireless that it had gone, and McCarthy had thought there might be some useful intelligence they could report from what they saw there. And, in any case, they were curious. What they saw was a torrent – water gushing out of the breach. The valley beyond was flooded, with bridges smashed, buildings ripped apart and submerged. The devastation looked to be incredible. Johnny Johnson could not help feeling a sense of satisfaction at such an astonishing achievement.

They did not stay long. It was time to turn for home. They headed north, back the way they had come towards Ahlen, but without the bomb the compass deviation had changed, and they were soon off course. Before they knew it, they were approaching a town, which, according to their compass bearing, should not have been there. In a trice, they realized they were flying over the Hamm marshalling yards. It was not a very healthy place to be.

McCarthy flew lower and lower – the only way was to keep going as low as possible. 'Who needs guns?' muttered Dave Rodger. 'At this height, all they need to do is change the points.'

As Martin, Maltby and McCarthy were heading for home, the rest of the First Wave were flying further away, south-east towards the Eder Dam. This involved another very tricky piece of navigation. For most of the journey across Holland and Germany, the landscape had been occasionally undulating but largely flat. It had meant that they never had to fly very high before they could pick out some visual fix, whether it be a road, a canal or a river. In the stretch of Germany between the Möhne and the Eder, however, lay the heart of the Sauerland, with its rising hills and twisting valleys. Towns and villages nestled in these valleys, one barely distinguishable from the other. Landmarks were much harder to pick out here. The only effective way to navigate was to set a course, take an occasional GEE fix if at all possible, and hope there was not too much mist in the Edersee. It was also an enormously dangerous place to fly over at low level. At least in flat and open countryside, it was mostly possible to see ahead – visibility in those moonlit conditions was about one mile – but over the Sauerland, with its dips and rises, peaks and valleys, power cables or smaller hills were all too often hidden by the silhouette of a larger feature beyond. Just getting to the Eder was quite some achievement.

Unsurprisingly, they all struggled. To make life harder, there was now a fair amount of mist in the valleys. Gibson managed to reach the western end of the long, narrow and snaking Edersee, and then had a highly precarious five-minute journey flying down it, its steep, curving sides rising either side of him. They found it very difficult to work out which was the lake and which were mist-covered valleys springing from it, but eventually they reached the dam, climbed a little and began circling, waiting for the others and taking note of the lie of the land.

They had all flown separately to the Eder; close cohesion had again been impossible. In *L-Leather*, Dave Shannon's crew had also struggled to find it and had been confused by the valley mists, but they thought they had found it and were about to make a dummy run when Gibson suddenly called up over the VHF.

'Hello, Cooler aircraft – can you see the target?'

Shannon immediately told him he thought he was in the vicinity.

Gibson then announced they would fire a red flare over the dam. Spotting it, Shannon's crew realized they had not been in the right place at all, but had been about to make a run at a bend in the lake that looked not dissimilar in the mist and moonlight. It seemed Maudslay, Young and Knight had also seen Gibson's flare because soon all five aircraft had joined *G-George* and were circling in a left-hand orbit.

The Möhne had its defences, the Sorpe its difficult approach, but while the Eder was undefended, it unquestionably posed the greatest flying challenges – challenges that had only sketchily been worked out beforehand thanks to the lack of a scale model. 'Nobody had seen it before,' says Les Sumpter. 'They didn't know what the situation was.' One of the reasons it was undefended was because the Germans considered it too difficult to attack by air. They had a point. Even manoeuvring in a small, light aircraft posed plenty of challenges, but in a thirty-ton Lancaster carrying a four-ton bomb, the task was of an even bigger order. A couple of orbits around the dam gave them a fairly clear idea, however, as to how to approach it. The biggest problem was the spit that curved around directly in front of the dam, and from which steep and wooded slopes rose, which meant the pilot could not turn before the spit then drop down the other side, because they would never be able to level off again at the required sixty feet in time. If they tried, they would plunge into the water. At ninety degrees to the centre of the dam wall, the spit was no more than 850 yards away – less than half a mile. Even to the very tip of the spit, it was only 1,275 yards – less than three-quarters of a mile.

That may sound quite a long way, but it was not in a thirty-ton, four-engine Lancaster. This was because of two things. The first was inertia, which was added to by the centrifugal force of the bomb – that is, the resistance of the aircraft to any change in motion. If a Lancaster was flying straight and the pilot wanted to bank to the left, he would have to anticipate the turn and allow plenty of space to make it, because the thirty tons of aircraft would still want to be moving straight ahead. As a rule of thumb, the smaller the aircraft, the easier it was to turn. Similarly, a Lancaster could not dive down over a hill and quickly pull up again. The second issue was the size of the Lancaster. As it turned, the aircraft tilted, but at low levels and with a wingspan of 102 feet, it could not tilt very far without one wing tip hitting the ground or water. Moreover, height would be lost in a turn. Furthermore, as it turned, the pilot was completely blind to what was on the other side of the tilt. Therefore, turning closely to a wooded slope, for example, was fraught with danger. And just as it took a while to make a turn, so it also took a while to come out of it again.

Around the lake, the hills rose quite sharply to some 400 feet above it. Standing sentinel to the north was the Schloss Waldeck, a castle standing perched on a promontory. To the west of this, running roughly north–south, was a gorge that ran down to the lake. This was the obvious approach route. Beyond the dam, there were further hazards, however, because a ridge of hills some 1,300 feet high and more than 500 feet above the dam curled round to the south only a third of a mile away and blocking their path. Attacking the Eder Dam was for highly skilled pilots only.

Gibson ordered Shannon to go first. Even trying a dummy run was going to be dangerous enough, because even the slightest misjudgement of the approach could prove fatal. With the town of Waldeck, behind the castle, as his start point, Shannon dived down the gorge towards the lake, then with the tip of the spit as his marker, made a left turn through ninety degrees, levelled out, tried to get to sixty feet and with just 450 yards to go, should have been in position to drop the Upkeep. He was not, however – he was still too high. Thundering over the dam wall, he put on full throttle and carried out a steep climbing turn to the right to avoid smacking into the rock face beyond. Watching from above, Gibson saw sparks from the engines on Shannon's plane as it lurched up out of the fray. 'To exit from the Eder Dam,' says Shannon, 'with a 9,000lb mine revolving at 500 revs was fairly hairy.' Having eventually cleared the hills, he banked away to the left and in a wide arc, swept around for another attempt.

Round he came again, the others orbiting above and well out of the way. Again, he could not get out of the ninety-degree turn at a height low enough to drop the Upkeep. 'You couldn't get the height,' says his bomb-aimer, Les Sumpter. 'You couldn't get down low enough to bomb, and by the time you had got the height, the towers were through the sights.' Twice more he tried, but twice more they were not in the right position to release the mine. Time was marching on. It was 1.30 a.m., they were deep in occupied Germany and with a long trip back home.

'OK Dave,' Gibson called over the R/T. 'You hang around for a bit and I'll get another aircraft to have a crack.' He called up *Z-Zebra*. Maudslay made two runs but, like Shannon, struggled to successfully clear the spit and level out again, so *L-Leather* was called upon to have another go. He made one dummy run, then, on his sixth attempt, both he and Les Sumpter felt they had at last got it right and released the bomb. It bounced twice, hit the dam wall, and then exploded, but as the water settled, the wall still held. Shannon was convinced he had made a small breach, although no one else had seen it.

At any rate, the dam looked as solid and immovable as ever as Maudslay now tried again. Gibson watched him running in, now straight and low towards the wall. His spotlights came on and merged, followed by the red flare; the Upkeep had been released. *Z-Zebra* hurtled over the dam wall, then a moment later there was a blinding flash as the Upkeep bounced and struck the parapet and exploded, and for a second the entire valley was lit up. Gibson could see the Lancaster quite clearly beyond the blast. 'It all seemed so sudden and vicious,' he noted, 'and the flame seemed so very cruel.' They all thought Maudslay's plane had been hit by the blast. Gibson quickly called him over the VHF. 'Henry – Henry. *Z-Zebra*. Are you OK?' There was no answer, so Gibson called again and this time received a faint voice in reply.

'I think so – stand by.'

Gibson heard nothing more. *Z-Zebra* had vanished into the night, but there was no second explosion, no tell-tale sign of a Lancaster crashing into the ground. Perhaps he had sustained some damage – not least to his VHF – so had flown on, clear of the others and towards home.

Meanwhile, the smoke from the explosion had filled the valley so they had to wait some more, circling overhead, for the fog of war to disperse. Eventually, it cleared, and now it was Les Knight's turn. Two highly experienced crews had tried and failed and now there was just *N-Nuts* left. Vainly, Gibson called up Astell at 1.47 a.m. and again three minutes later. He got no reply; Astell and his crew had been dead for over half an hour. So that left just one.

Last plane, last bomb. Last chance.

While the remainder of the First Wave circled around the Eder, the Reserve Wave were following the route the strike force had taken earlier. Ken Brown's crew in *F-Freddie* had crossed the Dutch coast around 1.30 a.m., once again a little to the south. Dudley Heal, the navigator, assumed this was due to a five-degree error in the compass; more likely, however, it was the northerly winds that had not been predicted, but which had caught most of them off guard.

The crew also had a new front gunner – their own was ill so they had taken Divall's, Sergeant Allatson – but despite this upheaval, the crew were working well. Brown's crew were among the least experienced and were only flying because Divall and Wilson had pulled out at the last minute. Even so, they were doing well so far with Dudley Heal, the navigator, and Steve Oancia, the bomb-aimer, working closely together, the latter calling out visual fixes as Heal plotted the course. They also flew a little higher than most – at around 150 feet rather than a hundred or below, which meant they could, initially at any rate, get GEE fixes.

As they were heading due east, south of the night-fighter airfield at Gilze-Rijen, they came under anti-aircraft fire for the first time. In the rear turret, Grant McDonald found this understandably unsettling. Just off the rear of the Lancaster, he saw red flashes shoot by. For a moment, he couldn't think what it was, then he saw searchlights swinging their beams and more tracer arced towards them, and then he knew exactly what was going on. He fired back for all he was worth. 'Flying that low,' he says, 'you can't go down and you can't go up, on account of the anti-aircraft fire – once you got up there, you're a goner, and, of course, you've got no room to go down, so you just had to plough through it.'

It was at this time, a short way to their port, that they saw *S-Sugar* get shot down by ground fire. There was an explosion, a ball of flame, which they then saw rise slightly into the air as Pilot Officer Lewis Burpee desperately tried to climb, and then the ball of fire began dropping again until it crashed into the ground with a massive further explosion as aircraft and Upkeep blew. All were killed; Burpee's English wife was expecting their first child. There had been something inevitable about one of the nineteen straying too close to Gilze-Rijen.

Poor buggers, thought Grant McDonald as they left the burning wreckage and the enemy flak behind and flew on towards the German border and the River Rhine.

1.47 a.m. At the Eder, Les Knight was carrying out his first run. Rather than feeling tense, at his navigator's station on board *N-Nuts*, Hobby Hobday was excited. He never really suffered from bouts of fear – unlike Gibson – and thought this attack was a great thrill. 'I learned to keep cool,' he says, 'and we were big headed enough to think that we were OK.' Just because two others had failed, their confidence had not been dampened.

This was not really shared by the other three still circling overhead, however, who in their tense concern began jabbering over the VHF with all manner of advice. 'We all joined in on the R/T,' noted Gibson, 'and there was a continuous back-chat going on.' Eventually, Les Knight switched the VHF off. 'It was a damn nuisance!' says Sid Hobday.

They tried one dummy run, after which Knight realized he needed to approach to the left of Shannon and Maudslay and to begin the turn earlier and wider.

And so he began his second run. It was now 1.52 a.m. This time he managed to line up the aircraft perfectly, and at the right height, and 450 yards from the dam the Upkeep was released, bounced three times, hit the wall and sank. As the Lancaster was screaming to clear the ridge of hills beyond, the mine exploded. Gibson, flying overhead, saw it all: the huge column of water rising a thousand feet into the air, and then the dam began to collapse. He thought it looked like a giant fist had punched a hole through cardboard.

'We could see the water gushing out,' says Sid Hobday, 'and all the masonry coming down . . . It really was fantastic. It's a sight I shall never forget.' Shannon agrees. 'We watched the water spew out,' he says, 'and as the valley flooded, everything in its path was carried away. A truly awesome sight.' From *L-Leather*, Len Sumpter also watched the extraordinary scene below and saw the breach getting bigger and bigger. 'The water was washing the sides out and also the wall below the water,' he says. 'There was just this great big flood all the way down the valley.'

They did not stay long. At 1.54 a.m., Gibson sent the signal 'Dinghy' – the codeword for a breach at the Eder, confirmed it again immediately, then answered the question from Group about whether there were any more aircraft to send to Target Z. Hutchison tapped out one word: 'None.' They followed the torrent for a short while, mesmerized by the crashing waves that tore down houses and bridges as though they were made of paper, and then told the others it was time to go home.

In the underground Operations Room at Grantham, when Wally Dunn announced that the Eder had also been breached, there was another outpouring of jubilation. An ecstatic Harris, any animosity he had felt towards the entire project now gone, decided to ring Portal in Washington. 'The telephone personnel,' he noted, 'seemed never to have heard of the White House, and there was some difficulty.' When he did eventually get through, he was intercepted and asked for an assurance that the person he was trying to speak to was reliable. On any other night, this might have caused an explosion from Harris, but he now patiently cajoled his way through a barrage of operators and eventually was rewarded. Portal was naturally delighted and promised Harris he would inform Churchill immediately. The timing could not have been better. It was the second piece of decidedly good news in four days, and both the victory in North Africa and CHASTISE had come while the Prime Minister and his Chiefs of Staff were in the United States for talks with their American counterparts. North Africa had been a predominantly British victory, CHASTISE an entirely British operation. These were timely successes.

26

Homeward Bound

WHILE THE SURVIVORS of the First and Second Waves were homeward bound, those of the Reserve Wave were still battling their way towards the target. The worst of the flak seemed to be where Gibson had made his warning just after midnight. At one point, Ken Brown was flying so low he saw the tops of the trees on one side of him being hit as the tracer scythed across them too high. 'It was so low,' says Grant McDonald, 'you could see the trees silhouetted against the searchlights.'

It was in this area, past Dülmen and north of Hamm, that Warner Ottley's crew were shot down in *C-Charlie*. 5 Group Headquarters had just sent a signal ordering them to attack the Lister Dam, which was acknowledged. Two minutes later, at 2.32 a.m., they sent the 'Dinghy' signal and ordered them to the Sorpe instead, but received no confirmation; in those ensuing minutes, *C-Charlie* was caught in lights and hammered by flak. The tail gunner was Sergeant Fred Tees, who had swapped positions with the front gunner at the tenth hour – a twist of fate that was to save his life. From his rear turret, he turned to see the inner starboard engine on fire, with long flames leaping past him. They were so low he knew there was no chance of successfully baling out and in any case, his parachute was in the fuselage and out of reach. 'I'm sorry boys,' he heard Ottley say over the intercom, 'we've had it.'

Moments later, the burning Lancaster crashed in a field next to a wood just north-east of Hamm.

Fred Tees was badly burned and knocked unconscious but somehow, despite the crash, despite the Upkeep exploding, and despite the usual fizzing and firing of .303 ammunition, he survived. It was nothing short of a miracle. Staggering away from the carnage, he was soon picked up by a farmer and a sixteen-year-old boy. The rest were dead, burned and flung from the plane. One of the crew had even been impaled on a nearby tree stump. It was another horrific and violent end.

There were now three attackers left. Cyril Anderson, in *Y-York*, had also, at 2.28 a.m., been ordered to attack the Sorpe, while Bill Townsend in *O-Orange* had, for some bizarre reason, been directed to the Ennepe. It was clear that Group Headquarters had no precise understanding of quite who was still flying, but even so, with the Sorpe having been struck just once, it made no sense whatsoever to attack anything other than the last primary target.

As Brown's crew turned at Ahlen for the final leg south, yet another Lancaster was about to be brought down. None of the rest of the First Wave had known what had happened to Maudslay's crew on *Z-Zebra*. Gibson had thought he had seen something dangling down from the Lancaster before Maudslay attacked the Eder, and most watching their attack thought they had suffered fatal damage when the Upkeep exploded on the dam wall. How much will never be known, but certainly they managed to fly on until, at around the same time that Ottley's plane was plunging to the ground, they were approaching the town of Emmerich, on the Rhine and very near the Dutch border. It was further south than the planned return route, which was to take them all back over northern Holland and over the Dutch coast south of Texel. Perhaps the aircraft was damaged; some of the crew may even have been wounded. At any rate, there were important oil storage facilities at Emmerich am Rhein and that meant plenty of flak as well. Attempting to fly directly over Emmerich, *Z-Zebra* was hit, caught fire, and crashed in a field to the north of the town. All seven were killed.

For the three remaining attacking aircraft, there was still a job to be done, however. In *F-Freddie*, Grant McDonald and Dudley Heal both reckoned they'd seen another aircraft going down – the flames and the explosion were something of a give-away. 'We were quite far away,' says McDonald. 'We didn't know who it was.' If they were right, it could only have been Ottley's *C-Charlie*. It was sobering, to say the least.

Shortly after, as they were approaching the Möhne, *F-Freddie* also received a message from Group, and this time they were directed to the last remaining primary target. It was not far to Sorpe – less than twenty miles as the crow flies from the Möhne – but finding it was quite another matter. By now, the mists that had plagued the strike force around the Eder had worsened. All they could see were the tops of the hills, so having reached what they thought must be roughly the vicinity of the Sorpe, they circled around. McDonald had noticed that the mist had been getting worse, but then they spotted an open passage in the blank sheet below and suddenly there was the water, dark and still and smooth below them, and at its blunt northern end, the dam itself.

All the problems that had confronted McCarthy now met Ken Brown and his crew, except that, if anything, the conditions were even worse. As they flew over, they could see the damage caused by McCarthy's Upkeep. Stonework at the top had been broken up and it seemed to have crumbled. They carried out several runs, each time realizing the damage by the first bomb had actually been quite considerable, even though the dam still stood. But they could not get down low enough; it was a recurring theme. Nor was climbing up clear of the wooded slopes at the far end settling nerves. They knew there was safety in keeping low, not exposing themselves to any prowling night fighters, who would certainly now be alive to the attacks that had already been carried out. After the third attempt, Brown climbed, then once clear dived and began another wide arc back again, only to run into mist that nearly did for them. By the time they were clear and back over the village of Langschied at the start of their run, the mist was worsening once more.

It was now nearly three in the morning. Mick Martin and David Maltby were around twenty minutes from home, Joe

McCarthy and his crew twenty-five. The crew of *T-Tommy* had somehow managed to get past Hamm unscathed, but once into the clear again had circled around trying to find a number of lakes near Dülmen, which were an obvious local landmark. Spotting them, they then realized they must be somewhere between sixteen and eighteen degrees off course of their track. Then McCarthy suddenly felt a thud and immediately asked the crew if they had seen anything. No one had. Nor could they smell any fire or anything untoward. Accepting that his compass was unreliable, McCarthy then decided to head back the same way they came – at least they would recognize certain key landmarks and already knew where to dodge flak. North of Broken, they turned north-west. After crossing the Rhine they were due to head back further south than the route they had come in by so as to avoid being lit up by moon reflection – which had obviously moved during the course of their flight to the Sorpe and back – when they reached the sea. 'Well, I figured it was the better of two evils,' says McCarthy. 'I felt I could compete with the fighters down at that level. But I couldn't compete with the defences I would have to go through.' A case of better the devil you know. Now, as they approached Scampton at last, it seemed the decision had paid off. The only scare had been as they'd approached the English coast and had run into a convoy. 'I wasn't gonna climb,' he says, 'because some of these navy shippers are real trigger-happy. We just picked our way through the formation.'

Some three-quarters of an hour and more behind were the rest of the First Wave. North of the Ruhr cities, Gibson ordered his flight engineer, John Pulford, to put *G-George* at maximum cruising. 'Don't worry about petrol consumption,' he said. He also decided to head back on a second planned return route, which meant crossing into the IJsselmeer at Elburg and out over the Dutch coast at Egmond aan Zee – this was a gap in the enemy defences he had used a number of times in the past, albeit never at a hundred feet off the deck.

The air speed indicator crept up to around 240 mph, then, from the rear, Trevor-Roper warned of an unidentified aircraft behind them, but they soon shook it off; it may well have been one of the others. He flew as low as he dared; his survival instincts were kicking in with renewed vigour. They had broken two of the dams; now he just wanted to get home and in one piece.

Almost 3 a.m. Gibson was just fifteen minutes from the Dutch coast. They were close now – over the sea they could begin to breathe a little easier, and yet, as Gibson was fully aware, anything could go wrong at any moment. Fifteen minutes was nothing and it was also an eternity.

He now decided to call up Dinghy Young, but received no reply. They wondered why.

Young had chosen the same return route as Gibson. In truth, there was barely a gap in the defences at Egmond. Flak positions were never far away – after all, there were some 10,000 heavy guns defending the reaches of the Third Reich and the same again of light anti-aircraft guns. It could take just one shell to knock a Lancaster down. Equally, the plane might be hit and barely notice the difference; or it might fly just a few yards to the right or left and be missed altogether. There were things a pilot could do to lessen the chances of being shot down – like extreme low flying, but then that threw up different risks, as Barlow's and Ottley's crews had discovered to their peril. In other words, random chance played a large part.

At 2.58 a.m., Young was approaching the sandy beaches around Castricum aan Zee, just five miles south of Egmond. He had tended to fly higher than some of the others, and that had meant less difficult – and in theory safer – navigation. But while Gibson would cross the coast unscathed fifteen minutes later, Young was hit within spitting distance of the open sea. The irony is that he was very probably flying extremely low here where the land is as flat as a board and with nothing but the sea up ahead. At any rate, the strike brought *A-Apple* down. Plunging to the sea it crashed on a sand bar just off the coast. And, once again, there were no survivors. The end of *A-Apple* meant eight of the nineteen had been lost on the raid.

In *G-George*, the open sea now lay just up ahead. Gibson thought it looked beautiful – at that moment the most wonderful sight in the world. But then Young would have seen the same view, and he and his crew had not made it. Gibson climbed to 300 feet, ordered full revs and boost from Pulford beside him, and then pushed the nose forward and dived with the air speed creeping up to 260 mph. Left of a small lake. Over a railway bridge. Along a canal. 'We flew low along that canal,' noted Gibson, 'as low as we had flown that day. Our belly nearly scraped the water, our wings would have knocked horses off the towpath.'

Ahead were the two radio masts that were their fix on the coast. Two hundred yards to the right. The sea drawing ever closer. Gibson tensed.

'Right. Stand by front gunner.'

'Guns ready.'

Suddenly they were hurtling over the coastal defences, the ditches and wire and beach obstacles, and the long stretch of sand, pale in the first grey shades of dawn, and heading out to sea, the enemy coast, grey and thin and ominous and still squirting flak, receding gradually behind them.

Back at the Sorpe, Ken Brown now hit on the idea of dropping flares, so asked Oancia, the bomb-aimer, to drop incendiaries which each crew carried through the flare chute the next time they went around. This would give them the markers they needed as they flew around for each run.

Dudley Heal had counted at least six dummy runs before finally, at fourteen minutes past three in the morning, both Brown and Oancia were satisfied they had the right line and height to drop the bomb. Away it fell, without spin, as Brown immediately pulled up to clear the trees at the far end, and landed not far from where McCarthy's had hit. 'We flew on round,' says Dudley Heal, 'heard the explosion and looked hopefully towards it but it hadn't gone. The damage was even more than it had been before, so we knew we had done the best we could.'

At the back of *F-Freddie*, Grant McDonald had seen enough. 'Get out of here!' he was urging Ken Brown. 'Go on – get moving!' They'd done the job they came to do, now it was time to head for home and sharpish. It would soon be getting light, there were bound to be night fighters about, as he was keenly aware, and whatever they had faced coming in, they probably had to face again going back. At 3.23 a.m., they sent the signal 'Goner 78C' – that is, contact with the face of the dam, but no apparent breach. They could not know it at the time, but their Upkeep had been the second and last mine dropped at the Sorpe.

This was because Cyril Anderson and his crew had already turned for home. Once again, it was the northerly corridor around the Ruhr heartland that had done for them. Taking evasive action from flak and searchlights, they had veered well off track and then could not get back on it again. GEE was jammed, mist was shrouding landmarks, and the rear turret guns were playing up. At ten past three, with dawn beckoning, and still hopelessly lost, Anderson had decided to turn back, retracing their steps as best they could back over the southerly route on which they had flown out.

The final aircraft to drop its Upkeep was *O-Orange*. The crew had had a harrowing flight to the target, and at one point had only avoided flak by flying down a narrow woodland fire break. Bill Townsend managed to find what he believed to be the mist-shrouded Ennepe Dam, no small achievement in itself, but it was another tricky one.* Furthermore, what had been marked as an island in the middle of the lake was, in fact, attached to the land by a narrow spit, which made the approach run even more difficult. The revolving Upkeep caused all the Type 464s to shudder, but on *O-Orange* it was really bad – because of the imbalance of the bomb – so much so that the crew began to feel really quite unnerved. They dropped their bomb on the fourth run. It bounced twice, then sank, short of the dam wall. It was now 3.37 a.m. Pulling up and circling, they saw the giant eruption of water, but when it settled back down again, the dam wall was still very much in place. 'Goner 58E' was the signal – bomb exploded fifty yards from the dam with no breach.

The last of the attackers had dropped his Upkeep. Now it was time to head home.

*

* There remains some debate over whether Townsend and his crew attacked the Ennepe or the Bever Dam, which looks very similar.

At Scampton, Harry Humphries had left the Mess and headed over to the squadron offices at No. 2 Hangar as soon as he heard more aircraft coming in. The first person he spoke to in the crew room was Dave Maltby, who told him Hopgood had been killed. 'We pranged it, though, Adj!' he added. 'Oh, boy, did we prang it!' He then asked Humphries whether Nigger had been buried. Gibson had asked Chiefy Powell to bury his dog at midnight. Humphries was not sure. In fact, he had asked LAC Munro to carry out the solemn deed, outside in front of Gibson's office. Hurrying out he was relieved to see freshly turned ground.

Joe McCarthy had finally touched down at Scampton at 3.25 a.m., safely, as it turned out, but not without drama. 'The right wing was very low,' says Johnny Johnson. 'The landing was very bumpy and the engineer looked out of the window and said, "We've got a burst tyre, Skipper."' It was only once they had taxied and come to a halt that they discovered the thud they had felt north of Hamm had been a 20mm cannon shell that had gone through the wheel on the starboard side, then on through the wing, and had hit the astro-navigation equipment above the navigator and then fallen down by his desk. At the time, they had had so much trouble with the aircraft already, the navigator, Don MacLean, had just assumed it was another bit of the aircraft falling apart. Not until they got back and saw the damage did MacLean realize the spent shell had virtually fallen into his lap. Such was the randomness with which aircraft could be hit; one crew's lucky escape was another's demise. 'A couple of feet one way or another,' says Johnson, 'and it would have been through a petrol tank and then it would have been bye bye McCarthy's crew.'

As McCarthy's crew were clambering from their battered replacement Type 464, Ken Brown's crew in *F-Freddie* were passing near the Möhne. Way up ahead, flak opened up, so they kept their distance, but were still able to see the huge devastation. The sight of all the water still gushing down the valley was, Dudley Heal thought, quite sobering. Ken Brown flew on north. They came under heavy flak near Hamm, but thereafter their journey back towards the north Dutch coast continued without any major alarms.

*

4 a.m. Harris, Cochrane and Wallis left Grantham and drove back towards Scampton. Hurtling north in his Bentley, and being driven by his chauffeur on this occasion, Harris banged his head on the roof as the car hit a bump in the road. His chauffeur later told him that he knew the raid must have been successful because he had heard no protest from his boss.

They reached Scampton shortly after half past four, with dawn creeping over the airfield. Dave Shannon and his crew had safely landed at 4.06 a.m. after a largely uneventful journey and there to greet them as they clambered down was the Station Commander, Charles Whitworth, congratulating them all and with a flight van waiting to take them to debriefing. Back on the grass they all congratulated each other, feeling pretty cheerful, and then clambered into the van.

Gibson and his crew touched down a little under ten minutes later, then at 4.20 a.m. Les Knight in *N-Nuts* landed safely, the last of the First Wave. They immediately headed for their debriefing; the promised beers had to wait just a little longer.

While Harris, Wallis and Cochrane joined the crews for the debriefing, the last three were clawing their way back. In *F-Freddie*, the largely uneventful nature of their journey was about to end as they crossed the IJsselmeer and passed over the last stretch of Holland before the sea.

As they passed over land once more, the navigator, Dudley Heal, realized they were slightly off track. It was beginning to get light, but before he could correct the error they were coned by searchlights and flak was pumping towards them from what seemed like all directions. 'That was where they really let us have it,' says Grant McDonald. 'That's where we got hit.'

Fortunately, the aircraft was still flying. In the cockpit, Ken Brown was quite blinded by the extreme glare of the searchlights, but despite this pushed the nose down, told Feneron, the flight engineer, to apply maximum boost, and flew on at no more than fifty feet off the deck. 'We flew on,' says Dudley Heal, 'and we could hear these shells or the bullets hitting the aircraft.' Somehow, they made it to the sea, and Heal stood up and peered from the astrodome and could still see tracers speeding past them, until suddenly they were clear and all was blissfully quiet once more except for the roar of the engines. Leaving his station, he clambered around to have a look and see what damage there was. The body of the aircraft just below the roof to one side was riddled with holes. Another few feet, he reckoned, and they would have been done for. 'We were just low enough,' he says, 'to avoid the worst of the damage.'

Cyril Anderson and his crew touched back down at 5.30 a.m., in the full light of dawn, and along with Les Munro, the only other pilot to bring a live Upkeep back to base. Three minutes later, Ken Brown safely landed *F-Freddie*. He was exhausted and had even handed the controls over to Basil Feneron for part of the journey across the sea. There to greet them as they clambered out was AVM Cochrane. 'So we realized then,' says Dudley Heal, 'how important this operation had been considered.'

There was a forty-minute wait for the last of the Lancasters. The crew of *O-Orange* had, like Ken Brown's crew, had a comparatively easy ride until they reached the Dutch coast. Crossing between Texel and Vlieland, they had then been lit up by the rising sun on what promised to be yet another lovely day. Flying at almost zero feet, they were astonished to discover the Germans were skipping shells across the water at them. They passed unscathed only to discover an oil problem with one of their engines, which Townsend promptly shut down. It was due to the loss of airspeed caused as a result that the final run for home took them so long.

6.15 a.m. *O-Orange* approached Scampton, and with the under-carriage lowered, Townsend gently brought her down. The battered Lancaster ran on, slowing gradually, then taxied towards dispersal, as Air Chief Marshal Harris, among others, hurried over to person-ally greet the arrival of the last of the returning aircraft. A few minutes later, the three Merlins were shut down and quiet once more returned to the airfield.

Operation CHASTISE was over.

OVERLOAD TANK
2COCKS

TRANSFER COCK

STOP COCK

FILLER

OIL DILUTION
VALVE

PRIM

LANCASTER I II III

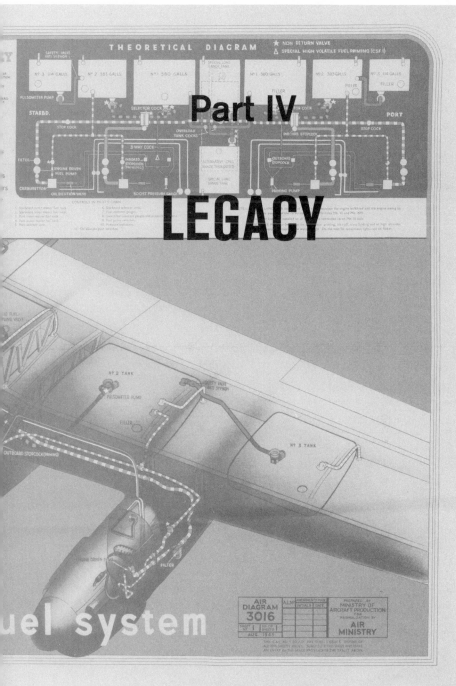

Part IV

LEGACY

27

After the Raid

FOR THOSE LIVING near the Möhne and Eder dams, the catastrophe that had engulfed them seemed barely credible. Within moments of the huge holes being punched through those immense walls, tidal waves of colossal power and destruction began thundering down the Möhne and Eder river valleys. At the Möhne, the power station at its foot had already been partly destroyed by Hopgood's Upkeep, but as the huge force of water plunged down upon it, the structure was simply smashed and swept away. Barely a minute later, the subsidiary hydro-electric generator at the end of the compensating basin had also been swept from the face of the earth.

The Möhne Valley was home to a large number of villages, homesteads and towns, all of which now found themselves in the way of the surging wall of water. Just two miles from the dam lay the village of Niederense, which had grown up from the banks of the river onto the rising slopes above. Warning sirens had not been uncommon in recent months, but the roar of attacking aircraft and heavy anti-aircraft fire most certainly were. At Niederense, many had retreated to their cellars or to shelters, but a number had also allowed their curiosity to get the better of them, and had hurried outside to see what was going on. There was confusion and bewilderment. Just what was happening at the dam? Could the enemy *really* be attacking such an enormous structure?

Karl-Heinz Dohle lived in the village and with his father had gone out into their garden to see. After each run, the Lancasters had swooped around and they could see them clearly in the moonlight and the lines of tracer from both their own guns and those of the attackers criss-crossing the sky. They also heard the explosions, then eventually a deep, thundering roar from the direction of the dam. Dohle and his father were gripped by a feeling of mounting unease and a compelling morbid curiosity. Leaving the house, they climbed up the nearby Kösters Ufer, a low hill that overlooked a bend in the river and the Cistercian Himmelpforten Abbey that nestled on the riverbank below. Its centrepiece was the Porta Coeli chapel, built in the thirteenth century and rich in art and treasures. Himmelpforten – and Porta Coeli – meant 'Heaven's Gate' but something decidedly hellish was now surging towards it.

Suddenly, Kohle and his father could see the immense tidal wave of water, some ten metres high, thundering down the valley with unstoppable force. Millions of tons of water, rock and debris now smashed down upon the abbey. 'All you could see,' says Kohle, 'was the tower sticking up out of the foaming water.' But not for much longer; ten minutes later, the spire slowly tipped over, the bell ringing out one final mournful, muffled peel, before disappearing for ever into the water.

Also living in Niederense was Elisabeth Lingenhöfer, a young mother of three whose husband was away fighting. She had only moved into her new family house two weeks earlier. It was a large timber-framed, three-storey house right by the riverbank, and they had the ground floor. That very day, Mother's Day, Frau Lingenhöfer had finished putting up new curtains. Earlier in the evening, she and her sister-in-law had cycled down the river to the town of Neheim to watch a new colour film called *Die goldene Stadt* at the Apollo. Back home later, she had just gone to bed when the sirens began to drone and soon after the aircraft arrived. Hurrying into the cellar with her three children, they heard the muffled roar of engines, the firing of guns, and explosions, then were suddenly aware of a rising roar. Hastily, she got them all out of the cellar, but no sooner had she done so than the house was swamped with water. She immediately knew that with three children in tow, she had no chance of escape, so she urged them up the stairs to the first floor and began shouting for help. The water was continuing to rise relentlessly, however, so they climbed to the second floor and then to the loft, but the water was soon around their ankles there too. Other women – her neighbours – were also sheltering there. The children were terrified, and crying and clinging to her. Elisabeth knocked out some tiles and then hauled herself up onto the roof itself and, with the help of the other women, pulled up the children one by one, and then her neighbours climbed out too.

With the children huddled around her, they sat on the roof and waited. The house was groaning and shifting from side to side. Around them, tree trunks were being swept by, some smacking into the side of the roof. An entire timber-frame house rushed past, as well as more trees and dead livestock. 'I just clung desperately to the roof,' she says, 'hoping that if it gave way I'd be able to swim off with the children.' She could not help thinking about the film she had seen earlier. One of the characters had been killed by falling into a bog and drowning. *It's all over*, she thought. *We're all going down into the bog together.*

Next to be hit was the town of Neheim, a few miles further on down the valley. A small town, it was nonetheless home to the Wohn- und Verpflegungslager eGmbH armaments factory, at which some 1,200 female foreign labour workers – mostly Poles and Ukrainians – worked. Their camp lay on the northern banks of the river, opposite the town. Ferdi Dröge was a sixteen-year-old plumbing apprentice living in the town with his employer and, when the sirens had begun, had gone with his boss's wife to the shelter at the Hillebrand lighting firm nearby, while his boss was on stand-by as an auxiliary fireman. There were over 150 people in the shelter, most casually drinking beer and playing cards, but after a short while one of the men, Johannes Kessler, ran into the shelter in quite a panic, and shouted, 'The Möhne's had it!'

Dröge instantly realized he meant the dam so ran out and hurried towards the bridge to see what was happening. As he was approaching he suddenly heard a terrible roar and then screams.

'The screams from up the valley came from the area of the Russian women's camp,' he says. He'd seen these women every day from his workshop because they were all working in the town. He now saw the wave rushing down the valley. 'It looked like a black block of flats with terraces,' he says. 'It was full of trees, pieces of wood and animals.' Then suddenly it was full of bits of smashed barrack blocks too, and screaming women. Lights were sucked into the tidal wave and disappeared. Kröge ran back up the road and to safety as fast as he possibly could, and only just managed to escape. As the wave thundered past, so it smashed the transformer station, which short-circuited and caused a massive flash of light across the valley. He now turned up Friedenstrasse, which led up the hill to the top of the town. 'Halfway up we stopped and followed the tragedy down in the valley,' he says, 'the crashing, the roaring, the smashing up and death cries.'

Just as a tsunami-like tidal wave had plunged down the Möhne Valley, so a second raced down the Eder with equally devastating force. Immediately beyond the dam, in the gorge, were a number of houses, nestling above the bank of the river. In the fifth house along lived the Bremmer family – Heinrich Bremmer, his wife and their eight children.

As soon as they had heard the aircraft circling overhead, they took shelter in the cellar. They could not quite make out what was going on, but heard a dull tremor and then a second and Herr Bremmer ran out, and then shouted to his family, 'The water is coming!'

They had less than a minute to get out, but, incredibly, they managed and were desperately scrambling up the steep wooded slopes as the water began surging through with rapidly rising force as the dam crumbled further and the breach widened. Suddenly, they could see a wave of water, some ten metres high, gushing down the valley. On they ran up the hill – it was their only chance. They could hear their neighbour's children calling for help, but there was nothing they could do. Eventually, they managed to reach the top and get to the village of Edersee, where Herr Bremmer's parents still lived. Below them, the first house from the dam had been literally sliced in half – the family had managed to clamber onto the roof and were sitting there, helpless.

The next village along, Hemfurth, had been largely inundated, buildings, trees and the bridge completely smashed and swept away. Next in line was Mehlen, another small village on the banks of the Eder. August Kötter was a young soldier, who had arrived back on leave from the Eastern Front only the day before and had sat up late in the family home with friends and relatives eager to see him and hear his news. He had not long gone to bed when he was woken to shouts that the dam had been hit, but he reckoned that with all the flak there, it would be a near impossible nut to crack; he did not know the guns had all been removed. Moments later, he looked out and saw a huge flash further up the valley towards the dam. This was the power station short-circuiting. The aircraft disappeared so Kötter had gone back to bed, only to be immediately pulled out again by his terrified wife. Moments later, they heard people screaming. The dam had burst!

Quickly, they got the children together and grabbed some essentials ready to hurry to the higher ground to the south of the village, but then Kötter remembered the pig. He hurried to untie it from the sty but it immediately ran out and straight into the house. His children had already left, urged to hurry on ahead to safety at their parents' insistence, but for Kötter and his wife – and the pig – it was too late. Looking out of the house, he saw a huge avalanche of water plunging towards them. Kötter was barely up the stairs before it had smashed through the front of the house and was up to his chest. The pig was squealing as a second wave hit them, forcing open the window and taking the pig with it as it rushed on. Kötter and his wife ran up floor by floor until they reached the attic. They stood there, terrified, listening, then with a huge groan the front half of the house caved in – Kötter only just managed to grab and hold onto his wife in time. 'Pieces of debris kept smashing into us,' he says, 'and you could hear crashes and gurgling noises as houses and barns went under.'

He could now see that the next house along was still in one piece, protected to an extent by their own. Unsure how long the barely standing remains of their home would survive, he managed to rip up the staircase and float it, and also pulled down the flag pole they had put up for the Führer's birthday. The stairs would be a makeshift raft, the flag pole an oar. Tying it to a beam so it wouldn't float away, Kötter now urged his wife to climb down the rope and clamber onto the raft on the water below them. As she did so, she burned her hands on the rope and then fell into the water. Diving in after, he grabbed her and managed to get her back onto the barely floating staircase raft. She was, by now, understandably paralysed with fear, but he did his best to comfort her. Abandoning the idea of floating free, they managed to clamber back into the remains of the house, praying they would eventually be rescued. 'It was ironic,' says Kötter, 'that I'd survived in Russia and nearly got drowned at home.'

A couple of miles further on, at the village of Giflitz, the sixteen-year-old Karl Schäfer had quickly dressed as soon as he heard people shouting warnings. Grabbing his bicycle, he rode towards the river. He had barely gone a few metres when way up the valley he heard and then saw a huge foaming wave of gushing water crashing towards the village. Hurrying home, he shouted the alarm to his parents.

'Boy, run for it!' they told him. 'Make sure you make it up the hill. We need to stay and untie the animals.'

Barely able to think clearly, Schäfer did as they told him. The railway line ran south from the river along an embankment over the low pasture that led to the bridge. Further south, the ground began to rise to a hill. As the water surged over the flood plain and swept on through the village, many were desperately trying to clamber up onto the railway embankment and then along it to safety as the ground rose either side of it. As he reached the railway embankment, Schäfer saw one of his neighbours, Frau Kleinertz, struggling with her young boy in her arms. 'Karl,' she said, 'I can't do this.' So he took the boy and left the bike and together they began hurrying along the embankment. Water was now swirling either side of them and threatening to rise over it altogether. Schäfer ran on, the boy in his arms, Frau Kleinertz beside him, frantically trying to escape the water. 'We barely made it up that hill,' says Schäfer. 'How we got through the water, I don't know. The people we'd passed by on the way were all washed away.'

Karl Schäfer was among the lucky ones who survived the tidal wave that still thundered on down the valley. For him, and for all those who did survive, it would be a night they would never, ever forget.

For those returning from the raid, the aftermath was slightly bewildering. Crews were handed mugs of coffee then went for their debrief, watched over in part by Cochrane and Wallis and even Air Chief Marshal Sir Arthur Harris himself. To see the C-in-C there was incredible to many. True, he had visited Scampton back on 6 May, but he was such a remote figure to most that to see him informally standing among them was an extraordinary sight. It had completely thrown an utterly exhausted Bill Townsend as he clambered out of his battered Lancaster. Harris was there to greet him and asked him how it had gone. With barely a glance, Townsend muttered that he would find out in the debrief, and then walked straight past. Harry Humphries thought he seemed an almost 'fictitious character', and had been equally stunned to see him.

After the debriefing, the crews went for their traditional meal of bacon and eggs, although in this case it really was almost breakfast time. From there, it was to the bar in their respective Messes. In the Officers' Mess, most were drinking beer. Photographers were there, catching the moment. The sense of elation was palpable, although very quickly most trooped off to get some rest.

While some continued drinking and others slept, three high-altitude Spitfires from 542 Squadron at RAF Benson took off to photograph the results of the raid. Flight Lieutenant Gerry Fray was first off, at 7.25 a.m., sent ahead of the other two because he had flown over there only two days earlier. He was briefed to be over the area by 8.30 a.m.

It was a perfect day for taking photographs, with clear blue skies and exceptionally good visibility. About 150 miles from the Möhne, Fray saw the industrial haze of the Ruhr and then what looked like a cloud to the east. As he drew closer, however, he realized that what he had first thought was a cloud was in fact the sun shining on the flood waters. 'I was flying at 30,000 feet,' he says, 'and

I looked down into the deep valley, which had seemed so peaceful before, and now it was a torrent, with the sun shining on it.' Just twenty-five miles from the Ruhr heartland, the whole valley of the Möhne was inundated. Only patches of high ground and the tops of trees, and buildings and church steeples stood out against the vast sheet of floodwater. Around them, the even flow of the water was broken as it rushed past.

Now nearing the dam, Fray reckoned the flood was about a mile wide. He was quite overcome by the immensity of it. 'When I realized what had happened,' he noted afterwards in his intelligence summary, 'I just wondered if the powers-that-be realized just how much damage had been done.'

Fray now began his photography, flying upwards towards the dam, where he could see water still rushing from a huge breach. What he assumed had been the 'Control House' – the power station at the foot of the dam – that he had seen two days earlier had completely gone. The water level in the reservoir had fallen dramatically, leaving a vast shelf of mud. On the upper reaches of the lake, it was completely dry already.

He then flew on to the Eder and once again had no difficulty in seeing the floods. The long, snaking lake above the dam had nearly drained and even from his position high, high above he could see the movement of water, stretching eastwards all the way to Kassel. Fray was stunned by what he saw: flooded villages, bridges completely swept away, power stations wrecked, railway lines and roads totally vanished.

As he was carrying out his second run over the Eder, he spotted two aircraft and decided to cut and run. At around 11 a.m., he touched back down at Benson only to see the Station Commander waiting for him. He immediately wondered whether he had done anything wrong, but all the CO wanted to know was whether it was true – that the dams really had been breached.

'Yes,' Fray told him. 'They've pranged two of them properly. The floods are spreading for miles.'

In the Eder and Möhne valleys, dawn had revealed an alien landscape. In Niederense, Elisabeth Lingenhöfer's ordeal had finally come to an end. Eventually, the water levels had begun to drop. Still clinging desperately to her roof, her children mercifully still beside her, she was at last able to tentatively lower herself, and then her children, back down into the loft, although the staircase leading to it had disappeared. Exhausted and suffering cramps and pains, she had to lie down for a while. Firemen and neighbours managed to free them after some seven hours up there in the loft. All the furniture had gone, all her possessions. Her home was ruined.

In Neheim, Ferdi Dröge was stunned by the level of devastation. He thought it looked as though a giant mower had been through the valley. The women's barrack blocks had gone – most of the 753 dead and missing had been electrocuted – and now their bodies lay strewn among the debris: the bits of torn houses, animal carcasses, personal belongings. Already the valley had a new name: 'Todestal'. Death Valley.

In Mehlen, August Kötter and his wife had also been rescued – by some army engineers, who had paddled out to them in a boat. Even his pig miraculously survived, but, as with the Möhne Valley, the devastation was phenomenal. Half the village had gone. The same was true of Giflitz and of most of the villages along the river. Karl Schäfer had stayed up on the hill all night watching his village largely disappear. The railway station was destroyed, and then with a crash the railway embankment also disintegrated and was washed away, although, soon after, the water levels began to recede. Every so often, he could hear a loud creak and groan and then another house would collapse. He had been terrified about what had happened to his parents. Fortunately, they had survived by climbing up a tree. 'And that one stayed standing, thank God,' says Schäfer, 'although many others were washed away.' It was a devastating blow, to lose not only so much of the home he had known all his life, but also so many friends and neighbours. 'We pretty much knew what they were having for supper the next day,' he says. 'That's how close our neighbourhood was.' Their world had changed for ever.

It had changed for ever for Barnes Wallis, too. Back at Scampton, he found the realization that eight crews would not be returning very hard to come to terms with. For so long he had been focusing on destroying the dams – it had all been about the weapon and the targets in his mind's eye; he had not really thought of the human cost that might be involved. Yet since arriving at Scampton on the Saturday afternoon, it struck home that the lives of many were at stake in this highly hazardous operation. Just the night before the raid, he had stayed up until midnight talking with Gibson, Hopgood, Maudslay and Young. It was shattering to think that of those young men, only Gibson was still alive. After the initial exultation, Cochrane found him in a terrible state and suggested he get some rest. It had been a long night for the crews, but for Wallis also, and Cochrane advised him to go to bed. He did so, heading back to Whitworth's house.

His rest was soon interrupted, however. Whitworth invited most of the pilots, plus a few select others, up to his house for a bit of a celebration. Drinks flowed, the mood was raucous, and before long a conga was moving through the house and up the stairs to Whitworth's room, where his pyjamas were snatched and waved around. Ann Fowler, who was one of those invited, had been joining in the fun when she suddenly noticed Wallis standing there in his pyjamas and dressing gown, looking utterly miserable and his eyes moist with tears. Later Gibson tried to reassure him, but he was inconsolable.

Gibson was less sympathetic to some of those who had returned early. During the party in the Mess immediately after their return, Gibson spoke to Les Munro. 'Well, what happened, Les?' he asked him. Munro told him he had been hit by flak.

'Oh, you were too high,' Gibson replied.

Munro was about to protest and give his side of the story, but Gibson had already turned and walked away. It rankled with Munro, who felt he had not been given a fair hearing. Nor did he feel he could raise the matter again; it was the last time either of them ever mentioned it.

Gibson was more forgiving of Geoff Rice, perhaps remembering how close he himself had come to hitting the dark waters of the Derwent Reservoir back at the beginning of April, but he showed less patience with Anderson, and was unconvinced by his reasons for turning back. Gibson always judged people by his own standards; he had found the Eder when there had been mist; and he had carried out fewer night-time navigation exercises than most of the other crews as well. If he could manage it, why not Anderson? But while Gibson may not have turned back, that does not mean Anderson did not have good reasons to do so. Time had been marching on. They had been able to see little and had become hopelessly disorientated. It was better to fight another day than kill oneself flying round and round looking for a dam that was eluding them.

Relief, exultation. Exhaustion, exhilaration. Exhaustion again, and, with it, more sombre thoughts. The returning crews experienced a range of emotions from the moment they touched down to the moment the scale of the losses began to sink in. Grant McDonald woke up later that morning to see the lorries coming around to pick up the effects of those who had not come back. 'And that was not a good sight,' he says. 'That was not a good sight at all.' Dave Shannon also felt a sense of 'depression to a certain extent' that they had lost nearly half the squadron.

Shannon's bomb-aimer, Len Sumpter, had drunk some whisky during the debrief, had waited around with Shannon and the others for the last of the crews to return, and then gone to bed. A few hours later, he woke up and stumbled down into the Sergeants' Mess. The other squadron aircrews came in and began joking. 'Had a good time last night, did you?' Sumpter said nothing. On the other hand, those who flew were used to comrades not coming back. 'Every time we took off,' says Johnny Johnson, 'we didn't know if we were coming back. That was part and parcel of the job.' Len Sumpter agrees. 'I don't think it put a dampener on things, really,' he says. 'You get in the plane and you take off, it's just fate whether you come back or not.' Les Munro thought that in many ways it was easier to deal with losses after the Dams Raid than it was on a more regular squadron or later on with 617. 'We'd only been together for six weeks,' he says. 'It was sad to know that some of these blokes, like John Hopgood, who I knew quite well and was a first-class chap, weren't coming back. There was sadness, but you got used to it and didn't let it get to you and affect your ability to carry out your duty on operations.'

And yet the cost had been high. On any op, one or maybe two might not make it back, but to lose eight out of nineteen crews was a massive loss. The squadron had been decimated; Bomber Command had not decided yet what should become of it, and yet there was no way it could function for a while in any case.

The losses were just so palpable. Each aircrew had its own groundcrew, who had nursed their aircraft and worked alongside the aircrews throughout the run-up to the operation. They had been a team, working together. Now eight sets of groundcrew no longer had aircraft to work on or crews to work with. The vacuum left was huge. Of those aircraft that returned, not one had made it back without a scratch. Some were barely standing. Ken Brown's aircraft was so badly knocked about it had to be taken away.

But while the Lancaster provided a visual sense of loss, aircraft could be replaced; young men could not.

Throughout the day, telegrams of congratulation sped down the telegraph wires between Scampton, Grantham, High Wycombe and Washington. There was one from Portal in Washington, from Slessor, the C-in-C of Coastal Command, whose 618 Squadron were still training for their planned Highball operation in the Mediterranean; from Ben Lockspeiser, from A. V. Roe, from RAF Manston; from Lord Trenchard too. There was also a message from Sir Archibald Sinclair, the Secretary of State for Air. 'The War Cabinet have instructed me to convey to you and to all who shared in the preparation and execution of last night's operations,' he wrote, 'particularly to Wing Commander Gibson and his squadron their congratulations on the great success achieved. This attack, pressed home in the face of strong resistance, is a testimony alike to the tactical resource and energy of those who planned it. To the gallantry and determination of the aircrews and to the excellence of British design and workmanship. The War Cabinet have noted with satisfaction the damage done to German war power.'

There was one further telegram of congratulation, and that was from Harris to Wallis. The C-in-C may have been vehemently opposed to the project back in February and right up to the moment it was launched he had remained a sceptic. Yet from the second the project had received its greenlight, he had done all he could to ensure the operation was a success. Of course, its success fitted in perfectly with his wider Battle of the Ruhr and reflected very well too on both him and his Command. Even so, his magnanimity was impressive. 'But for your knowledge, skill and persistence,' he wrote, 'often in the face of discouragements and disappointments, in the design, production and servicing of the equipment used in the destruction of the dams, the efforts of our gallant crews would have been in vain. We in Bomber Command in particular, and the United Nations as a whole, owe everything to you in the first for the outstanding success achieved.'

As Wallis returned home that evening, this most gracious and dignified message would, it is to be hoped, have made him feel just a little bit better.

There were, however, other telegrams that needed to be sent that Monday, 17 May. The task of sending telegrams to the families of those dead and missing was left to the Squadron Adjutant, Harry Humphries. Once the initial celebrations had died down, Humphries had washed, shaved and eaten a bit of breakfast, then had managed to escape the Mess without having beer poured all down him. When he reached his office at No. 2 Hangar he was amazed to discover all the squadron NCO staff there: Chiefy Powell, Jim Heveron, LAC Munro. Between them, they would write and send the telegrams and collect the personal effects. 'I felt frightfully tired and depressed with it all,' noted Humphries, 'but it had to be done.'

There were fifty-six missing in all. Notification that they were missing was sent to next of kin: parents or wives usually. Doris Fraser, married for a little over two weeks, received her 'It is with deep regret . . .' telegram that day. So too did Dinghy Young's wife, and John Hopgood's parents at their home in the quiet Surrey village of Shere. At the time, the squadron had no idea what had happened to many of them – they were 'missing in action', even those lucky three who had got out: John Fraser, John Minchin and Fred Tees. The messages that they were, miraculously, still alive would arrive later – much later.

But there was one person that day who did not receive a telegram. Charlie Williams's final letter, written in the last hours before he took off, would reach Bobbie Parfitt the following day, Tuesday, 18 May – a letter in which he spoke of the wedding he hoped would take place that week. A wedding planned but not yet undertaken – so she received no official notification that her beloved Charlie was among those who had not made it back.

28

Katastrophe

S ID BUFTON HAD accepted that if the raid were to be successful it
would receive great publicity, but put in place severe restrictions
as to who could say what, and that meant no one from Group or
Scampton breathing a word for the time being – after all, there was
the security of the ongoing Highball project to think about. Now,
however, with breathtaking photographs to prove the spectacular
success of the operation, there was no reason not to savour and
revel in what had unquestionably been an astonishing achievement. The official announcement of the raid was given in a
carefully worded BBC radio communiqué later that first day,
Monday, 17 May. At the Wallis home in Effingham, their youngest
daughter Elizabeth heard the news on a radio in the kitchen. His
older daughter Mary, at boarding school in Salisbury, was told by
her housemistress that her father had 'done it again'. She was rather
nonplussed by this, but eventually twigged and also sent a telegram
to her 'Wonderful Daddy'.

Not only was the news given to the press; so too were a number
of Gerry Fray's photographs, which made the front pages of news-
papers across the free world the following day. 'DAMS WERE BURST
OPEN BY ONLY 19 LANCASTERS', ran the headline in the *Daily Express*.
'RAF BLOW UP THREE KEY DAMS IN GERMANY', announced the *Daily
Telegraph*, which followed with, 'DEVASTATION SWEEPS DOWN RUHR

VALLEY – BRIDGES AND POWER PLANTS ENGULFED – ADVANCING FLOODS STILL SPREADING FAST'. It was even front-page news in the *New York Times*. The accompanying stories were intoxicating: a special squadron, training in secret, led by the ace commander Guy Gibson DSO, DFC. Details of the attack were written up in great, albeit not always accurate, detail. But who was going to quibble? The raid was sensational. It was brilliant. It was an act of un-imaginable daring and courage. And the photos were incredible – not bombed-out cities but breached dams and immense floods. With the Axis surrender in North Africa a few days before, those in the Free World were suddenly being fed a glut of successes from land and in the air. Fresh hope heralded the summer of 1943.

In Washington still, Churchill addressed Congress on 19 May, hailing his American allies, trumpeting the great victory in North Africa and reiterating the importance of the strategic air campaign that would continue to be carried out by British and US bomber forces side by side. 'You have just read of the destruction of the great dams which feed the canals and provide power to the enemy's munition works,' he told them. 'That was a gallant operation cost-ing eight out of the nineteen Lancaster bombers employed, but will play a very far-reaching part in German military output. It is our settled policy, the settled policy of our two staffs of war-making authorities, to make it impossible for Germany to carry on any form of war industry on a large or concentrated scale, either in Germany, in Italy, or in the enemy occupied countries.' At this, Congress erupted into cheers. For those in the US who had been critical of British bombing efforts, the Dams Raid provided a per-fectly timed riposte.

Over occupied Holland and France, news of the raid was dropped by Allied aeroplanes and heard about on the BBC via illegal radio sets. Britain was milking this for all it was worth, and why not? For Germany, the attack on the dams was a catastrophe. There was no other word to describe it. In fact, from the outset, the attack on the Möhne, in particular, was called just that: *Möhnekatastrophe.*

The Reich Armaments Minister, Albert Speer, was woken in the early hours of Monday, 17 May, and wasted no time in heading to the scenes of carnage himself. By dawn, he had flown around the Möhne and down the valley and then landed at nearby Werl. Soon after, he was motoring down to the dam itself, then carrying on to Sorpe. The levels of destruction were certainly immense, but from the outset Speer was determined that the Ruhr should never be abandoned and that whatever damage there was should be repaired as quickly as possible. This, however, would require a gargantuan commitment in terms of manpower, resources and, of course, money. With the Allies threatening to attack in the Mediterranean, and with the German offensive at Kursk about to be launched, such heavy commitment at home could not have come at a worse moment.

Throughout that day and into the next, the scale of the disaster began to be realized. In the Möhne Valley, houses and buildings had been destroyed up to forty-five miles away, and for thirty miles every single bridge had been destroyed. The Möhne River ran into the Ruhr, the Ruhr into the Rhine. At the junction of the Ruhr and Rhine, more than ninety miles from the dam, the crest of the wave of water was still four metres higher than normal. The great out-flow of water also flooded other sources of water supplying the Ruhr, which were then put out of operation as far as Essen. A large number of towns were temporarily without water, including Hamm, Hagen, Bochum and Dortmund. The immense flow of water, of course, did not just contain water: carried with it were vast amounts of silt, rock and smashed trees, plants, buildings, humans, animals and other debris. The silt covered everything it came into contact with, while equally problematic was that most factories, pumps and day-to-day facilities that depended on electricity were put out of action, not least because water and electricity simply do not work together. For example, the important pump storage plant at Herdecke, forty miles away on the River Ruhr, was flooded up to two metres. This power station had a capacity of 132,000 kW and was one of the most important stations of the Rhine-Westphalia Power Supply Company. It would require a round-the-clock clean-up and repair operation that would keep it out of action for two weeks.

In the Eder, the tidal wave had brought with it far-reaching destruction too. The region may not have been such a centre for heavy industry, but vast tracks of prime agricultural land now lay under water; the harvest that year had been completely ruined. The tidal wave had reached the River Fulda beyond the major town of Kassel, fifty miles away. As with the Möhne Valley, every bridge as far as Kassel had been destroyed, locomotives in the way of the wave rolled over like hay, large numbers of houses either destroyed or damaged. And that was just the start of it. What long-term effects this would have were hard to gauge in the first couple of days, but the clean-up and repair operation was going to take a long time and be extremely expensive.

In Berlin, reaction to the attack was one of barely contained shock and horror. The British and Americans had been sending over massed bomber formations, but what made this co-ordinated attack so especially troubling was the apparently small numbers of aircraft used and the fact that the weapons – whatever they were – had been delivered with precision and had clearly contained awesome power. Maximum damage caused by few weapons and carried out by a single or a handful of aircraft was in many ways the Holy Grail of the combatant nations. Arthur Harris may have pooh-poohed the panacea-mongers, but the Nazi high command did no such thing in Germany; on the contrary, scientists were given every assistance and support to develop weapons of mass destruction. What this new attack by the RAF appeared to show was that the British were possibly ahead of the game. That was a devastating psychological blow.

'The attacks of the British bombers on the dams in our valleys were very successful,' noted Josef Goebbels on Tuesday, 18 May. 'The Führer is exceedingly impatient and angry about the lack of preparedness on the part of our Luftwaffe. Damage to production was more than normal.' The Propaganda Minister had spoken to the nation in February, heralding a new age of total war. In the destruction wrought on the Ruhr and now on the dams, here was the proof.

In Britain, the accolades and celebrations continued. Air Vice-Marshal Cochrane officially visited Scampton on 18 May, then told the squadron they were all being given a week's leave. Not everyone left Scampton for a breather, however. Not Humphries, not the squadron office staff. And not Gibson. Getting Humphries to send the telegrams was one thing, but he took it upon himself to write personal paragraphs on otherwise form letters – and while others helped him with some, he added personal paragraphs on each. These took a great deal of time. His letter to Bill Astell's father, for example, was a page long. 'Flight Lieutenant Astell was a great personal friend of mine,' he wrote, 'and his assistance was extremely valuable in the organisation of this squadron.' On 20 May, he finally found time to write to Barnes Wallis. His hand-writing showed the signs of weariness and having written too many letters before it, but the words were heartfelt. 'I'm afraid I'm not much of a letter writer, but I would like to say just this. The weapon that you gave us to deliver worked like a dream and you have earned the thanks of the civilized world.'

Fay Gillon noticed Gibson seemed downcast during those days. He told her he felt bad about the losses, particularly of his friends who he had asked to join him at 617. There was a sense of anti-climax – everyone had gone, Scampton was half empty. And his dog had gone too. He had still not had any leave since ending his time with 106 Squadron.

There was, however, cause for cheer a few days later. On 20 May, Cochrane put forward a list of decorations, which were swiftly confirmed three days later. Thirty-four members of the squadron were given medals. There were Conspicuous Gallantry Medals for Townsend and Brown, and Distinguished Service Orders for all those pilots that made it to the targets. Dudley Heal had been at home having tea with his family when a telegram arrived. Bringing it back into his living room, he opened it and read it out. 'Heartiest congratulations on award of Distinguished Flying Medal. Wing Co.' Still at Scampton on 23 May, Gibson supervised the sending of congratulatory telegrams too. There was a DFM for Len Sumpter, for his part in the Eder attack; but, for Gibson, there was quite justifiably the top gong: the Victoria Cross.

There was more excitement to follow. With the squadron returning on 26 May, the following day the King and Queen paid

Scampton a visit. Barnes Wallis was also invited by Cochrane, although by that time he was back hard at work on both Highball and the Windsor bomber – he had spent three days in Scotland working on Highball and picked up Cochrane's letter inviting him to attend the royal visit on his return – three days after it had been sent. Nonetheless, he made it. May the 27th also happened to be David Shannon's twenty-first birthday; it was not one he would forget. The visit proved a great success and another wonderful photo opportunity – which in turn prompted yet more publicity. The King had been asked to choose one of two squadron crests and mottos. The first was of a hammer parting chains with the motto 'Alter the Map'. The second was of a lightning bolt over a broken dam and the words, 'Après nous le Déluge'. The King chose the latter. Almost overnight, it seemed, 617 Squadron had become the best-known squadron in all the RAF, and Gibson the most famous pilot.

Speer had returned to Berlin and assured Hitler that the damage would be quickly repaired and that he had already begun taking steps to get work under way. As a result, two days after he had first written of the attack on the dams, Josef Goebbels reported that the destruction did not seem quite so severe after all. What was certainly true was that initial reports of tens of thousands of deaths in the floods had clearly been exaggerated, but other than that the effects were still absolutely devastating on so many different levels. To suggest otherwise was utterly fallacious.

Still, putting a good spin on things was very much standard practice among senior Nazis. All had witnessed Hitler's rages when he was given particularly unwelcome news; they were also well aware that if they were to maintain their position they often needed to take matters into their own hands with the minimum amount of upset to the Führer and simply get on with resolving whatever the problem was. Speer was a master at this. His enormous energy, vision and drive ensured that herculean feats were often achieved without Hitler ever truly appreciating quite precisely what had been done.

Within a few days, a much clearer picture of the level of damage had emerged. In the areas affected by the Möhne, this amounted to ninety-six buildings completely destroyed, and a further 872 damaged; twelve war-production factories had been destroyed and a further ninety-one damaged; twenty-five rail and road bridges had been completely destroyed and a further eight severely damaged. Even at Hirsel, sixty miles away, a large railway bridge was destroyed. 'All rail bridges and road bridges over the Ruhr are either damaged or severely damaged as far as Herdecke,' noted a subsequent report.

Many power stations were also destroyed or were out of order due to flooding of important installations. Among these, and in addition to the power station at Herdecke, VEW's power plant at Dortmund, which provided 50,000 kW, had been closed down. Many of the Ruhr's towns were also without drinking water, and very short of water for the much-needed fire services. Without water, the tens of thousands of incendiaries dropped by the Allied bombers could not be extinguished. Harris made the most of this by ordering his bombers to attack Dortmund on the night of 23 May. It was the largest raid of the entire Battle of the Ruhr to date – 826 aircraft hit the city, which was showered with incendiaries that resulted in some 2,000 buildings destroyed. Four nights later, 518 aircraft hit Essen yet again.

Thus the problems caused by the smashing of the Möhne were threefold. First, there was the material damage. Factories, bridges, railways, buildings and, of course, the dam itself would all have to be replaced. The factory at Neheim, for example, comparatively small fry in the big scheme of things, had been massively damaged by the flood, but half the foreign labour work force had been killed and their barrack blocks wiped from the face of the earth. This camp alone had cost 1 million Reichsmarks. This was about £250,000, which equates to around £7m in today's money. In other words, just creating a labour camp for 1,200 women cost a fairly large amount of money. Some of the buildings and bridges would cost vast sums more. Replacing a labour camp was very much just the tip of the iceberg. Then there was the cost of replacing the dams themselves, which would be a massive, massive undertaking.

Second, there was the water shortage. Water was needed both as a power source and for the extraction of coal – and the Ruhr was Germany's coal-mining heartland too – and for cooling in other industrial processes. Water was also greatly needed for drinking and sanitation – without it the area's large population would ultimately die or become diseased – and for the fire services.

Third was the issue of manpower. Both the *Möhnekatastrophe* and the wider damage caused to the Ruhr by the Allied bombing campaign had left many dead, wounded and homeless, which in turn meant there were fewer people to go down mines or work in factories.

Within a few days, the Möhne Reservoir had lost 90 per cent of its capacity, but despite short-term deficiencies caused by the immense flood, water supplies were not likely to be critical that summer; there were reserves, from underground pumping stations, that could be used, while there were the other, albeit smaller, reservoirs in the area. The Sorpe, too, although damaged and although it would need to be completely drained, could at least be repaired at a time of German choosing.

No – the water shortage was unlikely to cause critical problems in 1943. There would, however, be a critical situation by the following summer should the dams not be repaired in extremely quick time, as Speer was well aware. The importance of re-establishing the reservoirs to full capacity was underlined in early June, when it was suggested that in future the reservoirs should be maintained at a lower water level, so that they would be harder to breach. Speer rejected this out of hand, securing Hitler's approval that only he had authority to lower the water levels in the lakes. Equally against the proposal was the General Inspectorate for Water and Power. 'The catastrophes at the Möhne and Eder dams in the Ruhr Valley,' it was stated tersely, 'have shown clearly just how every interference in the drinking and industrial water supply has a painful effect on national life and especially on industrial production and the traffic economy. For this reason, your proposal of lowering the water level of all the dams even partially cannot be met.'

The problem facing Speer was that these reservoirs needed to be ready by the autumn in order to collect the essential winter rains. That meant in just five months. The British had raced to develop Upkeep in time for an attack in May; now it was the Germans who were facing a race against time.

There was a further important, although very different, reason for repairing the dams as quickly as possible. The Möhne and Eder dams were iconic – two of the best-known structures in the entire Reich and symbols of German mastery and power. They *had* to be repaired. Even had they been of little importance at all – and that was most certainly not the case – the affront to German prestige simply would not allow them to remain standing with their huge, gaping wounds.

Speer acted with his usual swiftness, immediately seeking Hitler's permission – and being given it – to move large numbers of workers to the area. On 18 May, he formed the *Einsatzstab Ruhrgebiet* – the Ruhr Area Unit – under Einsatzgruppenleiter Adam, which was to be given 50,000 Organisation Todt (OT) workers and 20,000 armaments workers. A significant number of OT labourers – some 7,000 – were to be instantly withdrawn from the Atlantic Wall. The Atlantic Wall was a planned series of coastal defences that ran all the way from Norway and down the continental coast as far as the Spanish border. Understandably, it was designed to be heaviest along the Dutch and Belgian coasts, around the Pas de Calais and in Normandy. In the summer of 1943, however, it was still massively under-developed. The withdrawal of 7,000 labourers was significant. They could not be building coastal defences if they were rebuilding dams and factories.

On 21 May, Speer held a planning conference. Repair of the dams was of the greatest urgency, but equally pressing was to get as many factories and power plants up and running again as quickly as possible; at this critical moment, the Nazi war machine could not afford to falter. Speer and his immediate subordinates viewed the attack on the dams as very much part of the wider offensive against the Ruhr, although he appreciated that the specific attack on the dams had been the first attempt by the Allies 'to influence the course of the war by destroying a single nerve centre of the war economy'. This had always been precisely Barnes Wallis's intention. Therefore, the reconstruction work had to be seen as one massive operation, which included dams, factories, bridges and power plants. This huge amount of work, caused primarily by the RAF since Harris launched his concentrated air offensive at the beginning of March, would cost a cripplingly large amount of money. 'The sum of construction,' ran the report of the conference on 21 May, 'of the most important quota contributors amounted to roughly 756 million Reichsmarks.' That was a staggering £5.9bn in today's money.

On 30 May, Speer attended a *Führerprotokoll* in Berlin. He had, admittedly, already given Hitler a fairly detailed report on the damage caused by the Dams Raid, which apparently made a deep impression on the Führer. 'He kept the documents with him,' noted Speer. Speer had to make clear the severity of the situation yet at the same time provide grounds for optimism that the situation could and should be rectified. One of the problems hindering repairs to many of the flood-damaged factories and power stations was a chronic lack of spares, not least because what spare parts there had been in the Ruhr had been destroyed as well. 'Important spare parts and machines,' suggested a memo from the Reichsminister der Luftfahrt – the Aviation Minister – on 18 June, 'should therefore always be kept outside factories and in places and locations which are less vulnerable to air attacks.' This was a case of shutting the stable door after the horse had bolted. The only solution right now was to plunder other factories elsewhere in the Reich for crucial equipment and other machinery. These would be confiscated – no matter the consequences – so they could be used in the Ruhr. Hitler gave his blessing.

The damage to the Eder Dam and the valley beyond also had to be repaired and cleaned up. Initially, some 3,000 troops were hastily brought in to help, which was then quickly increased to 5,000. Large numbers of Hitler Youth were also recruited to join the clean-up operation. As the water began to recede, so the scale of the damage had been revealed. On the Eder Dam itself, Shannon and Maudslay's strikes had caused further damage that would have to be repaired. The banks of the Eder Reservoir were badly damaged in a number of places, as a result of the rapidity with which the water had drained. The equalizing pool beyond the dam had been breached in a number of places too. This would also require urgent repair. Further afield, the sluices of all seven accumulation lakes to the north and south of Kassel were silted up and no longer functioning. The flood water also started major earth movement in the River Fulda. Some 30,000 cubic metres of earth needed to be dredged to re-establish normal flow.

From the Fulda ran the larger and more important River Weser, which in turn flowed all the way to Bremerhaven on the North Sea coast. Even here, some fifty miles from the dam, further dredging was needed, while around a thousand groynes needed replacing. On the River Weser alone, three miles of collapsed riverbank had to be rebuilt and strengthened.

The task ahead of them was truly gargantuan and to get it all done in time for the autumn would be nothing short of a miracle.

29

Damn Busters

AFTER THE SETBACK in Russia in the first months of 1943, the Eastern Front had stabilized. From March, Hitler and his generals had begun planning a decisive counter-attack, which would begin with the destruction of the Kursk salient, an enormous bulge some 150 miles wide and a hundred deep. At the heart of the Russian salient, around 400 miles south-west of Moscow, lay the town of Kursk itself. Around it were wide, open, gently undulating green plains – ideal country for mobile armour, and with an attack in summer, when the weather was vastly more favourable, the Germans fancied their chances of driving the Ivans back rather as they had done in their victorious summer of 1941. The assault on the Russian salient was to be the starting point of a dramatic return to form, which would restore German prestige and prove that the reversals of the winter of 1942–3 were temporary setbacks only. 'This offensive is of decisive importance,' wrote Hitler in his operation order of 15 April. 'On the main axis the best formations, the better commanders and a large amount of ammunition must be used . . . Victory at Kursk will be a beacon for the whole world.'

The pause in the fighting, however, had been beneficial for both sides. While the Germans were building up their forces, so too were the Russians, which was why, despite a certain amount of Nazi confidence in the forthcoming offensive, it was absolutely imperative that the German build-up continue without any major setbacks. Bomber Command's pounding of the Ruhr was therefore precisely what Germany did not need at that time.

Operation CITADEL, as the attack on the Kursk salient was to be called, was to be launched in early July. By the end of June, a more precise assessment of damage caused by the attacks on the dams and the bombing campaign on the Ruhr was established. It did not augur well for the coming offensive.

'The grid gas supply situation in the month of May was severely affected by the enemy,' ran a report. 'Due to the effects of the Möhne Dam catastrophe on 17 May 1943, all consumers had to be radically throttled for a longer period because of the failure of many coking plants due to lack of water. This resulted in considerable losses of production.' As a result of the breach of the Möhne, the water supply to the entire Ruhr area had been affected 'to a threatening extent', the report continued. 'Many shaft mines, coking plants, smelting works, power stations, fuel plants and armaments factories were shut down for several days due to lack of water. The dependency of the entire extractive industry and key industry on a regulated water supply became especially obvious.' It was true that Speer had, by the end of June, ensured that many of those factories and power plants were working again, but other plants elsewhere in the Reich had paid for it.

Coal extraction had also fallen radically. This essential commodity was needed both at power stations and for the steel industry. Coal extraction had dropped by 813,278 tons in May alone, of which 416,464 tons was because of damage to coal pits, 242,870 tons was due to the Möhne catastrophe, and 153,944 tons was because of damage to miners' homes. Coal extraction 'is now at its lowest since the outbreak of war'.

On the Ruhr's waterways, the knock-on effect of the dams attack was also felt. For example, both the Duisburg and Ruhrort ports were closed for several days and canal traffic seriously affected. All this, unsurprisingly, had an effect on the armed services. 'Army production dropped strongly in some cases,' ran the report, 'due to the effects of the heavy bomb attacks on the Ruhr area and the Möhne Dam.' Ammunition production was down considerably, which was not at all good for the forthcoming offensive. The factory at Neheim produced mines – a large number were lost in the flood. The flood had caused a major delay in the shipment of tank turrets from the Stahlwerke Harkort Eicken. Production of tank turrets had been set back because of the damage elsewhere. And, as the report pointed out, even factories not directly affected were suffering from a lack of water, electricity and gas, and a depleted workforce.

'Luftwaffe manufacture was so affected,' the report continued, 'by the enemy air attacks on the industrial areas in Essen, Dortmund, Wuppertal and the Möhne Dam, that it was no longer able to maintain an upward sloping curve. The damages have mainly affected the extractive manufacture, meaning the effects on the output of finished products will appear in a few months when the stock of semi-finished products runs out.' This was not good news for CITADEL, or if the Allies made a landing somewhere in the Mediterranean.

Back in Britain, the image of the breached dams and the vast floods was one that stuck in many people's minds. Few people, however, had much appreciation of the enormous challenge now facing the Germans to get them repaired. For the men who had delivered this catastrophe to the enemy, it was enough to know that they had largely done what was asked of them and that they had done much to enhance the reputation of their Command.

The investiture of those rewarded with medals for their part in the Dams Raid took place in London on 22 June, for which Humphries had been asked to organize a special train to take everyone there. They arrived the night before, all in a terrific party spirit, not least because large amounts of drink had been taken from the Mess for the journey down. Many of them were half-cut before the train even reached Grantham and decidedly worse for wear by the time they pulled into King's Cross a little after six o'clock. No accommodation had been booked, but Harry Humphries, Les Munro and Joe McCarthy, among others, headed to the Savoy, were given rooms, then went out on the town. Humphries had little idea where they went that night. 'I only know,' he noted, 'that I kept getting in and out of taxis and meeting dozens of people I had never seen in my life before . . . I only know that it was one of the most terrific parties I had ever attended.'

Despite crashing hangovers, they all managed to make it to the palace, the decorated men of the squadron receiving their medals from Queen Elizabeth since the King was in North Africa. Gibson was given both his VC and the Bar to his DSO; it made him the most decorated man in the Royal Air Force.

The visit to the palace was followed by a dinner at the Hungaria Restaurant in Lower Regent Street, which was given by A. V. Roe. Many of those directly involved with the operation were there: Barnes Wallis, Mutt Summers, Whitworth, Cochrane, Roy Chadwick. Some of the backroom boys had also been invited – not only Humphries, but Fay Gillon, Chiefy Powell and Jim Heveron too.

After dinner came the cigars. While a cloud of tobacco smoke gradually filled the room, Tommy Sopwith, aircraft inventor and now chairman of Hawkers, presented Gibson with a specially made silver Lancaster. 'The Wing Commander's face,' noted Humphries, 'was a study: a mixture of pride and embarrassment.' The rest of the boys immediately began shouting, 'Speech! Speech!' He obliged, thanking those who had contributed to the great Dam Raid, and remembering to mention everyone, including the groundcrews and backroom staff. Even when a little drunk and overwhelmed, Gibson was never less than thorough.

More speeches followed and then finally there was a present-ation to Barnes Wallis, who was given a large photograph of the breached Möhne Dam, which Gibson and others then signed. It would adorn his office wall for the rest of his working life. For all his remorse at the loss of life, he could quite rightly still feel great pride at what he had achieved.

Signing Wallis's photograph was the catalyst for a mass swapping of signatures on each of the guests' specially printed menus.

And at the top of the card were two words: 'Damn Busters.'

In Germany, those battling against the clock to get the restoration work done could no doubt think of many worse expletives to use on the damned Dam Busters. By the end of June, nothing like the 70,000 workers promised had arrived, but the 7,000 workers from the Atlantic Wall had been transferred and more were to follow. Already, though, work had begun. The damaged sluices had been repaired and cleaned while existing work on two new pump stations on the River Ruhr had been accelerated with more parts requisitioned from elsewhere. Nor were the Eder and Möhne dams the only ones having urgent work carried out. A new dam, the Verse, had already been under construction, and work there was now to be massively accelerated with the implementation of double shifts and by making labourers work through the night.

By the beginning of July, rebuilding of the two great dams was well under way. In both cases, this required a quite phenomenal investment in materials, labour, logistics and money. At the Möhne, the first task was to repair the railway between Neheim and the dam; it was essential for bringing supplies and had been completely destroyed. Incredibly, this was up and running by 15 June, just a month after the attack. OT workers also had to rebuild a number of bridges in quick time, often single track and timber-piled. Frequently the wreckage of the previous bridge was left tumbled and broken beside the new wooden one; the essence of the operation was speed and joining broken links, not aesthetics. A number of new wooden bridges were built in the Eder Valley too for the same reason; work could not begin on the dams until access to them had been established.

At the Möhne, an entirely new narrow-gauge railway was built which led right up to the foot of the broken dam on a round loop and included no fewer than four stations from which materials could be unloaded. Barrack blocks for the thousands of labourers had to be constructed, with all the accompanying toilets, kitchens and other amenities. The same was true at the Eder, where new wooden viaducts were constructed, on which the railway was then built.

Both breaches were much the same size: 22 metres deep at the Möhne and 77 metres wide, and the same depth at the Eder and 70 metres wide. Work began with blasting the bottom of the breach with high-pressure hoses and clearing the rubble until a firm base was established. No corners were to be cut in the rebuilding process; the dams were also to be reconstructed using precisely the same method with which they had been built in the first place. Vast lattice works of scaffolding were erected – solid and strong enough to take the weight not only of hundreds of workers at any one time, but also of rails and wagons that delivered the stone. Stone also had to be cut out from the same quarries that had originally been used. The entire undertaking was quite breathtaking in its scale. The original dam had taken five years to build; it was being rebuilt in just five months in the middle of a total war.

Operation CITADEL was launched in the early hours of 5 July. Five days later, with the Germans having barely broken the crust of the Russian defences, the attack was already running out of steam. That same day, 10 July, the British and Americans launched the world's largest ever seaborne invasion when they landed at Sicily. Immediately, Hitler ordered the Mediterranean front to be reinforced, and especially with his air forces. Germany would lose 702 aircraft over the Eastern Front in July and August, but during the same period they lost a staggering 3,504 elsewhere, and most of those were in the Mediterranean. Germany would pay for the stalling of aircraft production in the Ruhr.

Two days after the invasion of Sicily, German forces at Kursk were fought to a standstill. The last great German offensive against the Soviet Union was over, and, with it, the opportunity to take back the initiative on the Eastern Front was lost for ever.

At the end of July, Air Chief Marshal Sir Arthur Harris decided the Battle of the Ruhr was over, and that it was time to concentrate efforts elsewhere. Since the beginning of March, Bomber Command had flown some 23,401 sorties and dropped more than 57,000 tons of bombs; the Luftwaffe had dropped 18,000 tons during the entire Blitz of September 1940 to May 1941. The Battle of the Ruhr had been expensive, however – 1,000 aircraft had never returned. Fighting an air war was a costly exercise, but 7,000 men was still as nothing compared to the losses in the First World War, something that was never far from Harris's mind. These figures

also put into perspective the eight crews that were lost during the
Dams Raid. As a percentage of the attacking force the cost was
certainly high, but when the losses were compared to the vast
amount of damage caused, the investment looked a lot better.
Indeed, such a small number of aircraft had never before achieved
quite so much in terms of material damage. It was one of the
factors about that raid that had so worried the Nazi High
Command.

Harris now turned his attention to Hamburg, the ancient
Hanseatic port on the River Elbe, home to important shipyards
and, with its access to the North Sea via the Elbe, a major transport
hub. On four separate nights, between the end of July and the
beginning of August, Harris sent more than 3,000 bombers to
attack the city and dropped around 10,000 tons of bombs. The US
Eighth Air Force also contributed a further 252 daylight sorties.
Among those taking part were Cyril Anderson and his crew, axed
by Gibson and back with 49 Squadron. They flew three times over
Hamburg, including on 27/28 July, when the attacks by nearly 800
aircraft caused a massive firestorm, which devastated much of the
old city. In all, 50 per cent of Hamburg was completely destroyed
in these attacks and more than 47,000 killed. No wonder Harris
called it Operation GOMORRAH.

Essen was given one more hammering and then, after
Hamburg had been left charred and smouldering, Harris turned to
other targets, and in particular to Berlin, which meant the reconstruction of the dams and the Ruhr could continue apace
without any serious interference.

Throughout the summer of 1943, RAF reconnaissance aircraft
continued to fly over, monitoring what was going on and seeing the
gradual rise of the dam walls once more. Both Speer and
Einsatzgruppenleiter Adam, whose task it was to oversee the reconstruction projects, were amazed that the RAF had not returned.
Clearly, there had been no chance of 617 Squadron returning
immediately after the raid, but some nuisance attacks by
Mosquitoes, for example, flying low and quickly, could have
wreaked havoc, both materially and in terms of morale. Destroying
some of those railways, or barrack blocks or the immense

lattice-work of scaffolding could have had a profound effect on the chances of having the dams ready before the winter rains. Why such raids were not undertaken is not clear; perhaps the improved defences meant the risk was simply too great.

In any case, no raid was ever launched, not even at night when work continued under floodlights. The urgency of getting the task finished in time was so great, the risk of continuing the rebuilding operation under lights was considered one worth taking. As a result, the thousands of workers at both dams were left in peace. Work continued round the clock, for twenty-four hours a day, seven days a week. The breach at the Möhne was closed on 25 September, just seventy-nine days after repairs had begun, that at the Eder a week later. There had been complications, too. There were fears that internal, invisible fissures had occurred at both dams, so liquid concrete was injected to help strengthen the original structures. At the Eder, this was inadvertently injected into the drainage channels inside the wall, which meant an entirely new set a drainage channels had to be bored, a major undertaking. Even when the dam was finally completed, these drainage and strengthening issues had not been entirely resolved. Not until well after the war was over would engineers be satisfied that it was safe to fill the reservoir once more.

Albert Speer re-inaugurated both dams on 3 October. By any reckoning, this had been a monumental achievement. The work was not complete yet, however. Having gone to such effort to rebuild the dams, the Nazis were insistent that they should never be breached again. This meant massive defences. Further guns were hastily brought in – both four-barrelled cannons and 88mm heavy anti-aircraft guns – with specially built concrete bunkers and pedestals constructed for the purpose. Searchlights and mobile flak were also deployed. Above the lake, barrage balloons were erected, while vast steel nets were put up, stretching thirty metres horizontally out of the side of the wall. Also now stretching across the width of the dams were hundred-metre-high anti-aircraft nets, metal cables that were suspended on masts and from which were hung, at seventeen-metre intervals, a row of contact mines. When eventually the water began to rise again, a massive, 400-metre-long mine-deflecting wall was floated out on wooden rafts, which, once in position, were sunk with concrete, while further lines of anti-torpedo nets were put in place. At the Eder Dam, it was planned that there should be three rows of anti-torpedo nets, one anti-aircraft net stretched from side to side, and four rows of bomb deflector floats.

Nor were these elaborate and extremely costly defences put in place only at the two great dams. Similar treatment was carried out at the Sorpe, Diemel, Ennepe, Lister and Agger.

By the time the dams were re-inaugurated, the front had shifted again in Russia – westwards, as German forces were pushed back. In the Mediterranean, Mussolini had been overthrown and Hitler's biggest ally, Italy, had sued for peace. In September, two weeks before the Möhne's breach was closed, the Allies invaded southern Italy. On every front, German forces were heading one way, and that was backwards.

A little over a month after the re-inauguration of the dams, Hitler ordered Feldmarschall Erwin Rommel to carry out an inspection of the Atlantic Wall, the planned series of defences that ran all the way from Norway down to the Pyrenees. It was clear that, at some point, the Allies would launch a seaborne invasion of north-west Europe. Hitler planned that the Atlantic Wall would stop them in their tracks. Equally obvious was that of all the possible invasion points, the Dutch, Belgian and northern French coasts were the most logical and practicable.

Rommel reached France on 18 December and was horrified by what he discovered. There were barely any defences at all, let alone any kind of wall, metaphorical or otherwise. And one of the reasons for this was that earlier in the summer, when the OT had been supposed to be building bunkers, gun positions, anti-tank ditches and beach defences, large numbers of labourers had instead been transferred to Germany to rebuild the dams. But workers could not rebuild dams and construct coastal defences at the same time. If as much energy had been put into building the Atlantic Wall as had been dedicated to reconstruction work on the dams and in the Ruhr, the Allied invasion of June the following year might not have been so successful. As it was, Rommel's defences were still woefully inadequate.

The cost of repairing the damage wrought by the Dams Raid of 16/17 May 1943 was absolutely enormous – psychologically, materially, logistically and financially. It was also one the Germans simply could not afford.

In no way should the achievement of the extraordinary Dams Raid ever be belittled.

Postscript

O N 1 JULY 1943, Edward Russell, of the Joint Liaison Committee in Washington, wrote to Flight Lieutenant William Teeling, an intelligence officer at the Air Ministry, quoting a comment from King Features, one of the biggest media syndicates in the United States. 'No one accomplishment in the war,' they claimed, 'appears to have generated public enthusiasm to the extent of the mining of the Möhne and Eder dams by the RAF. There is a demand for every scrap of information about the feat and about Wing Commander Gibson and his men.'

They would be given it, not least in Gibson himself, who in August was sent to North America, first to attend the Anglo-US QUADRANT Conference in Quebec, and then on a publicity tour promoting British war efforts in the US.

What was missing, however, was any mention of the Sorpe Dam, although why would it be mentioned? It was not breached after all – merely badly damaged and its crust 'crumbled'. This would, in time, mean that it had to be completely drained for essential repair work to be carried out, but the Germans did not have to do this at the same time as repair work was going on at the Eder and Möhne. Draining and repairing the Sorpe was a major and costly inconvenience, but it was not disastrous.

It is true that Upkeep had been developed for attack against gravity dams, yet Wallis always claimed that enough Upkeeps dropped in the right place could destroy the Sorpe Dam. Inasmuch as the key decision makers in the planning of Operation CHASTISE had recognized the importance of destroying the Sorpe in conjunction with the Möhne, the raid has to be seen as having been only a partial success. Nineteen crews took part in Operation CHASTISE, and ten were available to strike the Sorpe, but only two managed to reach it. Of those two, the strike rate was 100 per cent – in fact, of all the three priority targets attacked, the Sorpe had the greatest hit ratio. In other words, had those ten aircraft available actually reached it, then perhaps it could have been destroyed. Johnny Johnson swears blind that Barnes Wallis told him that six Upkeeps would be needed to destroy the Sorpe. Certainly, Wallis appears to have recognized that more than two would be necessary. Five aircraft were specifically directed to the Sorpe, which suggests that this was the number of Upkeeps he reckoned it would take to destroy it. Certainly, with every successful drop, the damage caused was likely to increase exponentially.

But could anything have been done differently? Little account appears to have been taken of the chances of valley mists, although the forecast weather conditions all pointed to this. The Reserve Wave took off two and a half hours after the first Lancasters had departed, but could easily have left at say, 11 p.m., rather than after midnight. This would have given them more time over the target area and a better chance of reaching the Sorpe before the worst of the valley mists developed. The time-lag was presumably to give the first two waves time to complete their attacks, and for Group to then make an assessment of the situation. Even so, a two-hour gap seems overly generous; it could easily have made all the difference to Cyril Anderson and his crew. Had Townsend then been sent to the Sorpe rather than a pointless 'last resort' target, that could have been two more Upkeeps on the Sorpe. Two more might have made all the difference.

Unfortunately, the Reserve Wave lacked the direction of the First, which was controlled at both the Möhne and Eder by Gibson personally. Back at Grantham, Group did not have a clear enough picture of what was going on, not least because each aircraft was told to maintain radio silence, except to send a signal once they had dropped their Upkeeps. Group had no real idea who was shot down and who had made it to the target. The situation had become hopelessly confused. A perhaps more sensible solution would have been to send both Second and Reserve Waves over together in much the same way as the First Wave, with the Sorpe as its primary target, since the dam was likely to be a tougher nut to crack. Dinghy Young, perhaps, could have been leader with the same role as Gibson with the First Wave. It would have meant attacking the Sorpe in controlled and concentrated waves, with successive attackers able to help and advise subsequent ones.

It is easy, however, to be wise after the event, although there is a sense of there being a degree of defeatism about the Sorpe; that Satterly had initially downgraded the target is telling. The truth is, the Upkeep was not really designed for a dam of the Sorpe's construction. This may well have influenced the final structure of the plan and in so doing helped create a self-fulfilling prophecy.

There was another area, however, where the planning seemed a little wanting, and that was the weather forecasting. The lack of forewarning about valley mists was consistent with inaccurate weather forecasting for the raid, which was almost certainly to cost Byers's crew their lives and could very easily have accounted for Gibson and the first three too.

On 7 June, Air Vice-Marshal Cochrane distributed a report on Operation CHASTISE which included a number of appendices, including 'Appendix E: Report of Navigation'. He reported that the weather forecast had been a north-westerly wind west of three degrees east of less than 6 mph, i.e. over the North Sea, and a north-easterly of as much as 35 mph over the target. However, this does not seem to have been the forecast given to the crews, because none of the navigators appear to have factored in a 6 mph north-westerly in their navigation logs. Flight Lieutenant Leggo, the Squadron Navigation Officer, who was flying with Mick Martin, recorded 'calm' west of three degrees east. It is also notable that not one of the navigators – or indeed any of the crews – who survived the raid ever mentioned the weather forecast given them by the Met Officer at the pre-raid briefing at Scampton, presumably because it was so unremarkable it was not considered worth recording. Most only refer to the fine weather that May Sunday.

At the time, the Meteorological Office produced an incredible array of forecasts, on a roughly three-hourly basis, which covered not only the British Isles, but continental Europe and out into the Atlantic. These changed little during the day, and both the morning and 1 p.m. charts for the British Isles showed that it was a warm and sunny day, just as the crews remembered. The forecasters clearly thought that, with high pressure over Britain, the temperature was likely to fall rapidly at night, which was typical of spring, and become very cold at surface level, all of which would suggest calm winds at that height. But, already, there were signs that the ridge of high pressure was just beginning to collapse.

Furthermore, the upper air chart showed clearly that there were already strong north-easterly winds at around 9,000 feet by early evening, while, across the North Sea, along the Dutch and Belgian coast and inland there were north-easterly surface winds already at 20 knots or more – that is, at the level the squadron would be flying. The combination of the high pressure over Britain and the strong winds across the sea suggested a northerly or north-easterly wind of perhaps 5–10 knots over the North Sea at the very least, and maybe stronger. For some reason, this was not forecast to the crews.

Interestingly, however, Cochrane in his Appendix E then listed the subsequent recorded weather forecast, which showed, as the maps had originally suggested at 1 p.m. on 16 May, that there had indeed been a northerly wind of 'up to 10 mph' and a north-easterly of some 14 mph over the Continent. 'All navigators, except one,' noted Cochrane, 'found winds.' The report on the raid concluded quite categorically that the six lost off the planned route were because of tracking error, and yet the squadron does not appear to have been properly briefed. 'As a whole,' noted Cochrane, 'the logs returned do not show as high a standard as they do on a normal high level night sortie.' Certainly, Leggo's nav log is particularly sparse on detail. On an operation of this importance, the Squadron Navigation Officer would have normally been expected to go through the route plan with every single other navigator, yet there are inconsistencies between Leggo's nav log and that of Vivian Nicholson in Maltby's crew, even though both flew the same course. There is no question that Leggo was a fine navigator – he would not have been made Squadron Navigation Officer unless he was – but the lack of information on his nav log and the inconsistencies are surprising, nonetheless.

Cochrane suggested a number of reasons for the slackness of the navigation log keeping, including crews feeling more 'jumpy' than normal because of the low-level operation they were flying, or navigators not being at their tables quite as much as normal because they were too busy map-reading. The last reason given, however, was the key one. 'In conditions of light winds,' suggested Cochrane, 'wind finding is not so important as it is if the winds are strong and changeable. On the operation in question, there was not enough wind to necessitate continual W/V [wind variation] checks.'

This is a far more convincing reason than being 'jumpy'. Drifts were used by some as they travelled across the North Sea – these were taken on flame floats that were dropped from the aircraft. Any deviation caused by wind could then be roughly worked out by looking at the position of the flaming float on the water behind them. These would obviously not be used as they approached the enemy coast for fear of being spotted, but since they had been told there would be calm winds in the North Sea and English Channel why would they need to carry out drift checks? The lack of navigational logging as the journey progressed certainly suggests they had carried out far fewer wind variation checks than they might otherwise have done.

They were able to use GEE for parts of the journey, although it involved climbing dangerously to use it, which meant most used it sparingly. They also repeatedly found that the GEE signals had been jammed by the enemy. At any rate, accurate weather forecasting might have made an important difference. Navigation was hard enough without being given the incorrect weather forecast.

Even so, despite the failure to destroy the Sorpe, there is no question that the raid was a phenomenal achievement. It was true that the squadron had accrued around 2,000 training hours, but, really, the preparation was decidedly patchy in parts. Only one, lone live Upkeep had been dropped before the raid; half the crews had never even dropped an inert one. That they should have been expected to head over enemy-occupied territory to drop a weapon that had been dropped once before by some and by many not at all is astonishing.

The standard of navigation was also incredible. That Anderson's crew were the only ones not to find their target was another astounding achievement. Low-level cross-country navigation was incredibly difficult even in daylight, but at night time and over occupied territory it was even more so. When I first flew over the dams, I was travelling at around 2,000 feet on a bright, clear day with good visibility. Travelling from the Möhne, we did find the Eder, but it was not easy, even at that height. At just a hundred feet, at night, with mists forming, it is extraordinary that they ever found it at all. Every current pilot I have talked to about this has reiterated just how difficult low-level navigation is without any modern navigational aids.

When I first visited the Eder Dam, I was similarly amazed as to how hard it must have been for those Lancasters to accurately hit the dam. The topography is so unforgiving. It took no time to walk from the dam itself to the end of the spit that curled round in front of it. Looking back to the dam wall, it seemed every bit as close as it was. A few months later, I was there again with a Beech 18 flying over at around 500 feet. This was a period two-engine aircraft with a similar tail to that of the Lancaster, although, overall, very much smaller. It also similarly lacked modern controls, hydraulics and navigational aids. The pilot had not flown over the dams before, and even in his smaller, lighter aircraft, and flying at 500 feet, he was surprised by how tight the turn was at the spit. He could hardly imagine how a laden Lancaster could achieve it and at a mere sixty feet off the water. 'It was wooded and rough land and scenically, it was rather beautiful,' Dave Shannon commented some years later, 'but not the sort of place to try and get into with a four-engined aircraft, and get out again and get down to sixty feet and do your run-up, get your speed at 232 miles an hour and then have a sheer rock face at the end of it to climb up over the top.'

The Sorpe was pretty difficult too, which is why both McCarthy and Brown repeatedly flew dummy runs over the length of the wall before finally dropping their mines. Much later, in the 1960s, Joe McCarthy visited the Sorpe with his son, Joe Jr, then a fast-jet pilot in the US Navy. Neither had been on the ground there before and suddenly, halfway across, Joe Sr stopped, his hands on his hips, and with a quizzical expression on his face looked back and forth along the length of the dam and at the rising wooded slopes one end and the village of Langscheid at the other. 'You know,' he said to his son, 'if I'd seen this dam from this angle before the raid, I would have said it couldn't be done.' Joe Jr later flew in the Vietnam War and continued his flying career afterwards, so has a good appreciation of what his father went through. He is in awe of what his father and those in 617 Squadron achieved. 'Especially that they were flying such a big, heavy aircraft, with flight controls that are just cables. It's not hydraulically boosted like controls are today,' he says. 'You really had to lug the thing around. You're dodging pylons, worried about flak, trying to stay on the route, you're making turns and to try and accomplish all these different things at the same time would be physically, physically, tiring.'

For 617 Squadron, there had been little flying in the weeks that followed Operation CHASTISE, but one thing was certain: the squadron was now here to stay, and although Harris had an instinctive mistrust and dislike of specialist elite units, it was clear that from its personnel and now fame, this was what it had become, as he was fully aware. 'It is my intention,' he announced on 3 June, 'to keep this squadron for the performance of similar tasks in the future.' Just how to use it had, however, not been quite resolved. The first operation after the Dams Raid was on two power stations in northern Italy on 15 July and included many of the originals, such as Les Munro, Joe McCarthy, Mick Martin and David Maltby.

Meanwhile, the Air Ministry and Bomber Command were considering using Upkeep mines again, although over land rather than water. The Dams Raid had demonstrated that there was a place for precision bombing and that attacks could be co-ordinated, rather as they were in land attacks, by a unit commander at the scene using VHF. This allowed for greater control at the target and increased flexibility to deal with an attack situation as it developed.

On 8 June, the Ad Hoc Committee had met once more following 617 Squadron trials in the New Forest using Upkeeps over land. The results had been encouraging and now Bufton, Bottomley and others began looking at fresh targets, not least the Rothensee Ship Lift, the Dortmund–Ems Canal and the Mittelland Canal. There were a number of issues, however, not least that more Type 464s would be needed. Upkeeps used on land would be more effective with forward spin, rather than backspin, which meant altering the rotors. Then there was the question of whether Highballs might be more effective on such targets than Upkeeps. Finally, there was the discovery that Norm Barlow's Upkeep had survived the crash intact and had been captured – and presumably dissected – by the Germans. All these factors contributed to a gradual erosion of enthusiasm for the weapon. Upkeep mines were not entirely discarded, but they were never used again. Not until after the war were those remaining large mines finally dumped into the sea.

Highball was never used either. After the cancellation of SERVANT, plans continued for an attack on the Italian fleet in the Mediterranean but the issues that dogged the trials in Scotland in May had still not been resolved by the time Sicily was invaded. The Italians threw in the towel before an attack could be launched. Testing continued but 618 Squadron could not be kept back for ever, and in September they were released for other duties. Not until the following year were all the issues with Highball finally resolved, and although 618 Squadron was later sent out to Australia in preparation for the weapon's use against Japanese shipping, it was never used operationally. Admiral Renouf, Highball's biggest champion, was retired just a month after CHASTISE. Highball demonstrated just how fine the line was between creating a weapon that could be used operationally and one that never saw the light of day.

Barnes Wallis has often been portrayed as a lone voice desperately arguing his case in the face of a wall of po-faced bureaucracy, but this was hardly the case. That Operation CHASTISE ever happened at all is testimony to the many people from different services and from different ministries and departments who helped support his idea and who ensured it bore fruit. Of course, there were those who opposed it but their opposition was perfectly valid, and even despite the success of the Raid, the fact that so much time and effort was put into a weapon that was only ever used once rather supports men like Linnell who were so sceptical initially. And, as it happened, the Windsor never did go into production; just three prototypes were made, but by then the Lancaster was delivering greater payloads than had initially been expected and assembly lines were running smoothly. The Windsor was simply not considered necessary any more.

No, Wallis may have been the inventor of the weapon and the driving force behind its development, but Operation CHASTISE was truly a team effort, and underlined Britain's willingness to harness science and innovation into winning the war. Far from being small-minded stick-in-the-muds, Britain's war leaders developed a culture of inventiveness and experiment that led to a staggering array of brilliant technological development. The bouncing bomb is testimony to this, and the decision to greenlight the project was an unquestionably brave one by Portal, but one which, again, demonstrates that Britain's war leaders were both modernists and risk-takers.

Although Upkeep would thus only ever be a one-operation weapon, Wallis quickly returned to his earlier ideas for a deep-penetration bomb. Just after the raid, he was approached by Sir Wilfrid Freeman, now Chief Executive at the Ministry of Aircraft Production, about his idea for the ten-ton bomb. 'How soon could you let me have one?' Freeman asked him.

'Five months,' Wallis replied, 'if I have all the labour available in Sheffield.' Even at the 8 June meeting of the Ad Hoc Committee, 'Item No. 10 – Deep Penetration Bomb' was being discussed. With Wallis's credibility now significantly higher, two such weapons would be developed: the six-ton Tallboy and the ten-ton Grand Slam, and both were to be used very effectively on a number of precision operations by none other than 617 Squadron, the Dam Busters.

Gibson left the squadron at the beginning of August and for a while 617 floundered. Squadron Leader George Holden took over, and although he had a hard act to follow, he was unpopular and his command was not a success. The next major operation by the squadron was an attack on the Dortmund–Ems Canal in September. The first time they tried, on the night of 14 September, they set off but were recalled due to bad weather and as they returned David Maltby and his crew were lost. Eight aircraft set out again the following night, once more in far from ideal weather conditions. Not only was the operation a failure, but five of the eight crews were lost, including those of Holden, Les Knight and Wilson and Divall. This was to be 617 Squadron's darkest hour.

Holden was replaced as CO by Wing Commander Leonard Cheshire – a man who rivalled Gibson's experience, and someone with vision, charisma, brains and charm. Les Munro reckoned Cheshire was the finest man he ever met; Johnny Johnson agrees. During the Cheshire era, 617 emerged from being the squadron who had performed one incredible mission to being the deserved elite squadron in Bomber Command. Men like Munro, McCarthy, Martin and Shannon became the core of this highly skilled, highly efficient precision-bombing unit. It was 617 Squadron that smashed the Saumur Tunnel, and the E-boat pens at Le Havre using Tallboys. On D-Day, with Munro and Cheshire sharing control, the squadron managed to execute a simulation of a cross-Channel invasion fleet to fool the Germans into thinking the main invasion force was heading for the Pas de Calais rather than Normandy. It was an operation that required the highest flying skill imaginable. Later, after Cheshire, Munro and the last Dam Busters had left the Squadron, it was 617 who finally sank the *Tirpitz* – the German battleship that had triggered such interest in the bouncing bomb in the first place.

The Dams Raid was never forgotten, but after the war it returned to the forefront of public consciousness, first with the publication of Paul Brickhill's *The Dam Busters*, and then, in 1955, with the film of the same name. It was a huge success and has remained one of the most popular war films of all time ever since. Post-war analysis of the raid has often been critical, however. 'The effects of this brilliant achievement upon the German war machine,' wrote the official historians of the Strategic Air Offensive

against Germany, 'were not, in themselves, of fundamental importance nor even seriously damaging.' This was a line repeated by
future historians. Goebbels's diary entry from 20 May, in which he
suggested the damage was not as bad as first feared, is also often
quoted, as are Speer's comments in his autobiography in which he
criticized the RAF for attacking the Eder and not the Sorpe more
heavily.

However, as I hope I have showed, the weight of German
evidence (not consulted by the official historians) does not support
this. It has been argued that the lasting effects of the Dams Raid
were minimal because they were rebuilt so quickly. This, however,
is to look at it the wrong way round: they would not have been
rebuilt so quickly or at so much cost had they not been important
targets. The tragedy is that the post-war downplaying of their
importance affected the way those who flew on the raid viewed
what they had done. The Dam Buster veterans were suddenly
expected to defend what they had achieved. Ken Brown, for one,
until his dying day, believed the losses had simply not been worth
what he had come to understand had been limited achievements. It
is time to put the record straight.

But what of the Dam Busters and those men who ensured this
incredible raid took place? Barnes Wallis lived a long and
celebrated life. After the war, he continued working for Vickers,
developing, among other things, the Swallow supersonic jet aeroplane. The photograph of the breached Möhne Dam hung on his
office wall at Brooklands for the rest of his working life.

Four years after the war, his old friend Sir Wilfrid Freeman
suggested to him that he should apply to the Royal Commission on
Awards to Inventors for some financial recognition for his work on
the destruction of the dams. Wallis refused; he felt very strongly
that the credit for destroying the dams was not due to him but to
the crews who carried out the mission. Always a man of deep faith,
he later heard in the church at Effingham a reading from 2 Samuel.
'Be it far from me, O Lord, that I should do this: is not this the
blood of the men that went in jeopardy of their lives?' It was a line
that summed up his view precisely. He was, however, eventually
knighted, deserved recognition not only of his extraordinary

wartime achievements, but also of an astonishing and long career. He lived on in Effingham until finally passing away in 1979, aged ninety-two, but his deep regret over the loss of life suffered on the Dams Raid was something he took with him to his grave.

Sadly, many of the Dam Busters did not survive the war. Gibson's crew were all lost flying with Holden on the Dortmund–Ems Canal operation. Geoff Rice later lost his crew on the raid on Liège in December 1943, although he survived, becoming a POW. Bob Hay was fatally wounded during an attack on a viaduct in southern France the following February. Mick Martin had made an unofficial pact with his crew that they would all finish together; Hay's death was the trigger for him to call time on operational flying. Cyril Anderson was also killed with his crew, during an attack on Mannheim in September 1943. On his grave, his wife had the following words inscribed: 'In my book of memory is marked the happy story of a love deep and true.'

Nor did Gibson survive the war. There would be no dream country cottage where he and Maggie – rather than his wife, Eve – could live out long, happy lives together. He went to America, as ordered, returning in December, thin, drawn and exhausted and assuming he would be returned to 617 Squadron. This was not to be. Instead, he wrote *Enemy Coast Ahead*, dabbled in politics, attended a staff course, and then pleaded with Harris to be allowed to return to operations. This did not happen, but he was posted to the staff of 55 Base at East Kirkby, the hub of three squadrons, where his duties were to be operational planning and liaison.

Almost immediately, Gibson found living and working at an operational base without actually flying a terrible kind of torture. Two weeks after arriving, he decided to get back in touch with Maggie, writing to her and then paying her a visit in Bognor Regis, where she was now based. He had not seen her in nearly a year, but the old feelings for one another were still very much alive. The war was finally drawing to an end and sometimes it occurred to him that he might survive it after all; perhaps he and Maggie did have a future. Perhaps Honeysuckle Cottage, their idealized fantasy home, might prove a reality. A couple of days after returning to East

Kirkby, he wrote her a card. 'The day was perfect. I love you now and for ever.'

Soon after, he flew again – unofficially taking the place of a Lancaster pilot from 630 Squadron in a raid on a V1 missile site. A couple of weeks after that, he was posted – this time to No. 54 Base HQ at Coningsby. It was here that he began flying – again unofficially – a Mosquito from 627 Squadron that was on loan to Coningsby Base staff from nearby Woodhall Spa, where both 617 and 627 Squadrons were based. Gibson had never been properly trained on a Mosquito, but on 19 September he appointed himself Master Bomber for an operation on Rheydt. It was a crazy decision and completely unnecessary, fuelled only by his urge to fly operationally once more. At any rate, he did not return from that mission. It may never be known what really happened, but Gibson's Mosquito crashed near Steenbergen in Holland, killing both him and his navigator.

It was a tragic waste and yet Gibson was in many ways a rather tragic, although undeniably heroic, figure. Like all the greatest heroes, he was flawed. He could be arrogant, was something of a martinet and could be horribly opinionated. Some, like Hopgood and Shannon, thought the world of him, others that he was insufferable. What is undeniably the case is that during the training for CHASTISE, and throughout the raid itself, Gibson's achievements were Herculean. Despite extreme mental and physical exhaustion, despite the immense responsibility, and despite being ill enough to be grounded, he moulded and formed the squadron and then, on the operation itself, led it with exceptional skill and bravery. His flaws only make his achievement even more remarkable.

There are now, at the time of writing, just four survivors of the 133 men who flew on the raid. Fred Sutherland, front gunner in Les Knight's crew, lives in Canada. Johnny Johnson, bomb-aimer on Joe McCarthy's crew, now lives in Bristol, having had a long career in the RAF, in which he rose to the rank of Squadron Leader before becoming a teacher. His marriage to Gwen, begun so hurriedly a few days after joining 617 Squadron, was a long and happy one. Grant McDonald, rear gunner on Ken Brown's crew, lives in

Vancouver. After the war, he left the Air Force and became a Customs officer, although he kept up with some of his old crew and to this day remains proud of being one of the original Dam Busters. 'It was something pretty different,' he says. 'It stayed with you, that's for sure.'

Les Munro was taken off operations in July 1944, after completing thirty-six operations with 617 Squadron and becoming 'B' Flight Commander. He was then appointed to command 1690 Bomber Defence Training Flight and flew Hurricanes for the next twelve months. Returning home after the war, he was employed by the State Advances Corporation, carrying out land valuation and the settlement of returned servicemen on farms. In 1961, he acquired his own farm, which he continued to run for the next fourteen years before downsizing to a smaller property. It was during this period that he became involved in local, regional and national Local Body Government. For this work, he was appointed a Companion of the Queen's Service Order and, in 1997, made a Companion of the New Zealand Order of Merit. He married his wife, Betty, a few years after the war, and together they had five children. Sadly, Betty died some six months after their fiftieth wedding anniversary. Munro retired to Tauranga on the Bay of Plenty, where he still lives.

For all the survivors, the Dams Raid remained an unforgettable moment in their lives. Historians may still debate the effects of the raid, but its legacy affected many people in more personal ways too. In Germany, Karl Schäfer says his generation never forgot the horrors of that terrible night. 'After that,' he says, 'we lost the will to carry on.' Even to this day, the breaching of the dams is still referred to as the *Katastrophe*.

The raid also profoundly touched the lives of John Fraser's family. After baling out of Hopgood's plane, Fraser managed to evade capture for a while, making use of the survival skills he had learned growing up on Vancouver Island. He later recalled making his way some 200 miles before being picked up near the Rhine. He spent the rest of the war as a POW. It was while in camp that he drafted a letter to Hopgood's mother, written in pencil in a small notebook. 'Mrs Hopgood,' he scrawled, 'we can wait and hope and pray, not only for our own dear ones, but for those others in distress, and in our waiting, we may be able to learn some lessons God is trying to teach us.' His time with Hopgood and the squadron was brief but had a profound effect on him. When he was finally reunited with his young wife and was able to take her to Canada and start a family, he called their daughter Shere – the name of the village where Hopgood had been raised. Tragically, John Fraser died in a flying accident in Canada in 1962, but later, through making a documentary about the raid, Shere Fraser Lowe met Joe McCarthy Jr and, in 2010, these two children of Dam Busters were married. They live not far from John's widow, Doris.

And, of course, many lives took a quite different course because of those who did not return from the raid. For three long months, Gwen Parfitt – Charlie Williams's Bobbie – desperately tried to find out what had happened to the man she loved, hoping and praying that he had somehow survived and been taken prisoner. Not until 14 August did she receive the terrible news that he had been killed on the night of the raid.

Gwen later married but had no children and certainly, by 1998, she was on her own and in need of funds for a place in a home. It appears to have been for this reason that she sold her letters from her beloved Charlie to the Queensland State Library in Brisbane, Australia. After all, she had no one to leave them to, while at a proper archive in Williams's home state they might be properly looked after. A place where Charlie might not be forgotten.

She sent the bundle of letters and the scrapbook Charlie had been filling before the raid with a covering letter, in which, on two sides of foolscap, she twice mentioned that they had been due to be married the week after the raid. She then wrote about how, some years later, she had the chance of visiting the Möhne Dam. 'It was a beautiful day,' she recalled, 'the sun was shining, children were laughing with ice creams and cakes. I stood drawing breath for a moment – it was as if it had never been – and knowing the young man so well, that is the way he would have liked to see it. I know. Perhaps it wasn't in vain.'

oh! what a lovely War !

Abbreviations

ACAS	Assistant Chief of the Air Staff
AM	Air Marshal
AVM	Air Vice-Marshal
BA-MA	Bundesarchiv-Militärarchiv, Freiburg, Germany
DB Ops	Director of Bomber Operations
C-in-C	Commander-in-Chief
CRD	Controller for Research and Development
SASO	Senior Air Staff Officer
TNA	The National Archives, Kew, London

Operation CHASTISE
Timeline

Sunday, 16 May

21 00	Very flare fired for First and Second Waves to start engines
21 28	*E-Easy* takes off
21 29	Munro takes off in *W-Willie*
21 30	Byers takes off in *K-King*
21 31	Rice takes off in *H-Harry*
21 39	Gibson takes off in *G-George* Martin takes off in *P-Peter* Hopgood takes off in *M-Mother*
21 47	Young takes off in *A-Apple* Maltby takes off in *J-Johnny* Shannon takes off in *L-Leather*
21 54	Munro crosses English coast
21 59	Maudslay takes off in *Z-Zebra* Astell takes off in *B-Baker* Knight takes off in *N-Nuts*
22 01	McCarthy takes off in *T-Tommy*
22 20	Gibson trio cross English coast
22 28	Maudslay trio cross English coast
22 56	Munro reaches Dutch coast
22 57	Munro hit

22 57	Byers hit
22 59	Rice crosses Dutch coast
23 00	Rice hits water
23 00	Wallis and Cochrane leave Scampton for Grantham
23 06	Munro returns home
23 02	Gibson, Hopgood, Martin cross Dutch coast
23 12	Young, Maltby, Shannon reach Dutch coast
23 13	McCarthy reaches Vlieland
23 21	Maudslay trio cross Scheldt
23 22	Maudslay, Astell, Knight reach Dutch coast
23 50	Barlow crashes

Monday, 17 May

00 07	Gibson trio encounters flak – Hopgood's plane hit. Gibson transmits flak warning
00 09	Ottley takes off in *C-Charlie*
00 11	Burpee takes off in *S-Sugar*
00 12	Ken Brown takes off in *F-Freddie*
00 14	Townsend takes off in *O-Orange*
00 15	Anderson takes off in *Y-York*
00 15	Gibson, Martin, Hopgood reach Möhne – Martin first
00 15	Astell shot down
00 15	McCarthy reaches Sorpe
00 16	Munro crosses back over English coast
00 26	Young trio reach Möhne Shannon arrives late
00 28	Gibson attacks
00 33	Hopgood attacks and is shot down
00 36	Munro lands back at Scampton
00 37	Gibson's first Goner 68A sent
00 38	Martin attacks
00 43	Young attacks – Goner 78A
00 46	McCarthy attacks the Sorpe

00 47	Rice crash-lands at Scampton
00 49	Maltby attacks Sorpe
00 50	Goner 78A signalled from Maltby even though dam already beginning to crumble
00 50	Young's Goner 78A signal received
00 53	Martin's Goner 58A signal received at Grantham
00 56	Gibson orders Nigger signal to be sent
01 30	Gibson arrives at Eder and fires Very pistol
01 30	Brown reaches Dutch coast
01 31	Townsend reaches Dutch coast
01 39	Shannon attacks Eder
01 45	Maudslay attacks Eder
01 45	Townsend evades enemy flak
01 46	Goner 28B sent
01 47	Gibson calls up Astell
01 50	Gibson calls up Astell again
01 52	Knight attacks Eder
01 53	Maltby crosses back over Dutch coast
01 53	Burpee shot down
01 54	Dinghy sent – Eder breached
01 55	Grantham asks for confirmation
01 57	Maudslay sends signal to Grantham
02 06	Shannon's Goner 79B message received at Grantham
02 10	Grantham asks Gibson if any from First Wave can attack Sorpe
02 22	Townsend ordered to attack Ennepe
02 28	Anderson ordered to attack Sorpe
02 30	Grantham tries to divert Burpee to Sorpe
02 32	Reserve Wave receives W/T signals from Grantham
02 35	Ottley crashes
02 36	Maudslay shot down
02 58	Young shot down
02 59	Knight crosses Dutch coast

03 10   Anderson turns for home

03 14   Brown attacks Sorpe

03 19   Martin lands

03 23   Goner 78C from Brown

03 25   McCarthy lands

00 37   Townsend attacks Ennepe

04 00   Wallis, Harris, Cochrane leave Grantham for Scampton

04 06   Shannon lands

04 15   Gibson lands

05 30   Anderson lands

05 33   Brown lands

06 15   Townsend lands

Operation CHASTISE
Codewords

Primary Targets

Target X   Möhne

Target Y   Eder

Target Z   Sorpe

Last Resort Targets

Target D   Lister

Target E   Ennepe

Target F   Diemel

Codewords Used on the Raid

Cooler   617 callsign for Operation CHASTISE

Pranger   Attack Möhne Dam

Nigger   Möhne breached. Divert to Eder

Dinghy   Eder breached. Divert to Sorpe

Tulip   Cooler 2 take over at Möhne

              Cooler 4 take over at Eder

Gilbert   Attack last resort targets

Mason   All aircraft return to base

Goner   Upkeep released and ...

1. failed to explode

2. overshot dam

3. exploded 100+ yards from dam

4. exploded 100 yards from dam

5. exploded 50 yards from dam

6. exploded 5 yards from dam

7. exploded in contact with dam

with results noted ...

8. no apparent breach

9. small breach

10. large breach

in Target . . .

A Möhne

B Eder

C Sorpe

D Lister

E Ennepe

F Diemel

For example, Goner 68A = Upkeep released and exploded five yards from the Möhne with no apparent breach.

Notes

61   'A solution to the problem . . .' Collins, 'Origins of the Attack on the German Dams'
61   'At present, I am working . . .' TNA AVIA 15/744

4 Sink the *Tirpitz*
65   'always inclined to nervousness . . .' TNA ADM 196/92
66   'The general argument . . .' TNA ADM 277/46

5 Sitting on the Fence
69   'Your prime objective . . .' OH Vol. IV, p. 153. This Directive was approved on 21 January 1943, but not sent to Harris until 4 February
73   'We have just worked out . . .' TNA AIR 14/840
75   'This is tripe . . .' TNA AIR 14/842

6 Bomber Boys
77   'most urgent attention.' OH Vol. I, p. 179
77   'I must bring . . .' Harris Papers, H81
78   'We are bombing Germany . . .' Cited in Harris, *Bomber Offensive*, p. 118
79   'Mr Dimbleby can talk . . .' Cited in Probert, *Bomber Harris*, p. 190
79   'in little winking flashes . . .' Dimbleby broadcast, IWM 2164
81   'You will find him absolutely first class . . .' Cited in Morris, *Guy Gibson*, p. 100
81   'A good trip . . .' TNA AIR 4/37
82   'Yes, but . . .' Cited in Morris, *Guy Gibson*, p. 127
87   'We finally landed . . .' Williams Papers, 31/5/1942, QSL
87   'We were glad to see them go.' Ibid., 26/6/1942
88   'It is really a most frightening sight . . .' Ibid., 26/9/1942
89   'We were all just about . . .' Ibid., 8/2/1943
90   'I don't want you to do this . . .' Cited in Morris, *Guy Gibson*, p. 134

7 Panacea Mongers
91   'DB Ops was requested . . .' TNA AIR 14/840
92   'After the operation has taken place . . .' TNA AIR14/840
94   'They should start training . . .' Cited in Melinsky, *Forming the Pathfinders*, p. 67
95   'I urge therefore . . .' Ibid., p. 68
96   'Sir, you will never . . .' Ibid.
96   'It was highly significant . . .' TNA AIR 2/9726
97   'This last letter . . .' Cited in Melinsky, *Forming the Pathfinders*, p. 75
98   'In the opinion of the Air Staff . . .' Portal Papers, Folder 9, 14/6/1942, Christ Church, Oxford
98   'at the dictation of junior officers . . .' Despatch on Operations, para. 20

8 Portal Power

103 'It is considered that the potential . . .' TNA ADM 116/484
104 'This is tripe . . .' TNA AIR
109 'What is it you want?' Cited in Morpurgo, *Barnes Wallis*, p. 248
109 'H. very much misinformed . . .' Barnes Neville Wallis Diary, 22/3/1943
110 'Mutiny!' Cited in ibid., p. 250
113 'Some aircraft failed to wait . . .' TNA AIR 27/767

9 Greenlight

114 'Conditions very good for bombing . . .' TNA AIR 4/37
114 'presumably factory' TNA AIR 27/767
114 'The trip took us . . .' Williams Papers, 26/2/1943, QSL
114 'A good but frightening trip.' TNA AIR 4/37
115 'I consider that the potentialities . . .' TNA AIR 20/996
115 'For this purpose . . .' TNA AIR 14/840
117 'Of the eight weeks available . . .' Ibid.

10 The Main Offensive

125 'You have set a fire . . .' Cited in Searby, *Everlasting Arms*, pp. 96–7
126 'Mr Hollis, the Managing Director . . .' D2/10, Barnes Wallis Papers, Science Museum Archives
127 'You will see . . .' Ibid.
128 'Everything is being done . . .' Ibid.
131 'Hey, Hutch. Turn off the heat . . .' Gibson, *Enemy Coast Ahead*, pp. 235–7
133 'Any Captain who completes . . .' Cited in Morris, *Guy Gibson*, p. 141
134 'How would you like the idea . . . ?' Cited in Gibson, *Enemy Coast Ahead*, p. 238. Gibson claims in his book that he had been posted straight to 5 Group, his leave cancelled, in order to start writing a book for the benefit of the would-be bomber pilot. It seems very unlikely that having completed a year in office at 106 Squadron he would have had his leave cancelled in order to produce something as non-urgent as a memoir. The 106 Squadron Operational Record Book also records that he was posted on 14 March and certainly he had already been appointed CO of a newly forming squadron by the following day. A Personal Occurrence Report filed in No. 5 Group Appendices records that S/Ldr (A/W/Cdr) Gibson was posted for operational duties (W/Cdr post) wef 15/3/43 – permitted to retain acting rank of W/Cdr. However, since 617 Squadron was not officially formed it might be better to say 'earmarked to form a new squadron'.

11 Special Squadron

135 'The former is much more important . . .' TNA AIR 14/840

136   'If the Möhne attack . . .' TNA AIR 14/840
138   'What kind of trip, sir?' Gibson, *Enemy Coast Ahead*, p. 238
138   'I asked you the other day . . .' Ibid., p. 239
143   'At the moment . . .' Cited in Morris, *Guy Gibson*, p. 146
143   'Sit down. The first thing . . .' Cited in Morris, *Guy Gibson*, p. 146
144   'That was not to my liking . . .' IWM 8177/1
146   'I think we were both wondering . . .' Gibson, *Enemy Coast Ahead*, p. 249

12 617 Squadron
152   'I spent quite a long time . . .' IWM 7298/1
153   'The loss rate . . .' Ibid.
155   'The engine got very hot . . .' Cited in *The War Illustrated*, 6/12/1943
156   'My reputation . . .' Cited in Thorning, *Dambuster Who Cracked the Dam*, p. 64
157   'Accurate navigation under moonlight . . .' TNA AIR 14/840

13 Certain Dams
161   'You're here to do a special job . . .' Gibson, *Enemy Coast Ahead*, p. 243. Gibson is not specific about when he gave this speech although he says it was after three days. Although he arrived on 21 March, the first crews did not reach Scampton until the 24th. Also, he says that Astell was ordered to photo recce lakes and reservoirs straight after and that definitely took place on 27 March. Certainly, it would have made no sense to hold a briefing earlier, because there were not enough crews until that date.
163   This paper can be found at TNA AIR 8/1238
166   'I could remember how . . .' Gibson, *Enemy Coast Ahead*, pp. 258–9

14 The Conquest of Nature
170   'For this reason . . .' TNA AIR 8/1238
171   'You will note . . .' TNA AIR 2/1238
175   'The English claim . . .' Cited in Kershaw, *Hitler: Nemesis*, p. 561, and Irving, *Goebbels*, p. 754
177   'The same guns could have well . . .' Speer, *Inside the Third Reich*, p. 382
179   'Listen boys . . .' Cited in Euler, *Dams Raid*, p. 152

15 Low Level
184   'every effort . . .' TNA AIR 20/4821
185   'It is very difficult . . .' IWM 7298
188   'But on 617 . . .' IWM 7372
190   'Caused the pilot to lose control . . .' Williams Papers, 11/4/1943
191   'But he was quite OK . . .' Ibid.

193   'Within half an hour . . .' Gibson, *Enemy Coast Ahead*, p. 260
194   'This worked just as well . . .' IWM

16   Trials and Tribulations
198   'The objective of the campaign . . .' Harris, *Bomber Offensive*, p. 147
198   'a .303 bullet has but little . . .' Cited in Roy Irons, *The Relentless Offensive*, p. 62
204   'Run up to 150 rpm . . .' Barnes Neville Wallis Diary, 3/4/1943
207   'My Own Sweetheart Darling . . .' Barnes Wallis Papers, 12/4/1943
210   'When an engine stops . . .' Gibson, *Enemy Coast Ahead*, p. 266
210   'I think they teach . . .' Ibid.

17   A Matter of Height and Speed
211   'Flight Sergeant Lovell . . .' TNA AIR 14/842
212   'This was the day . . .' John Fraser Papers
213   'I have not enlarged or boasted . . .' Williams Papers, 17/4/1943, QSL
213   'He'd do it in front of the squadron . . .' IWM 7298
214   'George, I want you' Cited in Humphries, *Living With Heroes*, pp. 4–5
215   'I only spoke to him once or twice . . .' IWM 7372
216   'life and soul of the party . . .' IWM 7298
216   'He was very strict . . .' IWM 8177
217   'I would be glad . . .' TNA ADM 277/46
217   'On the point of chances . . .' Ibid.
217   'From the Lancaster trials . . .' TNA AIR 14/2087
218   'wait a day or two . . .' TNA AIR 14/840
219   'Lunch on sandwiches . . .' Barnes Neville Wallis Diary, 18/4/1943
220   'You know the difficulties . . .' Cited in Gibson, *Enemy Coast Ahead*, p. 251
220   'There is little doubt . . .' TNA AIR 14/840
223   'You will wish to see . . .' TNA AIR 14/840
224   'This would undoubtedly . . .' TNA CAB 80/68
225   'Failure . . .' Barnes Neville Wallis Diary, 22/4/1943
225   'The best height . . .' Gibson, *Enemy Coast Ahead*, pp. 268–9

18   Scampton and Reculver
227   'Flying at sixty feet . . .' IWM 8177
228   'What price the last big raid . . .' Charles Roland Williams Papers, 18/4/1943
228   'The Mess is quite comfortable . . .' John Fraser Papers, 21/4/1943
229   'We have been drinking . . .' Charles Roland Williams Papers, 11/4/1943
229   'I intend to lead . . .' John Fraser Papers, 22/4/1943
230   'All the lawns neatly mowed . . .' John Fraser Papers, 21/4/1943

230   'Do you think I might learn something . . .' Charles Roland Williams
       Papers, 22/4/1943
230   'I did not enjoy it . . .' Ibid., 14/4/1943
230   'There was a big joke . . .' IWM
231   'Wish we were there now . . .' Charles Roland Williams Papers, 25/4/1943
231   'I am anxious to know . . .' Ibid., 22/4/1943
232   'Ht 60', rpm 500 . . .' Barnes Neville Wallis Diary, 29/4/1943
234   'No longer single . . .' John Fraser Papers, 2/5/1943

19 Bottomley Sets the Date
237   'Incidents such as this . . .' TNA AIR 14/840
242   'The time has now come . . .' TNA AIR 14/842
244   'How about radio telephony?' Cited in Gibson, *Enemy Coast Ahead*,
       p. 274
248   'The news must have shaken her . . .' Charles Roland Williams
       Papers, 7/5/1943
248   'What wonderful news . . .' Ibid., 7/5/1943

20 Air Ministry versus the Admiralty
250   'Weather still unsuitable' Barnes Neville Wallis Diary, 10/5/1943
251   'Will you please get down to it . . .' Cited in Sweetman, *Bomber
       Crew/Dambusters Raid*, p. 114
256   'There is considerable divergence . . .' TNA AIR 14/2088
257   'I found that with all your training . . .' IWM 7372
258   'Did you shave this morning?' Charles Roland Williams Papers,
       22/4/1943
259   'I was so certain that I would find you . . .' Ibid., 11/5/1943
261   'They looked rather like a huge oil drum . . .' IWM 8177
261   'It was hard to think . . .' IWM 7372
262   'Sir, it is my duty to report . . .' Churchill Papers, 20/111
265   'much regret having been forced . . .' TNA AIR 2/8395

21 Countdown
268   'Full dress rehearsal . . .' TNA AIR 4/37
268   '2nd Wave . . .' TNA AIR 14/844
270   'I am very glad, darling . . .' Charles Roland Williams Papers,
       15/5/1943
274   'That night Hoppy saved our lives . . .' Gibson, *Enemy Coast Ahead*,
       p. 276
277   'Then I was alone in my room . . .' Ibid.

22 Final Day
281   'Flying programme, Adj . . .' Humphries, *Living With Heroes*, p. 6
283   'None of us had any idea . . .' Joe McCarthy Jr

284   'They were very high, the Dutch pylons . . .' IWM 7372
287   'I will never forget . . .' Gibson, *Enemy Coast Ahead*, p. 277
287   'He was a very kindly man . . .' IWM 7298
289   'Can I have your egg . . .' Gibson, *Enemy Coast Ahead*, p. 279
289   'And when I do get that leave . . .' Charles Roland Williams Papers, 16/5/1943
290   'Always on the spot, Adj' Humphries, *Living With Heroes*, p. 10
290   'Hoppy, tonight's the night . . .' Gibson, *Enemy Coast Ahead*, p. 279
290   'Don't let us worry you!' Cited in Humphries, *Living With Heroes*, p. 10

23 Outward Journey
304   'The information we had . . .' IWM 16256
304   'GEE jammed something chronic' Maltby Navigation Log, c/o Rob Owen
305   'I was navigating all the time . . .' IWM 7298
305   'On one occasion . . .' Ibid.
307   'We are six miles south . . .' Cited in Gibson, *Enemy Coast Ahead*, pp. 284–5
309   'We always knew exactly . . .' Cited in Euler, *Wasserkrieg*, pp. 244–5
310   'In that light it looked . . .' Gibson, *Enemy Coast Ahead*, p. 26

24 Goner
313   'Aircraft were circling . . .' Cited in Arthur, *Dambusters*, p. 229
313   'Bit aggressive, aren't they?' Gibson, *Enemy Coast Ahead*, p. 287
316   'You're going to hit them . . .' Ibid., pp. 288–9
318   'a piece of cake . . .' Cited in *Vancouver Sun*, 23/2/1952
318   'OK, attacking . . .' Gibson, *Enemy Coast Ahead*, p. 289
319   'For Christ's sake . . .' Cited in Sweetman, *Bomber Crew/Dambusters Raid*, p. 165. The account of Hopgood's plane being hit comes from an interview with John Fraser in the *Vancouver Sun*, 23/2/1951
319   '*look awful damn close . . .*' Shere Fraser Lowe
324   'I hope they all come back' Cited in Gibson, *Enemy Coast Ahead*, pp. 277–8
325   'And then there was an excited yell . . .' IWM 8177
326   'I can hardly describe . . .' Cited in Euler, *Wasserkrieg*, pp. 239–40
327   'Wallis, I didn't believe a word . . .' Cited in Sweetman, *Bomber Crew/Dambusters Raid*, p. 168

25 The Hardest Target
330   'Nobody had seen it before . . .' IWM 7372
331   'To exit from the Eder Dam . . .' IWM 8177
332   'It all seemed so sudden and vicious . . .' Gibson, *Enemy Coast Ahead*, p. 295

334   'I learned to keep cool . . .' IWM 7298
334   'We all joined in on the R/T . . .' Gibson, *Enemy Coast Ahead*, p. 295
334   'It was a damn nuisance!' IWM 7298
335   'We could see the water gushing out . . .' IWM 7298
335   'We watched the water . . .' IWM 16256
335   'There was just this great big flood . . .' IWM 7372
335   'The telephone personnel . . .' Harris, *Bomber Offensive*, p. 158

26 Homeward Bound
341   'We flew low along that canal . . .' Gibson, *Enemy Coast Ahead*, p. 301
341   'We flew on . . .' IWM 13248
345   'So we realized then . . .' Ibid.

27 After the Raid
350   'All you could see . . .' Cited in Euler, *Dams Raid*, p. 119
351   '*It's all over* . . .' Cited in ibid., p. 120
352   'The screams from up the valley . . .' Cited in ibid., p. 125
353   'Pieces of debris . . .' Cited in ibid., p. 83
355   'fictitious character' Humphries, *Living With Heroes*, p. 33
355   'I was flying at 30,000 feet . . .' Quoted by Fray in an interview for
        Sean Whyte from his written intelligence summary
356   'When I realized . . .' Ibid.
359   'depression to a certain extent' IWM 8177
359   'You get in the plane . . .' IWM 7372
360   'The War Cabinet . . .' TNA AIR 14/208
361   'But for your knowledge . . .' Ibid.
361   'I felt frightfully tired . . .' Humphries, *Living With Heroes*, p. 39

28 *Katastrophe*
364   'You have just read . . .' Recording of Churchill's Speech to Congress,
        19/5/1943, or www.royalsignals.org.uk
366   'The attacks of the British bombers . . .' Lochner, *Goebbels Diaries*,
        18/5/1943
367   'Flight Lieutenant Astell . . .' c/o Ray Hepner
367   'I'm afraid I'm not . . .' Barnes Wallis Papers
369   'All rail bridges . . .' BA-MA RW 20/6/9
370   'The catastrophes . . .' BA-MA RL 4/366
371   'to influence the course of the war . . .' Speer, *Inside the Third Reich*,
        p. 383
372   'The sum of construction . . .' BA-MA RW 20/6/9
372   'He kept the documents . . .' Speer, *Inside the Third Reich*, p. 384
372   'Important spare parts . . .' MA-BA RL 4/366

29 Damn Busters

374   'This offensive is of decisive importance . . .' Cited in Chris Bellamy, *Absolute War*, p. 577

375   'The grid gas supply . . .' BA-MA RW20/6/9

377   'The Wing Commander's face . . .' Humphries, *Living With Heroes*, p. 53

Postscript

384   'No one accomplishment . . .' TNA AIR 20/4821

387   'All navigators, except one . . .' TNA AIR 14/2087

389   'It was wooded and rough . . .' IWM 8177

390   'It is my intention . . .' Cited in Webster and Frankland, *Strategic Air Offensive Against Germany, Volume II*, p. 179

392   'How soon could you let me have one?' Barnes Wallis Papers

393   'The effects of this brilliant . . .' *Strategic Air Offensive against Germany, Volume II*, p. 168

396   'The day was perfect . . .' Cited in Morris, *Guy Gibson*, p. 251

398   'It was a beautiful day . . .' Charles Roland Williams Papers, QSL

Sources

I have only end-noted sources taken from those other than my own; thus all quotations from my own interviews have not been noted. Nor have I end-noted statistics and figures, opting instead for a reasonably full list of sources here:

UNPUBLISHED

Author interviews
Shere Fraser Lowe
Elisabeth Gaunt
George 'Johnny' Johnson
Joe McCarthy Jr
Grant McDonald
Les Munro, CNZM, DSO, QSO, DFC
Mary Stopes-Roe

Bundesarchiv-Militärarchiv, Freiburg, Germany
RL 4/363: Captured German Documents May 1943–December 1944
RL 4/365: Correspondence General Inspectorate for Water and Power
RL 4/366: Correspondence General Inspectorate for Water and Power
RW 20/6/9: War Diary Armaments Inspectorate VI

Christ Church, Oxford
Papers of Lord Portal of Hungerford

Churchill College Archives, Churchill College, Cambridge
Barnes Wallis Papers

IMPERIAL WAR MUSEUM, LONDON

Documents
Papers of Bill Townsend
Papers of Charles Williams

Sound archives
7298 – Harold Hobday
7372 – Len Sumpter
8177 – David Shannon
13248 – Dudley Heal
16256 – David Shannon
17970 – George Johnson

Ray Hepner
Papers of William Astell

Richard Morris
Notes of interviews with Fay Gillon and Margaret North
'Who were the Dam Busters?' draft article

The National Archives, Kew, London
ADM 277/46: Lt Cdr Lane Papers
ADM 116/4843: Highball Bouncing Mine: Anti-Ship Trials and Counter-Measures
AIR 2/8395: Operation CHASTISE – Attack against Möhne, Eder and Sorpe Dams
AIR 2/9726: Correspondence on Despatch by Air Chief Marshal Harris
AIR 4/37: Logbook Wing Commander Guy Gibson, VC
AIR 8/1238: Destruction of German Dams – Economic Effects
AIR 14/707: Circus Operations
AIR 14/840: Attacks on Ships and Dams: Highball and Upkeep Executive Action
AIR 14/842: Upkeep – Progress Reports
AIR 14/2087: Reports and Analysis on Operation CHASTISE
AIR 14/2088: Operation CHASTISE
AIR 16/757: Fighter Command Operations
AIR 19/383: Dams and Reservoirs – Attack and Defence
AIR 20/994: Operations Highball and Upkeep Development Progress Reports
AIR 20/995: Operations Highball and Upkeep: Operational Planning
AIR 20/996: Operations Highball and Upkeep: Minutes of Meetings
AIR 20/4821: Highball and Upkeep Policy
AIR 27/453 and 449: 44 Squadron Operational Record Book
AIR 27/766 and 767: 97 Squadron Operational Record Book

AIR 27/833: 106 Squadron Operational Record Book
AIR 27/2128: 617 Squadron Operational Record Book
AIR 27/2130: 618 Squadron Operational Record Book
AIR 41/42: RAF Narrative. A Period of Expansion and Experiment (March 1942–January 1943)
AIR 41/43: RAF Narrative. The Full Offensive February 1943 to February 1944
AVIA 15/744: Barnes Wallis – Model Experiments on Dams
AVIA 15/1655 and 1656: Windsor Development
AVIA 15/3934: Upkeep Trials
AVIA 18/715: Lancaster Test Trials
AVIA 19/1263: Upkeep Trials
AVIA 19/1270: Upkeep Bomb: Reculver Trials
CAB 80/68 and 69: War Cabinet Chiefs of Staff Committee

Queensland State Library, Brisbane, Australia
Papers of Charles Roland Williams

RAF Museum, Hendon, London
Papers of Air Chief Marshal Sir Arthur Harris
Papers of Air Marshal Sir Robert Saundby
Papers of Group Captain Frederick Winterbotham
Diary of Barnes Neville Wallis

Robert Owen Papers, 617 Squadron Aircrew Association
Navigation Logs: F/Lt Jack Leggo; F/O McLean; Sgt Vivian Nicholson

The Science Museum Archive, Wroughton, Wiltshire
Barnes Wallis Papers

Dr Mary Stopes-Roe
Wallis Family Archives

Sean Whyte, SWA Fine Art
Interview with Frank 'Gerry' Fray, DFC

PUBLISHED WORKS

Books
Air Ministry, *Bomber Command* (HMSO, 1943)
Arthur, Max, *Dambusters: A Landmark Oral History* (Virgin, 2009)
Bateman, Alex, *No. 617 'Dambuster' Sqn* (Osprey, 2009)
Beck, Pip, *Keeping Watch: A WAAF in Bomber Command* (Goodall, 1989)

Bellamy, Chris, *Absolute War: Soviet Russia in the Second World War* (Pan, 2008)

Biddle, Tami Davis, *Rhetoric and Reality in Air Warfare* (Princeton University Press, 2002)

Bishop, Patrick, *Bomber Boys: Fighting Back, 1940–1945* (Harper Press, 2007)

Blackbourn, David, *The Conquest of Nature: Water Landscape and the Making of Modern Germany* (Pimlico, 2008)

Caddick-Adams, Peter, *Monty and Rommel: Parallel Lives* (Preface, 2011)

Carrington, Charles, *Soldier at Bomber Command* (Leo Cooper, 1987)

Cheshire, Leonard, *Bomber Pilot* (Hutchinson, 1943)

Cotter, Jarrod, and Paul Blackah, *Avro Lancaster: Owners' Workshop Manual* (Haynes, 2008)

Currie, Jack, *The Augsburg Raid* (Goodall, 1987)

Deighton, Len, *Bomber* (Pan, 1972)

Dildy, Douglas C., *Dambusters: Operation Chastise, 1943* (Osprey, 2010)

Escott, Sqn Ldr B. E., *History of Royal Air Force High Wycombe* (no publisher listed)

Euler, Helmuth, *The Dams Raid: Through the Lens* (After the Battle, 2001)

—, *Wasserkrieg* (Motorbuch Verlag, 2007)

Foster, Charles, *Breaking the Dams: The Story of the Dambuster David Maltby and His Crew* (Pen & Sword, 2008)

Fry, Eric, *An Airman Far Away* (Kangaroo Press, 1993)

Furse, Anthony, *Wilfrid Freeman: The Genius behind Allied Survival and Air Supremacy 1939 to 1945* (Spellmount, 2000)

Garbett, M. and B. Goulding, *Lancaster* (Promotional Reprint Company, 1992)

Gibson, Guy, *Enemy Coast Ahead* (Michael Joseph, 1946)

—, *Enemy Coast Ahead Uncensored* (Crecy, 2010)

Grunberger, Richard, *A Social History of the Third Reich* (Phoenix, 2005)

Gunston, Bill, *Fighting Aircraft of World War II* (Salamander Books, 1988)

Harris, Sir Arthur, *Bomber Offensive* (Collins, 1947)

—, *Despatch on War Operations* (Frank Cass, 1995)

Hastings, Max, *Bomber Command* (Book Club Associates, 1980)

Humphries, Harry, *Living With Heroes: The Dam Busters* (The Erskine Press, 2008)

Irons, Roy, *The Relentless Offensive: War and Bomber Command, 1939–1945* (Pen & Sword, 2009)

Iveson, Tony, and Brian Milton, *Lancaster: The Biography* (André Deutsch, 2009)

Jones, R. V., *Most Secret War* (Penguin, 2009)

Lochner, Louis P. (Ed./Trans.), *The Goebbels Diaries* (Hamish Hamilton, 1948)

Longmate, Norman, *The Bombers: The RAF Offensive against Germany, 1939–1945* (Hutchinson, 1983)

McKinstry, Leo, *Lancaster: The Second World War's Greatest Bomber* (John Murray, 2010)

Melinsky, Hugh, *Forming the Pathfinders: The Career of Air Vice-Marshal Sydney Bufton* (The History Press, 2010)

Middlebrook, Martin, and Chris Everitt, *The Bomber Command War Diaries: An Operational Reference Book 1939–1945* (Penguin, 1990)

Morpurgo, J. E., *Barnes Wallis: A Biography* (Longman, 1972)

Morris, Richard, '16/17 May 1943 Operation Chastise: The Raid on the German Dams', *Defining Moments: Dramatic Archaeologies of the Twentieth Century*, ed. John Schofield (Archaeopress, 2009)

—, *Cheshire: The Biography of Leonard Cheshire, VC, OM* (Viking, 2000)

—, *Guy Gibson* (Penguin, 1995)

Murray, Iain R., *Bouncing-Bomb Man: The Science of Sir Barnes Wallis* (Haynes, 2009)

—, *Dam Busters: Owners' Workshop Manual* (Haynes, 2011)

Neillands, Robin, *The Bomber War* (John Murray, 2004)

Noakes, Jeremy, *Nazism, Volume 4: The German Home Front in World War II* (University of Exeter Press, 1998)

Orange, Vincent, *Slessor: Bomber Champion* (Grub Street, 2006)

Otter, Patrick, *Lincolnshire Airfields in the Second World War* (Countryside Books, 2009)

Overy, Richard, *Bomber Command 1939–1945: Reaping the Whirlwind* (HarperCollins, 1997)

Probert, Henry, *Bomber Harris: His Life and Times* (Greenhill Books, 2006)

RAF Manston History Club, *RAF Manston Album* (Sutton, 2005)

Rivaz, R. C., *Tail Gunner* (Sutton, 2003)

Saward, Dudley, *Bomber Harris* (Sphere, 1985)

Sawyer, Group Captain Tom, *Only Owls and Bloody Fools Fly at Night* (Goodall Publications Ltd, 1982)

Searby, John, *The Everlasting Arms* (William Kimber, 1988)

Speer, Albert, *Inside the Third Reich* (Phoenix, 1998)

Stopes-Roe, Mary, *Mathematics With Love: The Courtship Correspondence of Barnes Wallis, Inventor of the Bouncing Bomb* (Macmillan, 2005)

Sweetman, John, *Bomber Crew: Taking on the Reich* (Abacus, 2007)

—, *The Dambusters Raid* (Cassell, 2002)

Terraine, John, *The Right of the Line* (Wordsworth Military Library, 1997)

Thorning, Arthur G., *The Dambuster Who Cracked the Dam: The Story of Melvin 'Dinghy' Young* (Pen & Sword, 2008)

Tooze, Adam, *The Wages of Destruction: The Making and Breaking of the Nazi Economy* (Penguin, 2007)

Ward, Chris, Andy Lee and Andreas Wachtel, *Dambusters* (Red Kite, 2008)

Ward, Chris, and Andreas Wachtel, *Dambuster Crash Sites* (Pen & Sword, 2007)

Webster, Sir Charles, and Noble Frankland, *The Strategic Air Offensive Against Germany, Volume I: Preparation* (HMSO, 1961)

—, *The Strategic Air Offensive against Germany, Volume II: Endeavour* (HMSO, 1961)
—, *The Strategic Air Offensive against Germany, Volume IV: Annexes and Appendices* (HMSO, 1961)
Wheeler, Edwin, *Just to Get a Bed* (Square One, 1990)
Winterbotham, F. W., *Secret and Personal* (William Kimber, 1969)
—, *The Ultra Spy: An Autobiography* (Papermac, 1981)

Magazines, pamphlets and journals
Boorer, N. W., 'Barnes Wallis Designer Memorial Lecture', *Royal Aeronautical Society*, March 1981
Brasher, Christopher, 'Master of the Skies', in *The Listener*, 22 November 1979
Collins, A. R., 'The Origins and Design of the Attack on the German Dams', in *Proceedings of the Institute of Chartered Engineers*, Part 2, 1982
Graves, David, 'Dambuster Model Safe amongst the Bluebells', *Daily Telegraph*, 10 May 1993
Hastings, Max, 'The Dambusters Raid was One of the Most Daring and Brilliant of the War But Did It Really Achieve Anything?' in *Daily Mail*, 17 August 2003
Irving, David, 'The Night the Dams Burst', www.fpp.co.uk
Jackson, Paul A., 'The Shipbusters', in *Aviation News*, Vol. 5, Issue 2, June/July 1976
Morris, Richard, and Robert Owen, 'Breaching the German Dams: Flying into History', Royal Air Force Museum, 2008
Nesbit, Roy, and John Sweetman, *The Dambusters*, supplement to *Aeroplane*, April 1993
Prins, Francois, 'Operation Chastise', *Wingspan* (date unknown)
Pye, Gerry, 'Homage to Comrades' in *Fly Past Magazine*, April 2002
Ramsey, Winston G., 'The Ruhr Dams Raid 1943', *After the Battle*, Number 3, 1973
Shortland, Jim, 'The Dambusters Raid – In Perspective', *Despatches*, April 2003
Spurr, Linda, 'Our Amy', *Rowing*, April 1975
Times, The, 'Sir Barnes Wallis', obituary, 23 November 1979
Wallis, Sir B. N., 'A Man and His Bomb: The "Dam-Busting" Weapon', *Aerospace Historian*, September 1973

DVDs, films, internet
The Dam Busters (Associated British, Special Anniversary Addition)
The Dambusters Raid (Delta)
The True Story of the Dambusters (History Channel)

www.cwgc.org
www.dambusters.org.uk
www.raf.mod.uk/rafscampton

Acknowledgements

There are a number of people I would like to thank for the help they have given me with this book. First, Rowland White, whose idea it was in the first place and who, as ever, has been a great sounding board throughout the research and writing. Rowland – thank you.

Second, I must thank the veterans and their families. Les Munro put up with me for two days in New Zealand and since then has put up with numerous further enquiries. He's a great man and a true gentleman. So too is Johnny Johnson, who has been grilled repeatedly and has been endlessly patient and helpful. In Vancouver, Grant McDonald allowed both me and a film crew to invade his house, and, again, he was hugely generous with his time and extremely helpful, putting me in touch with Ken Brown's wife, Beryl. Thank you to her as well, for talking to me about Ken. It really has been an extraordinary privilege to meet and get to know these heroes.

It has also been wonderful to meet two Dam Buster children – Shere Lowe and Joe McCarthy Jr, who not only welcomed me to their home in the States but have been enormously helpful and generous, allowing me to see and use their parents' papers and subsequently sending photos, old interviews and other material across the Atlantic. Thank you, Shere and Joe.

Enormous thanks are also due to Barnes Wallis's daughters, Elizabeth Gaunt and Dr Mary Stopes-Roe. Mary, especially, has been incredibly helpful, furnishing me not only with memories of her parents and childhood, but also with allowing me access to many of her parents' papers. I am indebted to you, Mary – thank you.

In Germany, Michelle Miles and her husband, Ingo, have once again been incredible in ferreting out key documents from the archives in Freiburg and doing quite superb translations. It was Michelle who found the crucial document containing the cost of the reparation work, a nugget of information I was desperate to find out from the start. I am enormously grateful to you both. I am also very grateful to Karl-Heinz Bremmer, Karl Schäfer and Ernst-Friedrich Gallenkamp. Closer to home, both Lalla and Tom Hitchings, and Elli Lanyon, have been brilliantly helpful in transcribing many hours of interviews. Once again, my heartfelt thanks.

Thanks are also due to the various archives who have helped: to Richard Hughes, Jane Fish and Roderick Suddaby at the Imperial War Museum; to Gavin Bannerman at the Queensland State Library; to the staff at the National Archives in Kew; to Peter Dye and staff at the RAF Museum, Hendon; to Cathy Pugh and the fantastic Second World War Experience Centre; and the staff at the Bundesarchiv-Militärarchiv in Freiburg.

A number of friends and colleagues have also offered advice along the way: Antony Beevor, Professor Jeremy Black, Seb Cox, Steve Prince, Guy Walters and Sean Whyte. Dr Peter Caddick-Adams has been an especially valued friend and someone with whom I have repeatedly chewed the cud. I would also like to thank Clive Denney, for all his help and his advice and, with John Dodd, for attempting to fly out to the dams. Having suffered engine failure over the Channel, he and John then managed to find a replacement Beech 18 in record time. This was flown by Carlo Ferrari and Gregor Schweizer, both of whom were quite brilliant. My thanks are also due to the inspirational Simon Keeling, whose expertise and meteorological wisdom have been a huge help. Thank you all. Another really big thank you goes to Professor Rick Hillum, a great friend and another person with whom I have regularly talked through various matters arising. Rick has a brilliant mind, knows more about scientific matters than anyone I know, and has once again been of enormous help. Thank you, Rick.

I am also indebted to everyone at Maya Vision. Making a television film helped the book enormously, allowing me to visit places and meet people that might not otherwise have been possible, so thank you to Mike Wood and Rebecca Dobbs, Sally Thomas, John Cranmer and Toby Farrell, and also to Keith Branch, Mick Duffield, Phil Bax and Jon Wood. Particular thanks, however, go to Freya Eden-Ellis for all her help, and I also owe an enormous debt of thanks to Aaron Young, with whom I have shared much of the ride. Thank you.

At Transworld, thank you to the incomparable Bill Scott-Kerr and Mads Toy, but also to Steve Mulcahey, Phil Lord, Vivien Garrett and everyone there who has helped with the book. My heartfelt thanks also to Mark Handsley, who yet again has proved a superb copy-editor. Thank you, as well, to Jake Smith Bosanquet, Alex Christofi and all at Conville & Walsh, and especially to Patrick Walsh – a great friend as well as agent.

There are two other people to whom I owe an enormous debt of thanks. The first is Richard Morris, Gibson's and Barnes Wallis's biographer and someone who has been incredibly generous with his own research, sharing many of his interviews with me and passing on critical pieces of advice. The second is Rob Owen, Official Historian of the 617 Aircrew Association. Rob has an encyclopedic knowledge of Operation CHASTISE as well as an unrivalled understanding of the subject. The amount of time he has spent on this book correcting, counselling, advising and generally pointing me in the right direction has been way, way, beyond the call of duty. Rob, I am eternally grateful for all that you have done, and the book would unquestionably have been a considerably lesser one without you. Thank you so much.

I also want to thank four very great friends, to whom this book is dedicated. We five are eternally fortunate that we were able to spend three wonderful years at university together, rather than having to go off and fight a war, and that we have remained friends ever since. I'm very grateful for that. So, to Si, Stu, Pete and J, thank you.

Last, but most certainly not least, I would like to thank my lovely family: Rachel, Ned and Daisy. Writing a book like this is a big undertaking, and requires a lot of forbearance and understanding from them; and they always give it to me. Thank you.

Picture
Acknowledgements

Every effort has been made to trace copyright holders; those overlooked are invited to get in touch with the publishers.

Endpapers in the hardcover edition only are taken from a contemporary pilot's map of the Dams Raid area.

Background illustrations on pages 18–19, 120–21, 278–79 and 346–47 are courtesy RAF Museum, Hendon.

ILLUSTRATION SECTIONS:

Section 1

Page 1
Barnes Wallis: Imperial War Museum/1284383; Squadron Leader John Nettleton: Imperial War Museum/HU_092988; Fred Winterbotham: Transport Road Research Laboratory/IWM; Nant y Gro dam: Wingnut Films; diagram from Wallis's *Note*: Wallis papers, Churchill College Archive, Cambridge.

Pages 2 and 3
Kaiser inspecting the Eder: Wingnut Films; Möhne and Eder dams: both Imperial War Museum; the Möhne, pre-war: © Crown Copyright; Vickers Wellington dropping prototype spherical bouncing bomb: Imperial War Museum/IMG039; Type 464 Lancasters drop cylindrical bomb at Reculver: both Imperial War Museum/FLM2365 and FLM 2343.

Pages 4 and 5
Four photographs of Type 464 Provisioning Lancasters on the ground: all ©
Crown Copyright; Lancaster in flight: Imperial War Museum; sketch of
features of Type 464: © Terry Lawless; background picture of Lancasters in
flight: Imperial War Museum.

Pages 6 and 7
Guy Gibson with David Maltby: Imperial War Museum/TR001122; Guy
Gibson: Imperial War Museum/CH_013121; Joe McCarthy and crew:
Imperial War Museum/TR001128; Les Knight and crew: Imperial War
Museum/CH11049; Grant McDonald: Imperial War Museum/CH9935; Les
Munro: both Imperial War Museum; David Shannon: Imperial War
Museum/CH_008474; Charlie Williams; John Fraser: both Imperial War
Museum; 'Mick' Martin and crew: Imperial War Museum/CH_009942.

Page 8
Sir Charles Portal: Imperial War Museum; Norman Bottomley: Imperial War
Museum/CH_000857; Francis Linnell: Imperial War Museum/10553210;
Ralph Cochrane: Imperial War Museum/CH14564; Sir Arthur Harris:
Imperial War Museum/CH_005491 and CH_013020.

Section 2

Page 1
Second Wave Lancaster taking off: Imperial War Museum/CH18006; British
weather forecaster: Imperial War Museum; wreckage of Hopgood's
Lancaster: both Wingnut Films; debriefing of Gibson's crew: Imperial War
Museum/CH9683.

Pages 2 and 3
The Möhne breached: Imperial War Museum/HV_4594; the Möhne
damaged: Imperial War Museum/CH_009687; Möhne damage downstream:
Imperial War Museum/CH_009720_A; flooding at Kassel: Imperial War
Museum/CH_009775; the Eder breached; destruction at Neheim: both
Wingnut Films.

Pages 4 and 5
After the flood: Wingnut Films.

Pages 6 and 7
Reconstruction work at the Möhne Dam: all Wingnut Films.

Page 8
Visit of King and Queen to Scampton: Imperial War Museum/100_2798; Les
Munro's menu card: courtesy Les Munro; sinking of the *Tirpitz*: Imperial War
Museum/C_004122; earthquake bomb: Imperial War Museum/CH_015374.

Index